Leslie Fiedler

Leslie Fiedler
Critic, Provocateur, Pop Culture Guru

Prem Kumari Srivastava

McFarland & Company, Inc., Publishers
Jefferson, North Carolina

LIBRARY OF CONGRESS CATALOGUING-IN-PUBLICATION DATA

Srivastava, Prem Kumari.
    Leslie Fiedler : critic, provocateur, pop culture guru /
Prem Kumari Srivastava.
      p.   cm.
    Includes bibliographical references and index.

    ISBN 978-0-7864-6351-0 (softcover : acid free paper) ∞
    ISBN 978-1-4766-0590-6 (ebook)

    1. Fiedler, Leslie A.—Criticism and interpretation.
2. Criticism—United States. I. Title.
PS3556.I34Z87 2014
814'.54—dc23   2014005364

BRITISH LIBRARY CATALOGUING DATA ARE AVAILABLE

© 2014 Prem Kumari Srivastava. All rights reserved

*No part of this book may be reproduced or transmitted in any form
or by any means, electronic or mechanical, including photocopying
or recording, or by any information storage and retrieval system,
without permission in writing from the publisher.*

Front cover image © Hemera/Thinkstock

Printed in the United States of America

*McFarland & Company, Inc., Publishers
  Box 611, Jefferson, North Carolina 28640
    www.mcfarlandpub.com*

For Gracious Huzur

*In dreams I see you clear
laughing with ones so near
and
smiling on others so far*

Contents

Acknowledgments ix
Chronology xi
List of Abbreviations xiv
Preface 1
Introduction 9

1. Fiedler's Credo: Literary and Critical; Socio-political and Pedagogical   29
2. Comradeship, Male Bonding or...?: Re-readings and Re-evaluations   68
3. Integration of the "Other": Indians, Jews, Blacks, Freaks and...   94
4. Toward Popular Culture: Establishment of a Pop Guru   137
5. Perspectives of the "Other": Postcolonial and Feminist Readings   171

Conclusion: Come Back to the Raft Ag'in, Fiedler Honey! 195
Chapter Notes 213
Bibliography 219
Index 237

Acknowledgments

I am grateful to many individuals and institutions who in various ways supported this project. At the top are two individuals who in their own way were closely connected to Fiedler. First, Professor V. N. Arora of the Indian Institute of Technology, Delhi, India, who, having personally known Fiedler, ignited my interest in popular culture enabling me to undertake a detailed research on Fiedler. This was more than two decades back. I would also like to thank the late Professor Ray B. Browne who believed in my project and Fiedler. My research would not have been possible without a post-doctoral research grant at the Advanced Centre for American Studies (ACAS), Osmania University Centre for International Programme (OUCIP), Hyderabad, India, in 2011 and the grant requirement to write a monograph at the end. It spearheaded the book to a fast, timely finish. In addition, I would like to thank many friends at ACAS such as the late Professor Vijayasree, Professor T. Vijay Kumar, Professor Kausar Azam, Professor R. S. Sharma and Professor Karunakar for productive conversations that enhanced my thinking about the challenges and possibilities of this different gaze on Fiedler. Earlier versions of some of the chapters published in this book were presented in many conferences where incisive scholarly responses (like the one from Bill Ashcroft in December 2011 at the AASA International Conference at Hyderabad and at USACLALS at Santa Clara, California, in April 2012) resulted in crucial revisions; others appeared as papers in journals.

The Department of English, Maharaja Agrasen College, University of Delhi, India, is responsible for keeping me academically engaged for almost two decades. Fruitful discussions with several of my colleagues there and many others helped me plug crucial gaps in my study. Their confidence in me helped me move forward, uninhibited and unafraid, much like the "Aunt Jennifer's Tigers" of Adrienne Rich. Thank you Anu and Gitanjali. Polite enquiries about my work and this book from many dear friends and loved family members helped refuel my energy. Many thanks Ajay and Sanjay Bhaiya, Prakash and Alpana, Jyoti and Shraddha bhabi, and Surat and Kavita. My own unmitigated cynicism and reservations about reaching the end of the road turned out to be a blessing in disguise. It kept me anxiously on my toes. Much sleep was lost cogitating over problematic patches at work and life—homework, guests, visits, illnesses, and the like.

I wish to express my gratitude to the *invisible visibles* in my life: my parents: Mr. Prem Dayal Prasad Srivastava and Mrs. Surat Kumari Srivastava, and my in-laws Professor Jai Prakash and Dr. Dayal Dei Prakash. I feel the aura and halo of their presence and *ashirwad* all the time!

This project wouldn't have been possible without the tacit and unconditional love, patience and excitement of two, now three, important constants of my life: Umang and Akshar, and later, Alakh who added sparkle and zing to those dull and low moments encountered by every researcher.

Above all, I would like to thank Amit, my husband and partner in life, for his companionship, loving approval, sustenance and confidence, which helped me sail and remain afloat all of the time, with the shore sometimes never in sight, but finally reaching it. His unstinting support helped me undo my mental, emotional and intellectual knots. I will forever remain grateful for his scrutiny of each and every word I wrote. This process was pursued with diligence repeatedly over the last several years. He sensitized me to not treat research as a bandwagon I could board easily with my pedestrian wares! I am thankful to him for helping me find my way out of many a labyrinthine passage. Thanks for being there, always!

I would be failing in my duty if I did not put on record my indebtedness for the hospitality shown to me by most respected Rani Sahiba. During my trying years of research at the Indian Institute of Technology, Delhi, my numerous visits found a home full of warmth, love and food.

Finally, I owe everything to Professor P.S. Satsangi Sahab of Dayalbagh who spotted the hint of research in me almost 30 years back. He is the inspiration behind every big or minuscule idea or concept related to my life. I bow down in *his* lotus feet for *his* continuous benign presence; a guiding force, without which, nothing is possible!

Chronology

1917	March 8, Leslie Aaron Fiedler born in Newark, New Jersey
1938	B.A., New York University
1939	M.A. University of Wisconsin, Madison Marries Margaret Shipley
1941	Ph.D., University of Wisconsin, Madison. Dissertation: "*John Donne's Songs and Sonnets*: A Reinterpretation in Light of Their Traditional Backgrounds."
1941–42	Assistant professor of English, University of Montana
1942	Enlists United States Naval Reserve
1946	Discharged from U.S. Naval Reserve with a rank of lieutenant, junior grade
1946–47	Rockefeller Fellow, Harvard University
1947–48	Assistant professor of English, University of Montana
1948	"Come Back to the Raft Ag'in, Huck Honey!" published in *Partisan Review*
1948–52	Associate professor of English, University of Montana
1951–53	Fulbright Lecturer, universities of Rome and Bologna
1953–64	Professor of English, University of Montana
1954–56	Chairman, Department of English, University of Montana
1955	*An End to Innocence*
1956	As Heavy Runner, named a chief of the Blackfoot Indian Tribe
1958	*The Art of the Essay*
1956–57	Christian Gauss Lecturer, Princeton University
1960	*Love and Death in the American Novel* *No! In Thunder*
1961–62	Fulbright Lecturer, University of Athens
1963	*The Second Stone* *Pull Down Vanity and Other Stories*

Chronology

1964	*Waiting for the End* *The Continuing Debate* (with Jacob Vinocur)
1965	Professor of English, State University of New York at Buffalo *Back to China*
1966	*The Last Jew in America* *Love and Death in the American Novel*, revised edition
1967	Arrested on charge of maintaining premises where marijuana is used
1967–68	Visiting professor, University of Sussex
1968	*The Return of the Vanishing American*
1969	Associate fellow, Calhoun College, Yale University *Being Busted* *Nude Croquet and Other Stories*
1970–71	Guggenheim Fellowship
1971	Visiting professor, University of Vincennes *The Collected Essays*
1972	Drug conviction reversed Named Samuel L. Clemens Professor, SUNY Buffalo *The Stranger in Shakespeare* *Cross the Border—Close the Gap* Divorces Margaret Shipley
1973	Marries Sally Smith Andersen
1974	*The Messengers Will Come No More*
1975	*In Dreams Awake*
1977	*The Leslie Fiedler Reader*
1978	*Freaks: Myths and Images of the Secret Self*
1979	*The Inadvertent Epic: From Uncle Tom's Cabin to Roots*
1981	*English Literature: Opening Up the Canon* (with Houston Baker, Jr.)
1982	*What Was Literature? Class Culture and Mass Society*
1983	*Olaf Stapledon: A Man Divided*
1991	*Fiedler on the Roof: Essays on Literature and Jewish Identity*
1994	Jay B. Hubbell Award for lifetime achievement by the American Literature Section of the MLA
1996	*Tyranny of the Normal: Essays on Bioethics, Theology and Myth*
1998	National Book Critics Circle Ivan Sandrof Lifetime Achievement Award, presented in a public ceremony at the NYU Law School on March 23
1999	Career Award from PEN West, a regional branch of the famed International Association of Writers
2001	Introduction to Fennimore Cooper's *The Last of the Mohicans*, Trade Paperbacks, Modern Library

2002	Introduction to Fennimore Cooper's *The Deer Slayer*, Trade Paperbacks, Modern Library
2003	Died on Jan. 30, just 38 days short of his 86th birthday. His desire was to write a trilogy of which the first appeared as *Fiedler on the Roof* in 1991. The last would have been *Back to Innocence* since in it he would have completed the circular process, which began with *An End to Innocence* (1955).

List of Abbreviations

Leslie Fiedler's works are quoted in the book using
the following abbreviations

AS—"Archetype and Signature"
CB—"Come Back to the Raft Ag'in, Huck Honey!"
CBCG—*Cross the Border—Close the Gap*
CE 1—*Collected Essays*, vol. 1
CE 2—*Collected Essays*, vol. 2
EI—*End to Innocence: Essays on Culture and Politics*
FR—*Fiedler on the Roof*
GDD—"Give the Devil His Due"
KR—*The Kenyon Review*
LD 1960—*Love and Death in the American Novel* (New York: Criterion Books, 1960)
LD 1966—*Love and Death in the American Novel*, rev. ed. (New York: Stein and Day, 1966)
MC—"My Credo"
NT—*No! In Thunder: Essays on Myth and Literature*
RVA—*The Return of the Vanishing American*
SS—*The Second Stone: A Love Story*
TAC—"Toward an Amateur Criticism"
TG—*To the Gentiles*
TSS—*The Stranger in Shakespeare*
UB—*Unfinished Business*
WFTE—*Waiting for the End*
WWL—*What Was Literature?: Class Culture and Mass Society*

Preface

This book admits a large part of my engagement with Leslie A. Fiedler and his cultural discourse, which began more than two decades back. Having revisited Fiedler, I discover that his articulations remain as challenging and engaging as ever. Brushed aside by the British critical establishment "as the man who ... accused Huckleberry Finn of being a nigger-loving liberal homosexual.... His stance ... is that of the bawdy, bearded western prophet, hurling contemptuous mischief at drawing room 'culture,' little magazines and the week's good cause" (Bryden 1969, 39, quoted in Winchell 1985, 5). My twenty-year-old affair with Fiedler has been bookended by two major research ventures: first one at IIT Delhi for my doctoral work in 1991 and the second as a postdoctoral fellow at ACAS in 2011. Intermittently, I have gone through several stages of relationships: from reading and understanding Fiedler intensely, to ignoring him, to doubting his shifty stances, to hating him, to embracing the vast corpus of his work once again. Over years, I have learned to love and hate Fiedler. Through Fiedler I got a glimpse into the dynamics and complexities of race in culture. Erasure and erosion, fissures and fusion, I realized were often called cultural collision by scholars. With him I understood the importance of re-readings and re-evaluations; of resurrections and insurrections. With him I learned to use the "I" in literature.

Though Fiedler seems to have become unfashionable since the '60s and '70s, "to writer Camille Paglia he was one of the three great thinkers, along with Marshall McLuhan and Norman O. Brown, who prepared America's mid-century culture for the wider and wilder world of cyberspace" (Timberg 2008). There was a time when no reputable literary critic either began or ended a sentence with the pronoun "I." A neat academic quarantining was often observed supporting the obliteration of any evidence of the author. Yet Fiedler announced in the preface to the first edition of *Love and Death in the American Novel*, "This is finally a very personal book" (LD 1960, xiii). Considered Emersonian in many ways, speaking in the first person lends Fiedler a kind of vulnerability and authority simultaneously (Schechter 1999, 134).[1] He negotiated both very well. I unashamedly say that this book too is personal in many ways. There are two stories meshed in this book. They exist in both private and public realms. Both share elements of smoke and mirrors, and both incorporate the fictive and the factual, demonstrating how constructions often are combinations of the real and the imagined, binaries that intertwine in the dialogic. This book in some ways can also be read as "my story." What this book does not strive to be is "objective and empirical." It chooses to present a "subjective and informed" narrative of my own encounters with Fiedler's writings and how I would like the readers to read him.

Let me begin this way. My engagement with the "other" continues. Twenty years back, with an All India Junior Research Fellowship (JRF) in hand, sitting in one of the plush offices of a senior professor in one of the premier institutions of India, the Indian Institute of Technology, Delhi, a gauntlet was thrown down before me, which ironically has ricocheted today. It was a challenge to encounter the "other" in American academia, Leslie A. Fiedler. Interestingly, several options of the "other" were also offered to me: a study of popular women's magazines of India (then, an other; definitely not literary); the impact of American popular culture in India (popular culture as a category has stood on the periphery perennially); women in Indian cinema; and spy fiction and best sellers in India (also outsiders to canonical study, at least then). From all of these I recoiled. After all I was an English literature person, trained in the school of Shakespeare, Milton and Wordsworth as well as Twain and Hemingway! For a full-length doctoral research study, anybody below the likes of these would have been blasphemy! Gently nudged by my professor, I encountered this "American gadfly" and "the *enfant terrible*," as many have called him.[2] The rest, as they say, is history. In 2011, when I was awarded another research fellowship by the Advanced Center for American Studies (ACAS), Osmania University Center for International Programmes (OUCIP), Hyderabad, for my research project "Leslie Fiedler: Without Margins, Beyond Borders," I felt that I had come back full circle, to Fiedler.

The purpose of this study is not just to establish him as an important critic, writer and scholar, both American and Jewish, but to revisit the Fiedlerian discourse as several hard-core Americanists' favorite stomping ground and to look for meaning in it not just for the Americans but beyond them. As a critic beyond the narrow confines of particularities of boundaries and borders he is to be seen as one who remained secular, and global in many ways. This critic's critical insights span not just six decades of American literary and cultural history but also several disciplines and library shelves. Way ahead of his times, the unstoppable Fiedler was constantly on the run to dismantle categories and unsettle hierarchies. "He had so much energy that he wrote standing up," remembers Jerome Richard (2004, 296). His center-margin paradigm chose to reach even beyond the periphery. He was always seeking to "cross the border and close the gap." Hidden in this agenda of "moving beyond" was a reconciliatory impulse: he wanted things to merge and shrink. Too much of a dreamer to envision only the possible, his critical corpus displays bridges, arches, conduits and passages that would enjoin and encase.

There exist two kinds of works about Fiedler. The first kind are his own writings published in numerous books (26 in all), journals, magazines, newspapers, most of them during his lifetime. In 2008, a collection of his essays was brought out by Samuele F. S. Pardini as *The Devil Gets His Due: The Uncollected Essays of Leslie Fiedler*. In the second category are critical notings and commentaries, primarily criticism on his life and works. Here we have only four exclusive texts: two books by Mark Royden Winchell, *Leslie Fiedler* (1985) and *Too Good to Be True: The Life and Works of Leslie Fiedler* (2002). The other two also constitute different categories by themselves: Kellman and Malin's *Leslie Fiedler and American Culture* published in 1999 and P. Marudhanayagam's doctoral thesis (1980) converted into a book on Fiedler's myth criticism.

Leslie Fiedler (1985), by Mark Royden Winchell, a full-length but slim book of 172 pages, attempts to introduce him to all readers, old and new. As Winchell says, he had to make hard choices with regard to emphasis on some apparent and obvious themes. The next is a one-off festschrift, *Leslie Fiedler and American Culture* (1999), edited by Steven Kellman and Irving Malin, to "mark the start of Fiedler's ninth decade." It is a collection organized into three sections: essays, statements and self-assessment by Fiedler himself; a collection of critical essays that analyze Fiedler's writings, examining him as more than just the author of *Love and Death in the American Novel* and *The Return of the Vanishing American* (among the subjects studied are Fiedler's literature textbook, his memoir, his fiction, and his studies of science fiction, of archetype, and of Shakespeare); and finally tributes by his admirers.

Winchell's second engagement with Fiedler, *Too Good to Be True: The Life and Works of Leslie Fiedler* (2002), published just a year before Fiedler died in 2003, is a captivating narrative in which the protagonist (Fiedler) almost appears fictitious. Winchell has managed to capture all the droplets that make the life of Fiedler. Towards the end, Winchell pens the unacknowledged and acknowledged overlaps that one finds in recent criticism owing much to this giant of a critic. The book is a rumination on Fiedler's life. It has the sincerity, intensity and concentration of a practiced meditation. Not aimed as a hagiography, Winchell's book is a testimony of one scholar's respect for the other. Written with great depth and detail, the book captures the most poignant, private and delicate moments of Fiedler's life alongside incisive critical commentary on his works. McLemee in 2002 when the book was published noted that Fiedler's feelings about the book were "very complicated." Later Fiedler added, "I feel delivered. It's a release to me that someone else has made a pattern of my life."

Fiedler readers will know that the next collection, edited by Samuele F. S. Pardini, *The Devil Gets His Due: The Uncollected Essays of Leslie Fiedler* (2008), does not represent his finest work but is a collection of several of his uncollected essays. Pardini in his introduction makes a strong case to go back to Fiedler by initiating a discussion of a kind of trampling of a literary world order of yesteryear, which has affected seminal critics like Fiedler. Pardini uses "crises in contemporary literary criticism" as a starting point to argue his sympathy for the devil.[3] But his greater worry is the absence of a "new, homegrown public voice with a background in literacy studies" and "the lack of proper memorialization of scholars who are part of and makers of the history of this valuable profession."[4] Zsolt Kelemen of Hungary, while reviewing Pardini's collection, finds the devil's (Fiedler's) indelible imprints in all the selections (2010). I join Pardini in bemoaning the fact that Fiedler does not stand in the ranks of those "other recently deceased or retired scholars who have been rightly saluted and celebrated both by colleagues and in academic journals (Edward Said and Jacques Derrida come to mind)." In fact, even many years after his death, no serious attempt has been made to properly "memorialize Fiedler's work" in any major academic journals or anthologies of theory and literary criticism (Pardini 2008, xiv).

The present book hopes to disrupt this mourning. Recent studies in all parts of the world show that his insights are alive and throbbing. This book gives many examples, but not to prove a point.[5] Fiedler would cringe. This book intersects, interjects and floats across the four books discussed above. Apart from discussing most of his writings, barring a detailed take on his fiction and writings on his writings, this book attempts to plug a hole with the goal of presenting Fiedler from a studied perspective. The readership constituencies that this book hopes to target are those who are seeing every day the important critical statements of Fiedler—on popular culture, personal voice, intertextuality and inter-disciplinarity—come alive in their own readings. Any new discussion on Fiedler cannot elide some of the essential aspects of Fiedler's criticism: his personal assurance of steadfast allegiance to his readers through his works; his ultra-consciousness of the avant-garde and kitsch; and his honest salutation to the "new": new mutants or new writers, novel interpretative strategies and pedagogies, or a new muse that plays to the market.

Within the context of American studies as practiced all over the world, Fiedler's criticism, writings and pronouncements continue to be an important subject of interest. They appeal to non–Americans too. The challenges he threw at the American critical establishment are also some that were bothering many other scholars outside America. Thus, despite the acrid attacks from within the establishment, most of his writings have such global relevance that it is difficult to pin him down to a location. Even when within the location, his contexts are bathed in rich vernacular and thus reach a much wider audience. Fiedler, his study, his writings, and his changing prerogatives need to be understood within the paradigmatic shifts that were happening in American studies in a postcolonial world. A widely travelled man, he felt those shifts and tremors and responded to them appropriately.

The pronouncement "Every age is an age of adaptation," said in a very different context by Linda Hutcheon (2004), aptly fits the schema of American studies as Leslie Fiedler would have wanted in America and elsewhere in the world. This is also a call to the American literary studies pundits to open up the canon of American studies in America, and globally. As a Fulbright lecturer himself at Rome and Bologna from 1951 to 1953 and the chair of the Department of English in the University of Montana from 1954 to 1956 during which time he fought against stalwart opposition to hire a black professor, he was concerned with the necessity for America as a nation to move from a state of innocence to a state of experience (or adulthood), a concern reflected in several of his books including *An End to Innocence* (1955), the famous *Love and Death in the American Novel* (1960), and *Fiedler on the Roof* (1991), and all through his seven decades of writing and scholarship. Fiedler epitomized the vision of Senator J. William Fulbright: "The Fulbright Program aims to bring a little more knowledge, a little more reason, and a little more compassion into world affairs and thereby increase the chance that nations will learn at last to live in peace and friendship." His relevance for India, America and the world has to be studied and then understood with a largesse of heart and mind, indefatigable.

This single author encompasses in himself not just seven decades (the lifespan of his literary-intellectual-academic-cultural-political-controversial-iconoclastic career), but centuries of American literary and cultural thought. With more than 26 books on American cultural-literary-political-pedagogical topics, an understanding of his writings is an understanding of a liberal newer America itself. It also signifies a fresh approach to the study of American culture and literature, an opening up of the canon, bringing home to the plethora of American literary courses in the universities across the world, a breakdown and a dismantling of sorts. According to him books cannot be monasticated in the sanctuary of a library. They need to come out of its confines to roam freely on streets and theatres, in art and sculptures, even in paintings. Bringing his refreshingly new and contemporary articulations center stage implies bringing American studies to the center. Maini, in his essay "The American Gadfly" (published when Fiedler was visiting India in 1987), rightly sums him up as

> the critic America was destined to produce ... to dredge up the American experience with that pitiless insight that often borders on gnomic utterances.... His critical antennae are sensitive enough to register even the faintest intellectual stirrings, and ... seldom short on riposte or response.... His astonishing penchant for provocative pronouncements, and for recognizing the winds of change ... the radical nature of his explosive ideas and rhetoric ... [makes him] ... an epic of critical epiphanies unequaled in modern American criticism [1987, 7].

The need for situating Fiedler today was also increasingly felt by me when several expressed a genuine skepticism towards my endeavor with almost the following question on their lips: "Is Fiedler of any relevance today?" Such a statement can only be the result of a comfortable ignorance and disdain accompanied by a sense of complacency that emanates from lack of interest and knowledge that exists in India about American studies in general and contemporary American critics in particular. Such ignorance about the lack of value in American literature has continually reminded me of what is at stake in discussing Fiedler.

In seeking to locate the politics of the myriad critical debates that Fiedler generated on the socio-political-cultural register of America and the world, one of the challenges for me from the start was to provide an afterlife to his work. For what Fiedler wrote survives into a new literary era and continues to flourish in a new cultural climate, which it may have helped to create. To adopt Fiedler, even if it is for a short time for reading this book, one has to adapt to his many peccadilloes.

Nudging the concept of borders once again, can we say that just because he spent his whole life within America as a part of academia, he cannot be taken seriously by the postcolonialists? Will his white skin be the albatross around his neck? Or isn't he the quintessential "un–American" American with a discursive position that is located territorially in the U.S. but ideologically outside the U.S.? Or does his position as an American professor who lived all his life in America disallow a consideration of him by the postcolonialists? Or am I reading too much into his dissenting voice, which was emblematic of the American sixties?

Not to make the entire effort a fetishization of marginalia—or a celebration at the expense of the core (often read as the dominant white male tradition, as spelled out in the canon wars of the academia in America), the book hopes to balance it out by its genuine treatment of Fiedler's American engagement with American core issues. So it is against such a backdrop—quite personal, in a sense; Indian, and a little global and contemporary—that I have embarked upon the study of Fiedler. What does not change, of course, is my position as a student of American studies located in postcolonial India. In all, I approach my subject from the twin vantage point of, first, a student of Fiedler's self-marginalized uniqueness within American literary studies and cultural discourse, and then, second, as a postcolonialist. My central concern is not to make an overarching postcolonial reading of all his works, per se, though a little of it is unavoidable. I would rather like to show what this project means for a postcolonial reader. The purpose is not to overwrite the postcolonial, nor be the palimpsest disclaiming the stature of Fiedler as an Americanist. His fiction and not-so-noted yet engaging poetry have not been given the kind of diligent reading that they should have, primarily because they require a full-blown critical study.

Although this book does not attempt the impossible task of covering all aspects of the gadfly that Fiedler is, I sincerely hope that its debates and arguments will stimulate and enable a second innings with the author. If this were a likely moment for the launching of "schools" in literature, Fiedler might be the starting-point of a new school.[6] He does at any rate mark an unexpected swing of the pendulum. Here in my opinion is the only writer of the slightest value who has appeared among the global intellectuals for some years past. Even if that is objected to as an overstatement, it will probably be admitted that Fiedler is a writer out of the ordinary, worth more than a single glance.

Out of the large body of criticism on Fiedler, one can hear many voices, and my voice is another. It is distinctly my own. I hope that there will be ears to hear it. Recently, in a pithy and restrained review of Pardini's book, Ray B. Browne regrets the loss of a "vital spark" to criticism of literature and indeed culture. This does not restrain him from calling Fiedler "the Serpent in the Garden who not only tempted but also urged" and even changed skins. Nailing Fiedler for his hasty, impulsive and wrongheaded criticism, he welcomes Pardini's not-so-full collection about an author, still "worthy to be heard" as a kind of beginning until a more comprehensive one is out (Browne 2009, 184).

Will this book be one?

Time will tell!

Introduction

He was nothing if not ambivalent.
—Fiedler to Scott McLemee, "Chronicle of Higher Education"

Often wrong, but never in doubt.
—Fiedler to Robert Boyers, "Thinking about Leslie Fiedler"

[H]e is on the one hand one of the creators of the modern orthodoxy and also one of the sources for the rebellion against it.
—James Seaton, "Innocence Regained"

Fiedler has traversed the academic promenade for more than six decades. His preoccupation with regression and the sexual boyhood fantasies of the American male is too well known to need exposition. Yet, read in conjunction with his other honest "other" preoccupations (racial, mythopoeic, psychological, cultural and postmodern), it clearly reflects his well-defined movement into a critical field, "free of all vestiges of the elitism and the Culture Religion," which can no longer be condescending to popular literature and must "resist all impulses to create hierarchies, even those implicit in what seem harmless distinctions of genre or medium" (CBCG, 4). It is one that does not reject that art "whose muse is the machine and whose fate seems more closely linked to the history of technology"(3).

So often repeated to the point of becoming a Fiedlerian jingle, the following is what defines Fiedler: oxymoronic to a point that his critics never trusted him, a specialist in hyperbolic statements, a regular rabble-rouser, the only person "who could or at least would quote Dante and the Talmud during a lecture on the literature of the American West.... His fearlessness in exploring new ground" (Richard 2004, 294) led him to do what he eventually and always did and for what he is notorious: carving out new, undulating roads, spreading novel vistas and looking beyond limitless horizons. In the same vein, William Van O'Conner categorically points out that Fiedler's subject is culture, popular culture, and shifts in culture and high art. He is as likely to refer to names of celebrities such as Marlon Brando or Al Capone as to literary figures like Guido Cavalcanti or William Blake (1960, 47).

Fiedler, who looked like a messianic figure, with almost a satanic gleam in his eyes, pontificated at the State University of New York, Buffalo, for more than three decades. Before that he was at Missoula, Montana, for twenty-three years in an intellectual wilderness that many feel encouraged the wildness in him (Kellman 1999, 8). Possessed of a robust and passionate intellect, he is known as an unorthodox and provocative interpreter of American literature. Over the years, in spite of much hostile criticism, Fiedler managed to find a cozy and significant place among the American intelligentsia. I am tempted to present a glimpse of the professor through the eyes of Benjamin De Mott:

> He rocks, slightly as he speaks ... a clever bearded, tanned face.... He seems, almost, to hum to himself ... self-enjoyment sweeps up the room.... Even in his moments of scrunched-up tortured, small-boy-cruelly-punished pain, the man's larger-than-life quality and relish of self are constant. Here before you, folks, here in this barrel torso sits the soul of the last appetitive, red-skinned, thoroughly non-academic academic on earth [1978, 29].

Starting with the publication of his first critical anthology, *An End to Innocence: Essays on Culture and Politics* (1955), Fiedler proved to be a thought-provoking scholar. In his distinguished, non-conformist academic career, Fiedler makes it impossible for us ever to read the classics of literature in the same way again. His exhibitionist discourse ruptures certain rhythms of the canon and his deconstructionist study of a mythical pattern of American males' insulated psyches makes an engaged reading of America's cultural contagion.[1] In his later critical phase, Fiedler believed that literature was no longer sacrosanct, to be monasticated in a sanctuary within the library and academia. The mass-commodified epoch has opened up immense possibilities for further problematization of literary hierarchies. His counter-culture accommodated, alongside the high mimetic mode of art, its obverse—the low mimetic—amply demonstrated in several of his path-breaking, nonconformist texts.[2] Encapsulated within Fiedler's subsuming cultural discourse is his pet project of opening up the canon of literature, stifled within the rubric of academia. Fiedler uses the center-margin paradigm to locate the "common and the periphery" in the arrogant history of highbrow cultural power.

By using such embarrassingly popular texts as *Gone with the Wind*, *Uncle Tom's Cabin* and *The Adventures of Huckleberry Finn* in a theory of literature that was at once disturbing and profound, Fiedler administered a brisk shaking to the staid and comfortable world of American literary establishment. His essay "Come Back to the Raft Ag'in, Huck Honey!" has been called notorious and written in bad taste, and his book, *No! In Thunder* has aroused considerable negative criticism. Actually the so-called offensive essay on homosexuality, "Come Back to the Raft Ag'in, Huck Honey!" which now in retrospect seems harmless, should have been sufficient warning to critics of the future direction of his writings. Most take off from the insights that were latent in this essay. Being chided for childish failings—"over statement, restlessness, and egotism"—was not unusual for this critic who was obsessed by the infantile in American culture,[3] as is evident in his next book, *Love and Death in the American Novel* (1960). But what it also brings to the fore is his public-centered, populist approach, as this review in *Times Literary Supplement* demonstrates: "He has written a long book.... [Not] content with a scholarly audience; he reaches out to the general public, for what he has to say bears not only upon the American novel but upon 'the American Experience,' so inextricably entangled are literature and life."[4]

In his attempt to negotiate between the elite and the popular can be seen a desire to subvert certain monolithic cultural ideologies and build an edifice of protest literature. He sees it as a kind of massive con-game on the part of the hegemonic discourse to ghettoize literature into conservative categories. Though critics perceive an overstated case of a lack of a sense of commanding perspective, the politics implicated in his critical position is populist, even anarchist, based on impatience with all distinctions of the kind created on the model of a class-structured society. "His influence has been so profound yet so diffuse that people don't even acknowledge it,"[5] says Mark Royden Winchell, a professor of English at Clemson University, whose biographical study of Fiedler, *"Too Good to Be True": The Life and Work of Leslie Fiedler*, was published by the University of Missouri Press in 2002. Fiedler, who never had the cautious, academic mien about him, even though Kenneth Rexroth once attacked him for "his membership in a small circle of extremely ethnocentric people—the self-styled New York Establishment," ably performed the part of the outrageous outlander, one who finds his secret self among Jews, freaks, Blackfeet, and other vanishing Americans (Kellman 1999, 8). Susan Gubar's summing-up is not too far from being perfectly apt:

> More of a free thinking "maverick" than a "maven," Fiedler could be relied upon to throw political correctness to the winds, to trample on many people's most cherished convictions of rectitude.... Gleefully provocative, he defiantly played out many of his most subversive maneuvers not in the name of feminism or queer theory or Jewish or Black Studies but under the banner of a visionary form of what today we would call Cultural Studies, but a Cultural Studies different from today's to the extent that its practitioners would eschew not only any narrowly political set of preordained assumptions but also the jargon and the pretentiousness of academe [1999, 169–70].

A "master of the hectoring overstatement" (Timberg 2008), Fiedler opened his first significant essay, "Come Back to the Raft Ag'in, Huck Honey!," published in *Partisan Review* in 1948, when Fiedler was 31, with a sentence that announced itself as a scandal: "It is perhaps to be expected that the Negro and the homosexual should become stock literary themes in a period when the exploration of responsibility and failure has become again a primary concern of our literature." But it is suggestive, "quasi-parodical prose," of these lines which seems to ridicule its own highmindedness. The first six words are pure ventriloquism as they echo the demurring perfected by older Jewish critics who feared they weren't mannerly enough to appropriate the "Anglo-American tradition." The drivel about "responsibility and failure" reeks of the ideological piety Fiedler was ready to explode (Tanenhaus 2003). Critics such as Chase have found his style "rapid and witty … often richly made, if occasionally pedantic" (1960, 12). Yet, accused of employing a highly elitist and sophisticated idiom for his writings, Fiedler offers his justification: "I speak the language of literary critics, explaining in literary idiom the nature and appeal of popular art" (Tanenhaus 2003, 10).

As the unclaimed hero that many feel he is and a man never apt to be mistaken for any other, Leslie Fiedler has always been a bit of a puzzle (Boyers 1999, 171).[6] He can be enjoyed like the taste of old wine alongside the newest thing in town. Celebrating difference and refashioning the canon, he is one without margins and beyond borders. Significantly, because of his ambivalence and penchant for newer themes for his books, he has been positively appreciated by critics as one "who redefines himself and his subject with each bold book" (Kellman 1999, 8). Fiedler did not shrink from boldness. "I'm very fond of words like *death* of the novel," he noted in an interview, "or an end to innocence" (Green 1981, 135). At one point, he proclaimed that the novel "is dead as a single genre.... [H]e was convinced that one of the gifts of a great writer of fiction is the gift of being possessed by hallucinations that he then translates in such a way that the reader accepts them as his/her hallucinations" (Walden 1999, 165). But he also knew many things academic people rarely bothered to learn, and he could talk about politics and popular culture without holding his nose or striking superior postures (Boyers, quoted in Kellman and Malin 1999, 171–72). For all of his tendency to categorize—no other literary man has given us so many amusing and suggestive terms with which to define and organize our experience—he has tried to explain how seemingly incompatible formations (the "magical, mechanical, psychological," the ego and the id, the heterosexual and the homosexual) are complexly related (172). His status as a wild man is matched by not a very long list: Harold Bloom with his sprawling, egomaniacal tomes; Stanley Fish with his "subversive" provocations; Frank Lentricchia in his muscle shirt; but he remains "the original chest-thumping extrovert of American criticism, and no one ever did it better" (Tanenhaus 2003, 17).

It is true that for so prolific a writer a large body of criticism has grown around his works. As his own comment to David Gates of *Newsweek* (1984) states,

The typical pattern of one of my books ... is that when it comes out everybody abuses it. Ten years later they're still abusing it, but they have begun to steal ideas from it. Twenty years go by, and they decide it's a classic, although nobody's ever said anything good about it.[7]

Thus it makes good sense to look at the body of criticism around Fiedler in about the same way. Initial reactions will be discussed largely in this chapter, whereas the concluding chapter will look at the recent body of work on him.

The early criticism that grew around Fiedler has a pattern. This pattern has a design that has been woven out of a number of threads. If one stands for denial, the other represents shock at his (Fiedler's) disclosures. The rest of the threads, entangled with one another, denote outright rejection. One almost invisible thread epitomizes grudging acknowledgment of his brilliant insights. Only some tiny invisible strands signify admiration and praise. Generally, these invisible strands gained illumination towards the latter part of his career. This came to him in different ways but never with overwhelming applause. So polarity of responses is the hallmark of the criticism that surrounds Fiedler. Interestingly, he was aware of it. Niela Sesachari points out, "The polaric responses that Fiedler generates in his readers are a result of his dynamic critical methods, for he has striven to strike at the roots of 'the new genteel tradition, with its emphasis on textual analysis, its contempt for general ideas and its fear of popular culture,' in order to deliberately democratise and 'Vulgarise' (in the best sense) his criticism" (1976, 17).

Most of the early critics claimed that Fiedler was an iconoclast, a shocker, and a scandalizer. They variously saw in him the negativist, the mythmaker, the pop critic, and the counter-culturalist. Relatedly, many of these critics also saw his various preoccupations with culture, literature and criticism as laden with an intense desire to shock. Hence his writings have been received with decided polarity of critical opinion, being described as both refreshing and offensive, provocative and tame, lively and tedious. A man of profound learning and knowledge, Fiedler evokes responses such as Perry Miller's—"Mr. Fiedler peremptorily reminds himself that he is obliged every fifth paragraph to make himself offensive to somebody or other" (Larson 1970, 135)—or Roger Sale's, that Fiedler is "always putting himself in situations where he is speaking against this fashion or that obsolescence" (1971, 10). *The New York Times Book Review* (May 23, 1971, 7) introduces Fiedler in these words:

> A list of great critics and historians of American literature in this century would have to include Leslie Fiedler, by far the least academic, the most voluble, diverse, uneven, divisive, rambunctious, and—to use his own word, heavy with irony, pride, and regret—"controversial."

Polarity and confusion notwithstanding, critics such as Stephen Donadio appear ambivalent: "Stylistically inclined towards the spectacular and facile,

Mr. Fiedler has a singular ability to make even important truths sound very much like gossip" (1964, 688). Donadio goes to the extent of saying that the "tendency to mingle fact with fiction often lends an air of unreality to Mr. Fiedler's observations; his comments conjure up an amusement park America in which the literary world is a side show" (1964, 670). Consequentially, it would appear that Fiedler's method is a frontal attack based on shock, entertainment and provocation, with a singular desire to gain attention. But this also makes his criticism interesting, lively and spicy, whether we agree with him or not. This also leads others (the luminous strands) who are overawed by his writings to say, "Do I have the nerve to do this?"[8]

William Van O'Conner, in his essay "Accent on the Negative," highlights Fiedler's pretentiousness in order to gain attention. He says, "Fiedler has a good eye for pretence, he can worry an idea like a cat toying with a mouse but he has a terrible need to be a show-off" (1960, 47). The same point is made by Granville Hicks, who calls him the wild man of American literary criticism, insisting that all Fiedler wanted to do was to give his readers a kick in the pants (1960, 14).

Most of the critics agree that Fiedler is a mythopoeic critic and that he is primarily concerned with myths and archetypes. In fact, if Larson is to be believed, "Fiedler has become what he set out to be: a living myth, a part of his criticism itself" (1971, 127). This comment of Larson's is in connection with the publication of two of Fiedler's essays in *No! In Thunder*, "Archetype and Signature" and "In the Beginning Was the Word: Logos or Mythos." Larson adds further, "Fiedler believes that each generation, each age, will temper the myths of the past to meet its own needs, and each generation will create new myths relevant for its specific age" (136). And, finally, he says, "This is the crux of the problem with Fiedler—everything becomes a myth" (141). Attributing to Fiedler all that he is known for, Winchell does not cringe to allot him a secondary spot where necessary. For example, in the arena of myth criticism, Winchell does not refrain from pointing out, "Although Northrop Frye has constructed a more comprehensive system of myth criticism, Fiedler has made more practical use of this approach in judging particular texts and in explaining the importance of song and story in human experience" (Winchell 2002, preface, ix). Some critics such as Winchell and Larson suggest that Fiedler has always been Huck Finn but unlike Huck, for Fiedler the territories the artist lights out for are always within, at a spot where dream and myth coincide, and Indians are really black men with red faces, and everyone at the bottom is a Jew.

Looking at Fiedler's total oeuvre, if Howe says, "Mr. Fiedler cares not about books and writers but about archetypes, myths, trends, depths, and sensations" (quoted in Larson 1970, 34), it does not hold much water because

Fiedler over and over again, in book after book, expanded his themes and has looked at innumerable writers, canonical and not so canonical, of America and Europe. John Hawkes, Henry Roth, Harriet Beecher Stowe, Margaret Mitchell, Alex Haley, and Olaf Stapledon are just a few names by way of example. In fact he can be said to have reinstated several subalterns of literature; *Call It Sleep* by Roth is just one example. It is true that Fiedler's approach in *Love and Death* was mythic and its attempt was to define a central American mythos. To call it "a depressingly bad job of criticism [and] written more to shock than illuminate" is just another example of the myopic early responses to his works (Levine 1967, 440). DeMott's sociological and humanistic thrust to Fiedler's Freudian interpretations in his essay "The Negative American" is also bigoted early on: "What his book says about American Novel is: there are no people here at all. In literature we have no passionate encounter of man and woman because we have (almost) no man and woman" (1967, 446). According to DeMott, Fiedler's main subject is the study of man, his losses and gains. What he—the man—loses can be measured in terms of his rights, his wholeness, his capability to speak truly. The symptoms that arise out of these flaws (which are also generally the main subject of most American novels) are flight from society, lack of interest in sex and full absorption in a single pursuit—love, hatred, intellectual stimulus or humor.

That there has always been "an element of absurdity or shock in Fiedler's work" that is often writ large by a "great number of generalizations, repetitions, and strained conclusions which so often have marred his frequently brilliant commentaries on American fiction" cannot be denied, but what is cumbersome is the disparity between his comments and method: "a frontal attack based on shock, entertainment ... and the destruction of shibboleths and prejudices we should have rid ourselves of years, if not generations ago" (Larson 1970, 133–134). It is true that "the desire to taunt, goad, and generally annoy the critical establishment has ... formed a major portion of Fiedler's intent in all his writings," but this is exactly what he wanted, "'the raised voice, the howl of rage or love' and what his own criticism accomplishes. If nothing else it never bores the reader" (Larson 1971, 50).

Along with Larson, there are a number of other critics who see numerous positive traits behind the façade of Fiedler's so-called provocative, shocking, and negative criticism. They all speak highly of his critical pieces and are sure of a place of eminence for him. Critics such as Richard Chase feel that he is "one of the most lively and interesting critics on the scene," but paradoxically his "cultural and literary judgments are sometimes profound and sometimes merely scintillating" (1960, 12).

The numerous adjectives attributed to Fiedler cannot just be brushed aside, as they quite appropriately decide Fiedler's position as a critic of American culture. Most of the critics, we discover, applaud Fiedler's critical evaluation of literature on the one hand; on the other, they also point out his highly controversial, provocative and diverse interpretations. But P. S. Prescott, who has devoted considerable attention to Fiedler's writings in "American as Innocents," draws up a list of Fiedler's weaknesses and strengths and points out that "among contemporary critics, Fiedler's strengths are unique." Prescott says of Fiedler, "He writes with vigor and style. He is arrogant, contemptuous of those who cannot see what he sees, but he has an uncommon wit and a talent both for satire and for pithy axioms." He also points out that Fiedler is "rarely boring. To be dull a man must be either modest or incompetent, and Fiedler is neither" (1971, 76). Humble enough, Fiedler "irritably disposes of talk of his brilliance, his skills at entertainment and polemics" in his writings. Fiedler's "true lust (there is no other word for it) is for connections, for the patterns of culture he finds behind the surface form of art," continues Prescott, pointing out the "theatrical jargon" that lends non-seriousness to Fiedler's art particularly in his essays on Joe McCarthy and the Rosenbergs (1971, 77ff). Unpretentious to the core, his works in general and *Love and Death in the American Novel* in particular elicited this response from *Times Literary Supplement*: "Throwing aside the caution and reticence that are commonly supposed to characterise the scholar, he speaks, with his own mouth, out of his own face. He addresses us, he says, without a mask" (March 17, 1961, 161). This trait is aligned well with his penchant for speaking in his own voice and writing in the first person.

Prescott further comments:

> Fiedler's essays with a narrow focus are generally acute, his broader essays may be in part mistaken but they are always exciting, prompting the reader (as Hercule Poirot would say) furiously to think. We have less need of critics who are right than we have of critics who are like Fiedler who set up a perspective that forces us to look again on art, on culture, we once thought familiar. Fiedler is part mystic, part romantic, part Hebraic truth-teller [1971, 77ff].

Finally, summing up his reflections on Fiedler, Prescott states, "Unlike most critics, Fiedler has sunk roots into American popular culture—into films and comic books—although he is often surprised that he likes it and is always more convincing when pop culture is the subject of his argument" (76ff).

Fiedler's belief that a poet's personality and his intention leave an impact on his creative effort evoked reactions not so wholesome and palatable. Wimsatt and Brooks in *Literary Criticism: A Short History*, as quoted by Larson (1970, 137), react sharply to Fiedler's comment "the poem is important as an event in the life of the poet." Notwithstanding their credo that a poem is a work of art, independent of its creator, some critics have not hesitated in commenting upon Fiedler's own autobiographical essays, both negatively and positively. More evidently autobiographical are those essays in which Fiedler deals with Jewishness, the Jews, establishment and his socio-political thinking (BB, 1967). Roger Sale says Fiedler has certain subjects—being a Jew in America is one of them—to which he returns over and over again. All his literature is covered with a thin layer of his ethnic identity as a Jewish writer in America.

Fiedler's study of Jewish heritage clearly traces the rise of the Jewish intellectual on the American literary scene. Moreover, a number of Fiedler's writings deal with the Jewish problem of alienation. Daniel Walden has devoted considerable attention to this aspect of Fiedler's writings. He points out that Fiedler, apart from his mythical preoccupations, has also dealt with the ethnic, racial and topological underlay of American life. Elaborating on his treatment of the Indian, the blacks and the Jews, Walden explicates, "He touched on the wellsprings of our national experience and the contradictions between what we say we believe in and what we practice" (1978, 208). Walden adds, "In spite of our protestations, we define outsiders all the time—by color or race or class" (1978, 209), and treat others accordingly.

Dealing with this Jewish aspect of Fiedler's critical faculty, I would like to highlight what Irving Malin brings to us in his book *Jews and Americans* (1965). In this book Malin has discussed seven Jewish-American writers, and Fiedler is one of them. Talking of Fiedler, the critic points out that Fiedler has always been concerned with Jewishness. His early fiction amply indicates this involvement. "Roman Holiday" (1954) and a number of essays in *Waiting for the End* (1964) and *To the Gentiles* (1971) indicate a positive commitment to Jews. In both the books, Fiedler is also concerned with elite and popular culture, and he feels that the Jews are closely associated with the latter. Malin goes to the extent of saying that Leslie Fiedler's myth criticism as represented in *Love and Death in the American Novel* (1960) and *No! In Thunder* (1960) is obliquely Jewish. Neila Sesachari in her essay "Leslie A. Fiedler—Critic as Mythographer" has also interpreted his Jewish preoccupations in terms of myths and archetypes (25–26). Malin says of Fiedler, "His criticism resembles a parable; through it he registers a 'representative' temper.... We may not agree with Fiedler at times—he may seem to be a propagandist—but his courageous interpretations are more valuable than 'automatic' explication" (1965, 167).

It has been noticed by critics and readers alike that Fiedler considers negativism important to the artist, the critic and serious literature. This element of dissent is present in almost all his writings, particularly in his preface to *No! In Thunder*. Examining the quality of dissent, D. R. Sharma's article "Leslie A. Fiedler: The Vitality of Negativism" is of great significance. Sharma examines Fiedler as an artist who looks upon literature as an earnest endeavor to investigate truth and whose literary criticism is not a means to obliging or supporting a guild but a defense of truth and the value of art. Sharma says,

"Fielder employs dissent as an instrument of differentiation between serious literature and the sub-literature of popular appeal ... and Fiedler pits his vital negativism to counteract the vulgarisation of culture" (1983, 15). Sharma says further that when Fiedler differentiates art, sub-art, serious literature and best-sellers, artist and anti-artist, his main idea is to "activate the dormant resources of creative and critical energies. He may not have the suavity of the 'American Scholar,' but he does manifest the passionate concerns of the 'chanticleer' to awaken us against the soporific drugs of sentimentality and conformism" (1983, 21). And, finally, Sharma sums up by saying, "It is the emotion of sincerity and compulsion to uphold the value of honest, unspectacular, and permanent protest against the affirmative assaults on art and life that imparts validity and precision to his hypothesis of vital negativism" (1983, 22).

To be abrasive, to say "No! In Thunder in as many different ways as he can," seems to be the hallmark of his critical enterprise (Sale 1971, 10). Dembo feels that Fiedler's major criticism is devoted precisely to discovering the archetypes and stereotypes—of women, Jews, Indians, negroes—that inhere in American life ... but the word No, sometimes in a thunder, sometimes in a whisper, sometimes merely in a gesture, echoes throughout" (1973, 139). Robert Alter in "Jewish Dreams and Nightmares" points out the characteristics of Fiedler's critical enterprise and in doing so, almost praises Fiedler's criticism, which has a paradoxical doubleness of effect. On the one hand, "because his favourite critical activity is the relentless pursuit of archetypes, an ill considered literary fashion of the fifties ... there is often an odd hint of datedness" in his writings. But, "one senses in Fiedler, on the other hand, a peculiar venturesomeness and energy of imagination that set him off from the academic mythmongers of the fifties, indeed, that endow his work with a perennial fascination" (1968, 61).

There is no doubt that critics have always been at a loss to assign an adequate and appropriate position to Fiedler, either as an elite critic or a critic of popular culture, and sometimes his negativism is seen by one set of critics as a revolt against literary standards that have become rusted, old and obsolete. Another set of critics see his negativism as an attempt to achieve a higher, more real truth, which is a kind of fulfilling self awareness: self achievement. Whatever the critics might say initially, they unanimously regard his negativism as one of the strengths of his criticism, but only when it manifests itself in restraint. Otherwise it is seen, by critics, as an attempt to shock rather than to illuminate, an attack to annoy the critical establishment rather than disagree and present his own viewpoint.

Roger Sale comments on Fiedler's "chutzpah and puduer," the two impulses that Fiedler sees lying behind a great many works of art. "Chutzpah" is the brazen impulse, oral, loud, and assertive, and "puduer" is the impulse of hiding, as seen by Fiedler. Through this essay Sale makes some interesting disclosures about Fiedler's critical enterprise. Fiedler's controversial revelations about American art and the artist are seen by Sale as characteristic of the brazen Fiedler, filled with chutzpah. Trying to explain the various shifts of opinion of Fiedler, Sale says:

> Fiedler has always been delighted to hurl himself into the immediate moment, not just to live that moment but to rewrite history or politics or mythology from the perspective of that moment.... Fiedler never tires of setting out a current problem or issue, comparing it to something else a decade or a generation ago, redefining the problem giving the context of the past, then projecting a large scale present and future from the redefinition [1971, 10].

Further, Sale points out that when Fiedler does things this way, he inevitably changes his mind a lot, and "has never been one to try to hide his many shifts in opinion and emphasis over the years" (1971, 10). This in itself is an act of chutzpah that shows Fiedler as a man who has responded and reacted to the moment without any pretense.

With an affective hint of chutzpah, Sale claims that Fiedler's relation with literature has remained "essentially impure," which implies that "much of what he writes dates rather quickly" (10). Fiedler also makes contexts control works rather than the other way round, in the process "overrating whatever will fit his context" (10). Perhaps the penchant for battle and for immersion in the present need not always be at odds with the penchant to tell truths, to be wise and impersonal. They are not always at odds in Fiedler's work. But the habit of battle is a punishing one, as is clear to anyone who finds himself becoming a little weary of Fiedler's otherwise splendid and necessary chutzpah (10).

The above assessment made by Sale can be considered worthy of attention. The assessment is balanced and a little harsh, yet Sale's style matches the style of the one he is evaluating. Both seem to be filled with chutzpah. A similar brazenness is seen in the following: "Fiedler is an incorrigible rascal, but to forbid his tricks would deprive us of the often brilliant insights he has up his sleeve" (Edwards 1968, 606).

Having been given the stature of a pop critic, one who heralds the shift from the "whisky culture to the dope culture," is seen as one who attempts to cross the border and close the gap between elite and popular literature. Critics are also constantly in a fix defining this multifaceted personality and his critical pieces. He "closes the gap," says Russell Reising, "between literature and society by suggesting that this revulsion from adult love and the subsequent refuge in a nightmare of neurotic evasions as portrayed in American fiction ... affect the lives we lead from day to day" (1986, 131). While he has been called an advocate of "opening up the canon of American literature," his own selectivity in *Love and Death in the American Novel* has led Irving Howe, among others, says Reising, to accuse Fiedler of "simply ignoring those writers and books that might call his thesis into question" and to remark that "what Fiedler disregards ... is awesome" (1986, 132). It is true that critics have not hesitated in criticizing Fiedler for his personal choices, but Fiedler himself has also not hesitated to offer justification and explanation for his very own preferences. Dembo elaborates the same point when he says that Fiedler's "tour-de-force" suffers from one major problem: "literature is used as evidence to support a sociological or cultural thesis and major and minor works are given importance in the perspective of this thesis rather than in terms of their inherent literary quality. Fiedler seems to have little concern for the integrity of an art-work" (1973, 140).

These pieces of criticism of Fiedler, read in continuation with Roger Sale's interpretations, suggest that Fiedler's judgment of literature could be, to a certain extent, partial to the presentation of his own thesis and point of view. But, whatever it is, critics have not hesitated in pointing out the high caliber of his interpretations of American literature. Commenting upon Fiedler's critical corpus, Maini points out, "He has steadily and strenuously held on to his intellectual faith in the beauty, richness and value of pop art" (1976, 8). Whatever the high priests of high art and culture may have to say with regard to the lowly comic and the crime thrillers, or in relation to the kitchen-maid romances and covert erotica and pornography, comments Maini, Fiedler is prepared to defend these literary outcasts as "an expression of a subculture that is as vital to the health of society as any moral hygiene." In short, to sum up Maini, Fiedler has used his formidable knowledge-machinery and industry to confront the critical Establishment, and forced it to take notice of his subversive aesthetic (1976, 8). In this way, Maini establishes Fiedler as a critic at war with the "pundits or high priests" of elite art.

Some critics have tried to give Fiedler the hard pat that he deserves. R. Z. Shippard, in his essay "Leslie Fiedler's Monster Party," opines:

> Critics of the critic suggested that Fiedler was playing to the crowd with a limited script based on pop, Freud, Jungian archetypes. His enthusiasm for discovering mythic power in such popular arts as movies and comic books was not appreciated by guardian of high culture. Yet Fiedler outflanked them by describing himself as a hybrid of Chutzpah (Yiddish for nerve or gall) and Puduer (French for modesty or reserve). This itself was an act of inspired Chutzpah that cast Fiedler as a cultural freak [1978, 95].

Winchell, in his book *Leslie Fiedler* (1985), alludes to *Being Busted*, in which Fiedler defends his pot bust and tells us that Fiedler was persecuted not for "what he did" as a supporter of the young but for "what he was—or what he was believed to be ... a pot-smoking communist professor." Winchell, who has written an authoritative account of the writer's life, *Too Good to Be True* (2002), in his 1985 book on Fiedler declared, "He did not smoke pot, had long since become disillusioned with the Soviet Union, and has never been comfortable in the pontifical role of professor" (1985, 2–3).

Winchell brushes aside these attributes with a speed that characterizes his other evaluation of Fiedler and says "such misunderstandings have plagued Fiedler for his entire career (but he remains undisturbed) ... as long as he cherishes the role of barbarian and disturber of the peace" (1985, 2–3). Barrie Hayne tries to sum up Fiedler's status as a critic by giving a plausible explanation for his being a controversial figure:

> Call him Freudian, Jungian, Archetypal, Mythic, Cultural critic (all these terms have their limitations) he is projecting the cultural dream and bringing his readers into contact with them. To be asked to look at one's comfortable assumptions, especially as they concern self and country is painful enough; to be confronted with one's national and personal dream, the repressed products of one's hidden recesses, is infinitely more painful which is why some regard him as "Controversial" [1979, xi].

His negativism, often regarded as one of the strengths of his criticism when manifested with restraint, is also seen by critics as an attempt to shock, rather than to illuminate.[9]

In a contemporary assessment of Fiedler what irks Witholt is the fact that "Fiedler has been largely forgotten by scholars and the public alike. Detractors suggest that he rode the waves of popular trends until his flimsy raft was shipwrecked on the shore. Recent trends in literary and cultural studies would instead suggest that Fiedler had found solid footing long before the crash" (2009, 71). For Witholt, "Unlike other academics, Fiedler seriously studied and wrote on popular culture ahead of his time. Ideas like those he had in 1952 on comic books have only recently received acknowledgment as literary scholarship" (2009, 72). As Fiedler's popularity peaked in the 1960s and '70s, Fiedler focused inward to reflect on the impossibility of playing both the worldly wild child and the institutional critic. Perhaps foreseeing his own decline, in a 1964 essay, "The Death of *Avant-Garde* Literature," Fiedler writes, "No writer can have the rewards of a book-club adoption and of alienation at the same time" (CE 2, 455). Focusing on Fiedler's own statement in "Leslie Fiedler Reintroduces Himself," published soon after his reflective *Being Busted*, a social critique-cum-memoir written after being arrested for letting marijuana be smoked in his house, Fiedler proposes three stages of his life: "first into radical dissent, then into radical disillusion and the fear of innocence, and finally into whatever it is that lies beyond both commitment and disaffection" (Witholt 2009, 72).

More recently, Gore Vidal described Fiedler as "America's liveliest full-time professor and seducer of the *Zeitgeist*." A sprinter and a long distance heavy runner, this "seducer of the *Zeitgeist* was ahead of his time, but he also defined and clocked it. An ageless child of the century, he has become one of its venerable ancients" (quoted in Kellman 1999, 8). He was indeed "the garrulous and provocative critic of literature who could write equally well on Nathaniel Hawthorne and circus freaks" (Timberg 2008).

Fiedler's subject is culture, popular culture, and shifts in culture and high art (O'Conner 1960, 46–47). He is as likely to refer to names of celebrities such as Marlon Brando or Al Capone as to literary figures such as Guido Cavalcanti or William Blake. In Fiedler "there is the culture analyst and commentator, there is the literary historian and there is the literary theorist and critic.... In fact, Fiedler is at his best as a cultural analyst and at his worst as a literary critic. The cultural analyst is to be seen (mostly) in earlier writings" (Chase 1960, 13).

In a Darwinian milieu, responding to the epoch of hegemony of commodities and commercial art, pop artists, including Fiedler, "have become self-consciously outrageous entertainers for a society demanding more and extravagant and intricate form of amusement" (Donadio 1964, 672). Whatever the high priests of high art and culture may have to say with regard to the lowly comic and the crime thrillers, or in relation to the kitchen-maid romances and covert erotica and pornography, Fiedler is prepared to defend these literary outcastes as "an expression of a subculture that is as vital to the health of society as any moral hygiene." In short, Fiedler has used his formidable knowledge-machinery and industry to confront the critical establishment, and forced it to take notice of his subversive aesthetic. In this way, Fiedler redounds as a critic recusant with the pundits of elite art. Maini also points out, "He has steadily and strenuously held on to his intellectual faith in the beauty, richness and value of pop art" (8). "If literary blogs had been around in Fiedler's day," said Richard Nash, who published the new collection by Pardini, "he would have been just loving it, in the sense of being a provocateur. He'd have been on nerve.com or had his own blog" (Timberg 2008).

Justifying the title, *The Devil Gets His Due* (2002), of the book about this "subversive scribbling devil,"[10] Kelemen quotes Pardini, "It is ... not a coincidence that Fiedler's critical career began in the Devil's home, Dante's *Inferno*, right where the informed imagination challenges the limits of knowledge, of the physical world and man's place in it. To look backward at a criticism based on these critical presuppositions and give the Devil his due may as well be a way out of the crisis of literary criticism" (Pardini, 2008, xvii).

Until some years back, Fiedler was still scandalizing the academic elitists and delighting the students at State University of New York (SUNY), Buffalo. Whether Fiedler had mellowed, or the rest of the world had simply caught up with him, is hard to say, avers Winchell.

Critics have examined him and his writings from various angles—as an iconoclast, a mythmaker, a champion of the Jews, a naysayer, a pop critic, and more. All these critics directly or indirectly talk of Fiedler's elitist position as a critic and the definite interest in popular culture—popular literature to be more precise—that dominates most of his writings. When he moves away from the elitist position, he is labeled an iconoclast, and a shocker. His myth criticism, on the one hand, borrows certain elitist ideas of formalist criticism, and on the other, his concern with the populace,[11] his undaunted belief that myths and archetypes join all, takes him toward popular culture. Richard Chase, in his essay "Leslie Fiedler and American Culture," says that in Fiedler's personality "there is the culture analyst and commentator, there is the literary historian and there is the literary theorist and critic.... In fact, Fiedler is at his best as a cultural analyst and at his worst as a literary critic. The cultural analyst is to be seen (mostly) in earlier writings" (1960). Some critics such as O'Conner, Dembo, Winchell, and Maini have tried to illuminate the shift in interests, or trace his movement from elite to popular culture. A full-length study of this organic growth in his criticism can be treated as a significant intervention in the not-so-many unbiased lists of discourses on American literature. This book can be treated as a sure step in this direction. I begin with no a priori notion; my approach to Fiedler has been open-minded. Hence, this book is in the nature of an exploration as well. In "My Credo," Fiedler proposes "a mode of criticism more congruous with the sort of literature we admire, a criticism as wary of bureaucratization, as respectful to the mythic and the mysterious, as dedicated to a language at once idiosyncratic and humane as, say, *Moby Dick* or the novels of Kafka" (1950, 561–62). He is "on the one hand one of the creators of the modern orthodoxy and also one of the sources for the rebellion against it" (Seaton 1989, 93). In *Waiting for the End,* Fiedler talks of Europe as a retreating horizon of the west, "a place difficult to remain" (1964, 25), the place of a "dream" from which we wake in pleasure or terror. Alternatively, it is viewed as an object of "romantic flirtation" (1964, 25). Most typically, Europe is represented as a "woman we cannot hold: a saint to be worshipped from afar, or a whore to be longed for and left" (1964, 25). In the essay "Jewish-Americans Go Home," Fiedler writes, "No American, not even a Jew in pursuit of Utopian Americanism, can escape European culture completely" (WFTE 1964, 105).

That Fiedler has raised a storm over the years with his incendiary revelations and provocative opinions is a truism few will disagree with. Yet, in talking about America, its culture, popular culture, myths and archetypes, the Jews, the Negroes, university and education, his only stand is that "to know the weakness and failures of all ... and speak them out is the only way of repaying the debt one feels" (Walden 1978, 208–09). Like Bellman, we find his dynamic rereadings and re-evaluations of literature "compelling," and it is because of "his views on the position of the artist in his own society, his emphasis on the importance of myth, authorial biography and the historical moment in shaping a literary work" that his work enjoys a unique position in contemporary American literature (Bellman 1963).

Much has been said about the evolution of Fiedler from an elitist critic to a popular culture critic. Fiedler's major concern, literature—political, social, and literary—constitutes a record of Fiedler's lifelong affair with dismantling categories and edifices; from his populist, man-in-the-street approach to the much more academic-cum-liberal vantage point of the Professor become Pop Guru. Often critics look at the Fiedlerian discourse as that of the "cultured" about the culture of those with/without "culture." Critics who debunk popular culture argue that viewed from the splendid heights, popular culture appears as a commercial wasteland. To this, Fiedler once responded with a characteristic tongue-in-cheek retort:

> The fact is that even economic security; high expertise and high culture seem threatened by what may be called "marketization." Lately there has been a rejection of literacy itself in certain communities. Most people do not read with pleasure and ease. Nevertheless, they do read images on the screen with pleasure, and that is why cinema and TV are popular [Maini 1987, 9].

It is evident from the discussion above that the evolution in Fiedler's writings is recognizable but for the deviations and aberrations, crests and troughs. He does not necessarily cross over all of them.

It may be a paradox, but still true, that Leslie Fiedler is claimed by both; high priests of elitist tradition see him as a member of their clan and the svelte swingers of the pop tradition stoically confirm his affiliation to their group. In his critical writings, he has reflected practically every color of the spectrum. What is true about his ethnic identity is even more evident in his professional identity. An academic Jew for most of his life, Fiedler in his written work has refused assimilation into the WASP community of scholars, an assimilation, he notes in *Waiting for the End,* that has claimed a myriad of his fellow urban Jewish intellectuals.

Demolishing the constructed conservative identity of literature, he problematizes the reconstructed identity of literature with an accommodation of interests of the marketplace. He unraveled the interests of the "common" encapsulated and suffocated within the rubric of watertight dead-end categories. His academic nonconformist stance was affected by the Bowling Green University critics—the advocates of popular culture, calling out for a breakdown and dismantling of categories. He talks of "a counter-tradition, liberating rather than repressive," and calls for a "qualitative alteration and a cultural revolution" (WWL 1982, 111). He advocates an accommodation of counterculture, a literature outside the academy—science fiction, soap opera studies, media and film studies, comic books, and says that it does not mean "opening the gates to the barbarians" (111). It is a battle in Fiedler's long war against genteel criticism and scholarship to defend the tower of pop art. Fiedler twits at the literary establishment and charges the literary artist with falling into the "hermeneutics of nostalgia" with its veneration of the past and classical models of scholarship. Perambulating the academic boulevard for decades, in his discourse on majority and minority cultures, his democratic leanings are evident.[12] His bourgeoisie discourse centers on consensus. I concur with this aptly worded statement of Camille Paglia, in a blurb from a recent edition of *Love and Death in the American Novel*: "Let's turn back to Fiedler and begin again" (cited by Timberg, 2008).

Towards this end, in this book an attempt has been made to unveil some of the myriad dimensions of the kaleidoscopic Fiedler. The mosaic created by him requires a study of the varied colors of the broken stained glass that constitutes it: his beginnings in the tradition of highbrowism and elitism, but soon changing color to a more democratic and counter-culturalist approach; matching with it is his sensibility of literary archiving and digging, which unsettled the existing paradigms of American literature and culture tackled through his Freudian-Jungian theory of the unconscious converted into a homoerotic thesis of male bonding. His quintessential "other" radar quickly captured the trope of "outsidedness" and othering in other "others" not really outsiders, yet "others" among the Jews, blacks, Native Americans and WASPs as well. The study of *sva* (self) and *para* (other) is so unique to Indian culture that one understands why Fiedler the Jew studied himself always in relation to others. He astutely saw that American literature was basically a literature of escape in which the WASP male escaped from domesticity, women and responsibility into the primeval world of forest and water, where he found companionship with a non-white male. This, according to Fiedler, is a typical American myth, which pervades all classics of American literature and popular literature as well. Further, Fiedler saw that myths join all, elite and pop, and in the last phase, he plumbed and chose to write more and more about popular culture. It can perhaps safely be said that the liminal space between elite and popular, lowbrow and highbrow is the one that harbors the most fraught debates to this day. What is relevant for our purposes here is to locate the evolutionary turn that such discourses have taken to bring us to certain understandings of "cultures."

It made obvious sense to introduce Fiedler and survey the early critical studies on Fiedler in the Introduction. Chapter 1 delineates Fiedler's early critical stance on criticism, i.e., his credo. This chapter looks into Fiedler's early critical stances on the nature of criticism, the artist, and negativism, which appear to have elitist leanings. This chapter also attempts to unearth the seeds of popular culture in his writings. In chapter 2 in continuation with his preoccupation with alienation, which started with the publication of his first essay on this theme, "Come Back to the Raft Ag'in, Huck Honey!" in 1948, Fiedler traces the myth of the runaway WASP male, alienated from home, domesticity and women, shrugging off the responsibilities of marriage and sex, escaping into the wilderness in the company of a colored male. Chapter 3 deals with the aspirations and the fears of the "other": the Indian, Blacks, Freaks and particularly the Jews and their attempts at assimilation through the Jewish-American writings which had become a unique force in American literature. Continuing his preoccupation with alienation, Fiedler traces the myth of the runaway WASP male, alienated from home, domesticity and women, shrugging off the responsibilities of marriage and sex, escaping into the wilderness in the company of a colored male.

In his last few decades, in his genuflection to the young in all ways possible, Fiedler took up the gauntlet even if it ricocheted in a way he had not imagined. As one of his early admirers—a disciple-turned-critic and later, one who gave up on Fiedler—says, in this later phase Fiedler moved from the status of guru to "freak" (Pinsker 1999, 186). He sought their adulation in all ways possible and in that process almost lost his "barbarian within the gates" status. Whether he left the gates or they opened the gates for him can be debated *ad nauseam*. Chapter 4 showcases Fiedler's well-defined movement into popular culture. Its beginning is noticed in his concern with the distinction between elite and popular literature, and later his shift to popular literature establishes him as a pop guru. Chapter 5 makes postcolonial and feminist readings of the work of this "other." The Conclusion assesses Fiedler and ends on a prophetic tone heralding a second coming (no Christ-like connotations!) of Fiedler. This chapter brings in the impact of Fiedler on a vast generation of young scholars that he tutored and advised in their graduate, postgraduate and doctoral days. Some of them have worthy positions today as critics, academics, celebrities, and writers. This material has been placed towards the end primarily for these reasons: had I written about these laudatory obituaries, inspirational writeups, sometimes hyperbolic tributes, and exaggerated praise right at the beginning of the book, it would not have been fair to my readers. After all, just as seeing is believing, reading is believing. Thus, having read through the pages of this book and made a somewhat tentative estimation of the writer by revisiting him, it is befitting to present the assessment of his admirers and students. To further categorize this list, I indulge in the following: There are those who have been taught by Fiedler and admired him as a teacher. They acknowledge his influence on their lives and writings, even their personalities. He has been the beacon guiding them or showing the path ahead. The other set include writers, scholars, and critics; his long-time associates or short term colleagues at Montana and SUNY Buffalo; or those whose writings were critically commented upon by Fiedler and who found his incisive comments true and to have stood the test of time, thus shaping their future writings.[13] But just as Tolstoy endures in the image of the aging sage of Yasnaya Polanye, Fiedler seems destined to play the perpetual role of academic Peter Pan, the evergreen insurgent who never grew up. He even outlasted the Bolshevik Revolution, which occurred a few months after his birth, on March 8, 1917 (Kellman 1999, 7).

A need for, and the existence of room for, more research is validated by Tony Bennett's famous theoretical argument that every new interpretation of a literary work is often its richer interpretation, which adds verve and substance to it. With the above viewpoint, this research can be based on the premise that

> every spectator's interpretation of the text is in effect a new construction of it, based on the formation of reading competencies. They do not act solely upon the reader to produce different readings of the same text, but also act upon the text, shifting its very signifying potential so that it is no longer what it once was (and conceived) because in terms of its cultural location, it is no longer where it once was [Bennett 1990].

This book is going to be well grounded, encompassing most of the critical and literary produce of Fiedler as well as critical notings on him. But, unlike the Fiedlerian pronouncement regarding *Love and Death* that since "the tale it seeks to tell is mythic rather than factual, poetic rather than prosaic, I eschewed such conventional academic trappings as footnotes and bibliographies" (Fiedler 1990a), my tale is generously laced with "academic trappings" such as endnotes and a bibliography, and at places an annotated one.

It is within such a framework that Fiedler is to be seen as "the critic" of this age, as a man for all ages. Whatever the critics might say—that the recalcitrant Fiedler is a shocker and an iconoclast, provocative and scandalizer—and in spite of all his protestations too, this *force majeure* of American culture constitutes a one-man fifth column in the elitist citadel to earn the nickname of the Pop Guru. He fought the colonizing impulses of the academy like a expunger, decolonizing the minds of many. It appears as if Fiedler had pledged to turn the colonial (to be understood very broadly) page. He did, to the chagrin of others.

I hope this book turns not one but many.

CHAPTER 1

Fiedler's Credo

Literary and Critical;
Socio-political and Pedagogical

"Some great works of criticism are, of course, great works of art: *Don Quixote, Werther, The New Eloise, The Man with a Blue Guitar, Madame Bovary*; but even discursive critical comment dares not forget its relationship with literature."
—Fiedler, "Toward an Amateur Criticism"

Fiedler is often a harsh critic of readings that seem to him dumb, misleading, or vicious. He readily resorts to terms of derogation like "philistine," "middlebrow," "pious," "pretentious," "genteel," and "solemn." There is much that Fiedler dislikes, much that seems to him to armor us unduly against the shock of the new or disturbing. Attitudes, like pacifism, that might seem noble or otherwise admirable can seem to Fiedler ridiculous or unworthy because, in the present state of the culture, they are safe, predictable, or "compulsory."
—Robert Boyers, "Thinking About Leslie Fiedler"

Right or wrong, he most often did not play it safe or hedge or second-guess himself into silence.
—Brady Harrison, "Love, Death, and the Deep, Abiding Happiness of Edgar Allan Poe...."

As Fiedler was an "inheritor and a maker" of the very long history of literary criticism in the U.S., it is only befitting that the discussion of Fiedler's literary and cultural preoccupations should be prefixed by the salient features of his critical ideology and principles: his "Credo."[1] To understand, read and evaluate his credo in the contemporary context, a necessary excursus is required to his Montana phase and some of the key essays of his early criticism. The wild Montana phase, as many have called it, was one of the most productive early phases of his criticism, as it was also a phase responsible for establishing a reputation that many call "controversial."[2] Pinsker writes that after the publication of his essays about Alger Hiss and the Rosenbergs in *An End to Innocence*, the word *controversial* "was quickly attached to Fiedler's name and it has hung securely around his neck—as an albatross, a noose, or defining adjective" (1999, 182). Quite on his side, Benjamin DeMott noted in a review of *Love and Death in the American Novel* that Leslie Fiedler, "though not yet called to any of the genuinely voluptuous chairs of American literature, has consolidated his position as the most controversial professor of literature of America since Irving Babbitt" (Winchell 2002, 181–182). So this phase and the early essays and writings will undeniably form the fulcrum on which this chapter and the next two will rest. While this chapter is not concerned with debates about the validity of the arguments in those essays or their relevance in the contemporary climate of "posts" (modernism, colonialism, structuralism, multiculturalism, cosmopolitanism, etc.), these remain the abiding concern of this book and are discussed elsewhere. For the purposes of this chapter, and attending to the call of systemic analysis, Fiedler's credo will be discussed within the ambit of the four critical matrices that surrounds his criticism. They are literary, critical, socio-political, and pedagogical. Of course, the axes around which these rotate are the use of "I" (the personal voice that he advocates and adheres to) and the quality of dissent ("No! In Thunder") in his writings. They underscore the vitality of his convictions, ideology and principles. When juxtaposed with his later writings, these writings indicate his initial elitist bearings; nevertheless, there is a slow but sure and definite movement toward a note of rejection and dissension and, later on, his preference for popular culture.

Literary and Critical

It is only when infuriated by some stupid or malicious argument or harried by an importunate editor (usually both) that I can begin to write.
—Fiedler, Preface to *End of Innocence*

Stepping back from the above for a while, a glimpse of Fiedler's relationship with *Kenyon Review* would help us understand his credo. Although his earliest essays appeared most often in *Partisan Review* and the *New Leader*, Fiedler had submitted work to John Crowe Ransom's *Kenyon Review* from the very beginning of his career.[3] Winchell writes that when none of these early submissions were accepted, Fiedler expressed his pique at Ransom in a letter dated October 19, 1947:

> Yours is the only publication from which in my year and a half of submitting material I have received nothing but the dumb rebuke of a firm rejected slip....

These anonymous pale slips of yours irk, annoy (and even, though I am a resilient fellow, discourage) me. I like, in general, your taste, but am equally fond of my own piece. What is it? [Winchell 2002, 87–88].

He further states that this letter produced a detailed reaction to the story submitted with it, along with Ransom's invitation to review for his magazine. Over the next decade, Fiedler was a frequent contributor to the *Kenyon Review* and was even named a Kenyon Fellow in Criticism for 1956 (Winchell 2002, 87–88).

It is true that when Fiedler began making a name for himself as a literary critic, the dominant approach to all kinds of reading (fiction, poetry and even drama) was a version of aesthetic formalism that many linked with John Crowe Ransom and the *Kenyon Review*. Winchell gives Christopher Clausen's view: "A bright student who knew little history, no philosophy, and no foreign languages could learn to analyze literary structures in terms of a small number of technical concepts. After that, nothing more was needed than a good anthology..., a supply of paperbacks, and perhaps, for the adventurous, a subscription to the *Kenyon Review*" (1999, 88).

With this as a backdrop, it is appropriate to point out that the mainstay of his criticism, summed up by Fiedler himself, is "a mode of criticism more congruous with the sort of literature we admire, a criticism as wary of bureaucratization, as respectful to the mythic and the mysterious, as dedicated to a language at once idiosyncratic and humane as, say, Moby Dick or the novels of Kafka" (TAC, 561–62). Fiedler's own assessment was that he thought of himself "as primarily a literary person though one whose interest in works of art is dictated by a normal passion rather than a cooler technical concern" (EI, xiv).

Fiedler is quite against the anti-romanticism of criticism that entails contempt for the imagination. His attempt is to search for strategies that oppose "Scientific Criticism whose methods are mining, digging or just plain grubbing" (TAC, 561). He establishes that the chief enemy of criticism is the liberal, scientific mind. He advocates strategic criticism, which is for him "not a rival to the attempt to achieve final hierarchies, but rather a handmaiden. The only way to find out if a poet is immortal is to kill him; Milton and Wordsworth slain have risen. Cowley and Shelley are rotting in their tombs" (TAC, 570). By definition, the amateur critic would be one who loved literature and conveyed a sense of pleasure in writing about it. In two important respects, his vocation is similar to that of the poet: "First, he must join in irony and love what others are willing to leave disjoined, and second, he must be willing to extend awareness beyond the point where the lay reader instinctively finds that quality profitable or even possible" (562). The critic also possesses a third responsibility that is only an option for the poet—the obligation to be comprehensible. Hence, all critical positions, according to him, are generally strategic; in fact, a critic should be frank enough (like him) to state his strategies. The greatest advantage of strategic criticism, which he proposes, is the unraveling of the "truth" for all to see. The role of the practitioner of that criticism is to oppose ineptness and falsity through his criticism, and this the critic should do with full conviction and force. In "My Credo" (1950) he writes that unlike the poet, "the critic has an obligation to be explicit, patient and humble.... He is responsible for all misrepresentations of what he asserts except those arising from absolute stupidity, but including those possible of deliberate malice" (562). The point that Fiedler emphasizes frequently is that the critic writes for the people. He should be "loyal to the work of art and pledged to good faith towards an audience conditioned to banalities" (563). The critic speaks directly to that general reader for whom the critic ideally writes. Fiedler explains further: "In intent, the good critic addresses the common reader, not the initiate, and that intent is declared in his language ... to speak as if to men and not to specialists" (563).

Just as he is opposed to scientific criticism so is he opposed to its language, which is "assumable to analysis in terms of currently honorific vocabularies of various sciences" (561–62). In "My Credo" he clearly states that the true language of criticism should be the language of conversation. To achieve the above, "criticism must be free to leap, to yoke in the flash of wit what has always seemed alien" (572). Regarding the language of the critic, he says that it should be "humane" and like "the law of God, he must speak in the language of men" (572). Fiedler is certainly not implying that a critic is totally forbidden the useful terminology of sciences, but that he is forbidden to make his art and language "a jargon in the image of such terminology" (573). In "My Credo" Fiedler emphasizes the role of the critic as a mediator between a poem and its audience and says that the duty of the critic is to mediate between the lay public and any area that illuminates or is highlighted by a work of art. So "connect" is the motto that renders the art of an artist, unique, according to Fiedler. And it is for the critic to connect.

Herbert Feinstein, who interviewed Fiedler in 1961, finds Fiedler's negativism as an evolution, a developmental stage of his strategic criticism. In reply to Feinstein, Fiedler says, "The negativism of the writer which I recommend is essentially a strategy for presenting the only kind of affirmation which is possible without sentimentality and falsification" (84). The key word here is "strategy." What Fiedler proposes is that the negativism of a writer is a deliberate attempt, a conscious effort to present the truth. This remark uncovers a very significant pattern of the evolution of Fiedler's stance on negativism. Negativism, hence, is almost an offshoot of the practice of his strategic criticism.

No! In Thunder (1960)

This important critical stance of his career reaches a crescendo in *No! In Thunder* (1960). In the introduction to this book, he says, "It has taken me a long time to realize that the obligation to praise does not contradict but complements the necessity to say no. This collection records my first gestures at putting that small wisdom into practice" (NT, xi). Therefore, serious fiction, "to fulfill its essential moral obligation," must be negative. Earlier too, Fiedler had pointed out that "the practice of any art at any time is essentially a moral activity.... I do not know how to begin to make a book or talk about one without moral commitment" (NT, 3). So the moral element at this juncture assumes great importance for Fiedler and becomes a major component in producing serious art, literature and criticism.

To come back to his negativism, Fiedler says, "Insofar as a work of art is, as art, successful, it performs a negative critical function; for the irony of art in the human situation lies in this: ...Some men—are capable of achieving in works of art a coherence, a unity, a balance, a satisfaction of conflicting impulses" (NT, 7). But when these relationships are attempted to be represented in art, they are revealed in intolerable inadequacy. The image of man, in art, is the image of failure. Hence, a self-conscious writer, in order to achieve coherence in art, presents "essentially [a] negative view of man." But, to gain readers publishers write on the book jacket, "beneath the shattering events of that book ... lies a passionate affirmation." Fiedler is against this affirmation. "Demonic, terrible and negative; this is the modern muse" (NT, 8). Elaborating his views on negativism, he quotes James Joyce (who chose for his slogan Satan himself: "Non Serviam, I will not obey..."), Henrik Ibsen (whose final words were "on the contrary..."), and Herman Melville (whose *Moby Dick*'s secret motto was "I baptize you not in the name of the Father, the Son and the Holy Ghost, but in the name of the Devil"). According to Fiedler, most explicit is Melville's comment in a letter to Nathaniel Hawthorne in which Melville tries to describe the essence of his friend's art, but which actually reveals the deepest source of his own art:

> There is this grand truth about Nathaniel Hawthorne. He says No in thunder! but the Devil himself cannot make him say yes. For all men who say yes, lie, and all men who say no—why, they are in the happy condition of judicious, unencumbered travellers in Europe; they cross the frontiers into Eternity with nothing but a carpetbag—that is to say, the Ego [NT, 8].

Such pronouncements heckled several critical quarters. One such example is pertinent to our discussion here. As soon as *No! In Thunder* was published, reactions as this one poured forth: "All writers say both yes and no. Even Fiedler in *Love and Death in the American Novel* says yes to what he regards as ideal.... The book would be nonsense if there were not this affirmation to give meaning to all its negations" (Hicks 1960, 14). Corollaries were drawn from renowned writers: D. H. Lawrence and Samuel Beckett both say yes loudly and as often as they say no. But Hicks' contention that Fiedler clings to this dogma because "he enjoys saying no, which in a way reveals the temperamental basis of his negativism" (14) requires a deeper probe. In the next breath, Hicks makes Norman Mailer a kin of Fiedler:

> They are two of a kind.... Like Fiedler he has a compulsion to shock people; he too thrives on disagreement. Both men are afraid of approval. Both men work hard to convince themselves as well as others that they are Simon—pure rebels. Their rebellion is acutely self-conscious and they worry about it all the time, resorting to larger and larger doses of outrageousness.... The noisy negativism of Fiedler and Mailer is, I am sure, a significant comment on the intellectual atmosphere of the fifties and sixties [Hicks 1960, 14].

This diatribe by Hicks is a symptomatic and reflective sample of 1960s America. But by no means can Hicks' comments be disregarded; for example, when he says that all writers negate and affirm in their writings, he is stating a basic reality of criticism.

However, Fiedler differentiates the definitive "No! In Thunder" from the lesser no, pseudo-no or subtle no, which is actually a surrogate yes, in his theory of "No! In Thunder." Defining the nature of this "No! In Thunder," Fiedler says that Mark Twain's attack on slavery in post–Civil War *Huckleberry Finn* or in Harriet Beecher Stowe's pre–Civil War *Uncle Tom's Cabin* has "a certain air of presumptive self-satisfaction" (NT, 9), an assurance of being justified by the future. Fiedler also says that the contemporary American writer can abjure negativism only if he is willing to sacrifice truth and art, because the pursuit of the positive means stylistic suicide whether the novelist is major or minor. Referring to William Faulkner's *The Sound and the Fury,* Fiedler writes that the point insisted upon bluntly and obviously is that life is a tale told by an idiot, full of sound and fury, signifying nothing. He continues:

> Yes "nothing" is not quite Faulkner's last word, only the next to the last. In the end, the negativist is no nihilist, for he affirms the void. Having endured a vision of meaninglessness of existence, he retreats neither into self-pity and aggrieved silence nor into a realm of beautiful lies. He chooses, rather, to render the absurdity that he perceives, to know it and make it know. To know and to render, however, means to give form and to give form is to provide the possibility of delight [NT, 20].

This delight for the audience and the self is the affirmation that a negativist renders in his work of art. This continues to be Fiedler's mission, and he has continued to convey that mission as a dream, quixotic though it may sometimes be (Hayne 1979, xi). It is his candor, ingenuity, honesty and consistency that render validity and precision to his theory of vital negativism (Sharma 1983, 13).

Reising gives, perhaps, a better analysis of Fiedler's negativism in these words: "Fiedler's campaign against social and political writing and criticism fits into the larger, culture context of his work" (1986, 140), by attributing the role of "professional nay-sayers" to American artists, "to disturb, by telling a truth which is always unwelcome" (Reising 1986, 139). Reising sums up his views in these words: "Fiedler's shocking pronouncements on American culture are trivialised by his voyeuristic sensationalism.... His refusal to approach literature's adversary aspects in social or political terms has rendered his critique impotent and safe" (Reising 1986, 139). This bid to lash out at authorities is more visible in his fiction, according to Malin, but it requires a full-length discussion and it will suffice to say here that the recurrent peculiar battle between father and son, one as a symbol of authority and the other as anti-establishment and anti-authority, gives his fiction a boyish tone. Fiedler, to his chagrin, is charged with adolescence and immaturity. And the irony is that throughout *Love and Death in the American Novel* we have Fiedler commenting that mythic America is boyhood and all American literature is juvenile in nature. Reising calls him the "good Bad Boy, the Tom Sawyer of the current generation, crying at all the windows, 'Come on out and play'" (1986, 140). In contrast, Fiedler uses the instrument of dissent to enable people to see the other side of the coin. As Larsen points out, "Willing to dissent, Fiedler is always telling us, 'No, there is another way of looking at things'" (1970, 136).

Fiedler's writings constitute a "long war against 'genteel' (formalist) criticism and scholarship, approaches that allegedly exist in a cultural vacuum and, though they shed the light, lack the head necessary for life"[4] (Dembo 1973, 138–9). This battle is evident in much of his criticism published in *Waiting for the End* (1964) and *To the Gentiles* (1971). Thus, Fiedler's criticism works in such a way that it can be called a process of cancellation. He refutes and opposes what others have said, and then, after he has won the debate (at least, to his own satisfaction), he knocks out his own theories. One side of Fiedler's mind seems honestly drawn to his commitment to *No! In Thunder.* The other side is satisfied only when he can show he's the sharpest and wittiest guy in class[5] (O'Conner 1960, 46).

Examining him as nay-sayer and a dissenter has its high points because one finds that Fiedler's negativism also fits into the larger framework of his criticism as a strategic instrument of real and serious art, and "it seems to disturb people in a way which is to me satisfactory," chuckles Fiedler (Feinstein 1961, 89). Thus, negative criticism creates a fruitful kind of disturbance and people wrestle with the problem thrown up by the negativist. And this appeals to Fiedler.

In presenting various facets of his negativism the attempt was to illuminate and highlight this important critical stance as an evolution of the practice of his strategic criticism. From 1950s to 1960s, Fiedler remained consistent in his view regarding strategic criticism, which was to be used as an instrument for practicing the art of criticism.

Love and Death in the American Novel (1960)

The task that he took upon himself earlier in *No! In Thunder* was to re-evaluate criticism and writers who had "cemeteries to defend." In *Love and Death in the American Novel*, he re-revaluates literature and says, "American Literature is distinguished by the number of dangerous and disturbing books in its canon—and American scholarship by its ability to conceal this fact. To redeem our great books from the commentaries on them is one of the chief functions of this study" (LD 1960, 11). In this work, once again, he emphasizes the necessity of the moral element in literature. "Literature is more than a grace of life ... it is the record of those elusive moments at which life is alone ... fulfilled in consciousness and form" (LD 1960, 15–16). In fact, Fiedler goes to the extent of saying that literary criticism is nothing but an act of total moral engagement, in which tact, patience, insolence, and piety consort strangely but satisfactorily together. This is almost a reiteration of his stance in *No! In Thunder*.

In his preface to the second edition of *Love and Death in the American Novel* (1966), he refers to criticism practiced then as "the last examples of the new genteel tradition, with its emphasis on textual analysis, its contempt for general ideas, and its fear of popular culture" (8), traits which now strike us as irrelevant and remote. So, Fiedler was striving to move away from conventional literature, something that he tried in his later critical writings and accomplished. To continue further, the issues and problems taken up in "Second Thoughts on *Love and Death in the American Novel: My First Gothic Novel*," according to Fiedler, are not "merely" literary. He bemoans that it is one of the scandals of American criticism that literature has become unexciting and dull. According to him, "It is a standard indignity of our life that middlebrow allrightniks have typically produced the standard analysis of books written by highbrow eccentrics," or that those writers who have dealt with a few books have "somehow considered it desirable to make them seem less exciting than they were—perhaps out of the conviction that good form demands more tedium than our ill-mannered novelists ever provide at their best" (1967b, 9). Fiedler adopts a stance against conventional criticism and further writes that most of our sensitive and ambitious critics try to buck the genteel tradition and insist that our classics are respectable and politically imbued with "O.K. liberal sentiments" (10). The genteel tradition that Fiedler is referring to is the one in which "Poe was not really a drunkard, or Hawthorne a melancholic or Whitman a homosexual" (10). "All those kindly and comforting lies *Love and Death* has eschewed—rejecting the conventional reasonable voice of our typical criticism along with its clichés of politics or good taste" (10), retorts Fiedler. He also says that this book is "wildly gothic," full of "grotesque jokes," and that its form is "novelistic" and is a long, darkly comic study. Commenting on the validity of criticism he says, "Indeed, all criticism when really valid is literature, not amateur philosophy or inflated journalism" (10). He concludes that what is of utmost importance regarding *Love and Death in the American Novel* is that "here at last is a critical work compatible with the style and tone of the works it proposes to discuss, a breakthrough in the last stronghold of WASP 'good taste'—the criticism of our own great untidy, unruly, but mythically potent fiction" (11).

In a symposium on the American novel in 1970, he says that a writer is a dealer in illusions and a magician because every book deals with a world that is real to the person who writes it. The writer has to persuade an audience that that world is real to them, too. What books in fact create are myths, or imaginative fictions that can then be taken out in the world to see what happens (Fiedler 1970d, 200).

He continues in a vein that to my mind is extremely important to discussions about the art of writing. He says, "Writers dream books and critics dream over books.... It's not a question of inventing a vocabulary, it's a question of finding the secret language that we all know, which is the language of our dreams" (1970d, 200).

He then goes on to give two examples about two books that were written at that time, beginning with totally different assumptions: *In Cold Blood* (1966) by Truman Capote and *Why Are We in Vietnam?* (1967) by Norman Mailer. In *In Cold Blood*, Fiedler says, "the author pretends that he's not there at all, that he's not going to indulge his fancy or fantasy one bit, that he's going to write about something that really happened and he's going to report it as it really happened." But in the other book, according to Fiedler, "the author is present and playing games about who he is." Then Fiedler makes a significant point about the similarities between these two books:

> The interesting thing is that when you look at these books, one which presumably came out of somebody's deepest released free fantasy and another one which came out of the newspapers and facts, it turns out to be the same dream: a white man and an Indian are walking down the road together. There's a gun someplace in the picture and one beast or another is going to get killed, the two favorite beasts of Americans, a grizzly bear and a white woman, a clean white girl in the case of Truman Capote's book [1970d, 205–06].

This dream, according to Fiedler, is being "compulsively" dreamt over and over again since Ken Kesey's *One Flew Over the Cuckoo's Nest*. Then he says,

"What we ask of writers finally is to dream our deepest dream, which we don't even confess to ourselves, to disguise it in such a way that there is a way for each of us to have access to the same deep dream" (1970d, 205–06).

Both *No! In Thunder* and *Love and Death in the American Novel* were published in 1960; hence, Fiedler's thrust on literature, as an act of moral pursuit and endeavor, is obvious in both these writings. In "My Credo," Fiedler reproached critics for dullness, distrusted autonomous judgment of art, and critiqued Arnold's touchstone method. According to him, the act of evaluating a work of art is, nonetheless, the vital center and the most important part of criticism, but in order to practice it, one must have faith and firm conviction in the reality of the true, the good and the beautiful. And the reader should also respect the existence of men of taste "in whom a disciplined sensibility is capable of making discriminations among experience" (566). We shall notice an evolution in this stance in "Second Thoughts on *Love and Death in the American Novel*: My First Gothic Novel." Attempting to blur the boundaries between critical and creative faculties, in this essay he says that what justifies a critic is "not his methodology much less his scholarship but his taste—his ability to anticipate and even influence the literary preferences of sensitive readers in his own time and afterwards" (1967, 10). The persistent endeavor of the critic is to reach the common man and influence his taste. On the one hand, the critic perceives himself as least likely to be a victim of pride, and on the other hand, he is considered most likely to be such a victim when he first opposes popular taste with a new stance and claim. The critic should face such a charge boldly.

Examining his literature on a much broader canvas, it is seen that his naysaying continues even in his choice of approach to criticism. Quite early in his literary career, Fiedler shrugged off the burden of the Marxist approach to literature from his shoulders. He did not even take kindly to the social approach to criticism. From the forties onwards, he was quite wary of the structuralists and then in the fifties, he openly derided the new critics. This way, he discarded the bearings of these older schools of thought and said a hard no to New Criticism.

In his introduction (1960) to *No! In Thunder* (second edition), the critical stance that Fiedler adopts is opposed to that adopted in *An End to Innocence*, in which he listened to "the Zeitgeist rather than to my own inner voice which spoke in Myth and Metaphor, rather than slogan and statistics" (NT, x). The result is that the former book, *An End to Innocence*, is highly political and *No! In Thunder*, quite literary. If Fiedler listened to his own personal voice, then *No! In Thunder* is bound to be autobiographical as well. Fiedler comments in *No! In Thunder*, "It is, I suppose, towards such general criticism that I began moving ten years ago … turning from the examination of texts … to an exploration of the contexts, social and psychological, in which literature was written and read" (NT, x). He even confesses that this book is hence "an autobiography, a confession, the record of my sentimental education" as well as "an account of the world in which I am being educated" (NT, xiv). He says that it is precisely because of this reason that "I try to speak always in my own person, never objectively as if I were the voice of an institution or an era" (NT, xiv). Fiedler unhesitatingly contends that wherever he uses "we" it represents not the desire to hide behind the editorial plural, but his awareness of the fact that by using "we" he might be speaking for a group, or community or section of society, which is joined to him by age or color or religion or just common indignation or common cause. Yet, for Fiedler behind his use of "we" always remains the first person singular pronoun "I."

"Archetype and Signature" (1952)

This belief takes us, further, to his important essay, in which he openly acknowledges his preference for the biographical approach to criticism. In "Archetype and Signature," which originally appeared in the spring 1952 issue of the *Sewanee Review*, he adds, "the word 'Archetype' is more familiar to him and he uses it instead of the word 'myth': ... to mean any of the immemorial patterns of response to the human situation in its most permanent aspects: death, love, the biological family, the relationship with the unknown, etc., whether those patterns be considered to reside in the Jungian Collective Unconscious or the Platonic world of Ideas" (AS, 319). He elaborates further that the archetypal "belongs to the infra- or meta-personal, to what Freudians call the id or the unconscious; that is, it belongs to the Community at its deepest, preconscious levels of acceptance" (AS, 319). By the term *signature* Fiedler implies "the sum total of individuating factors in a work, the sign of the Persona or Personality through which an Archetype is rendered" (AS, 319). Hence both myth and archetype tend to become a subject of as well as a means to the poem. Literature "can be said to come into existence at the moment a Signature is imposed upon the Archetype" (AS, 319).

The distinction between archetype and signature is not the distinction between content and form or the distinction between impersonal and personal signature. It belongs, according to Fiedler, to social collectivity as well as to the individual writer. The signature is a joint product of the expectations of a community as well as the idiosyncratic response of the individual poet. Also, what differentiates signature and archetype, according to Fiedler, is that the signature element is conscious. You consciously impose the personal stamp on a work of art, whereas the archetype is unconscious.

"Archetype and Signature" is important for many reasons, feels Winchell

(1999, 92). First, it helped Fiedler to differentiate his position from that of the New Criticism. Second, the essay posits as an affirmative rationale for myth criticism. Third, it is a spirited attack on what Fiedler regards as the inevitable excesses of a purely intrinsic approach to literature. Last, it became one of Fiedler's best known and most frequently anthologized works. Even though he may have been somewhat reticent in naming names, the New Critics were never in doubt that Fiedler had them in mind when he attacked the "antibiographists" in "Archetype and Signature." And Fiedler was nonchalantly happy with that distance. Winchell avers that Brooks and other New Critics of an orthodox Christian persuasion accept the conventional Judaea-Christian separation of the sacred from the profane. Fiedler, however, subscribes to the mystical tradition that sees religion not as a specific category of experience, but as the underlying reality of all experience. Although Fiedler speaks of mythos and archetypes (terms that do not carry the sectarian baggage of religion), he is clearly dealing with what he regards as spiritual and metaphysical realities (Winchell 1999, 96).

"In the Beginning Was the Word—Logos or Mythos"

In another essay, "In the Beginning Was the Word—Logos or Mythos," Fiedler explains myths, logos and archetype without signature. In this essay, Fiedler talks of the existence of ideas in a work of art. According to him ideas exist prior to their poetic expression, and poetry is representative of myths in a much less direct way than philosophy is of logos. Fiedler defines myths as "intuition in the Crocean sense," and says, "The intuited in Myths are the Archetypes, those archaic and persisting cluster of image and emotion which at once define and attempt to solve what is most permanent in the human predicament" (NT, 301). He connects archetype and myth, and says, "Archetype is a term somehow too modern and abstract to encompass the total richness of myths"; hence he uses a word "hopelessly compromised by fashion"—myth. He says that there is no word that can suggest the relationship of mythos to the myths—those ancient Greek stories that are our archetypes par excellence, preserving for us the assurance that belongs to ritual alone: that what is done below is done above, what is done here and now is done forever, what is repeated in time subsists unbroken in eternity" (NT, 302). Hence a myth is an archetype without signature. A true critic, then, is alert to both myth and signature.

Fiedler's preoccupation with myth can be traced to 1950. In his essay "My Credo," for the first time Fiedler aligns himself with myth criticism. He acknowledges, "It is to myth criticism that I find myself more and more drawn"

(573–74). His view is that myth criticism forms a common area where experts from all genres—the critic, the anthropologist, the psychoanalyst, the philosopher and the literary theorist—meet. He also says that is in myth alone that "we find not only the recognition that the springs of art creation are ultimately a mystery grounded in truth, but also a new basis for evaluation in the assessment of mythoplastic power, that goes beyond the merely formal without falling into the doctrinal and dogmatic" (572). Fiedler believes that writers such as Charles Dickens and R. L. Stevenson "reveal the source of their persistent power over our imaginations in the light of myth doctrine" (574). Myth becomes a kind of mediator for the critic and the work of art. The critic finds it possible to speak of the profound interconnections for the artwork and other areas of human experience, without translating the work of art into unsatisfactory equivalents of ideas or tendencies (574). Fiedler asserts that the myth helps not only in "exploring the meaning of the imagination and the persistence of archetypes," but also provides an infinite number of new critical metaphors that will not deceive too grossly any work of art. And finally myth can bolster and nourish that "dreamed-of" language that is common to the creative mind and is pledged to truth and also to the "liberal" scientific mind, which is actually distrustful of absolutes. Myth, according to Fiedler, helps in the interpretation of these minds. Fiedler says, "In a world where they do not ordinarily find it possible to communicate, there is work enough for the critic" (574). Fiedler closes this essay on these futuristic lines. At another place he dismisses the myth approach as any kind of panacea, yet cautions,

> In the hands of the scientizers it becomes, like many other approaches, merely an excuse for another jargon, just one more strategy for avoiding evaluation. But intelligently exploited, it can open new possibilities for exploring the meaning of the imagination and the persistence of archetypes; it can provide a fund of new critical metaphors that will not betray too grossly the work of art. And finally it can bolster and nourish that dreamed-of language, common to the creative mind, pledged to the daemonic and the mystery of Truth, and the "liberal" scientific mind, distrustful of absolutes, and incapable either of salvation or the tragic appreciation of its own doom. Our especial need is the interpenetration of these minds [TAC, quoted in Pardini 2008, 12].

Fiedler was drawn to myth criticism in 1950, and later we discover that all his books have the mythical element. He interprets both life and American character in terms of myths. In fact, according to Niela Sesachari in "Leslie A. Fiedler: Critic as Mythographer," "Fiedler has become a unique force in myth criticism in America. Barry Wallenstein calls him a "mythopoeic critic" (1972, 589). In fact, all the tenets of Fiedler's criticism—strategic criticism, his allegiance to truth and serious art, metaphoric language—find validity in myth criticism. At this juncture I shall not undertake a journey into all his critical anthologies, but will only say that in the past thirty years Fiedler's allegiance to myth criticism remains stable, resolute, determined and unshakable. The evolution noticed in this stance is actually a developmental growth of the same idea. For example, in *The Return of the Vanishing American* he explores four main myths found in American literature. Everything in Fiedler's criticism can be examined in terms of myths, and this is not an exaggeration.

Many critics maintain that the essays "Archetype and Signature" and "In the Beginning Was the Word—Logos or Mythos" (which conclude his anthology *No! In Thunder*) are two of the finest pieces he has written. For instance, Larson points out that conceptually both begin as an attack on New Critics, on the poem-should-not-mean-but-be school of criticism. But these essays also elaborate the limitations of any piece of writing, if the conditions under which it is written are ignored. Fiedler means precisely that if "signature" is missing then a whole lot of meaning is incomplete.

The Personal Voice

Most of his writings, we discover, are his very personal utterings. In his preface to the first edition of *Love and Death in the American Novel* he calls it "a very personal book" and says, "I attempt to say with my own voice, out of my own face (all masks abandoned) what I have found to be some major meanings of our literature and our culture" (13), thus permitting himself, as he confesses, "to indulge in high rhetoric and low humor. For this reason, the reaction of more conventional scholars was overwhelmingly negative, as it was to the three succeeding volumes, *Waiting for the End, The Return of the Vanishing American* and *What Was Literature?* So that for while it seemed as if I were to be doomed forever to be labeled a disturber of the peace, an *enfant terrible*, the 'wild man of American Letters'" (1999a, 24). In the same vein he openly acknowledges the influences over him of C. S. Lewis, Marxian critics, Freud, Jung and D. H. Lawrence (LD 1960, 14–15). It is true that the personal element is very evident in *Love and Death in the American Novel*. If this element is borne in mind, then, what Fiedler has all along offered "in the guise of criticism is, in loose sense, a spiritual autobiography: a confession of the impact upon him of the American experience."[6] An autobiographical tendency in Fiedler dominates "as a disturbing force" which does not let him reach the accolade of an ideal critic, which he actually is (Wallenstein 1972, 590). Fiedler's "I" is sometimes louder than the "we"; it drowns the "we." But then Fiedler boldly faces these charges. Over the years, Fiedler does not change this critical stance—the importance of personal voice in criticism. According to him, this "personal voice" enables the critic to have a greater rapport with his audience, a practice that he followed in his criticism. Look at this example:

> Looking back over my own brief critical practice, I find that it has been rather consistently based on presuppositions fashionably called "obscurantist." Though I should hate to call myself a Romantic, I am opposed to the dogged anti–Romanticism of much contemporary criticism, which leads to a contempt for the imagination, and is often grounded in a kind of *lumpen-nominalism* that would grant only a second-class "reality" to works of art. The discrepancy between the metaphors typical to the creative mind and those typical to the critical mind in our world (and this is true often in the single individual who practices both as poet and critic) indicate a quietly desperate cleavage [1950e, quoted in Pardini 2008, 3].

It can safely be said that his insistence on the use of personal voice catapulted him to be an "agent of change" (Kellman 1999, 74). Against the new critical ideal of impersonality that still dominated intellectual life in 1960, particularly Eliot's position in the essay "Tradition and Individual Talent" (1921), Fiedler announced, heretically, that *Love and Death* "is finally a very personal book, in which I attempt to say with my own voice out of my own face (all masks abandoned) what I have found to be some major meanings of our literature and our culture" (1960b, 13).

By the end of a tumultuous decade, the conventions of academic discourse were changed utterly. (Kellman 1999, 74). Fiedler ably bore that responsibility. As one who heralded "change" in the way critics became the omnipresent invisible objective voice of criticism, Fiedler's supporters and admirers (progenitors would be an exaggeration!) have in many ways followed him. Susan Gubar, his admirer, in her famous *Mad Woman in the Attic* with Sandra Gilbert uses "we" quite often. Baring her intent, she writes, "... we must particularly do this in order to understand literature by women because, as we shall show..." (1979; 2000, 597)."

Being Busted and the Use of "I"

It would be irreverent not to discuss *Being Busted* (1969) as an exemplary piece of personal writing. It is thus befitting that it be considered in the chapter that discusses Fiedler's credo, with its emphasis on the personal voice, the use of "I," and importance of dissent. *Being Busted* is a painful apology, as some critics say, of an aging professor who got mixed up in a police frame-up for maintaining premises where marijuana was used. But according to Fiedler, "I had no crimes on my conscience and fight was what I had longed for, real contact between real men over real issues" (Norman 1970, 77A). *Being Busted*, despite its autobiographical form, is a book that depicts Fiedler as a wounded literary soldier fighting for justice. In this book, he spoke at length about the cultural and social change between 1933, when he was about to be arrested for a public demonstration, and 1967, when he was actually arrested. Whatever it is, when *Being Busted* was published in Buffalo, it made Fiedler a public figure, and put him at the center of a number of misunderstandings. Parents of his students became a little wary of him and took him to be a sort of "aging swinger," whereas youngsters, says Fiedler, "are likely to assume that because I have been busted, I am not merely Kosher, but a real Head in professor's clothing" (BB, 232). What he got in return was something that he had not bargained for, says Albert H. Norman in *Newsweek*: "Fiedler's testimony is relevant not merely in the academic province of 'freedom of expression' or 'the right to be left alone' but more important, in the real world, where every Fiedler has the right, nay the obligation, to get involved with 'real men over real issues'" (1970, 77A).

As rightly pointed out by Kellman, *Being Busted* stands tall as a vivid evocation of several times and places—not only Newark, Missoula, and Buffalo, but also Colorado and China, where Fiedler spent World War II in navy intelligence; Harvard, where he studied on the GI Bill; Italy and Greece, where he lectured and hectored; and Amsterdam, southern France, and Brighton, where he travelled while his marijuana case was making its way through American courts. *Being Busted* can also be read as a "polemical memoir organized around the theme of dissidence" (Kellman 1999, 7). "I like disturbing the peace, whenever that peace seems to me the product not of meditation but of torpor and fear" (BB, 55), explains Fiedler, who recounts numerous instances in the United States and Europe of his success at disturbing the peace and who, in recounting those instances, sets out to disturb the reader's torpid, fearful peace (77).

Early on, he says of the book: "Its true subject is the endless war, sometimes cold, sometimes hot, between the dissenter and the imperfect society" (BB, 7). That would appear to situate Fiedler firmly in the camp of the dissenter, except that he also finds himself at odds with organized dissent. He depicts himself as "a pharmacologically abstemious *pater familias* manifestly uncomfortable when hailed as champion of pot-smoking polymorphous perversity. He was, along with Buckminster Fuller, Che Guevera, Timothy Leary, and Benjamin Spock, one of the very few figures over thirty trusted by the young. And he was trusted by them merely because he was so mistrusted by his own generation, a fact that undercut any trust he had for either" (Kellman 1999, 77).

Kellman tells us that Fiedler has been compared with another outspoken American Jewish author, Norman Mailer, who was demonstrating his own estrangement from conventional political polarities by ascribing to himself the oxymoron "Left Conservative." *Armies of the Night* (1968) is Mailer's account of being busted at an anti-war demonstration outside the Pentagon, and it shares many qualities with the book that Fiedler published a year later, not least the author's discomfort with being cast in the role of guru to Jacobin youth. Both works are self-conscious performances by eristic literary celebrities who place themselves at the center of the drama and at the margins of respectability. Mailer's epic description of himself, as "a warrior, presumptive general ex-political candidate, embattled aging *enfant terrible* of the literary world, wise father of six children, radical intellectual, existential philosopher, hard-working author, champion of obscenity, husband of four battling sweet wives, amiable bar drinker, and much exaggerated street fighter, party giver, hostess insulter" (153), matches Fiedler's auto-portrait:

> Not just, not even primarily, the professor who was busted for pot and maligned, much less the pot-happy corrupter of the young, but a refugee from the urban East, as well, who lived in Montana for nearly a quarter of a century, a thirty-years married father of six kids; a critic, teacher, and committee-member; a writer of fiction and verse; a maker of jokes, good and bad; a translator of Dante [BB, 230].

Kellman rightly writes that *Being Busted* is not the first instance of personal writing published by an American professor; Margaret Mead and Joseph Wood Krutch, among other scholars, had earlier abandoned the formalist fiction of *impassibilite*. *Being Busted* anticipates many of the qualities celebrated three decades later in the autobiographical narratives of Cathy Davidson, Henry Louis Gates, Jr., Sandra Gilbert, Alice Kaplan, Frank Lentricchia, Susan Rubin Suleiman, and other faculty authors (Kellman 1999, 75–76). *Being Busted* often also considered the New Leftism as self-aggrandizing (Tanenhaus 2003). In many ways it is indeed an act of restoration to one's own self; a "selective memoir," a page lifted from the book called life (Kellman, 79). In many ways, it is a state of combat in which, after progressive setbacks, Fiedler emerges victorious.

Working within the binaries of dark and light, *Being Busted* displays an astute mind at work that uncovers as much as it hides. The private and the public remain insulated from each other with few overlaps. With businesslike precision the marijuana bust that is the proximate basis for the book is discussed in detail even as he withholds essential information about his family. His own identity also remains the anonymous "I." However, he proclaims his Whitmanesque ambitions (Kellman 1999, 7a) by adding: "But 'I' is, of course, the true name of us all, of the reader as well as the other actors in the book, or at least would be in the similar books each of us might write" (BB, 7, quoted in Kellman, 79). Call him Ishmael, or call him simply "I," he is the articulate proxy for the troubled reader, declares Kellman (79).

Being Busted is more a work of the poetic imagination than it is a legal brief; however, zealous prosecutors were quick to introduce passages taken out of context to demonstrate Fiedler's criminal intent. As a meditation on the first fifty years of Leslie Fiedler's life, *Being Busted* is an engaging book, which inhabits some middle ground between the light of common day and a dream landscape (Winchell 2002, 220).

Problematizing the charge "maintaining a premise," in one passage, ignored by the jurors, Fiedler writes, "Once deciphered, 'maintaining a premise' turns out to mean creating a context, a milieu, an intellectual atmosphere in which the habits of the young are understood rather than condemned out of hand; their foibles responded to with sympathy and love rather than distrust and fear; the freedom necessary to their further growth sponsored and protected rather than restricted and crushed by an appeal to force and the intervention of the police" (BB, 159).

Writing in the *New Republic,* Reed Whittemore makes a dubious comparison in expressing his admiration for the Fiedler persona: "What interested me in his book," Whittemore observes, "more than the details of his being busted, and the implications for all of us of the experience to which he has been subjected, was his massive cool. I don't know how cool he was really in the face of the recent indignities, but with pen in hand he displays enormous detachment from his own problems.... The book might better be called *The Education of Leslie Fiedler,* with the chief lesson being learned that the spoken word is dangerous after all" (Winchell 2002, 220).

In late 1980s, almost twenty years after the publication of *Being Busted,* James Seaton compared Fiedler with a previous version of Fiedler's own self, writes Winchell. The critic who had urged an "end to innocence" and argued for a "liberalism of responsibility" in 1955 now seemed to be arguing for the virtues of innocence and irresponsibility. Winchell draws attention to the conclusion of *Being Busted*, where Fiedler writes, "That judgment was and remains 'innocent': collectively and individually innocent, not only of the absurd police charges (about which there was never any real doubt), but also of having in any essential way failed our own personal codes." "To make this clear to everyone," he continues, "my wife and I intend to keep insisting not just that we are 'not guilty,' which is a legal formula only, but that we are 'innocent,' in the full sense of the word" (BB, 249).

In response to this declaration, Seaton writes, "But such protestations of total innocence were exactly what troubled Fiedler about Hiss and the Rosenbergs. The issue is not whether anybody in Fiedler's house ever smoked grass. The issue is to what extent Fiedler regained the pose of innocence that in *An End to Innocence* he had ascribed to his own generation. In *Being Busted* and in later works Fiedler indeed assumes a pose of political innocence, of one unimplicated in the complexities of political life, the pose of a permanent outsider" (Winchell 2002, 221–22).

Pinsker states that Fiedler's countercultural bravado made him an accident waiting to happen; and when it did, he turned a very bad patch (financially and otherwise) into a piece of New Journalism that could hold its own with the best practitioners of nonfiction's latest wrinkle. More important perhaps was the way that the book generated sympathy—not for Fiedler's embattled circumstances, but also for a more enlightened, less up-tight response to where the country itself was headed (Pinsker 1999, 186).

The book thus is a telling observation only if one disregards the specific circumstances of the situations involved. It is one thing for a Soviet spy to deny charges of espionage; it is quite another for an indulgent parent to deny that he is running the legal and moral equivalent of an opium den. To believe that Alger Hiss and the Rosenbergs were metaphysically "innocent" one must believe that spying for the Soviet Union should have been a legally permissible activity. To believe in Leslie Fiedler's "innocence," one need only hold that a parent ought not to be jailed for failing to inform on an offspring for using a substance that shouldn't have been banned in first place (Winchell 2002, 222). After a long battle, in 1972 Fiedler walked free.[7]

In all, *Being Busted* continues to remain one of Fiedler's most personal works. Larson sums up the significance of the signature element:

> Fiedler's critical writings have never been mere charts and tables. Rather, they are critical evaluations—often far-fetched, often illogical, often strained, often brilliant—but always marked indelibly with his own eccentric signature, a signature which tells us over the over again that just as the poet and the novelist has his own myths to live, so too the critic may become the scapegoat of his own fellow critics [1970, 143].

From the foregoing discussion of his early writings it becomes clear that Fiedler displays early leanings toward formalist criticism and an inclination toward and preference for "form" in literature, yet as Winchell points out, "As his critical stance has grown more aggressively anti-elitist, Fiedler has begun to feel profoundly uneasy about his theoretical essays" (1985, 13) mainly "Archetype and Signature" and "In the Beginning was the Word—Logos or Mythos." Later in *What Was Literature?: Class Culture and Mass Society* he said that they were academic affectations or rather put-ons, but his movement towards this realization had happened as early as the introduction to the second edition of *No! In Thunder* (in which the essays were originally published), published also in his *Collected Essays*, vol. 1. He finds the two essays on literary theory "the most offensive ... demihoaxes from the start" (CE 1, 213). This way he once again spells out his credo. Fiedler states that the title essay of this collection *No! In Thunder* "remains for me still alive and close to the center of my vision of myself as a writer and general critic of society" (CE 1, 213). This title essay happens to be "Dante: Green Thoughts in a Green Shade." It consists of reflections on the Stony Sestina of Dante Alighieri. But can these essays be dismissed outright? I don't think so. This deliberate run-down of excellence cannot be readily accepted mainly because for a "one off" critic such as Fiedler, ideologies cater to a commitment to truth, which is of relative excellence and importance. And sometimes critics are constrained to claim to having put on the mask of an academic amateur in order justify their later divergences, which actually are nothing but a part of their evolutionary process.

Socio-Political Credo

The unafraid Fiedler seemed to be constantly at work in the early days of Joseph McCarthy, Richard Nixon, the Red Scare and the widespread distrust—and even active demonizing—of intellectuals, liberals, Jews, homosexuals, and countless other so-called subversives or threats to the American body politic. Although conservative pundits sometimes like to portray English professors, at least today, as a bunch of radical, no-goodnik pinkos dedicated to dismantling democracy and capitalism,... we are, in fact, a pretty tame lot; given his time and place, Fiedler perhaps puts any number of today's tenured radicals to shame (Harrison 2008).

In the history of twentieth century America, there have been some important moments that have captured the attention of intellectuals for decades. Two such cases, apart from many others on which Fiedler's critical enterprise turned into socio-political commentary, were the Alger Hiss case and the execution of Julius and Ethel Rosenberg on June 19, 1953. Some of these political pieces were published in *An End to Innocence* (1955). Referring to Fiedler's contention in *An End to Innocence*, his first collection (and his first book), in which he made no bones about the fact that the essays contained within would tell "about my world and myself as a liberal, intellectual, writer, American, and Jew," Pinsker writes,

> Good as his word, the essays did precisely that, unpacking painful truths about a generation of intellectuals who simply could not bring themselves to believe that Alger Hiss had lied or that Ethel and Julius Rosenberg were traitors. After all, these were people of good will, people on the left, people, in short, like them. Hiss and the Rosenbergs couldn't be guilty as charged because if they were, then so too were they. Even the prospect that this just might be true was enough to cause many liberal intellectuals to close ranks and to engineer distinctions between the larger Good (to which Hiss and the Rosenbergs were presumably devoted) and what they characterized as small legal infractions [Pinsker 1999, 182].

With Fiedler then was a generation on trial along with Hiss, and "not, it must be noted, for having struggled toward a better world, but for having substituted sentimentality for intelligence in that struggle, for having failed to understand the moral conditions that must determine the outcome" (Pinsker 1999, 183). Thus, Fiedler early on declared himself as one who was persuaded, however reluctantly, to put away ideological certainty for a more complicated movement from a "liberalism of innocence to a liberalism of responsibility" (182).

Both these essays need to be understood within the larger framework of liberalism. According to Adamowski (2006), demoralization of liberalism in America may have begun in the work of men and women involved with *Partisan Review* and New York literary culture. Within the larger framework of Adamowski's contention is his hypothesis that Fiedler along with Trilling and Mailer may have been a key participant and contributor to the debate and later crisis and demoralization of the liberalism ideology, before and after the World War II. Adamowski quotes Fiedler's account of how he understood a liberal:

> To the liberal-intellectual, "we" consisted of the supporters of trade unionism, social security, and the rights of Negroes, Jews, and other minorities, including socialists and even Communists; while "they" consisted of "Red-baiters," readers of Hearst, supporters of Franco, Pinkertons, ... members of the Catholic hierarchy, ... the A.F.L., Southern Senators and football players, American Legionnaires, etc. [EI, 68, quoted in Adamowski 2006, 885].

It is believed even now by many that twentieth century American liberalism is at least in part the creation of American Jews. Leslie Fiedler took it upon himself to write essays fiercely critical of American liberals for their groupthink responses to the Hiss and Rosenberg cases, and Fiedler's essays are entirely in keeping with the work of a literary critic.

Adamowski points out in his essay on Hiss that Fiedler's targets were both Hiss and his progressivist sympathizers (2006, 893). For Fiedler—in one of the central words of his critical vocabulary—Hiss is the *archetypal* "popular front" intellectual, convinced that his actions are justified by the unassailable rectitude of his ends. Far beyond mere family or national ties, he is a citizen of the world. For Fiedler, however, he is also a liar and a traitor, and perhaps even a coward. This is to say that Fiedler *reads* the Hiss of the various transcripts as he would a character in a novel, whose social position dooms him to one of the worst nightmares a good communist can have:

> He had by then too much to lose; for, without ceasing to be a Bolshevik, he had become a "success," a respectable citizen. To acknowledge that Russia could be fundamentally wrong would have changed the whole meaning of his life, turned what had perhaps seemed to him his most unselfish and devoted acts, the stealing

of State Department documents, into shameful crimes—into "treason!" Only the conviction that there was no final contradiction between his activities, public and private, could have made Hiss's life tolerable [EI 11, quoted in Adamowski 2006, 894].

Adamowski is not interested in the accuracy of Fiedler's account of Hiss's private torments; he is rather intrigued by the literary dimension of Fiedler's reading. In Fiedler's rendering, that huge and innocently receptive audience is unable to imagine that either itself or its favorite character can be—or have gone—wrong: "Certainly, a generation was on trial with Hiss" (21). Adamowski suggests that Fiedler's essay is written from the position of a kind of Conradian narrator, who, knowing that Hiss is wrong and that history will not exculpate him, must represent for us Hiss's mental agony:

> No wonder Hiss was inaccessible to Chambers' arguments against the party! No wonder he seemed scarcely willing to admit Chambers' existence, refusing him his very name! It was as if Hiss had wanted to shrug off his accuser, not like a real being in the outside world, but like a nightmare. Indeed the persistent voice of the man he had once admired must have seemed to him to possess the quality of a nightmare, speaking in its characteristic half-whisper the doubts, thrust down in himself, that could destroy his self-esteem [EI 12, quoted in Adamowski 2006, 895].

"Afterthoughts on the Rosenbergs" (1953)

Shortly after Julius and Ethel Rosenberg were executed on June 19, 1953, for conspiracy to commit espionage against the United States, the then-young literary and cultural critic Leslie Fiedler presented what was in effect a retrospective justification of the government's action, based on an evaluation of the letters that the Rosenbergs had written to each other while they were incarcerated in separate cells in Sing Sing Penitentiary. His discussion includes the following summary judgment: "It is a parody of martyrdom they give us, too absurd to be truly tragic, too grim to be the joke it is always threatening to become" (1953a, 38; Hite 1993). Like the executions themselves, this edict marks a key moment in the articulation of Cold War doctrine. The electrocution of the Rosenbergs was a stunning overreaction to a purported crime—passing the "secret" of the atomic bomb to the Soviet Union—and which could have had little effect in any case, according to such nuclear physicists as Albert Einstein and Harold Urey, who maintained that there was no secret to the atom bomb and thus nothing of importance that a spy ring, even if one existed, could have passed on to the USSR (Hite 1993, 86). According to Hite, Fiedler's pronouncement represents a strategy characteristic of postwar anticommunist intellectuals, who needed to maintain a sense of their own decency and tolerance while at the same time supporting an increasingly hard governmental line on the question of suppressing dissidents.[8] The phrase "parody of martyrdom" trivializes the political significance that the Rosenbergs tried to assign to their own deaths. But Fiedler goes further, insisting on the ultimate unreality of the event. He declares the Rosenbergs so ontologically lacking that their deaths are not, properly speaking, deaths at all: his essay climaxes with the rhetorical question, "What was there left to die?" (Fiedler 1953a, 45).

In "Afterthoughts on the Rosenbergs," a commissioned article in 1953 for the first issue of *Encounter* (the CIA-funded magazine conceived as a highbrow weapon in the war for the "hearts and minds" of the European intelligentsia), Fiedler presents as an "open-and-shut case" that the Rosenbergs were guilty of spying on behalf of the Soviet Union (25; Tanenhaus 2003). Interestingly, Fiedler's concern are not the "real Rosenbergs," although clearly guilty and deserving of the death penalty; he would rather focus on his position as a literary critic. He would rather engage with the "symbolic Rosenbergs" who supplanted them and have to be dispatched after the executions by other means. These other means involve expunging any residual effect their prison correspondence, published as *The Death House Letters of Julius and Ethel Rosenberg*,[9] might have had on national and international opinion. Like his fellow cultural critic Robert Warshow, Fiedler thus concentrates on the "painfully pretentious style" of these letters, which, he argues, is the "literary equivalent" of the cynical and manipulative politics that the Rosenbergs embody (Fiedler 1953a, 40). Fiedler is more concerned with the Rosenbergs' awkwardness in appropriating and then misusing forms of discourse, emblematized by their failure to distinguish between private and public genres. He writes, "The letters consist almost equally of intimacies which should never have been published, and lay sermons which should never have been written to each other by a husband and wife," and concludes, "The line between the person and the case, between private and public, had been broken down for them long before and could not be redrawn even in the extremest of situations" (41).

Thus, in his "mythic commentary" on the national trials in which the public came to terms with the imperatives of the Cold War, Fiedler sees them "as great symbolic events in which a whole society objectifies and acts out its inner conflicts, its most pressing archetypal terrors" (163). During these trials, the collective fears left over from World War II were objectified in the Soviet threat. The Russians' possession of the bomb elevated these fears into mass hysteria, while the Korean War organized mass hysteria into a miniature version of the total war everyone feared (163). In popular mythology, the Rosenbergs represented one version of the enemy, Joseph McCarthy exemplified a way to search them out, while Alger Hiss and Whittaker Chambers actualized in their relationship the new social bond of internalized distrust. Taken together these figures constituted as a mythological configuration the Cold War mentality. Throughout his commentary on these figures, Fiedler treated this popular mythology and the Cold War mentality it represented as dual symptoms of a psychological complex in need of dissolution rather than as a set of political questions in need of judgment. To differentiate his commentary from that of other American intellectuals, Fiedler distinguished, at the outset of his essay, what he called the factual from the legendary Rosenberg case (Fiedler, CE 1, 31).

Fiedler, throughout his essay, denounced Julius Rosenberg's sacrifice of his private person to an ideological cause as a form of political victimage and concluded that the reduction of persons to political causes "betrays" their "essential humanity." To open up the bonds of what he calls "essential humanity" to a nation whose collective mentality had set "us" against "them," Fiedler believed he had to break apart the bonds joining "us" together. If his characterization of the Rosenberg case exemplified Fiedler's willingness to break apart the bond he shared with the intellectual class, his analysis of the psychological basis for those bonds argued for a different relationship between the intellectuals and "essential humanity" (165).

For Fiedler, the actual Rosenbergs had already been "sacrificed" through this conversion to psychological symbol. Also, in Fiedler's reading of the phenomenon, McCarthyism was the pathological symptom of the disrelation between the intellectuals' explanations of political events and the public's experience of them (166).

Tanenhaus finds the analysis acute, but the manic tone frightened even so fierce a polemicist as Sidney Hook, who advised Irving Kristol, *Encounter*'s editor, to run a disclaimer saying Fiedler's meditation "should not be construed as an attack against human beings who are dead." Thanks to Fiedler, the entire print run of the magazine, 10,000 copies, sold out in a week. The embarrassed editors wished they could have had them back and set them ablaze. Why couldn't Fiedler have written an essay like Robert Warshow's sober piece in *Commentary*? It was just as critical of the Rosenbergs—in fact it made the identical argument—but its tone was nuanced, deliberative, clinical (Tanenhaus 2003).

Placing these writings alongside the vast oeuvre of Fiedler's other writings, I find a kind of tabloid honesty in them. Tanenhaus points out that the essay's vulgarity heroically subverts its very thesis and exposes the ugliness of using taste as an instrument of moral judgment. Thus did Fiedler turn the obsessions of "the family," punitive anti–Stalinism and reverent High Modernism, inside out? Let the genteel critics make pained gestures of "reconciliation" toward

America—the miniature Tocqueville who contributed to *Partisan Review*'s 1952 symposium "Our Country and Our Culture," the born-again capitalists and celebrants of middle-class values, the purveyors of "American Exceptionalism." Fiedler instead roared off on a Hell's Angels road trip through the desolate highways of the national psyche, in search of its demons, its appetites, its lust (Tanenhaus 2003).

Donald E. Pease in his essay "Leslie Fiedler, the Rosenberg Trial, and the Formulation of an American Canon" (1990) links up Leslie Fiedler's account in *Love and Death in the American Novel*, published in 1960, of what constitutes a representative work of American literature, and his critical interventions, written over a decade earlier, in the collective debates over the significance for American cultural life of the national public trials involving the Rosenbergs, Hiss, Chambers, and McCarthyism. Pease is thus trying to state that while formulating the canon, Fiedler constructed a "cultural imaginary" whose contentions changed in a span of 10 years in the sense that it enabled him and his readers to imagine themselves reconstituted within an alternative cultural realm, and that this alternative to the Cold War mentality inevitably turned Fiedler into a subject of that mentality. One result of these debates was "the blurring, in the name of national security interests, of the distinction, traditional to liberal democracies, of the private and public realms [a]s ... every American individual was definable as either an agent or an enemy of the state" (155–156). Pease explains that by "cultural imaginary" he means

> a realm wherein abide not the images of already existing social materials but the "undetermined abstract materiality of society itself.[10] In relation to the Cultural Imaginary the things, objects, and individuals that society brings into existence can be said to be themselves only insofar as they are figured from out of this realm. Here social principles and beliefs are held to be self-evidently true, hence beyond debate [155–56].

In constructing his "cultural imaginary," Fiedler transformed into psychic registers the charged materials of the collective debates in which he had earlier participated (Pease 1990, 156). This collective fantasy was structured in terms of two reversals of the Cold War mentality. Whereas the Cold War mentality designated every American citizen as a symbolic representative of the House Un-American Activities Committee, Fiedler's fantasy involved freeing individuals from an ever-present domestic tyranny. But whether this interethnic bond of freedom that Hawkeye, or Ishmael, or Huckleberry Finn shared with Chingachgook, Queequeg, or Jim was psychically compensatory in relation to the collective surveillance for signs of the enemy within was not so much to Fiedler's point as was the alternative inner life represented by this collective fantasy (156–57), stresses Pease.

According to Pease, Fiedler's "cultural imaginary" was not merely imaginary. It produced what might be called a cultural pre-conscious, where persons whose experiences and relationships are insufficiently assimilated by official culture can abide. Fiedler implicitly describes his work in terms of the political pre-conscious throughout his essays and explicitly in the following passage: "'Sub-minds' would be a more precise way of naming the laws of myths and is it not well to remind ourselves in this regard of the differing weights of mind and sub-mind, conscious and pre-conscious factors in the case of the Negro and Jew?" (CE 2, 165, quoted in Pease 1990, 157). In *Being Busted*, Fiedler brings what Pease called his "cultural imaginary" into explicit relationship with the Cold War mentality:

> I am, in fact, adverse to politics itself as ordinarily defined, so that when I am not, like my favorite models Rip Van Winkle and Huckleberry Finn, I am neither pledging allegiance to the red-white-and-blue, nor chanting, "Ho-Chi-Min" [BB, 234].

Obviously, Fiedler has stuck to his stance of negation practiced in *No! in Thunder* in a very different way here. Pease finds that Fiedler models himself after Huck and Rip Van Winkle, and claims that his true crime against culture inheres in his refusal to position himself within the terms of its controlling opposition. Pease tracks the genealogy for that refusal in autobiographical terms, by bringing a day from Fiedler's boyhood on Bergen Street in Newark, New Jersey, in the time "before the Spades had taken over from the Jews, the role of most visible disturber of the peace" (BB, 14), a day when he ran from the police breaking up a Marxist rally, into relation with a day on Higgins Avenue in Missoula, Montana, a generation later, when he led a revolt against a college president. In bringing his flight from engagement with the police in 1933 together with the revolution he led against a college president in 1958, Pease finds that Fiedler recognizes both incidents as the reactivation in his personal life of the cognitive logic he had earlier criticized in his essay on the Rosenbergs (1990, 159).

Reflecting on his motives for fleeing the scene of revolution as a boy and organizing one as a professor, Pease quotes Fiedler's remark that "maybe what moved me, even more deeply, was my old desire, which had survived my old politics, to play the part of society's victim at long last" (BB, 62).

According to Pease, in consenting to play the part of society's victim Fiedler in his personal life had agreed to the political terms he claims his work had refused. *Being Busted* brings his personal self, constructed within a social realm supervised by the Cold War opposition, to the judgment of his creative self, constructed out of the "cultural imaginary" (1990, 160). Fiedler continues to articulate the terms of that refusal in the form of a dual misrecognition of his Americanness: "Face to face with Italians [during his stay in Europe], I knew myself to be an American simply because, compared to them, I was something else; and what other name is there for the European's Other.... Face to face with the Indians, however, my Americanness seemed called into question once more—rooted as it was not in the land their ancestors had hunted for thousands of years, but only in a language which even my grandparents hardly knew." Caliban to Europe's Prospero, Prospero to the Native Americans' Caliban, Fiedler's dual misrecognitions—of his Americanness by the Italians, of the Indians' different Americanness by Fiedler, himself—became the discovery of Fiedler's new American identity. Interestingly this identity reformation did not take place in society but in the context of his re-reading *Huckleberry Finn*: "Between them, the Italians and the Indians managed to convince me of the truth of what Mark Twain had first suggested to me: that no one was born an American even in America, only adopted or reborn as one; since America was a myth created in the dialogue between those who at any point inhabited our land and those who remained outside" (BB, 51). This is, by far, one of the most significant contributions that Pease's understanding of Fiedler's cultural imaginary has made.

In addition, Pease states that *Being Busted* leads him to a different understanding: that to engage "the dialogue between those who at any point inhabited our land and those who remained outside ... is to seem a double agent to those who need to believe in clearly defined sides: the Past, the Present; Right, Left; America, Japan [or any ideological Other]; Male, Female; Straight, Queer; Them, Us; You, Me.... At least one party in every dialogue must be an interpreter, which is to say, a traitor to those for whom any peace is a betrayal" (BB, 46).

In the discussion of both his and Fiedler's "cultural imaginary," Pease brings to the fore the twin lining of Fiedler's American narrative. He tells us that throughout *Being Busted*, Fiedler develops a double-narrative logic to signify the dual placement of his person. As a dissenting American he finds himself subjected in 1967 to the same mentality he had written about with the Rosenberg case. In many ways, then, the real trial in *Being Busted* can be taken as a reenactment in his personal life of the great national trials he had written about in the late forties and early fifties. It appears as if Fiedler's understanding of Julius Rosenberg's ordeal helped him to "describe his own work solely in ideological terms and to set the innocence of his vision against the corruption of the official culture" (Pease 1990, 161).

Donald Pease's article in many ways established for several who had started writing of Fiedler as just a phenomenon come and gone that Fiedler's credo of America's "cultural imaginary" needed to be understood through some of his major socio-cultural-political writings of and commentary on the

1950s and '60s. In addition, the duality of his identity as an American was corroborated by the critiques of similar nature in his writings.

Pedagogical Credo

At the end of his tether, just a year before his death, in his 85th year, it is amazing that Fiedler's desire to connect to students and public remained unflagging. When Scott McLemee asked if he had withdrawn from the classroom, quick came the response: "I still do teach, one on one, and will give an occasional lecture. Talking is something I love to do. So long as I can still make some sounds, I'll be making them in public" (2002).

In one of his visits to India, in an interview with Jeet Thahil published in *Indian Express Magazine* (Feb. 1987), Fiedler states his own position—primarily that of a teacher who writes, rather than a writer who teaches. He says that in the classroom, he brings other books to life. A scholar dedicated to teaching, Fiedler is quite apprehensive even about the thought of relinquishing teaching: "The notion of not teaching again appalls me. I don't think I can bear the life of a lonely writer where my only audience is a hypothetical one and I am only confronting a piece of paper" just as a writer or novelist has to. As a teacher in the classroom, one actually interacts with "living bodies, responding to you, talking back at you. It's a relationship that becomes personal, carnal, almost erotic" (6). Some years back, in a Salon.com piece, Paglia (quoted by Timberg, 2008) described Fiedler as a thinker who did not impose his system "but liberated a whole generation of students to think freely and to discover their own voices."

But turning back the pages would uncover that Fiedler's pedagogical credo has been much governed by the impact that some of his teachers had on him. In the preface to *Love and Death*, he pays glowing tributes to his teacher, William Ellery Leonard of the University of Wisconsin. As "a great and, I hope, unforgotten teacher, as well as a rebel poet, translator, and essayist," Fiedler eulogically attributes to his teacher his own treatment of literary criticism as "an act of total moral engagement, in which tact, patience, insolence, and piety consort strangely but satisfactorily together" (1960, 15–16). Kellman points out that the disjunct felt by Fiedler between American literature and being an American is also because of the influence of Leonard (1999, 75). Fiedler pays extraordinary tribute to William Ellery Leonard:

> It was he who first not merely told but showed me—the rich, tragic quality of his own being as well as by the excitement that he engendered in the classroom—that literature is more than what one learns to read in schools and libraries, more

even than a grace of life; that it is the record of those elusive moments at which, life is alone fully itself, fulfilled in consciousness and form" [LD 1960, 15–16].

This grandiose but glorious defense of literary criticism as something more than mere interpretive proficiency, "an act of total moral engagement," is a fitting prologue not merely to Fiedler's impassioned attempt to examine the tradition of the American novel, but also to the currents of American culture. It is a gloss on all the author's twenty-something books, not least on his most personal, *Being Busted*, an enduring blend of tact, patience, insolence, and piety (Kellman 1999, 75). What he spelled out here was only a reiteration of his own commitment to literature as a "grace of life" in *The Art of the Essay*, published in 1958. Another teacher from whom Leslie believed he actually learned something was an English professor named Mallory, who had gone to Oxford on a Rhodes scholarship from New Mexico (Winchell 2002, 21).

Many of his students-now-turned-professors, academics and scholars, feel that as a teacher, Fiedler might well serve—at least at first glance—as a model for the eccentric yet brilliant professor. One such student-now-turned-professor recalls,

> He liked to smoke cigars in his office ... and smoked so incessantly that his cardigan front was most often covered in ash and burn holes; he was so little concerned with matters of fashion that he appeared to wear the same clothes everyday.... He never managed to order books for his classes but gave students extensive reading lists and left it to them to track down the assigned texts (not necessarily an easy task in the days before internet booksellers, especially since Fiedler's classes were most often over-enrolled); in lieu of detailed lecture notes, he would usually bring a matchbook-sized scrap of paper with some scribbles on it to his three-hour graduate seminars, and yet stayed on track, both in class and over the course of a semester. He seemed to have read everything, from the Romans to the Victorians to contemporary writers of the American West, and he enjoyed and admired the lowbrow as much or more than the highbrow, and sought (decades before the rise of Cultural Studies in American universities) to get his students to do the same.
>
> Most of his students recall that though more often than not he would appear for a class looking like he's just been hit several times by lightning—his hair stands on end ... and yet proceeds to dazzle his students (*and* the frequent visitors from the community who were always welcome to attend his courses) with his wit, erudition, and passion [Harrison 2008].

While it may be fun to think of Fiedler as a nutty professor, he certainly wasn't a cartoon figure, but rather an exceptionally generous, encouraging, and open-minded teacher and mentor, as Brady Harrison, Casey Charles and Nancy Cook (the latter two were colleagues who knew Fiedler well from their days as graduate students at SUNY-Buffalo) attest. In conversation with Brady, both noted not only *l'eau du cigare* that followed Fiedler around, but the fact that he held far more office hours a week than any of his colleagues, open not only to students but to anyone who wanted to stop by to discuss ideas about literature and culture. More, Fiedler was incredibly patient and kind toward his students, encouraging them to make what connections they could: "who knows where an idea or leap may lead? ... He pushed his students," according to Cook, "to think harder and to make (unexpected, wide-ranging) connections"; and, because he had, he "made me read everything" (as quoted by Harrison 2008). As evidence of his dedication and generosity toward his students, he served on committees and mentored students on topics as diverse as Renaissance literature, Twain, the history of the book, and Stephen King. As a teacher, he was by all accounts as great a listener and guide as he was a lecturer and public speaker.

Charles, the chair of the University of Montana's department of English in 2008, shares an important genial and populist approach that Fiedler had in his interactions with students. He recounts Fiedler's unassuming and supportive populist approach towards his students, which speaks volumes about his pedagogical credo, which in many ways was open and embracing, encouraging new ideas and thoughts. Charles recalls a graduate seminar on Whitman at SUNY-Buffalo as a graduate student in the late 1980s in which the same populist ethos was at work. He recounts, "Leslie was nothing if not intellectually and socially magnanimous, and I often wondered—as he taught this class on America's most famous poet—if he felt some personal affinity with the author of that 'wonderful and ponderous book' that appeared in 1855, the poet who wrote 'Do I contradict myself? / Very well then ... I contradict myself / I am large ... I contain multitudes.' There was something of Whitman's big embrace in Leslie Fiedler" (quoted in Harrison 2008). Like Emerson, he possessed a mind on fire (and, like Emerson, he certainly did not mind offending people (Harrison 2008).

Geoffrey Green, who was a doctoral student at Buffalo, recalls a few of the typical pedagogical enterprises of Fiedler: "Meet two, three, sometimes four times a week—it was a Fiedlerian form of psychoanalysis ... mutual schmoozing, the most essential activity to Fiedlerian learning [and] the broadest possible engagement with the world of culture activity, an engagement that reflects the best sense of humanism: no boundaries; no high or low; nothing is forbidden" (1999, 178–79).

His varied, wide-reaching critical oeuvre was best uncovered in his teaching. Jerome Richard, who was Fiedler's student at Montana and later taught at Montana in the sixties, left to pursue his doctorate with this advice from Fiedler: "Don't confuse getting a Ph.D. with getting an education." He writes,

> Unlike many senior professors who begrudge the teaching part of their jobs, Leslie loved it. At Montana, throughout his career, he taught the introductory humanities course with an enthusiasm that was evident to his students. There

was a dramatic quality to his lectures. Pacing his platform, speaking without notes but often glancing at the back of his left hand as if ideas were written there, or running his hand through the curling, gray Mosaic locks of hair that surrounded the great vault of his forehead, nurtured by his street corner oratory as a young radical and fed by his suppressed acting ambitions, each lecture was a performance. Professors whose audiences tended to doze off found that another reason to disparage what he had to say [2004, 295].

Fiedler was particularly interested in why some works endure in popular regard despite having been dismissed by critics. That led him to cross the boundary from canon to popular literature. This did not mean any lowering of standards. When students told him how much they loved Richard Bach's *Jonathan Livingston Seagull,* he protested that it was "pretentious banality" (Richard 2004, 295). This was explained in *What Was Literature?*—that the effective teacher "must show himself capable of responding not only to those works which his students are not likely to discover without his guidance, but also to those which have persisted in spite of critical disapproval" (Richard 2004, 114). Fiedler, trying hard to bring about a consensus regarding the artificial division of literature into high and low in "Is There Counter-Tradition?" (WWL) says that his is not the only voice speaking against "elitism"; he is joined by a number of those who are teaching pop literature in American universities today. But Fiedler despairingly notices that such teachers are regarded as second-class citizens. He pleads with American universities to accommodate "without betraying its heritage ... courses in both high and popular literature" (WWL, 108). And he says, "It is all a matter of time ... everything is changing" (109).

This is no longer regarded as quite so startling an idea as it was in the fifties and sixties. In fact, the very idea has itself been canonized to such an extent that in his speech accepting the Modern Language Association's Hubbell Award for lifetime achievement he said: "I am now routinely quoted in jargon-ridden, reader-unfriendly works I cannot bring myself to read, am listed honorifically in the kind of footnotes and bibliographies I have always eschewed" (Winchell 2002, 333).

That of course was an exaggeration, but only an exaggeration. It was often the way he made his point. He did think the ivory tower should be more of a multi-story pavilion, and for that he was considered a danger to the Academy. As one of the graduate students at the SUNY at Buffalo in the spring of 1968, Rocco Capozzi recalls the unconventional teacher that Fiedler was, advising students to go home and watch "soap operas" and other popular TV shows, in order to study the new, modern "myths" offered by the "mass media" (Capozzi 1991, 332).

When asked by Capozzi in an interview if he can talk about both overall expectations in proposing new approaches to looking at literature and at culture in general, Fiedler responded that as a published writer, a teacher, and a speaker, he has been trying to function as a repairer, "trying to repair the cultural damage done by the rise of Modernism and the domination of High Culture by the academy: the splitting of the audience for song and story into hostile camps."

Baring his pedagogical enterprise once again, he says,

> I have been doing this in the classroom and from the lecture platform as well as in print—"boring from within," as it were; which is to say, operating from inside the university community and the elitist critical establishment. I have never, of course, despised the masterworks of recent High Literature, much less the classics canonized in the curriculum of classes in literature. Instead, I have tried to reread such authors as Joyce and Shakespeare in the context of popular culture, pointing out their indebtedness to the despised popular genres of their time. Simultaneously, I have attempted to reread writers like Edgar Rice Burroughs, Margaret Mitchell, and Stephen King not as symptoms of the decay of taste or the tyranny of the marketplace, but as works of art in their own right.

For this he has worked out "new classroom strategies—teaching books from both sides of the great divide in the same courses, rather than segregating them in ghettoized ones." Then making an important point on the use of language, he says,

> I have ... found it necessary to reinvent the language of criticism by finding a non-hermetic, non-pedantic vocabulary for evaluation and analysis understandable to the widest possible audience. I have, therefore, sought to avoid formalism of all kinds, from the New Criticism to Deconstruction, since these inevitably lead their practitioners to translate what they have to say into a code penetrable only by a chosen few. I have not, I must confess, been completely successful in becoming either a pop pedagogue or a pop critic—but at least I have tried [Capozzi 1991, 332].

Commenting on present-day professors, old and young, Fiedler feels that they have learned to win the confidence and hold the attention of their students by displaying their knowledge of soaps, sitcoms, cop shows, comic books, and the like. They tend, moreover, not to make the invidious distinction between print and post-print media, the latter of which their students disconcertingly read with more ease and pleasure. Nor do they have any sense that they are shamelessly pandering or uneasily slumming when they do so (Capozzi 1991, 333–334).

Finally, Fiedler "still considered himself a teacher who wrote rather than a writer who taught" (Winchell 2002, 184). It must be noted that over thirty-six years after his departure from Missoula, he was one of sixteen professors featured in an article titled "Teachers Who Change Lives" on the university's official website. From the time he first stepped in front of a college class at the

University of Wisconsin in 1939, he tried to enlighten and entertain his students or at least to allay their boredom. As a writer and public lecturer, he simply addressed an expanded audience of students—the reading and listening public. In *What Was Literature*? he says, "The teacher, that professional amateur, teaches not so much his subject as himself. If he is a teacher of literature, he provides for those less experienced in song and story, including the reluctant, the skeptical, the uncooperative, the incompetent, a model of one in whom what seemed dead, mere print on the page, becomes living, a way of life—palpable fulfillment, a transport into the world of wonder" (WWL, 114; Winchell 2002, 184).

In spite of his tryst with films, theatre, and television talk shows, his role of college professor was his most enduring presence on screen, not in an absurd low-budget fairy tale, but in the mainstream film *Exposed*—in which Nastassja Kinski clutches a copy of *Love and Death in the American Novel* to her bosom, and a fictional teacher writes a sentence from that book on a fictional blackboard. It was a role he redefined for an age in which the boundaries between education and entertainment were becoming blurred (Winchell 2002, 257).

The Art of the Essay (1958)

But superimposed on all these laudatory observations is a classic piece of pedagogical enterprise, the only textbook that Fiedler ever wrote: *The Art of the Essay* (1958). In the ensuing pages, I discuss a work of Fiedler's that has not been commented upon by many. This work, like the several that it followed and many that will follow later, brings to the fore some of the key elements of his critical enterprise: his credo. Not only this, I read this textbook, which appeared a few years before *Love and Death in the American Novel*, as an important component of his pedagogical credo. This in many ways also establishes that his pedagogical credo was in sync with his others: his literary, critical, cultural and socio-political credos. Viewed as part of his canon, *The Art of the Essay* uncovers, once again, some of the universal key elements of his critical enterprise: the unabashed use of "I" in writing; the "sense of connect" with the reader that he is most concerned about; his continuous engagement with America and its culture and his movement from "high," as he chooses to call it, culture to popular culture.[11]

In 1999, Malin drew attention to *The Art of the Essay* in his co-edited anthology titled *Leslie Fiedler and American Culture*. Malin bookends his essay "The Prophetic Textbook" with two significant observations: "It's ... an 'occult' autobiography ... an intriguing document, one that, like his dissertation on Donne, offers a 'secret' passage into his written world and clarifies Fiedler's abiding interests and obsessions." The second is that the textbook—which is usually not listed in the Fiedler canon—is as close to autobiography as *Being Busted*. It is a thrilling achievement filled with the ironic joy of an academic fighting the academic world by employing a textbook to declare his profound other side, his peculiarity (Malin 1999, 37–46).

The book is divided into three large sections: "The Discovery of the Self"; "America" (containing "Americans on Native Places," "As Europeans See Us," and "Coda"); and "Ourselves and Our Culture" (containing essays on mass culture and high culture). Fiedler offers introductions to each section, selections of essays, and even a series of questions about the essays.

As in his other works containing famous personal prefaces (EI, NT LD), here also Fiedler offers a personal confessional introduction, refreshingly surprising for a textbook. He refers to the essay as a "kind of printed confession," a transaction, an exchange, between "our best 'I' and an ideal 'you'" (Malin 1999, 37).

Fiedler attacks the academic world—it consists of "boredom" and "dullness"—and he hopes to save it by offering the student a fresh way of perception, a mode of looking at school and world as fields of energy, formal beauty, and "grace of life" (37–38).

Then, Fiedler makes another point that the "peculiar" is what interests him. He is crossing genres or, at least, questioning rigid lines of demarcation. No wonder that he later refers to *Love and Death* as a kind of gothic novel, to the other book as the "inadvertent epic" (38).

The selected essays and the authors, "be it Montaigne's or ... his own essays are full of tension, they are ambivalent gestures of intimacy and secretiveness. (There is a sense of opposition, of battling forces.) They are 'midway' texts: bold explorations, not final solutions" (Malin 1999, 38). All the selections are linked with a common thread: a sense of inwardness: His introduction ends with "the hope that by reading the essays he has chosen, the student will 'search' for the self: the search for the self becomes the search for the child one was, and in some disconcertingly essential way still is" (38–39).

In section 1, "The Discovery of the Self," Fiedler's choice of essays is remarkable. They are Montaigne's "Of Presumption"; Lamb's "Two Letters to Coleridge" and "Two Attempts at an Autobiography"; Fitzgerald's classic "The Crackup"; Greene's "The Revolver in the Corner Cupboard"; Baldwin's "Stranger in the Village"; and an excerpt from Stein's *Autobiography of Alice B. Toklas*. The last line of Baldwin's essay is "This world is white no longer, and it will never be white again." Isn't the line an oddly prophetic one for the reader of Fiedler's future works?

In section 2 in his introduction to "America," Fiedler suggests that "the search for identity leads outward as well as inward, and the sensitive observer turns his eye on the place he knows least: the place from which he begins or the one in which he chooses to end, the place from which he has fled or the one to which he comes after his flight." These words have mythological resonance. Although each person has his own identity, his signature, he seems to be acting in a recurring, universal drama (41). Fiedler includes his own well-known "Montana: or The End of Jean Jacques Rousseau" (1949).

In the selections included in "As Europeans See Us," we find three essays that are especially significant. Matthew Arnold writes one entitled "America Is Not Interesting"; D. H. Lawrence writes "The Spirit of the Place" (a chapter from *Studies in Classic American Literature*); and Sartre writes "American Cities." These essays are valuable for several reasons.

Arnold's essay, excerpted from *Civilization in the United States*, makes a long list of things and ideas that America lacks: fine paintings, so that it depends on imitations of European art; grand, European-like architecture (instead it is "pretty and coquettish"); and distinction, as it is full of "tall talk," "inflated sentiment," "elevation," and lofty idealism. The placement of this essay is crucial to the understanding of America for many young students.

Lawrence, in opposition to Arnold, understands that America is a special, spectral place—the home of new myths, new masks. Lawrence is, without doubt, an influence on Fiedler (43).

Sartre begins his description of America by admitting, "My eyes were not accustomed to the skyscrapers and they did not surprise me; they did not seem like man-made, man-inhabited constructions but like rocks and hills." He mentions "turbulent soil." He describes American communities: "communities are born as they die—in a day." Sartre notes shrewdly that in America nothing is "definitive," nothing is arrested. Malin tells us that Arnold, Lawrence and Satre act as good counterpoints and bring a kind of wholesomeness to the discussion on America.

In the third section, "Ourselves and Our Culture" (divided into "Mass Culture" and "High Culture"), according to Malin, Fiedler again plays with opposition. He writes in his introduction: "The essayist cannot consider for very long the relationship between the self and the society which forms it without coming to terms with the ways in which most men become aware of that relationship. 'Ordinary people' act out; their scripts (life-scripts) come from what they see daily: television. Television, athletic 'rituals,' films 'celebrate the beauty of violence.'" Fiedler is perhaps easy here because he doesn't indicate the "ugliness" of violence, of "acting out," but he recognizes that we are spectators, not readers. When he speculates at length about "sub-art," he relates it to dream. He implies that our existence is at times so filled with dream that we can barely recognize fact. Popular culture, whether we like it or not, is always before us, and it forces essayists to find the secrets for its verve and appeal.

Liebling's essay, "Ahab and Nemesis," on the match between Rocky Marciano and Archie Moore, subtly conflates high art and violent entertainment. He refuses to write in newspaper language, to use such simple words as "crushed" and "bloody." Perhaps he actually believes that a "fight" is our equivalent to ancient ritual. Norman Podhoretz's essay, "Our Changing Ideals, as Seen on TV," is a complex investigation of the American family in sitcoms.

The section "High Culture" has three well-known essays—well-known now—by Baudelaire on Poe, Poe on Hawthorne, and Melville on Hawthorne. When these essays were written they were bold assessments of "new writers." The mark of a significant critic is that he dares to recognize genius before others. I am particularly thinking of Fiedler on Barth and Hawkes.

If we were to see these essays as "reflections"—on the anthologist's or the author's part—then we would be capable of recognizing the reasons for the choices. Fiedler is using them, in fact he is using the entire textbook, as an "occult" guide to the literary work he was writing at that time: *Love and Death in the American Novel*.

The textbook collection is a journey into the Fiedlerian world of literature, culture and criticism. His selections are a reflection of himself; the essays of writers chosen act as his doubles because, as Malin says, "Don't the best choose to write about their 'doubles?' Don't we feel the strong attraction? Am I surely not one of the 'best' critics, writing on Fiedler because he led me to the Gothic, to American Jewish writers?" (45).

Like a detective unraveling a mystery, Malin prowls around the textbook looking for hidden, secret, and coded messages (clues) that shall lead him finally to a resolution, the unpeeling of the truth, layer by layer, which is that the textbook is an "occult autobiography" of sorts.

Chutzpah and Pudeur (1969)

Towards the end, I draw attention to the real Fiedlerian credo that according to many defines all his works. It is unmistakably Fiedler's "Chutzpah and Pudeur." This challenging, eclectic essay was originally written in 1969, but is the concluding selection in "Cross the Border—Close the Gap." When we consider that, in 1960, "Archetype and Signature" and "In the Beginning Was the Word" occupied a similarly climactic position in *No! In Thunder*, we might well regard "Chutzpah and Pudeur" as an index of how far Fiedler's theoretical sensibility had developed over the watershed decade of the 1960s, says Winchell (2002, 246).

In "Chutzpah and Pudeur" Fiedler identified these two terms: one the Yiddish term for nerve or gall, and the other a French term for civility or gentility, signifying the polarity in "our very understanding of what constitutes art and literature." He called most literary theory *"pudique"*—too genteel, bashful, obscuring. He issued a mandate for more "chutzpahdik" criticism; and indeed, among Fiedler's contributions to the field of literary studies has been the introduction of the feisty persona of the chutzpahdik critic (Rubenstein 2003, 160).

An example of the chutzpahdik Fiedler, the critic, can be drawn from a reading of his essay "Hemingway in Ketchum." Hemingway's suicide made Fiedler a celebrity. In his Montana period, Fiedler made a pilgrimage to Ketchum, Idaho, months before Hemingway killed himself. After Hemingway's death, Fiedler traveled the country, reminiscing about his day at Ketchum, pretending it was an ordeal to brood so publicly about what he'd seen and that he could bring himself to do it only after the third or fourth drink. In fact he savored the details, as the essay he wrote makes all too plain: "The Hemingway who greeted us, framed by the huge blank television screen that dominated the living room, was an old man with spectacles slipping down his nose. An old man at sixty-one.... Hemingway's handclasp I could scarcely feel; and I stood there baffled, a little ashamed of how I had braced myself involuntarily for a bone-crushing grip" (Tanenhaus 2003). Winchell writes that Harold Bloom's theoretical apparatus was not really needed to understand that Fiedler is feasting on Hemingway's ebbing powers—that the critic has defeated the novelist. But then, this has always been criticism's message. It is a contest between gifted writer and gifted reader. Fiedler spelled it out with appalling literalness. He was chronically unable to leave anything unsaid—or unshouted. And this was his genius (Tanenhaus 2003).

Tracing a decline in Fiedler's position from an "intelligent" critic to a "freaky" one, but establishing his *locus standi* very much in the academy, Pinsker points out that Fiedler is part of the literary establishment, however much he prefers to think of himself as a "barbarian *within* the gates." After all, he makes out syllabi, holds forth at appointed hours, sets examination questions, gives grades, and not least of all, picks up a healthy paycheck. Real barbarians—within the gates or beyond them—do none of these things. Pinsker bemoans that Fiedler as a pedagogue at this juncture was reduced to "a mere approval, worse, their adulation" seeking professor. Yet, "Fiedler's vision is unashamedly utopian. It posits a university that bridges all gaps—teachers and students, fathers and sons, literatures both High and Low, cultures both majority and minority—and teaches the wider world to do likewise" (Pinsker 1999, 188).

But the superscript on his pedagogical credo was his attitude towards the margins: people and credos. An example of this can be lifted from the pages of his post-retirement teaching days. In 1989, Fiedler celebrated his fiftieth anniversary as a college teacher. Even at seventy-two he was not ready to retire from the profession he loved. Instead, he stopped teaching conventional classes and began taking tutorials. In many ways, it was an ideal situation, because he ended up working with only those students who sought him out with a project that interested both of them. Even as his health began to deteriorate in the next decade, he kept coming to campus three mornings a week. In his later teaching days, the American students who sought him out were often on the margins of society (Winchell 2002, 325). One entire class consisted of disabled persons who studied the treatment of physical abnormalities in literature. As one might expect, this was not a class of meek-spirited Tiny Tims. "We're not 'handicapped' or 'disabled,'" they would say, "Goddamit, we're cripples and proud of it." By the end of the semester, a dwarf anarchist had given a huge engagement ring to a girl with flipper arms (Winchell 2002, 325).

This is what he remained: for the margins always.

The kind of pedagogical credo that emerges includes honest commitment as a pedagogue to his job and his students, personal and political commitment to populism, Fiedlerian qualities of generosity, capaciousness of mind, and openness to others and new ideas; these make his credo stand apart and tall.

In a conversation with Geoffrey Green in 1981, Fiedler stood his ground about his literary, critical and pedagogical credo. Still concerned with biography and personal stamp he voiced his views against the structuralists: "I'm a cryptoanalytic critic: I take every text as being primarily interesting for its encoded meaning, rather that its apparent meanings" (Green 1981, 135). Thus, Fiedler says that the end product is as important as the means and ways by which that end product has been achieved. For him, imagination, biography, and influence on a work of art are as important as the work of art itself. Fiedler's views on the artist also exemplify a remarkable evolution in this dialogue published by Green. He points out that even the critic tends to create a fictional self and that self overtakes his writing. Fiedler says that the critic becomes the victim of the first fiction that he creates of himself as a critic, as a novelist, as a short story writer. According to Fiedler, the "I" is as much an invention on the part of the critics as the "hes" and the "shes" and the "yous" that he talks about. He clearly acknowledges, "I decided that I was going to be an 'I' critic instead of a voice 'ex cathedra'" (Green 1981, 134–135).

If Fiedler's warning against critical jargon was useful in 1950, it sounds downright prophetic nearly half a century later. When in "Archetype and Signature" Fiedler refers to his enemies as "anti-biographic," Fiedler argues that formalist critics, of whatever stripe, have made a fatal error in reducing the poem to mere words on a page. When I. A. Richards defines a poem as an "experience," he is rejecting the notion that it might also be an "imitation," or a "communication." If, as Richards strongly implies, literary language is nonreferential, then it is divorced from the rest of human experience. Although no one could have foreseen it at the time, it was precisely this notion that laid the philosophical groundwork for the deconstructionist contention that all language is simply an arbitrary system of linguistic signs with no objective meaning (Winchell 1999, 89, 93).

Jerome Richard points out, "Leslie understood that literary criticism was not brain surgery, that a mistake was not fatal and one could therefore take chances" (Richard 2004, 294).

He took several chances, but all in the favor of the public against the private, intimate and personal, calling for a middlebrow cult, and he did succeed. This will be seen in the next few chapters.

CHAPTER 2

Comradeship, Male Bonding, or...?

Re-readings and Re-evaluations

> Do you still believe that st-st-stuff about Huck Finn?
> —Ernest Hemingway to Fiedler, *Collected Essays*

> It is easy to see why critics were in a constant flap in those days when Fiedler was just beginning to publish his literary criticism. He says, for example, 'the dressing of Jim in a woman's gown in Huck Finn ... can mean anything or nothing at all ...' just enough to upset his critics.
> —C. R. Larson, "The Good Bad Boy and Guru of American Letters."

> Even more tiresome than ... constant mythicizing of heterosexuality is the pre-occupation with homosexuality.
> —William Van O'Conner in Charles R. Larson, "Leslie Fiedler: The Critic and the Myth, the Critic as Myth."

One can never say, even today, when we are into the twenty-first century by more than a decade, that the final word has been said on Fiedler's preoccupation with regression and the boyhood sexual fantasies of the American male. Needless to say, they will always need exposition, more so when read in conjunction with his preoccupation with the "other" to be dealt with in the next chapter. It clearly reflects his well-defined movement into racial and mythic concerns. Fiedler perceived the WASP American male as an alienated and runaway male, seeking refuge in the company of a colored male. Stated without a hint of hesitation, his robust, bold and energetic critique continues to exasperate and unnerve, concurrently engage and interest scholars. So much so that over the years its insights have repeatedly been used as theories by researchers all over the globe. His formulation that the mythic American condition was boyhood, as the American fictionists were afraid of dealing with adult heterosexual love and their literature, which depicted the American male's flight from society into the wilderness, in the company of a non-white male, in retrospect appears to be hardly a bold thesis at all.

I wonder if it is too much of a stretch to see the early rejections of his bold critical statements on major mainstream American texts as symptomatic of a will to exclude all that undergirds the entire predictable institution of American literary historiography beginning with F. O. Matthiessen's *The American Renaissance* and R. W. B. Lewis's *The American Adam*; or if contrapuntally, he really had a genuine thesis to tell. "Time will tell," critics cried hoarsely more than half a century back. Time has told. More and more, younger writers of today are using his thesis to further their own interpretations, which shall be discussed in the following pages.

So, one cannot not use his first essay, which earned him so much of notoriety and ill will, as the starting point of a theme. The essay in retrospect appears harmless now: "Come Back to the Raft Ag'in, Huck Honey!" (1948). The field of literary scholarship has certainly changed a great deal since 1948. Like all criticism of real consequence, ridding *Adventures of Huckleberry Finn* of its Fiedlerian stamp proved difficult, if not impossible. No matter that Fiedler's proudest boast was that he had effectively added a line to Twain's classic (as careful readers discover, Jim never utters the words of Fiedler's title), or that responsible Twain scholars felt his chutzpah was the very essence of irresponsibility; the essay took hold (Pinsker 1999, 183). In it, he argued that American culture during the frontier era had been dominated by the male quest to flee what Washington Irving dubbed "petticoat government." One form of escape from domesticity (read: fatherhood) could be found in Rip Van Winkle's hillside nap, or Thoreau's solitude at Walden (183). But Fiedler also pointed to the recurrent motif of white heroes forming extremely close emotional bonds with men of other races. While European novelists of the nineteenth century wrote about the problems surrounding heterosexual love, classic American literature projected a fantasy of interracial harmony in a world without women—"innocent homosexuality," as he put it. To a later generation, it seems impossible to overlook the erotic overtones of, say, Ishmael's relationship with Queequeg, his Polynesian bunkmate, in *Moby-Dick*. But as Winchell documents, the argument was quite upsetting at the time. He cites the greeting of Ernest Hemingway upon meeting Mr. Fiedler: "Do you still believe that st-st-stuff about Huck Finn?" (McLemee 2002).

The Montana Wildness and Tryst with *Partisan Review*

It is said that it was at Montana that Fiedler shot to notoriety and ill fame. It also produced his landmark critical corpus. Brady Harrison calls the work produced while in Montana "the Montana Wildness" (2008). Jerome Richard, who knew Fiedler at the University of Montana (then Montana State University) when he taught there in the early sixties, recounts that there were two warring camps that existed in the English department at Montana: "the pro and anti Leslie forces." The reason was once again a campaign that Fiedler had launched against the university president, which led to the president's resignation. This fight resulted during Fiedler's stint as department chairman when he tried to hire an African American professor, Charles Nylon, and the president turned down the appointment. Richard rightly points out: "The incident demonstrated several things about him [Fiedler]: his principle, his passion, and his obliviousness to odds. It also demonstrated his ability to stir up passion in others. His literary criticism often had the same effect. Henry Nash Smith who wrote the seminal study *Virgin Land*, once described him to me as 'a wild man'" (Richard 2004, 294). This is just one example of the way people spoke of Fiedler. But as stated earlier, he attracted attention in many other ways too: by inviting famous writers such as Faulkner to lecture at Montana and later, of course, his infamous Fourth of July parties in Buffalo. Jerome recalls that at Montana Federation he was "active in the teachers' union (American Federation of Teachers) and though not particularly observant in his religion, conducted Seders when a minyan was sometimes difficult to round up. Perhaps it was finding himself, a Jewish boy from Newark, in Montana that made him look at things differently. Initially disappointed that this remote outpost of academia was the only job he was offered out of graduate school, he developed towards the state something of the attitude that Faulkner held towards Mississippi" (Richard 2004, 296).

Many scholars including Winchell feel that even if he had not been a Jew, Fiedler's identity as an Easterner would have eventually posed problems for him, especially since he seemed to have a compulsive urge to publish whatever was on his mind. At that juncture, often it was in *Partisan Review*, the kind of little magazine in which publication (in those benighted times) was still more of a hindrance than a help to academic advancement (Fiedler 1999a).

The Montana Phase

During the two decades that he lived in Montana, nothing that Fiedler wrote stirred more controversy, global and local, than his two essays "Come

Back to the Raft Ag'in, Huck Honey!" (1948) for global stirrings and "Montana; or the End of Jean-Jacques Rousseau" (December 1949) for local discomposure, both published in the *Partisan Review*. They made him one of the most famous scholars and intellectual provocateurs in the nation (Harrison 2008). A discussion of the essay "Montana; or the End of Jean-Jacques Rousseau" will best be suited to the next chapter, whose larger theme is "outsidedness." In this chapter an analysis of the first would rest. Fiedler also included both these essays in the only textbook that he wrote, *The Art of the Essay* (1958). Montana is, for him, not the Romantic paradise. It is a dangerous place because it doesn't conform to the usual descriptions. It, like Hollywood, is full of nervous contradictions. (Consider that Montana and Hollywood are partially *mythical* places.) It offers contradiction between "actuality and the dream," writes Malin (1999, 39). In his autobiographical account *Being Busted*, Fiedler wrote that he "had come to love that absurd place" (BB, 62, quoted in Richard 2004, 296).

"Come Back to the Raft Ag'in, Huck Honey!" (1948)

The other essay that is linked with Montana and the *Partisan Review* was written in 1948, in his first year back in Missoula after his service in the navy and post-doctoral studies: "Come Back to the Raft Ag'in, Huck Honey!" This essay expresses the central insight of his trilogy *Love and Death in the American Novel, Waiting for the End,* and *The Return of the Vanishing American*, in which I shall trace the rest of the development of this theme. But as an interesting aside, let me recount in Fiedler's own words the genesis of this essay. It is true, and Fiedler claimed as much, that he was no Americanist. He says in the Hubell Award acceptance speech (1994),

> Unlike most of you and those you have thus honored before, I am not a professional scholar, specializing in American literature, but an unreconstructed amateur, a dilettante who stumbled accidentally into your area of expertise. I have, as you are surely aware, never been a member of the American Literature Section of the MLA.

He further goes on to say,

> In graduate school I took no courses and wrote no papers on American literature, concentrating instead on the poetry of the Middle Ages and the English Seventeenth Century under mentors who believed and sought to persuade me that only second-rate minds wasted their time in studying American books.

In the same speech he reveals the genesis of his most controversial product:

> I had been reading to my two sons (then seven and nine), as I was accustomed to do at bedtime, a passage from *The Adventures of Huckleberry Finn* about Huck and Jim on the raft; and afterwards between sleeping and waking, I found myself redreaming Twain's idyllic dream of inter-ethnic male bonding and the flight from civilization. Then, I awoke fully to realize how central that erotic myth was not just to our literature but to our whole culture and rushed to my desk to get the insight down before it vanished forever. The little prose lyric which it insisted on becoming I sent off immediately to the *Partisan Review*.

Turning the pages of "Huck Honey!" today, it seems to begin with, as Harrison says, "a Kafka-like precision": "It is perhaps to be expected that the Negro and the homosexual should become stock literary themes in a period when the exploration of responsibility and failure has become again a primary concern of our literature" (413). According to Harrison, if this opening does not pack quite the same jolt of the unexpected as, say, the first line of "The Metamorphosis"—"As Gregor Samsa awoke one morning from uneasy dreams he found himself transformed in his bed into a gigantic insect" (2008, 89)—Fiedler's gambit certainly gets the reader's attention (even today), and precisely announces the terrain and concerns of his analysis. Fiedler continues:

> And yet before the continued existences of physical homosexual love (our crudest epithets notoriously evoke the mechanics of such affairs), before the blatant ghettos in which the Negro conspicuously creates the gaudiness and stench that offend him, the white American must make a choice between coming to terms with institutionalized discrepancy or formulating radically new ideologies [413].

As early as the late 1940s, Fiedler addresses both white racism and the taboo subject of male homosexuality, and makes clear the cultural and political terrain of his analysis. Before Fiedler, few critics had discussed classic American literature in terms of race, gender, and sexuality (Winchell 2002, 53). Unlike some of his peers, Richard points out, he eschews the apolitical, anti-historical, eyes-half-closed, text-only approach of the New Criticism, and sets out the larger issues before he turns to his consideration of Twain, Melville, and Cooper:

> The situation of the Negro and the homosexual in our society pose [sic] quite opposite problems, or at least problems suggesting quite opposite solutions. Our laws on homosexuality and the context of prejudice they objectify must apparently be changed to accord with a stubborn social fact; whereas it is the social fact, our overt behavior toward the Negro, that must be modified to accord with our laws and the, at least official, morality they objectify. It is not, of course, quite so simple. There is another sense in which the fact of homosexual passion contradicts a national myth of masculine love, just as our real relationship with the Negro contradicts a myth of that relationship; and those two myths with their betrayals are, as we shall see, one [2004, 414].

Fiedler attributes a psychological meaning to the American male's problem of love, as this theme evolves in the books of Twain, Melville, and Cooper. This American male, whom Fiedler calls a runaway male from women (petticoat government) and domesticity (home and hearth), unconsciously wanted to be loved and pampered by the people he had most offended and oppressed—the blacks and the Red Indians. Fiedler gives mythic and archetypal significance to this triangular relationship of woman, man and colored man. His books, Fiedler has said, "have become for a new generation of teachers in universities, colleges and high schools, the basis for a new understanding of our classic books and of our culture in general as well as the model for critical studies which do not even bother to acknowledge their sources—as if everyone had always known what was really at issue between Huck and Jim on the raft" (EI 1955, ix). In this brilliant, albeit quirky, reading of American archetypes, Fiedler gradually unearthed the seeds of popular culture in them.[1] According to him, these books have great popular appeal and lasting significance and they serve as guides to the large body of popular literature written today.

In "Come Back to the Raft Ag'in, Huck Honey!" Fiedler appeals to white Americans to formulate radical "new ideologies" regarding homosexuals and Negroes because "homosexual passion contradicts a national myth of masculine love" (EI, 143). He says that the very existence or presence of overt homosexuality in American life "threatens to compromise an essential aspect of American sentimental life: the camaraderie of the locker room and ball park, the good fellowship of the poker game and fishing trip, a kind of passionless passion at once gross and delicate, homoerotic in the boy's sense, possessing an innocence above suspicion" (EI, 143). Fiedler comments that such a relationship is "simple, utterly satisfying yet immune to lust; physical as a handshake is physical" (EI, 143). There seems to be a "characteristic 'Fiedleresque' pronouncement in this essay,... finely balanced, incisive, yet ambiguous" (Wallenstein 1972, 591). The ambiguity is seen by Wallenstein in Fiedler's comment that the "White American must make a choice between coming to terms with institutionalised discrepancy or formulating new ideologies" (EI, 142). Wallenstein finds Fiedler lacking the specialized wisdom of a political theorist and finds that he formulates no new ideology. At best, he does illuminate the discrepancy that is actually the prevailing gap between illusion and reality.

In *Love and Death in the American Novel* (1960) Fiedler clearly states, "It is not homosexuality in any crude meaning of the word," nor is it competing with man-woman passion. He reiterates, "There is an almost hysterical note in our insistence that the love of male and male does not compete with heterosexual passion but complements it" (LD 1966, 368). Here is no juvenile effort to outrage the Philistines, but a serious and impressively well-informed attempt to look at American fiction in a new way (Hicks 1960a, 16). So we notice that, by and by, Fiedler tries to clarify the ambiguity present, if it is there at all, in his early commitments to his readers. Some critics have tried to penetrate deep, like Wallenstein, who says, "The gap between love as it is dreamed of and frequently enacted e.g., in *Adventures of Huckleberry Finn*, and love as vulgar imagination, is the subject of 'Come Back.'... Rather than being an eccentric attempt to prove the relationship between Huck and Jim a homosexual one, it recognizes that in the finest and most disturbing literature, the true depth of our capacity for love emerges" (591). An air of "good clean fun" overhangs the sessions of this "purely male society" (CB, 144), yet "this self-congratulatory buddy-buddiness, its astonishing naivete" breeds "endless opportunities for inversion and the terrible reluctance to admit its existence" (CB, 144).

This was way back in 1948, when Fiedler wrote that essay. R. W. B. Lewis makes an interesting evaluation of Fiedler's works, mainly *Love and Death in the American Novel*, and examines his theory of "chastely homosexual" relation between a white and colored male. Lewis says, "Mr. Fiedler's ... explanation (the historical guilt sense of the American male) is fragile ... but the phenomenon of this recurring relation remains, and Mr. Fiedler is the one who required us to acknowledge it" (Lewis 1960, 613).

In the same essay, Fiedler explains the reasons that give rise to this sort of a relationship. The main reason according to him is "the regressiveness ... of American life, its implacable nostalgia for the infantile" (CB, 144), as depicted in American fiction. He says that the two most "popular, most absorbed" books of America are found on the shelves of the children's library. He is referring to Herman Melville's *Moby Dick* and Mark Twain's *The Adventures of Huckleberry Finn*. Fiedler calls them "boys' books." Fiedler also refer to Cooper's *Leatherstocking Tales*, Dana's *Two Years Before the Mast*, Hawthorne's "hell-fired book" *The Scarlet Letter* and writers such as Stephen Crane and Hemingway who, according to him, cater to the taste of boys. According to William G. Coleman, the only contemporary author that Fiedler discusses in terms of this pervasive theme of male-bonding, seen in earlier novelists, is Saul Bellow. According to Fiedler, Bellow re-imagined Huck Finn as a young Chicago Jew in *The Adventures of Augie March*, where "everything goes except the frank description of adult heterosexual love. After all, boys will be boys!" (CB, 144). These books, he adds, "proffer a chaste male love as the ultimate emotional experience" (CB, 144–45). In Cooper's book it is the affection of Natty Bumppo and Chingachgook; in Twain's book it is Huck's affection for Nigger Jim, and Melville's *Moby Dick* is called a love story of Ishmael's love for Queegueg, the harpooner. The point that Fiedler is putting forth is that generally we are used to, or accustomed to discovering in all the world's great novels some heterosexual passion, platonic love or adultery, seduction or rape or a long drawn-out flirtation. But in an American novel, says Fiedler blatantly, "We come instead on the fugitive slave and the no-account boy lying side by side on a raft borne by the endless river toward an impossible escape" (CB, 145). Ishmael in *Moby Dick* tells us frankly,

> I found Queegueg's arm thrown over me in the most loving and affectionate manner. You had almost thought I had been his wife ... he still hugged me tightly, as though naught but death should part us twain.... Thus, then, in our heart's honeymoon lay I and Queequeg—a cozy, loving pair.... He pressed his forehead against mine, clasped me around the waist, and said that henceforth we were married [CB, 145].

Fiedler takes this example from Melville's *Moby Dick* because in this book the relationship is most explicitly rendered, almost openly explained, "not by a change phrase or camouflaged symbol," says Fiedler, but by a full written explanation of the entire ritual of the marriage ceremony. In fact, Fiedler explains the connubial relationship :

> The initial going to bed together ... that great tomahawk-pipe accepted in a familiarity that dispels fear ... finally, a symbolic portrayal of the continuing state of marriage, through the image of the "monkey rope" which binds the lovers fast waist to waist (for the sake of this symbolism, Melville changes a fact of whaling practice—the only time in the book) a permanent alliance that provides mutual protection but also threatens mutual death [CB, 145].

Notwithstanding these apparent explications, DeMott in his essay "The Negative American" has a different view point. He says, "The chapter on *Moby Dick* is not really about the holy marriage of males" (1967, 445). Of course, according to DeMott, its theme is, as most of the critics say, the fight of a single person, the desire to master, to rationalize, to fight the absurd, to know a final truth—it is Ahab's fight for supremacy. DeMott's argument does not seem to be very convincing, because no one can refute the special relationship between Ishmael and Queequeg. In fact, talking of Fiedler's treatment of this theme, particularly with reference to Twain, DeMott says, "Neither is the chapter on Huck Finn about innocent homosexuality. It is about a condition that Fiedler rather awkwardly calls, 'outsidedness'" (1967, 445–46), an idea to which Fiedler has devoted considerable attention and that will be taken up in the next chapter. Nevertheless, what Fiedler continuously emphasizes is that the relationship, though physical, is somehow ultimately innocent. He says that a "child like ignorance" lies between the lovers:

> Ishmael's sensations as he wakes under the pressure of Queequeg's arm, the tenderness of Huck's repeated loss and refinding of Jim, the role of almost Edenic helpmate played for Bumppo by the Indian—these shape us from childhood. We have no sense of first discovering them or of having been once without them [CB, 146].

This pure mutual love of a white man and a colored man can only be experienced at this infantile level, when class, color or caste has no meaning. This kind of a thesis, discarded by many, found sponsors too. Fiedler finds a supporter in Prescott, who says, "Fiedler extends his theme of innocence—I think accurately—to cover a certain ignorance and regression in American culture, an implacable nostalgia for the infantile" (Prescott 1971, 76). According to Prescott in "Americans as Innocents,"

> Most of Fiedler's major themes touch upon Innocence, either in our literature or in our politics and the tenacity with which we hold on to it. We put our best books on the kiddies shelf in the library, he says, meaning *Huck Finn, Moby Dick* and *The Last of the Mohicans* whereas—Oh, irony!—the secret message of these books concerns the homoerotic attachment between a white and a black, red or brown man, an ennobling or redemptive love, to be realised only between males fleeing both women and civilisation, and a mature sexual relationship, if there is one in our major fiction, does not jump to mind [Prescott 1971, 78].

Commonly, critics point out that Fiedler has an uncanny habit of abandoning themes or ideas after a span of time. But that is not true of this theme. He reiterates his concern in *Love and Death in the American Novel* as well: "In our native mythology, the tie between male and male is not only considered innocent, it is taken for the very symbol of innocence itself" (LD 1966, 350).

This concern is evidenced in a series of essays that he wrote called "The Eye of Innocence" (1958). These essays discuss at length the role of the child (a symbol of innocence) in literature. In Greek art, the icon of the downy-cheeked boy is wrought in many tender works of sculpture; for example, the undraped adolescent, bent to remove the thorn in his foot, or lying with his back to the beholder. Here, he is considered a love object only, and not a prophet of or a guide to lost innocence. In Judeo-Christian tradition, any trifling with the erotic image of childhood is condemned. It says, "He who offends the least of my little ones" will be cast in the sea with a millstone round the neck. In the Old Testament, there is a reference not to exploit the possibilities of a child. In the New Testament, there are image of appealing babyhood, the pure infant situated between beasts and wise men. In the Renaissance, the child fulfills its significant image—the infant as innocence itself. But, says Fiedler, in the Catholic faith the child was still peripheral. Dante used an abused child to arouse pathos. It was impossible to conceive of a child as hero. In addressing this phenomenon, in "The Eye of Innocence" Fiedler once again ventures into literary anthropology (Winchell 1985, 28).

One of the major shifts in modern thinking brings the child to the center of life. For the bourgeois, there was one symbol of protest and impulse: the child. In "Boys Will Be Boys," an essay that is part of the larger essay, "The Eye of Innocence," the child represents "not only a search for projections of pure impulse, but also a rejection of the themes with which the bourgeois novel began, themes rooted in sexuality" (NT, 268).

It is important to trace the entire cult of the child as sketched by Fiedler to actually show the evolution in his writings since 1948, when he wrote "Come Back to the Raft Ag'in, Huck Honey." In "Boys Will Be Boys" he says, "The child remains still, what he has been since the beginning of Romanticism, a surrogate for our unconscious, impulsive lives" (NT, 293). In 1958, when he wrote these essays on innocence, Fiedler takes a literary anthropological dive, to trace the cult of the child since Greek literature, to actually locate its bearing on modern literature. Packed with information and undaunted spirit, Fiedler further illuminates the growth of the role of the child over the years. The child is a very important character in most of the novels. The child is always there—peeping, listening, observing so much so that we are chiefly aware of him only when he is absent. Sometimes he is the hero himself—Tom Sawyer, Huckleberry Finn or Holden Caulfield. Fiedler says that the figure of the child is ubiquitous—a product of the needs of the culture, and also a product of the imagination.

The holiest icon of the cult of the child is the Good Good Girl, the blonde, asexual goddess of the nursery or orphanage, reincarnated from little Nell to Mary Pickford. The Good Good Girl fulfills the Protestant resolve to celebrate premarital chastity, the northern European wish to glorify the fair and debase the black. This Good Good Girl is imagined not in the hands of the mother, but the father, not at the time of birth but at the time of death. The basic image in most of the novels, according to Fiedler, is the white-clad girl dying or dead in the arms of the old man or a tearful father or grandfather or woolly-haired male slave. This white slip of a girl (Fiedler's humor at its best) is too good to be in this wicked world, hence she leaves for the next. Allowed to grow up, she would become wife, mother, widow—tinged, if only slightly, by the stain of sexuality. Though the essential theme of such novels is love, she is never spared the rod of death, for example little Eva in *Uncle Tom's Cabin* (1852). In Dickens, his symbols of offended innocence include boys, too. He is convinced that all of adult society is in conspiracy against childhood.

Now the Good Bad Boy is America's vision of itself, says Fiedler. It is "Authentic America, crude and unruly in his beginnings, but endowed by his creator with an instinctive sense of what is right; sexually as pure as any milky maiden, he is roughneck all the same, at once potent and submissive.... No wonder our greatest book is about a boy and that boy is 'bad'" (NT, 265). Fiedler sticks to his view of Huck Finn, projected in "Come Back to the Raft Ag'in, Huck Honey!"

According to a sentimental approach to childhood, the one characteristic that is common between the Good Good Girl and the Good Bad Boy is, as Winchell puts it, "the lack of sexual imagination" (1985, 30). Fiedler has all along been laying emphasis on this fact. In the essay "The Eye of Innocence," he says, "Twain blurred adolescence back into boyhood to avoid confronting the problem of sex" (NT, 276), and at another point he says the book on Huck and Jim is an "idyllic vision of childhood on the Mississippi" (NT, 266). As an outcast of society, the Good Bad Boy forms alliances with adults who are also outcasts or symbolic aliens. And he adds, "Huck is closer to Jim than to Tom—that is, closer to what the white world of gentility fears and excludes than to what it condescendingly indulges in the child" (NT, 266). Accordingly to Fiedler, the Good Bad Boy is symbolically Twain himself. The memory of all the boy Twain was is Tom Sawyer and the memory of all he was *not*, and wished to be, is Huck Finn. Hence, both the characters are two aspects of the same man, what he has become and what he has escaped from becoming.

In modern times, the image of the child has been remade by homosexual sensibility into an object of lust and desire. Fiedler says, "Once the child has been remade by homosexual sensibility into the image of an ambiguous object of desire, the lust for the child is revealed as a flight from woman, the family, maturity itself" (NT, 286). J. D. Salinger trifles with this theme in his fiction where one of the characters fondles with the figure of a child, kisses her feet, and so on. Another development in modern literature is the image of a girl or boy as a peeping Tom, witnessing erotic scenes between two adults, for example in Faulkner's works, or Vladimir Nabokov's *Lolita*. Henry James, according to Fiedler, establishes the child as a peeping Tom—eye to the crack of the door, an innocent observer who stumbles upon the murderer bent over the corpse. Real initiation of the child in an American novel is through violence rather than sex. Fiedler poses this question: why have our writers welcomed this sort of initiation of the child into the fallen world, this sort of child's passage from innocence to experience? The answer lies in the refusal to portray the child as an actual sinner and the desire to establish his symbolic innocence.

Taking the same theme, the role of the child as a symbol of innocence itself, let us consider Fiedler's other major work that falls into our chronological order of selection, *Love and Death in the American Novel*. In the preface to the book, he says,

> Certainly, my earliest formulation of this theory in "Come Back to the Raft Ag'in, Huck Honey!" has met with a shocked and, I suspect, partly wilful incomprehension. I have been accused of impiety, grossness, a contempt for the classics of childhood, even a disturbing influence on private lives. I trust that the full development of my contentions in these pages will obviate ... misunderstanding, and that my additional comments on the importance in our literature of brother-sister incest and necrophilia will not stir up new protests of a similar kind [LD 1966, 12].

At the very outset of this book he says that the novel in America differs from that of Europe in one way. It is "innocent, unfallen in a disturbing way, almost juvenile. The great works of American fiction are notoriously at home in the children's section of the library, their level of sentimentality, precisely that of a pre-adolescent" (24).

Fiedler, as should be well known, is a man of many parts, and many changing views. Starting from a fascination with "innocence"—"It's the original chaos, the unorganized, the intuitive, the impulsive," he said in an interview; he added later, "I think of innocence as being at the heart of the thing" (Green 1981, 136, 148; Walden 1999, 161).

Many critics including Reising would like us to believe that Fiedler is highly indebted to and enlarges D. H. Lawrence's famous argument about the infantile surface of the classic American literature into a theory of the novel in *Love and Death in the American Novel*.[2] Even if it is to be believed, there is enough to prove that this thesis was not to be simply airbrushed out of existence. Reising adds that this sort of adolescent literature consumed by adults has turned adults into their own inmost images of themselves as children. He makes a very pungent remark: "Twain blurred adolescence back into boyhood to avoid confronting the problem of sex, the newer writers, accepting the confusion of childhood and youth, blur both into manhood to avoid yielding up to maturity the fine clean rapture of childish 'making out'" (1986, 290). In effect, Fiedler claims, white American novelists have resorted to these pairings in order to contain, if possible, any implications of homosexuality: what better way to negate any hint of queerness than to hit that taboo with an even more egregious one—at least in nineteenth century American culture—the fear of miscegenation (Harrison 2008).

In Fiedler's other two works taken into consideration in this chapter, *Waiting for the End* (1964) and *The Return of the Vanishing American* (1968), though there is no direct reference to the cult of the child in literature, the child-aspect is never really ignored. In one of his last few interviews, given to Rocco Capozzi in 1990, Fiedler says,

> When I finished *What Was Literature?* I pledged publicly that it would be my last full-scale book of criticism; and I have kept my word. But I have recently gathered together the shorter critical pieces that I have written over the past fifteen years or so and have discovered that they make three substantial volumes. The first of these, which is due to appear at the beginning of next year, I have called *Fiedler on the Roof*; and the third will be called *Back to Innocence*—since in it I will be completing the circular process which began with the publication of *An End to Innocence* in 1955, thirty-five long years ago. It has taken me a long time to grow young [Capozzi 1991, 336].

An overdose of the adolescent fiction offered by American novelists is the result of a flight from "woman." I shall trace the evolution of this aspect from his earliest essay, "Come Back to the Raft Ag'in, Huck Honey!" to *The Return of the Vanishing American*, here, but also take its discussion to a later chapter on feminist readings of Fiedler. In "Come Back to the Raft Ag'in, Huck Honey!" Fiedler says that the myth of the Immaculate Young Girl or the fair maiden archetype or the Good Good Girl type, all these myths regarding woman have failed to survive today. And "in the dirty jokes shared among men in the smoking car, the barracks, or the dormitory, there is a common male revenge against women for having flagrantly betrayed that myth" (CB, 143). The key words are "male revenge against women." This revenge is taken by assuming a relationship with another man, which is satisfying and though physical yet has a "passionless passion" and a "childlike ignorance," contrary to the man-woman relationship. He writes, "Just as the pure love of man and man is in general set off against the ignoble passion of man for woman ... the dark desire which leads to miscegenation is contrasted with the ennobling love of a white man and a colored one" (CB, 147). In this essay, Fiedler refers to Natty Bumppo of Copper's *Leatherstocking Tales* who flees from "the defilement of all women" into the woods amongst the Indians (CB, 148). As we go through these works chosen for this study, precisely because they throw light on this aspect, we discover that Fiedler talks of this aspect in great detail. What was "revenge" in "Come Back to the Raft Ag'in, Huck Honey!" became "flight" in "The Eye of Innocence." He says that Huck, the symbol of America itself, is running away from "all the reduplicated female symbols of religion and 'sivilization'" (NT, 266).

Not content to rest on this early exercise in critical chutzpah ("chutzpah" remains the term one most often sees in criticism of Fiedler's work), he soon enough turned to what may be his most important, sustained study of American literature, *Love and Death in the American Novel* (1960). Alongside such works as F. O. Matthiessen's *American Renaissance* (1941), Alfred Kazin's *On Native Grounds* (1942), R. W. B. Lewis's *The American Adam* (1955), Richard Chase's *The American Novel and Its Tradition* (1957), and a handful of other seminal studies, Fiedler's *Love and Death* helped shape our understanding of what was then canonical American literature and made clear the obsessions of the canonical male authors. But where his scholarly forebears somewhat politely explored notions of art, nature, and the American self, Fiedler dove right between the sheets (if there were any) and from there to the subterranean reaches of the unconscious and found, in his words, that

> The failure of the American fictionist to deal with adult heterosexual love and his consequent obsession with death, incest and innocent homosexuality are not merely matters of historical interest or literary relevance. They affect the lives we lead from day to day and influence writers in whom consciousness of our plight is given clarity and form. Paul Bowles, writing highbrow terror-fiction in the mid-

dle of the twentieth century, cannot escape the limitations that plagued Charles Brockden Brown at the beginning of the eighteenth; and Saul Bellow, composing a homoerotic *Tarzan of the Apes* in *Henderson the Rain King,* is back on the raft with Mark Twain [xi].

Fiedler finds American literature, in other words, to be a fairly twisted affair, a corpus incapable of exploring adult sexuality and pathologically consumed with subjects, including incest and death, that would make Edgar Allan Poe blush (with happiness, we might presume). Needless to say, his analysis and the connections he makes between literature and culture—which were the obsessions of writers, even the obsessions of most Americans—offended a great many scholars and readers, but Fiedler called it like he saw it, and too bad for those who took offense. Deservedly, *Love and Death* put Montana State University on the literary map of America.

His early feminist critique, which very few acknowledge, states that though most American novelists were competent in dealing with issues of indignity and assault, and loneliness and terror, they avoided or failed to treat the passionate encounter of man and woman. In this deliberate moving away from women, elaborated in *Love and Death in the American Novel, Waiting for the End* and *The Return of the Vanishing American,* presides Rip Van Winkle and his flight from petticoat government. It continues with "Latter-day Rips," the Hemingways and Faulkners (Winchell 1985, 56). And it is within this framework that Fiedler finds a motif for the interracial theme of homoeroticism—from Ishmael and Queequeg to Huck and Jim.

I am not dealing with the theories of myth criticism, because it is not my primary concern here. As a tool, Fiedler makes ample use of myth criticism to shoot forth his thesis. What I am concerned with, primarily, is Fiedler's emphasis on myth as a recurrent pattern of responses and desires that are universal in nature. And Fiedler has tried to see this pattern in American literature. Moreover, theories of myth criticism have already been explored by P. Maruddanayam in his thesis on Fiedler (1980), in the chapter "Theories and Foundations of Fiedler's Myth Criticism."

As we know, these relationships in an all-male society can only exist in the contradiction of adulthood that finds a "difference in color sufficient provocation for distrust and hatred" (Fiedler 1976, 146). This love, hence, can survive only "in the obliquity of a symbol, persistent, obsessive, in short, an archetype: the boy's homoerotic crush, the love of the black fused at this level into a single thing" (EI, 146). Fiedler gives a mythic complexion to this relationship in "Come Back to the Raft Ag'in, Huck Honey!" Accordingly to Fiedler, mythic patterns are universal in nature. World literature reflects this eternal triangle of man/woman/other woman (or man). What is different in Fiedler's thesis is precisely this: this triangle has been reversed or altered beyond imagination to woman/man/other man. And this other man is a nonwhite male. As he clearly states in *Love and Death in the American Novel*, "In dreams of white men, psychologists tell us, the forbidden erotic object tends to be represented by a colored man ... so in the communal American dream of love ... the spouse of the pariah is properly of another race, a race suppressed and denied, even as the promptings of the libido are suppressed and denied" (LD 1966, 365). In *Leatherstocking Tales* it is the dispossessed Indian; with Huck Finn, it is the Negro slave; and in *Moby Dick* we have the uprooted Polynesian. The marriage between the two companions has a sociological as well as psychological and metaphysical significance. The elopement of these companions stands for the healing of social conflicts that irk us. It is not a tie between servant and the master but a tie between equals. Such unions, according to Fiedler, join soul to soul, rather than body to body. And the superiority of this love is shown by the stigma, disgusting as well as forbidden, attached to the colored rival of the wife. Chingachgook wears a death's head on his chest, Queequeg is tattooed and bears with him a phallic god and shrunken head, and Jim is black.

Yet, in the myth of homosexual sensibility, the white man turns to the love of a colored man, only in the role of an outcast, ragged woodsman, or despised sailor ("call me Ishmael") or unregenerate boy (Huck) or as a pariah. Now this vision of the white American as a pariah does not correspond with the long-held public image of the world's most successful people. Fiedler tries to give a plausible answer, and Fiedler's fund of originality is as enormous as his capacity to startle (as some critics would say) is unflagging. Fiedler says, "It is perhaps only the artist's portrayal of himself, the notoriously alienated writer in American at home with such images, child of the town drunk, the hapless survivor" (EI, 150). Fiedler gives a fresh perspective to it and says further, "Ishmael is in all of us, our unconfessed universal fear objectified in the writer's status as in the outcast's sailor's: that compelling anxiety ... that we may not be loved, that we are loved for our possessions and not ourselves, that we are really—alone" (EI, 150). Fiedler brings it to tragic proportions by illuminating the deep sense of fear of isolation and alienation present in the American psyche. And it is this underlying terror that explains the American "boyish modesty." Fiedler puts forth precisely this: "Our dark skinned beloved will take us in ... without rancour or the insult or forgiveness. He will fold us in his arms saying, 'Honey' or 'Aikane,' he will comfort us, as if our offence against him were long ago remitted, were never truly real" (EI, 150). Yet this reconciliation is made unbelievable by letting the colored man become a victim, of death or torture. Dana's Hope is shown dying of the white man's syphilis, Queequeg is portrayed as racked by fever and later death, Crane's Negro is disfigured totally, Cooper's Indian smolders to the end, conscious of the imminent disappearance of his race, Jim is shown loaded down with chains.

And the most interesting fact is that this archetype recurs. Fiedler says that each generation plays this impossible mythos because the American children play it: the white boy and black boy wrestling affectionately on any American sidewalk, along which they walk in adulthood, eyes averted from each other, full of suspicion and rancor, unwilling to touch even by accident. Yet it is only a dream of the white man's acceptance at the breast he has most utterly offended. The dream recedes; the immaculate passion and the astonishing reconciliation becomes a memory, yet "it is a dream so sentimental, so outrageous, so desperate, that it redeems our concept of boyhood from nostalgia to tragedy" (EI, 151), says Fiedler. Hence, the alarming reality behind the American fictionists' depiction or celebration of this white and colored man's harmonious union is that the basis of this relationship is unreal and is attained by "dreaming." He gives examples of "the texture of a dream" with passage in and out of darkness and mist on the river, the constant confusion of identities (Huck's ten, twelve names), the sudden intrusion of violence without past or future, which gives the book a dreamlike atmosphere. Even Cooper's book has the motif: the childish impossible dream. According to Fiedler, Lawrence saw in Cooper's writings the boy's Utopia. Rip Van Winkle's flight is also that of a "dreamer," a flight from domestic strife to a world of fear and loneliness, a haunted world. Hence, Fiedler develops his thesis by saying that the American novel is preeminently a novel of terror. Though the natural man is waiting for him in the green heart of nature—Queequeg, Jim or Chingachgook—they are a dream and a nightmare at once. The other face of Chingachgook is Injun Joe, and Nigger Jim's is Babo of Melville's *Benito Cereno*. In Cooper, the colored man is the "spirit of the alien place" (LD 1966, 101).

In *Waiting for the End* (1964) Fiedler enlarged the "white man's dream of reconciliation" of Thoreau's book *Walden*. This dream of reconciliation is attained by running away from civilization into the heart of nature. Flight, hence, has all along been emphasized by Fiedler as an important part of the American male's personality, since his earliest formulation of this theory in "Come Back to the Raft Ag'in, Huck Honey!" The evolution seen in *Waiting for the End* is a greater insight into the elements that constitute this flight.

There are three elements that constitute this flight: The first element is simply the American desire to escape America and other Americans; the second element is seen as an equally American tendency to confuse some particular place with an imagined Utopia; and third is the identical hunger for an absolute freedom that brought the first Americans across the Atlantic and sent later generations trekking west after that, as Fiedler says, which "can be sought but never found. All three impulses obviously are self-defeating, as well as authentically American" (WFTE, 173). In his *Love and Death in the American Novel*, Fiedler referred to Hemingway, for whom the West was from Switzerland to Africa, to the mountains of Spain, but he does not elaborate the idea further. Hence "dream" and "flight" are two components that merge into a single whole, each incomplete without the other, in Fiedler's theory of the American novel.

This bond was imagined by American writers in a paradisal world in which there were no heterosexual or giving-in marriages. Fiedler comments, "Nature undefiled—this is the inevitable setting of the sacred marriage of males" (EI, 148). Hence, this bond is generally placed in a setting of make believe, a world most familiar in our dream—the wilderness, the sea, the forest or the past; for example, Ishmael and Queequeg arm in arm, about to ship out, Huck and Jim swimming beside the raft in the peaceful flux of the Mississippi—here it is the motion of the water that completes the syndrome, the American dream of isolation afloat. In *Moby Dick* and *Huckleberry Finn* water is the texture used in the novels; in *Leatherstocking Tales*, it is the virgin forest. What Fiedler is emphasizing is that these symbols still survive in our fiction. Gore Vidal writes of the reverie of a lover running away to sea with his dearest friend. Hence, in each generation the archetype reappears. Yet by the end of each book such heroes are remanded back to reality: Ishmael alone escaped to tell the story; Gordon Pym writes his tale of adventure in the end; Huck Finn lights out into the territory "ahead of the rest."

Bringing in an example of Alfred Kazin's *On Native Grounds*, the passionate, personal encounter with the literary tradition of the United States that he published when he was only twenty-seven, according to Kellman, Fiedler's *Love and Death in the American Novel* has forever "altered the terms of the country's literary conversation." And it, too, seems a young man's book, the radiant thoughts of an author whose ardor has not yet been tempered by demands from a world oblivious to the whiteness of an imaginary whale. Yet Fiedler was already forty-three when, in 1960, he published the book that propelled him into the role of *enfant terrible* of American letters. It is true that *Love and Death*, as Emerson noted about the first edition of *Leaves of Grass*, "had a long foreground somewhere, for such a start": its germination is already evident in the bravura essay (which we have already discussed in detail) "Come Back to the Raft Ag'in, Huck Honey!" (1999, 7).

Fiedler has covered so much ground in "Come Back to the Raft Ag'in, Huck Honey!" and *Love and Death in the American Novel* that it appears that no evolution takes place in his latter works such as *Waiting for the End* and *The Return of the Vanishing American*, taken up for discussion in this chapter. An in-depth reading of these texts reveal certain key ideas not taken up before. A study of these books is imperative for without them, this chapter would remain incomplete. I have already pointed out the evolution in certain ideas like those on "woman," "child," "dream" and "flight" in his "male camaraderie critique" as major principles that govern the American psyche. *Waiting for the End* and *The Return of Vanishing American* disclose that Fiedler is not through with this subject as yet.

In *Waiting for the End*, Fiedler examines this relationship more broadly. He interprets it in terms of the frontier. In the mind of Americans there exists a nightmare of race-relations that actually constitutes a legend of the American frontier of the West (where the second race is the Indian) or of the South (where the second race is the Negro); and this dream and nightmare, at once, have been portrayed for decades in American popular films and fiction. Positing this in the backdrop of his theory of the alteration of consciousness in *Waiting for the End*, he says that the rejection of the male role of home and bar can take place by taking drugs—a practice that is an alteration of consciousness, a theory developed by Allen Ginsberg. Homosexuals, "pursuing the phantom of youth and immune to the responsibilities of a family" (WFTE, 182) have a "certain contempt for whisky ... and a complementary taste for dope" (WFTE, 19), says Fiedler. Ginsberg's theory of the alteration of consciousness is rooted in the shift from the whisky culture to the dope culture. Fiedler analyzes it further and says that the only way to alter the consciousness is by taking drugs on the one hand and following the techniques of oriental adepts on the other. This sort of writing was not appreciated by some university professors and it resulted in Fiedler's arrest (in 1966) for supposedly maintaining premises where marijuana was used.

Contrary to the above, in *The Return of the Vanishing American* Fiedler problematizes race-relations and talks of the WASP male's confrontation with the Indian, the Red Indian's return to America. (This will be discussed in greater detail in the next chapter.) He interprets American geography mythologically by creating a mythicized North, South, East and West and their various characteristics. The Western story in the archetypal form is made up of four basic myths: the first is love in the woods, the story of Pocahontas and Captain John Smith; the second is the myth of the white woman with a tomahawk, the account of Hannah Dustan, a New England lady who, snatched out of a bed by an Indian raiding party, fought her bloody way to freedom; the third is the myth of good companions in the wilderness, the story of a white man and a red man who find solace and sustenance in each other's love, identified with the encounter of Cooper's Natty Bumppo and Chingachgook; and the fourth is the myth of the runaway male, given its archetypal name in 1819 in Washington Irving's "Rip Van Winkle": the tale of a man who deserted his wife for a twenty years' sleep and returned to find her (happily) dead. Fiedler's explorations in this book are, as rightly said, a continuation of his desire to explain the terrors and desires of the American psyche. The fact that one can raise objections to certain arguments regarding this aspect of the

American male as probed by Fiedler is not a fatal flaw. Whether we agree with him or not, Fiedler proves to be highly flexible and convincing. He makes it impossible for us ever to read the classics of American literature in the same way again. Tellingly, he told DeMott:

> I always say something which seems to me so sweetly simple, so seductively obvious, that if I just say it, everybody will say, yes, yes, yes. That is the way I felt about "Come Back to the Raft Ag'in" when I wrote it originally, and it turns out that people not only find what I say difficult to accept and in some ways shocking, but that they accuse me of saying it just in order to shock [1967, 447].

Philip Rahv, who was co-editor of *Partisan Review* when "Come Back to the Raft" was published, tried to absolve himself of responsibility by claiming that he "thought the essay a 'put-on'" (Winchell 2002, 55). And in this opinion the writers of the first fan letters it occasioned concurred, referring to it (troubled elitists turning typically to French) as a *boutade,* a *canard,* a *jeu d'espirit* (WWL 15, quoted in Winchell 2002, 55–56).

Brady Harrison, a faculty member at Montana State University, recalls his initial reaction to "Come Back...": "One superb provocation.... So this ... was criticism: sly, comic by turns, yet deadly serious and ... dedicated both to saying what needs to be said and to saying what needs to be said in the service of human dignity" (2008).

It would not be a fair hearing if we considered all his writings as just rereadings and reevaluations (Pease 1990). Nor is it necessary that everything that Fiedler has said should be difficult to accept. Several articles and recent researches amply prove the point. Granville Hicks points out, "Fiedler has refused to tie himself up in his system; he has other insights and he uses them. Furthermore, he makes no claim that he has said the last word.... We may not always, we may only rarely, accept his view in its entirety, but it is unlikely that our own will remain unchanged (1960a, 16). In addition, Norman Mailer, in "Huckleberry Finn, Alive at 100," writes, "Reading 'Huckleberry Finn' one comes to realize all over again that the near-burned-out, throttled, hate-filled dying affair between whites and blacks is still our great national love affair, and woe to us if it ends in detestation and mutual misery" (1985, 19). Relatedly, in 2002, Scott McLemee in an interview with Fiedler recounts his influence on the young and how he still remains "a combatant in the culture wars." Recently, on *The Sopranos*, Mafia daughter and Columbia University undergraduate Meadow shocked her mother, Carmela, by stating that Herman Melville's novella *Billy Budd* concerns a gay relationship, citing a recent guest lecture at her university by Leslie Fiedler. "Well, she's wrong," responds Carmela, indignantly (McLemee 2002). When asked by McLemee about Fiedler's pervading influence on the young, and if he watched *The Sopranos,* his answer was in the affirmative. When asked if he enjoyed being name-checked, Fiedler responded:

I was astonished. I was undone. It made me question the difference between reality and fiction, at least for a moment. I had no notion it was coming. It was amusing that one of the things they picked up on was that ambiguous first name of mine. I keep getting letters addressed to "Ms. Leslie Fiedler." And I always write back, "I prefer to be called Mrs." The other thing that made it pleasing was that most of my children and some of my grandchildren were watching.

McLemee questioned Fiedler on his interest in the show, to which Fiedler replied that he shares an affinity with the setting of the show, "so when I watch the show, I see familiar faces." He reminisces about his old neighborhood in Newark, and the fact that the idol of the kids was "the local gangster" who during the Depression had set up a soup kitchen and fed the unemployed. He particularly remembers that "our mothers looked with longing eyes at his mother, who wore the most-expensive fur coats." McLemee refers to some recent episodes of *The Sopranos* in which the homoerotic undercurrents of the gangsters' intimate circle have been explored. Fiedler responded by displaying his command on topical issues and his little note on Freud:

> Certainly male bonding is one of the major things in the show. It makes good sense, in some ways, that the writers would move in that direction. All my life I've been interested in what traditional psychiatrists have had to say on the subject. Just a few hours before I saw that episode on the air, someone gave me a present—a statue of Sigmund Freud. I think of him as joining me to them. *Freud's the link between me and the mob* [emphasis mine].

Thus, so close to his end, Fiedler's allegiance with the common and the "mob" remains unflagging and spirited.

However, taking into consideration the larger framework of the evolution of Fiedler as a critic in the popular culture tradition, this theme substantiates, to a large extent, his growth as a pop guru. By looking for homosexual meanings in classics of American literature, Fiedler made a departure from the older school of thought, which called these books children's books to be studied in classrooms. Fiedler discovers in them a popular theme, writ large in all popular fiction in America, imbued with popular sentiment and thought. To the chagrin of elitists, Fiedler almost devaluates these books. Working on the classics of American literature through myths and archetypes, Fiedler gradually discovers the seeds of popular culture in them. According to him, these books have great popular appeal and lasting significance and they serve as guides to the large body of popular literature written today. In fact, not only literature, even television and cinema—all domains of the popular—have for their essential theme male bonding. By giving this new interpretation to American literature, Fiedler clearly crosses over the border from elite to pop. On the other hand these can also be considered as rereadings and reevaluations. After all, "Huck Honey!" does work as a provocation to reread, but even more it works as a piece of intellectual, literary analysis. Somebody had to ask what these pairings meant, and Fiedler looked closely at the literature that many thought to be the best the nation had ever produced. Likewise, in *Love and Death,* he was not being churlish; he was serious: what does it mean when a nation produces a body of literature that seems incapable of dealing with adult sexuality, whatever its forms, and that appears obsessed with death? If Fiedler took risks in his subject matter, he took even greater risks in thinking in ways others could not or would not; he clearly enjoyed his jabs at fellow scholars and readers, but even more he seems to have enjoyed trying to change how others read or saw the world, themselves, and their nation (Harrison 2008). In 1994 in the Hubbell Award Acceptance Speech, Fiedler refers to the essay "Come back..." in this way:

> A half century later, however, that much-maligned essay has refused to die. I myself reprinted it in my first book, *An End to Innocence,* where it was flanked by a dozen or so other pieces, some literary, some autobiographical or political—but all more like what academics of the old school would have called "mere journalism," rather than "true scholarship." Yet it has appeared since in many languages; and, in another ironic turn of the screw, has become assigned reading in university classes on literature. In addition, it was this volume, that persuaded those with no sense of where I was really coming from or heading to, that I was—however misguided and perverse I might be—a would-be scholar of American letters.

And it has not. In many ways, Fiedler, in his critique of racial and sexual discrimination, and in his heralding of equal rights for both blacks and queers, is years ahead of his time (at least in terms of literary and cultural scholarship), and he approaches these charged issues through the novels then at the core of the American literary curriculum (Harrison 2008). I am presenting only some examples out of many to show how Fiedler lives, in texts, theories, criticism and minds.

It would indeed be worthwhile to enter into a discussion about the famed responses of the queer theorist Christopher Looby and Winchell's analysis of them. As a literary critic specializing in eighteenth and nineteenth century American literature and a professor of English at UCLA, Looby asserts that Fiedler's claims in "Come Back" stem from a twentieth century urban perspective and do not adequately address the nineteenth century time period when Huck was written. This is when Fiedler has already expressed his exasperation with readers who persist in thinking that he was "attributing sodomy to certain literary characters or their authors" (LD, 349). Taking this argument further, Winchell makes some interesting observations. According to him, as things turned out, people who knew nothing else about Leslie Fiedler were convinced that he believed Huck and Jim—and a host of other characters in American literature—were "queer as three-dollar bills" (WWL, 15, quoted in

Winchell 2002, 56). Moreover, the matter also offended righteous heterosexuals. In an overturn, the homosexual lobby itself was also displeased with Fiedler's position. Their objections to "Come Back to the Raft" are forcefully presented in Christopher Looby's essay "Innocent Homosexuality: The Fiedler Thesis in Retrospect." Winchell rightly avers that Looby renders Fiedler the dubious tribute of taking him quite literally. Refusing to see homoeroticism as some kind of metaphor, he asks: "What's so interesting about claiming that, after all, Huck and Jim are just good pals?" (Looby, 538, quoted in Winchell 2002, 56). Winchell tells us, Looby argues that it is anachronistic to try to understand the sort of male relationships that existed on the American frontier in terms that are more appropriate to late-twentieth-century urban life. He goes on to cite anecdotal evidence suggesting that intimate physical contact between males in the early nineteenth century was too common to indicate anything as portentous as sexual orientation. It is only in our own time that we have fallen from the garden of polymorphous perversity into the wasteland of homophobia (Looby, cited by Winchell 2002, 56). Moreover, Fiedler's constant references to "innocent homosexuality" and "chaste" male love simply mark him as a man of his time—a secret fag hater posing as an enlightened liberal (56–57).

I agree with Winchell that the case that Looby makes for Fiedler's alleged homophobia rests largely on Fiedler's use of the term "innocent homosexuality." "The implication," Looby writes, "is that there is some other, 'guilty,' form of homosexuality" (Looby, 538, cited by Winchell, 57). But an American culture and literature reader who has, as Winchell says, "even a nodding familiarity with Fiedler's work" must realize that the Fiedlerian reference to "innocent" sexuality—homo, hetero, or whatever—is a reference to unconsummated desire. He is perhaps alluding to that baneful tradition in Western thought that would label all sexual activity, including procreative relations within the sacrament of marriage, as evil. It is understood that the saintly young girl of nineteenth century fiction must be killed off before the onset of puberty. Our male heroes escape the implications of heterosexual domesticity by finding their freedom in the wilderness. Like all myths, this one is immune to the tyranny of both logic and political correctness (Winchell 2002, 58).

To support his thesis, Winchell brings in Kenneth S. Lynn, who, while reviewing *What Was Literature?* in the January 1983 issue of *Commentary*, comments on the "sinister" subtext of "Come Back to the Raft" in relation to Alfred C. Kinsey's *Sexual Behavior in the American Male*, published the same year. Lynn writes:

> So eager was [Fiedler] to challenge both the folk wisdom of the American people and the clinical wisdom of the psychoanalysts, so fervently was he dreaming of a Kinseyesque America of sexual pluralism and guilt-free self-indulgence that he

found it easy to convince himself that every important American writer from Cooper to Faulkner was on his side. The authors of the Kinsey Report believed in their dubious statistics no more firmly than Fiedler did in his fraudulent vision of American Literature [Lynn 1983, 68, quoted in Winchell 2002, 58–59].

As the following argument proves, the reality is not very pleasant. Winchell says it in so many words:

> Right-wing critics did not need the issue of homosexuality—innocent or otherwise—to find fault with Fiedler's controversial essay. They were sufficiently offended by the notion that Huck—and, by implication, Mark Twain himself—was pronouncing a wholesale condemnation on American society. Although Fiedler might not have said this explicitly, he had come to represent all critics who found Huck's decision to "light out for the territory" to be a profound act of social criticism. When Kenneth Lyn attacked this interpretation of *Huckleberry Finn*, half a dozen years before his review of *What Was Literature?* he titled his essay "Welcome Back from the Raft, Huck Honey!" even though it makes no specific reference to Fiedler" [Lynn 1983, 42].

Winchell's contention is crucial to this discussion precisely because both Lynn and Fiedler offer a thesis which, according to Winchell, is more logically correct in former's case and more mythically true in the latter's. As Fiedler reminds us, there is pathos as well as triumph in Jim's declaration to Huck: "It's too good for true, honey, it's too good for true" (Twain 1884, reprint 1995, 98, quoted in Winchell 2002, 58).

On the same register, Betina Entzminger applies the Fiedlerian theory that "mythic America is boyhood," used in various American novels, to James Dickey's 1970 novel *Deliverance*, which presents middle-aged men trying unsuccessfully to reclaim their lost authentic selves (2007, 98). Entzminger points out that much like Twain's novel, *Deliverance* centers on men floating down a river, but in this twentieth century version, the environment refuses to restore an incorrupt identity. Fiedler sees Twain's river as a mythic conception of American identity as well as a metaphor for the self. Unlike *The Adventures of Huckleberry Finn*, *Deliverance* reveals a more complex conception of society and the self, particularly with regard to gender and sexuality. In *The Adventures of Huckleberry Finn*, while Huckleberry Finn heads out to new territory ahead of the rest to escape the "civilizing forces" of his society, Entzminger suggests that Dickey's novel hints that there is no free territory and, as Judith Butler would confirm with regard to identity, perhaps there never was. In this process Entzminger makes two significant points that are of interest to us. Firstly, *The Adventures of Huckleberry Finn* and *Deliverance* offer similar truths about the self through the symbolic journeys downriver. Both novels suggest to readers that identities of race, class, and gender are social constructions (Entzminger 2007, 101). The dark "other" is a central part of Fiedler's thesis. The dark "other," according to Fiedler, is our shadow self, and love of this "other" is figuratively love and acceptance of that darker part of our own natures: "Our dark-skinned beloved will take us in, we assure ourselves, when we have been cut off, or have cut ourselves off, from all others, without rancor or the insult of forgiveness. He will fold us in his arms saying, 'Honey' ...; He will comfort us, as if our offense against him were long ago remitted, were never truly real" ("Come Back to the Raft Ag'in" 11). As his tone here suggests, Fiedler recognizes this portrait of acceptance as naïve, wishful thinking on the part of the authors. Ultimately, through the love of the "other," this bond that is outside the normal conventions of society, the authors reveal a desire to love and accept the wayward part of the self, that part of the self which has sinned. As Arthur Petit observes, Huck's recognition of Jim's humanity is tantamount to a recognition of his own identity: "In a society of mixed blood in which the central preoccupation is with purity of blood, denial of the dignity and worth of blacks and mulattoes becomes, inevitably, a denial of the self" (Entzminger 2007, 154). By extension, as we rise above the societal definitions of such concepts as the race, class, and gender of the "other," we free ourselves from the definitions that confine and limit us.

Secondly, *Deliverance* presents a more overtly sexual dynamic, which replaces the homosocial bonds Fiedler sees underlying *The Adventures of Huckleberry Finn* and other texts. And this has been explained thus. In *Deliverance* the others through whom the protagonists consciously or unconsciously confront hidden aspects of themselves are not African American, like Jim in *Huckleberry Finn*, but poor white mountain folk. The novel links these hillbillies to their natural setting; they are, in a sense, violated nature responding with violation. The violation the mountain men enact is a violent homosexual rape, suggesting that modern man has raped the land and is now suffering nature's retribution. However, extending the metaphor further, nature (including the hillbillies) becomes a part of the protagonist's self, a violated self, responding with violation. The rape is the violent eruption of homosexual desire that, despite the protagonists' refusal to acknowledge it, underlies the trip from the beginning (Entzminger 2007, 98–99).

Deliverance has much in common with *Huckleberry Finn*, from the all-male journey down river, to the blurring of gender distinctions, to the suggestion of homoerotic bonding. It presents dark, unacknowledged shadow figures, characters who are of the same socio-economic class as Huck Finn, and the mountain men also resemble the protagonists of *Deliverance* more closely than Jim resembles Huck in that the hillbillies and the Atlantans are of the same race (101). The takeaway from this discussion is that Fiedler's theories related to male bonding are important academic substances for serious research. Their use in new avatars is seen repeatedly in literary and extra literary researches.

"Huck Honey!" still receives attention today, and scholars such as Constance Penley have pointed to the continuation of this pattern into the twentieth century: the Lone Ranger and Tonto, Captain Kirk and Spock, Maximus and Juba in Ridley Scott's film *Gladiator*, and so on (Harrison 2008). David Greven, in his article "Contemporary Hollywood Masculinity and the Double-Protagonist Film" (2009) uses Fiedler's formulations on American masculinity to understand the double-protagonist film, a genre that has emerged in the past two decades in which two male protagonists, each played by a film star, vie for narrative dominance.[3] American manhood is depicted as fundamentally split, a split that can be understood as a conflict between a narcissistic and a masochistic mode of masculine identity. The central conflict is a complex negotiation for power between *two* protagonists, each played by a star, both of whom lay legitimate claim to narrative dominance.

Several Ph.D. scholars in the last two decades have used Fiedler's argument that adolescence serves well in the American novel to express themes of independences, rebellion and initiation. Molly Childers (1999) uses Fiedler's insights on adolescence, masculinity metaphors, female stereotypes, and native images in the American novel to study female adolescence in Henry James's *The Bostonians* (1886), Nabokov's *Lolita* (1955) and Joyce Carol Oates' *You Must Remember This* (1987) and has conducted exemplary research.

Casey Charles, the chair of the University of Montana's department of English in 2008, comments on Fiedler's openness to the then-new approach to gender:

> I overcame my trepidation on a few occasions to come in and talk about Shakespeare and homoeroticism, and to my surprise found him unassuming and supportive. I think he was pleased to hear about scholars who were expanding the notions of male relations he began to develop in *The Stranger in Shakespeare* and other works.... I gave my presentation on the Calamus poems and, believe it or not, had little support from students on my gay approach to these works. Only Fiedler and a few students supported these readings, now widely accepted in the critical discourse. Later in a seminar paper on "The Sleepers" I received an equally open attitude toward looking at the great American Poetic Icon through a queer lens [Harrison 2008].

Such was the academic largesse of Fiedler. A man who could anticipate the direction that the new breeze would take was also an endearing mentor of the young.

Michael Snyder's essay (2007) on "crises in masculinity" discusses the homosocial desire and homosexual panic in the critical Cold War narratives of Mailer and Coover provoked in the American fifties and sixties by anti-communists' discourse, which rhetorically linked communism and sexuality (and thus, in the psychiatric and popular imaginary, effeminacy and narcissism) as "perversions." The essay identifies Robert Coover's novel *The Public Burning* and Norman Mailer's novels of the sixties, *An American Dream* and *Why Are We in Vietnam?* as Cold War critical narratives. More importantly, the essay borrows the Fiedlerian concept of homophobia to conclude that Coover's use of subversive Bakhtinian carnival laughter offers a more devastating and comprehensive critique of Cold War rhetoric than Mailer (250).

Coming back to his first essay, "Come Back...," many years later after its publication, in the Hubbell speech (1999a) Fiedler reminiscences the reactions when he had sent out "Come back..." to *Partisan Review*:

> To my surprise, however, it was widely read (or more often misread) and responded to in the academy as well as out. Not that it was generally admired. On the contrary, it was either dismissed as a *boutade*, a joke in bad taste, or condemned as a calumny of the tradition it purported to explore and a travesty of scholarship. Needless to say, among those condemning it on the latter grounds were the sort of scholars who had at that point been awarded the honor you bestow on me today.

Fiedler, who thought of himself as a comparativist, a mythographer, a literary anthropologist, anything but an "Americanist," when on a Fullbright fellowship to Italy to teach a course in American literature, said,

> I felt disconcertingly at ease in that new role. This was I have come to realize, because as a stranger in a strange land, I was able to teach our books as a literature in a foreign tongue.... What I ended up trying to do was to translate the parochial insights I had sketched out in "Come Back to the Raft" into more university terms; which is to say, treating our literature not in isolation but in relation to Western culture as a whole—specifically, to deal with it as the first postcolonial literature of the modern world [1999a].

Is it true? Can this comment be taken seriously?

CHAPTER 3

Integration of the "Other"

Indians, Jews, Blacks, Freaks and...

> If my concern had been the relation of fathers and sons, or mothers and sons, or even brother and brother, there would have been no way not to deal with Hamlet at considerable length. But I have been concerned rather with the relations between America and Europe, white men and black, Gentiles and Jews, masters of arts and savages, males and females, and within the family, as it has turned out, between fathers and daughters.
> —Fiedler, Preface to *The Stranger in Shakespeare*

> Fiedler's career—as critic, teacher, fiction writer, and lecturer has been a series of provocations. Though Kenneth Rexroth once attacked him for "his membership in a small circle of extremely ethnocentric people—the self-styled New York Establishment," Fiedler has in fact performed the part of outrageous outlander, one who finds his secret self among Jews, freaks, Blackfeet, and other vanishing Americans.
> —Kellman, Introduction to *Leslie Fiedler and American Culture*

> If ... Fiedlers would always be *outsiders* [emphasis mine] in Missoula, Leslie sensed that that would be true anywhere they lived.
> —Mark Royden Winchell, *"Too Good to Be True": The Life and Work of Leslie Fiedler*

In this chapter I shift my gaze to the "other" as Fiedler saw this "other." This 'other' can be variously called the "stranger" or the "outsider." Alternately it can also be called a phenomenon of "outsidedness" and symbolic alienation. Read the following to understand how the gaze of the other is a sweeping one, bringing in other aspects of his writings:

> In the troubled sleep of Americans, there came two myths. One, life can be endurable for white men, transplanted from their native habitat of Europe to this continent, living in the presence of Indians from the beginning and after awhile

in a presence of transported black men from Africa, only by eliminating the "other." The only answer to a myth, to a Hitlerite myth, or a native American genocidal myth, is not sweet reason for another myth, a countermyth. And that other myth is a myth of a kind of mingling or brotherhood, which has been in the American mind just as long, and just as deep. This is the myth that has been in our literature from the beginnings and the dream we dream when we wake from the nightmare of history [Fiedler 1970d, 206–7].

Fiedler admits that he has, alongside ancient Greek tragedy, the classic Chinese novel, old Provencal poetry, the English Victorian novel, Kafka and James Joyce, Jaroslav Hasek and Chrétien de Troyes, and especially Shakespeare and Dante, "also dealt with subjects as remote from my presumable field of expertise as theology and psychology, voting studies and the war in Vietnam, Japanese woodblock engravings, pornography and comic books, sideshows and circuses, bioethics and organ transplants." He says that he has "talked about them, moreover, not just in the classroom and at gatherings of my fellow-academics, but to trade-unionists, nurses and dermatologists, as well as on talk shows presided over by Dick Cavett and William Buckley, Merv Griffin and Phil Donahue—earning myself a listing in Who's Who in Entertainment" (1999a). Several of these also stand at the "margins" in academia, perpetually waiting in the wings to be called center stage.

This "understudy" is actually a reflection of his abiding interest in the "other." It is apparent from Chapter 1 that Fiedler could never really shrug off the mantle of elitism from his shoulders, but as his literary career advanced, certain other preoccupations took hold of him. These apparent preoccupations or themes unify or serve as guides to the large body of his criticism. In 1958 when he wrote his only textbook, *The Art of the Essay*, he spoke of the self and the other. Then at another juncture he spoke of the "othering of the self." Fiedler's reevaluations of American literature revealed that alienation was writ large on the cultural ethos of America, which he uncovered in his bold thesis presented in *Love and Death*. Being a Jew himself, he perceived his fellow Jews as strangers on the American soil, as depicted in his early writings. This theme has been explored in a large body of his works: anthologies and essays, particularly *To the Gentiles* (1971), *The Stranger in Shakespeare* (1972), and *Fiedler on the Roof* (1991). In his early essays, the Indians (natives) stand as outsiders. Later, his sensitivity perceived the blacks as the "other" (*Love and Death, Waiting for the End, The Return of the Vanishing American*). Finally, his concern with strangers or aliens made him wear a new lens in *Freaks: Myths and Images of the Secret Self,* dealing with the nature's outsiders, and *Tyranny of the Normal* (1982). Not only this, his literary antennae sighted some of the literary outsiders, neglected texts by less-known writers, and he attempted to integrate them by writing about them. So once again in his role of an upholder of the neglected and the lost, he resuscitated a number of these dying or dead texts.

Thus, this chapter takes us to several of his earliest essays: on Montana, the Jew as outsiders, the Negro-Jew conflict, Jew versus Gentile, and the Jew in the American novel. This major concern, the problem of integration, runs parallel to his principal concern of the sixties, the emergence of the Jewish intellectual on the American literary scene. Several of these essays consider the shifting relations between Negro and Jew in America. With this introductory backdrop, let me look at his obsession with the "other."

The Indian, the West and the Western: *"Montana; or The End of Jean-Jacques Rousseau"* (1949)

The first essay of Fiedler's Montana phase, during which he imprinted his concerns about the "othering" of an insider on the American soil, and registered his shock at "a perverse psychology at work in the state" (Harrison 2008), one that upset many when it first appeared (and that perhaps continues to upset people, even today) is "Montana; or The End of Jean-Jacques Rousseau." The timing of its publication was coincidental. The time that Fiedler was at Missoula was that phase when the Indians were very much a persecuted minority. Harrison narrates that under antimiscegenation laws aimed at the state's negligible black population, the Indians were also targeted. In many towns, Indians couldn't purchase a drink at a saloon. Ethnic stereotypes branded them as dirty, deceitful, and even subhuman. As the civil rights movement began to heat up in the rest of the country, Montana liberals had only the Indian to defend. Then as Winchell points out, "both popular legend and the Book of Mormon have long held that the Indians are the lost tribes of Israel" (2002, 144). So, even if his views were not politically motivated, he almost certainly would have identified with the ancient sense of tradition and ritual and the presence of myth in their culture, says Winchell. This led him to write the essay.

Winchell makes a strong case when he says that right at the outset, in his bid to urge the Montanans to move from myth to reality, the essay outlines three stages in the evolution of the frontier. The first stage is a paradox: the force of the fight for survival is so intense that the settlers have neither sufficient time nor energy to ruminate the appalling incongruity present in between their romantic dream of utopia and the barrenness of their present surroundings. However, when the schoolmarm moves out from the East, displaces the whore, and marries the rancher, "the dream and the fact confront each other openly" (CE 1, 133). This confrontation results in the perceived need "for some kind of art to nurture the myth, to turn a way of life into a culture" (CE

1, 133). As a result, the West in its refurbished form dons the sentimentalized image of the frontier purveyed in pulp novels, Western movies, and fake cowboy songs. At the time that Fiedler was writing, Montana was coming to the end of this second phase of frontier development and moving into a third. The most recent transformation exploits the images of pop art for purely commercial purposes. In effect, popular mythology has become so powerful and so pervasive that life begins not only to imitate art, but also to forget that any discrepancy exists between the two:

> Certainly for the bystander watching the cowboy, a comic book under his arm, lounging beneath the bright poster of the latest Roy Rogers film, there is the sense of a joke on someone—and no one to laugh. It is nothing less than the total myth of the goodness of man in a state of nature that is at stake every Saturday after the show at the Rialto; and, though there is scarcely anyone who sees the issue clearly or as a whole, most Montanans are driven instinctively to try to close the gap [CE 1, 136, quoted in Winchell 2002, 61].

In the mythology of the frontier dream and Montana's position on the last frontier, geographical eschatology inevitably gave way to fantasy. The real cowboy imaginatively recreates himself as Roy Rogers, while the upper-class Montanan identifies himself with even older prototypes of frontier nobility— the pioneer and mountain man. Some who are of a liberal or romantic sensibility even try to redeem the image of the Indian as Noble Savage, without really coming to terms with the presence of today's Indian, "despised and outcast in his open-air ghettos" (Winchell 2002, 141). Fiedler urges his fellow Montanans to make the painful but necessary adjustment from myth to reality: "When he admits that the Noble Savage is a lie, when he has learned that his state is where the myth comes to die (it is here, one is reminded, that the original of Huck Finn ended his days, a respected citizen), the Montanan may find the possibilities of tragedy and poetry for which he so far has searched his life in vain" (CE, 141, quoted in Winchell 2002, 62).

This essay, apart from tracing the myth of the frontier that was discussed in the last chapter, also disparages the predicament of the state's Indian population, trapped, as Fiedler puts it, in open-air ghettos. Traveling across Montana in the 1940s, he finds writ large on its tracks atrocities committed by whites against Indians. With verve he writes:

> The cruelest aspect of social life in Montana is the exclusion of the Indian; deprived of his best land, forbidden access to the upper levels of white society, kept out of any job involving prestige, even in some churches confined to the back rows, but of course protected from whiskey and comforted with hot lunches and free hospitals—the actual Indian is a constant reproach to the Montanan, who feels himself Nature's own democrat, and scorns the South for its treatment of the Negro, the East for its attitude toward the Jews [21].

Fiedler continues his tirade:

> To justify the continuing exclusion of the Indian, the local white has evolved the theory that the redskin is *naturally* dirty, lazy, dishonest, incapable of assuming responsibility—a troublesome child; and this theory confronts dumbly any attempt at reasserting the myth of the Noble Savage [22].

Fiedler does not hesitate in uncovering the fact that in the Montana of the 1940s, the myths and realities of the West worked together to reduce the Indian to an abject outcast; the Noble Savage had become the "troublesome child." Brady Harrison writes that Fiedler's analysis does not, by any means, acknowledge the agency of Montana's first peoples or accurately reflect the complexities of life on or off the reservation—he makes no note, for example, of efforts to protect or recover language, culture, history, religion, and more. Unafraid and quick to contribute his bit to "debates on race and culture then taking place in Montana and across the West," his most odious comments, particularly to the Montanans, are on what he dubbed the "Montana Face," and the posture and tone he adopted appeared to many as that of an outsider:

> What I had been expecting I do not clearly know; zest, I suppose, naiveté, a ruddy and straightforward kind of vigor—perhaps even honest brutality. What I found seemed, at first glance, reticent, sullen, weary—full of self-sufficient stupidity; a little later it appeared simply inarticulate, with all the dumb pathos of what cannot declare itself: a face developed not for sociability or feeling, but for facing the weather [16–17].

It is intriguing to many who, precisely, Fiedler had in mind with these remarks on the "Natives of Montana" (his colleagues? Indians? Whites? Ranchers? Missourians?). His thunderous statements would be disapproved, he certainly must have known, particularly coming from an Eastern, Jewish intellectual who found himself among people who, he thought, "had never seen an art museum or a ballet or even a movie in any language but their own" (17). He rather disingenuously remarks, in a footnote later added to the essay, that he had supposed his remarks on the Montana face to be "quite unmalicious" (17). One cannot help admiring his characteristic chutzpah. Right or wrong, he most often did not play it safe or hedge or second-guess himself into silence (Harrison 2008).

Though few of his neighbors at Montana read highbrow Marxist literary reviews, those who did quickly spread the word that this Eastern ingrate—in the South he would have been known as a carpetbagger—was biting "the fine, generous Western hand that was feeding him" (CE 2, 331). The passage the locals found most offensive was Leslie's description of the "Montana face": "developed not for sociability or feeling, but for facing into the weather" (Winchell 2002, 61).

Brave Heavy Runner

It was at Montana in 1956 that the Blackfeet Indians adopted him in recognition of his civil rights work and gave him the name Heavy Runner. Winchell writes in his biography of Fiedler that, when he was given a traditional Indian bonnet during the induction ceremony, he thought that he would take it home with him as a souvenir. "They put it on my head," he recalls, "faced me into the sunset, said a formula, pushed me and told me to stumble, and I stumbled into Indianhood" (2002, 143). Fiedler was named by the Blackfeet as "the Heavy Runner" after a famous chief of the tribe for whom a mountain is named in Glacier National Park. Winchell writes of the time when his family later went to an Indian dance in Missoula that featured a girl named Eleanor Heavy Runner; his kids kept screaming, "That's our cousin, that's our cousin!" Later Fiedler was told in the ceremony "that Heavy Runner had gone east and come back with the 'weapons of his enemies.'" Winchell recalls, "Leslie was struck by the fact that he was then preparing to leave Montana for a year's appointment at Princeton. The new Heavy Runner was to fill in for Richard Blackmur and to give the prestigious Christian Gauss lectures. Already he was challenging the received critical orthodoxy by asserting the primacy of myth in literature. What weapons he might bring back were anyone's guess."[1] When he arrived in Buffalo he received a letter from a former colleague (of Montana presumably) informing him that "an old Indian fighter" had said, "I always knew he would run out on us some day" (Richard 2004, 297).

Paying a tribute to his writings in 2003, the year Fiedler died, Jerome Richard writes, "Now he has run out on us all. But he has left this behind for everyone (or almost everyone) who has ever read him or heard him speak: his criticism never had the quality of an autopsy. In fact, he left literature more alive than any other critic" (297).

Montana was so deeply entrenched in his psyche that once after a trip back to Missoula, Fiedler observed, "It is a Montana landscape I see when I close my eyes, its people I imagine understanding, or more often misunderstanding me. And in this sense, I have to think of myself as a Western writer" (Wakeman 1975, 469). It was in his second novel, *Back to China* (1965), that Fiedler had first used the Montana setting in his fiction. Here, the contemporary Mountain West serves as time present, against which the memory of China immediately after World War II is juxtaposed. The novel's protagonist, a philosophy professor named Baron Finke Stone, has had himself sterilized in atonement for the bombing of Hiroshima and spends the next twenty years seeking to maintain his youth by doing dope with his male students and sleeping with his female ones (Winchell 2002, 193). In one of his last interviews with Bauman in 2003 for Salon.com, Fiedler applauds the uniqueness of the only neatly organized book in American literature, *The Great Gatsby*, with *The Scarlet Letter* coming at a close second. But considering himself a truly "old Montanan," what had a special appeal for him was Fitzgerald's short story "A Diamond as Big as the Ritz" (Bauman 2003, 3).

Toward the end of the 1960, Fiedler noticed that the Indian, who was a more truly invisible part of American national life than Ralph Ellison's Negro, was beginning to appear with astonishing frequency in mainstream American literature in the writings of John Barth, Thomas Berger, Ken Kersey, David Markson, Peter Matthiessen, James Leo Herlihy, Leonard Cohen, and "the inspired script writers of *Cat Ballou*." The artists (and Fiedler himself in *The Last Jew in America*) had "been involved in a common venture: the creation of the New Western, a form which not so much redeems the Pop Western as exploits it with irreverence and pleasure, in contempt of the 'serious reader' and his expectations" (RVA, 14). Fiedler explores this phenomenon in his third venture into literary anthropology, *The Return of the Vanishing American* (1968).

Early on, *The Return of the Vanishing American* makes the Fiedlerian assertion that "geography in the United States is mythological." Hence, much of its literature has "tended to define itself topologically, as it were, in terms of the four cardinal directions: a mythicized North, South, East and West" (16). In some ways, this borderless man was writing about borders.

Winchell explicates that when Fiedler speaks of the American West, he is thinking of the region between the Mississippi River and the Rocky Mountains: "The heart of the western is not the confrontation with the alien landscape (by itself this produces only the Northern), but the encounter with the Indian, that utter stranger for whom our New World is an Old Home" (RVA, 20). Because of the radically strange and alien nature of the Indian, he is the one element of the American experience that Europeans have never been able to assimilate. "Whether he is a survivor of the Lost Continent of Atlantis, a remnant of the wandering tribes of Israel, or some extraterrestrial being, he is the ultimate other. He may have a soul, but—as D. H. Lawrence concluded—*not* one precisely like our own, except as our own have the potentiality of becoming like his" (RVA, 22).

According to Fiedler's definition, the Western refers neither to a region nor a direction, but to our encounter with the savage "other." "So long as a single untamed Indian inhabits it," Fiedler writes, "any piece of American space can become to the poet's imagination an authentic West" (RVA, 26). Of course, the corollary of this notion is that once the Indian has disappeared as a mythic presence in the American imagination, "the Western will become a defunct genre (a fate that already seems to have befallen the Northern and the Eastern)." And yet, the Western is so deeply embedded in the American subconscious that it is constantly being resurrected from two directions: from the past in the form of historical fiction—even of the debunking variety, such as Thomas Berger's *Little Big Man*—and from the future in the form of science fiction tales, which are really crypto–Westerns, "space operas" instead of "horse operas," says Winchell (1985).

In *Return*... Fiedler argues that four myths arose that form the American image of the Far West. These are "The Myth of Love in the Woods," or the story of Pocahontas and Captain John Smith; "The Myth of the White Woman with the Tomahawk," based on the experience of Hannah Duston, a New England woman who was captured by Indians and fought her way to freedom; "The Myth of the Good Companions in the Woods," the Paleface/Redskin version of the Huck-Honey motif, derived from the youthful friendship of fur trader Alexander Henry and the Indian Wawatam; and "The Myth of the Runaway Male," which was first imagined by Washington Irving in "Rip Van Winkle." In Winchell's analysis, Fiedler sees the roots of the "New Western" in Hemingway's first published novel. A farce about Indian life masquerading as a parody of Sherwood Anderson, *The Torrents of Spring* exploits "the clichés and stereotypes of all the popular books which precede it ... bringing the full weight of their accumulated absurdities to bear in every casual quip" (RVA, 147). The next example that makes the Western into self-conscious camp can be found in Nathanael West's satirical description of a drugstore cowboy and a Yiddish Indian in *The Day of the Locust*. For reasons that seem to baffle Fiedler, this inchoate genre did not reach fruition until 1960 when John Barth's *The Sot-Weed Factor*—a burlesque of the Pocahontas myth—gave rise to a whole spate of New Westerns, which produced neither a new myth nor an anti-myth, but rather an anti-stereotype (204). When the vanishing American returns, it is not as Chingachgook or even as Tonto, but as Chief Bromden, tossing a control panel through the asylum window in *One Flew Over the Cuckoo's Nest* before returning to the privileged insanity of his tribe, opines Winchell (1985).

Venturing deep into anthropology, *The Return of the Vanishing American* decidedly shows some sort of evolution in respect of his theory of the Red Indian's return to America: his native land. Today, the notion that the vanishing American is staging a comeback seems pretty tame, particularly when after more than half a century of publication of his book, the First Nations are, after all, vanishing all the more. Maurer writes:

> Archetypes, after all, are *supposed* to stick like chewing gum on the unconscious.... Fiedler is certain that a radically alien "other," a dark man, haunts us all: "everyone who thinks of himself as being in some sense an American," he says, "feels the stirrings in him of a second soul, the soul of the Red Man—about which, not so very long ago, only an expatriate Englishman, his head full of Natty Bumppo and Chingachgook, had nerve enough to talk seriously" [Maurer 1968, 26].

In *The Return of the Vanishing American*, therefore, he tracks down Mohicans, Chinooks, Chickasaws, Beatniks, and other lost Indians—from legend, history, literature, and the social scene. He text invites criticism, as Maurer notes, "for if reviewers often have been giddy-headed (when they have not been downright rancorous) about his previous ventures in literary anthropology, their high-pitched responses were perhaps natural in the face of concerns that even Fiedler admits are a 'peculiar form of madness'" (1968, 26).

Fiedler's connection and concern with the native Indian is visible in many other texts. In *Unfinished Business* (1972) he probably deals with all aspects of American culture. In the typical Europe-America relationship, the Indian once again makes an appearance in one of his most provocative essays, "Caliban or Hamlet: A Study in Literary Anthropology." As his old *Partisan Review* editor Philip Rahv had done in his famous essay "Paleface and Redskin," Fiedler attempts to divide classic American writers into roughly Apollonian and Dionysian categories. He goes beyond Rahv, however, in relating this distinction to the images the Europeans harbor of Americans and that Americans harbor of themselves. Because these images are rooted in literature but have extraliterary ramifications, Fiedler draws upon what he calls literary anthropology to argue that Americans have been viewed alternately as either Caliban or Hamlet (Winchell 2002, 240).

As Fiedler reminds us in *The Return of the Vanishing American* (which was published two years after original appearance of this essay), "America" was a realm accessible to the European imagination for nearly three hundred years before the "United States" came into being (Winchell 2002, 240). During this time, one of the most mythically potent attempts to visualize the "brave new world" across the sea was *The Tempest*, a play Leo Marx has called "Shakespeare's American Fable"[2] (2002, 241). Even today, many Europeans share Shakespeare's vision of the indigenous American as Caliban, "an already existing mythology transplanted to the New World: part Indian, part Negro, all subhuman" (RVA, 293). Thus, when Americans—particularly American writers—are most primitive, nativist, and provincial, they are closest to validating the European stereotype of them.

The Hamlet analogy, like that of Caliban, is influenced by its relationship to Europe. It enables the Americans to play, however, not the rebellious slave, but the wronged son. According to Winchell, "when we feel the tug of the umbilical cord that ties up to our Old World mother, we become that second Adam, Christ, or even that second Christ, Hamlet: For archetypally speaking, Hamlet is Christ after the death of God" (292). America's compulsion to save the rest of the world (particularly the Western or European world) from whatever particular monster is the impulse of a dutiful son.

Although indigenous Americans are not immigrants, they have also experienced displacements that are diasporic in nature. Native Americans throughout the Americas have both voluntarily, as a result of economic pressures, and involuntarily, due to genocidal institutional policies of the settler nations who currently occupy this hemisphere, left their homelands and adjusted to harsh conditions in unfamiliar locations where resources are scarce. Yet even when indigenous communities advocated for universal citizenship, as Native Americans did following World War I, and were eventually granted citizenship by the U.S. government in 1924, many aboriginal people remain dislocated from their homelands and live as often invisible outsiders within countries such as the United States, Canada, and Mexico. Fiedler's treatment of the natives as outsiders is also a significant intervention to this ensuing debate.

The Jews, the Blacks and the Gentiles

My own subject position as a South Asian Hindu, with bookish knowledge of Christianity and Judaism, is an interesting dichotomy in itself. Although I seem to have read most of the works of Fiedler, I don't pretend to know everything about his Jewishness. So I did what any neophyte would do: I consulted my Jewish friend Serge Liberham in Australia. And there arrived emails and a treasure trove of Jewish encyclopedic entries on Fiedler that I am most grateful for. I must quote Serge's email (Jan. 2012):

> Although I possess two of his most important and probably influential books in their time—*Love and Death in the American Novel* and *Unfinished Business*—I don't pretend to know much about him. So I consulted Wikipedia. While the lead article is illuminating to a dabbler like myself—what versatility and sheer fecundity of his writings he displayed (see his curriculum vitae)—more interesting and alive are the external links relating to Fiedler, in particular Bruce Jackson's piece, "Conversations with Leslie Fiedler" and another link telling how "he turned American criticism on its head." What a character he must have been! But what does account for his decline? His "Being Busted" for alleged possession of marijuana and hashish and the ensuing consequences? The imputation that he was "sex-obsessed" or that, as the writer in the Encyclopedia Judaica states, "he tended to regard a literary work as the expression of the author's psychosexual desires, minimising the importance of its structure and linguistic texture?" Or has he just been too eccentric or too radical for his peers in some of the literary and social causes that he championed? I did say that, on returning to Melbourne, I would follow through this seeming eclipse. I just thought I'd write and thank you for alerting me to him. Quite a character—and scholar—indeed!

This was a response from a first-time reader of Fiedler's literary story.

The Jew

Since his early writings, Fiedler has been at pains to establish his position as a Jew. In his preface to *An End to Innocence* (1955), he states his position as "a liberal, intellectual, writer, American, and Jew." He further clarifies:

> I do not mind, as some people apparently do, thinking of myself in such categorical terms; being representative of a class, generation, a certain temper seems to me not at all a threat to my individuality. As one who dearly loves a generalisation ... I relish all that is typical, even me; and I like to think of myself as registering through my particular sensibility the plight of a whole group ... the groups for which I think I speak often, regard me not as their appointed mouthpiece but as a rather presumptuous apostle to the Gentiles; and this (I confess) I do not find altogether distasteful [EI, xiii].

In the 1960s every Jewish graduate student knew the fairy tale of Fiedler: exiled in Missoula, Montana, where he wrote and taught before returning to the East to SUNY Buffalo; in his life and work he thumbed his nose at the academic establishment and parochial historical criticism and what he saw as the narrow formalism of New Criticism, while making a very substantial reputation based primarily on one important book, *Love and Death in the American Novel* (Schwartz 1999, 99). Thus, to hear the sounds, squeaks, guffaws, loud pronouncements of his outsidedness, of freakishness, of other cultures, people—Indians, Jews, blacks, nature's outsiders, literary outcasts, whatever the case may be—one will have to go back to his essays, right to the early ones.

Several of Fiedler's essay on the Jewish experience have been published in his early anthologies: *An End to Innocence* (1955), *No! In Thunder* (1960), *Waiting for the End* (1964) and later *To the Gentiles* (1971), which was republished in the section entitled "To the Gentiles" in volume 2 of his *Collected Essays*, published in 1971. Many others can be found in his 1991 collection entitled *Fiedler on the Roof: Essays on Literature and Jewish Identity*. He also wrote on such "Jewish" subjects as Ethel and Julius Rosenberg and the *Partisan Review*, which were discussed in Chapter 1. He became particularly interested in the vast body of cultural production that he termed the "middlebrow," which he argued had become the special province of the Jewish writer. The Jew in America, he proclaimed, had come to stand in for the American experience; the Jewish writer, in turn, had become the creator and mediator of American popular culture: the Superman comic strip, science fiction, Marjorie Morningstar, and Holden Caulfield, Fiedler was the first to point out, had all been created by Jews. Fiedler's early articulations that hold much validity even today on the topic of Jewish literature and the Jewish writer are "The Jew in the American Novel," "Negro and Jew," and "Master of Dreams: The Jew in a Gentile World."

The earliest expression of his views on the Jews and their problems came forth in the form of essays on writers such as Peretz, Kafka and Malamud. In a 1948 essay, "Kafka and the Myth of the Jew," Fiedler hits upon his major concern: "The artist ... still concerned with his alienation, finds in the Jew, inseparable from the dignity of his ultimate exile, the noblest metaphor of the outsider" (NT, 101). The same year he published another essay, "Peretz: The Secularisation of the Absurd," in which he talks of the assimilation of the Jews in America. He says, "We have become aware that we must achieve, if we are unwilling to become shadows of shadows, a double assimilation, back to a stable past as well as forward to a speculative future" (NT, 98). In "Roman Holiday" (1954), an essay about his personal experience in Rome, Fiedler is distressed to discover that the Jews have become very much like the Gentiles. In this essay, Fiedler, an orthodox Jew at heart, emerges as a man disillusioned with reality. This essay is an important landmark in Fiedler's early Jewish writing. Malin says that "Roman Holiday" clarifies Fiedler's commitment and strength, which led him to explore in detail the ambiguities of his "Jewish-American Identity" (Malin and Stark 1961, 23) and establishes "Exile" as a crucial moment for the Jews. In *Waiting for the End*, a collection of essays published in 1964, Fiedler reiterates the same point: "All flights, the Jewish experience teaches, are from one exile to another," and it is this dream of exile as freedom that has made America; but "it is the experience of exile as terror that has forged the self consciousness of Americans" (WFTE, 25). And, according to Fiedler, it is the Jew who has been able to translate this old wisdom (that home is exile, and it is the nature of man to feel alienated everywhere) in terms valid for the twentieth century Americans.

Similarly, Fiedler writes of a major concern of his fiction, which represents various attempts to come to terms with the world of experience: the Second World War itself, the problem of being a Jew in contemporary America, and being an intellectual and a writer in a society that at once adulates and fears him. Hence, we notice that Fiedler's writings till this point of time depict a kind of struggle to establish the identity of the Jew in America, to the point of assimilation.

Winchell writes that Fiedler's own sense of himself as a Jew remained intense, even as he lived in an almost exclusively Gentile region of the country. Perhaps more troubling was what struck him as the pervasive anti–Semitism of the literary canon he revered. In a fit of youthful courage (or brashness), he dealt directly with this matter in a letter to T. S. Eliot, dated December 13, 1948. Although that letter has been preserved, Eliot's reply of January 14, 1949, is currently housed in Fiedler's private files. Essentially, Eliot sees the charges against his own poetry as a matter of geographical and generational sensitivity. Neither the Jews he has known in England nor his older Jewish friends in America have ever mentioned evidence of anti–Semitism in his work. (The poems in which the word Jew appears were all published by Jews—in England by Leonard Woolf and in America by Alfred Knopf and Horace Liveright.) In any event, those poems were written many years ago, before racial sensibilities had become as polarized as they are today. Eliot then concludes on a personal note. "Incidentally, and last," he writes, "as you say that you are Jewish: I hope that you will not consider it an impertinence of me to express the hope that you are diligent in attendance at your synagogue (if you are so fortunate as to have one in Missoula), that you observe Law and read the Scriptures. And that you cherish the faith of your fathers" (Winchell 2002, 60). Fiedler, however, used Jewish culture as a referent and employed a Jewish sensibility even when he addressed such canonical writers as Shakespeare and Joyce (Rubenstein 2003, 159). In *The Stranger in Shakespeare* Fiedler devoted a chapter to *The Merchant of Venice* (the "stranger" in Shakespeare, in Fiedler's argument, being Jews, blacks, and women). The collection *Fiedler on the Roof* showcases his interest in Leopold Bloom, the Jewish protagonist of Joyce's *Ulysses* (in "Bloom on Joyce; or, Jokey for Jacob," and "Joyce and Jewish Consciousness"), as well as his provocative reading of the centrality of Jewishness to that most "goyish" of myths, the Grail Legend (in "Why Is the Grail Knight Jewish?").

Fiedler's own fiction also taps into his general concern with the alienated and marginalized, and his more particular concern with the Jew in America. "The Last Jew in America" takes place in the fictional Lewis and Clark City, located somewhere between Montana and Idaho. One of the three first Jewish men to settle the city is dying in a Catholic hospital, and the second tries to convince the third to organize a bedside Yom Kippur service for the dying man. The subject of the story, as of many of Fiedler's works of fiction, is the cultural and spiritual impoverishment of the city's (and America's) assimilated and secularized Jews. Even Jacob Markowitz, the protagonist of the story, who thinks of himself as the "last Jew in America," no longer observes the tenets of his faith, and his only childhood memory is of deliberately breaking the Yom Kippur fast. The stories "Pull Down Vanity" and "Nude Croquet," as well as Fiedler's first novel *The Second Stone*, all deal with the theme of love among the intellectuals, most of whom, in Fiedler's fictional universe, happen to be Jewish.

Towards the end, Fiedler began to argue that Jewish-American literature was a genre that was ephemeral by nature. By 1991, in his preface to *Fiedler on the Roof*, Fiedler began to believe that Jewish-American writers had ceased to remain central to American literary thought.

The Jew and the Negro

Continuing his preoccupation with the question of identity for the Jews, Fiedler elaborates on the Negro-Jew conflict, both facing a crisis of identity in America. In 1956, Fiedler published "Negro and Jew—Encounter in America," originally a review of James Baldwin's book *Notes of a Native Son*. Boyers comments on the contemporary relevance of such an essay, written five decades ago, principally in three ways: firstly, it is interesting as "a historical document," for it uncovers for us "what American intellectuals were saying on this subject forty years ago" (Boyers wrote this essay in 1999). Secondly, the essay is still a work of compelling vitality by a "great American original." Thirdly, Boyers admits, "If it is occasionally wrong-headed or dubious in several respects, well, that is generally what we always felt" about the work of Fiedler (Boyers 1999, 173).

As will be apparent from the discussion of this essay, Fiedler very enthusiastically puts forward his own views, for he says, "To write with less involvement or risk of pain would be an offense" (NT, 233). Winchell points out, "Because Newark was what we now euphemistically call a 'changing community' the complex social relations between Jews and Blacks (only recently become a matter of national interest) was part of the fabric of Fiedler's early life" (1985, 3). The same year Fiedler published another essay, "Negro and Jew." Though the thrust of the two essays is different, Fiedler calls them an extension of comments on the Negro-Jew problem of identity. "Negro and Jew," which was included in Fiedler's book *No! In Thunder*, considers the shifting relations of two American "minority" populations. Those relations, Fiedler writes, have been exacerbated by the fact that Negroes and Jews have been "so alike and so different." How alike? At least "in the complicated fear we stir in the hearts of our neighbors," and in the "restrictions" as to "what clubs and fraternities they can join" and as to "whom they can marry." The two groups have been alike as well in existing always "for the western world ... as archetypes, symbolic figures ... projecting aspects of the white, Christian mind itself" (Boyers 1999, 173).

In the fifties, it had become important for the Jewish writer to reimagine the Negro in terms that removed him from the old WASP clichés, which were both sentimental and vicious. And the Negro writer himself was unable to invent a new Negro, as Harriet Beecher Stowe, Mark Twain, D. W. Griffith and William Faulkner had invented the old Negro in Uncle Tom and Jim. As a result the Jewish writer started dealing with the Negroes from the fifties onwards, which led to greater misunderstanding and tension between the Jews and the Negroes.

Unlike the Negro, the Jew does not feel himself to be the *native son* of the soil but a sojourner, an outsider in America. Of course, by assimilation and adaptation the Jew can become an American, like anyone else, but he knows he has played no part in creating what he has become. The Jew is a latecomer to America. When he came, America had its own identity. Giving a symbolic meaning to the relationship, Fiedler says, theirs is a marriage of the middle aged. The guilts and repressions, the boasts and regrets of America, are already formulated and are waiting for him when he debarks. Americans' genesis goes back to an experience Jews do not share; and the Jew himself is determined by quite other experience—twice determined, in fact, by the dim pre-history of Eretz Yisrael and by the living memory of Exile (NT, 233–34). Primarily concerned with "time: Fiedler takes us back to the beginning; he assumes that the Negro and the Jew accept roles which they have played no part in creating" (Malin 1965, 69). So, the Jews came to America with a history, "but the Negro arrives without a past, out of nowhere" (NT, 234). Further, Fiedler says, "out of a world that he is afraid to remember.... Before America there is for him simply nothing" (NT, 234). The fault lines in this essay are too obvious to be stated. Nostalgia and a return to roots was the anthem of black power movement and the Harlem Renaissance writers. On the contrary, as rightly pointed out by Fiedler, "white America scarcely exists until he (Negro) is present" (NT, 234). So the Negro and the white share a very special relationship. But unlike the Jew, the Negro can never forget that he was a salve and the cause of a civil war that set white Americans against each other and created a bitterness that has not yet been forgotten.

No other foreigner came to America like the Jew, on a dead run, universally branded and harried. Fiedler writes, "We fled to the Golden Door not merely from poverty and hunger, but impelled by an absolute rejection and threat of extinction" (NT, 235). Fiedler places the Jews on a high pedestal when he writes that Americans wince when the word "Negro" is mentioned, thinking of slave ships; they stutter when the term "Indian" is mentioned, remembering the encroachment of lands, and they squirm at the mention of "Japanese," recalling the concentration camps of war. These Americans "can cite the Jews with pride. We are (it is fashionable to forget this now, but salutary to recall) the boasts of the United States, as the Negroes are its shame" (NT, 235–6).

Coming to the physical traits, Fiedler points out that the Negro is a "prisoner of his face." No amount of skin bleaching, plastic surgery, nose straightening or shortening, or hair straightening can free the Negro from himself. Whereas, within a decade or two, the Jew is born with a new face in America. Hence, this realisation lies between the Negro and the Jew "that for one (whether he finally chooses or not) there is always a way out, by emigration or assimilation; for the other there is no exit" (NT, 238). Fiedler, as we notice rightly, develops the intricacies of the Negro-Jew relationship and gives a well-balanced view of the two, supported efficiently by his ability to compare and contrast, a fact that lends strength to his argument.

But Fiedler does not stop here. He says that the Negro and the Jew exist

3. Integration of the "Other"

"in the timeless limbo of the psyche," as symbolic figures and archetypes, but actually projecting aspects of the white Christian mind itself (NT, 238). Fiedler distinguishes the two archetypes and points out that "the myth of the Jew is a European inheritance, a persistence; while the myth of the Negro is a product of American experience, and of a crisis in the American mind. The image of the usurer and bad father with a knife that lies behind Shylock existed long before even the dream of America" (NT, 238-39). On the contrary, the key archetypes of the Negro are purely American: Uncle Tom and Nigger Jim, "those inspired and infuriating inescapable images that in the best American tradition belong really to childhood" (NT, 239). In *Waiting for the End* Fiedler points out, "Certainly the Negro is the Jew's archetypal opposite, representative of the impulsive life even as the Jew is the symbol of the intellectual" (107). In "Negro and Jew—Encounter in America" he says that the Negro and the Jew are opposites: law and lawlessness, the eternal father and the eternal child (NT, 239). Delving into Freudian analysis, Fiedler says that one stands for the superego (Jews), the other the id, and both are felt as "other" by the white Gentile ego. Hence we discover that Fiedler is throughout concerned with this "otherness" faced by the Jew and the Negro, simultaneously, in the Gentile world. Notwithstanding their separateness, the Negro and the Jew are bound together and condemned to a common fate: in the quality of exclusion they are one. Every Jew knows that the printed injunction "For Whites Only" is for him too, because of the fear of "contamination of blood." Hence the Jew tells the Negro, "We are taboo people … so unlike and so different" (NT, 241). "The best thing about Fiedler's essay is not the categorical element, however much it permits him to establish long perspectives and to frame his more immediate observations. Here, as in many other instances, we value most Fiedler's way of speaking candidly on a subject bounded by taboos" (Boyers 1999, 175).

In America, particularly in the ghettoes, the emancipated Negro fleeing the South, the plantation and poverty and the emancipated Jew fleeing exclusion, extinction and Europe become neighbors. The ultimate ghetto, though, is reserved for the Negroes, as the place of real belonging is that of Gentiles only. The Jew inhabits the in-between space. Economically superior, the middle-class Jew despises the Negro for lagging behind in the ghettoes (which they had emptied for the Negroes to move in); at the same time they resent the Negroes for pressing too close. Fiedler recalls the voice of a mild, horrified old Gentile lady discussing over her tea: "First the Jews, then the Negroes" (NT, 251). According to Fiedler this is the comedy and pathos of the plight of the Jews. "As he to me," the Jew thinks helplessly, "so I to them" (NT, 251). This is a very poignant sketch by Fiedler of the difficult triangular relationship of the Negro-Jew-Gentile. According to Fiedler, the Negro is the "shadow," the "improbable caricature" of the Jew, whom the Jew hates only at the price of hating himself. He also realizes that his own human dignity depends upon the Negro. "No Jew can selflessly dedicate himself to the fight for the equality of the Negro; when he pretends that he is not fighting for himself, he is pretending that he is indistinguishable from a goy" (NT, 252).

According to Robert Boyers, Fiedler accounts for the origin of the troubled relationship in a way that may well have seemed doubtful even to early readers of his essay. It is easy to say that Fiedler got it all wrong when he contended that blacks arrived here without a past. And it is easy to say that many American Jews were in flight from their own dark Eastern European or German past and thus closer to the Negro and to other immigrant groups in wanting rapidly to become a part of America.

Fiedler may well have underestimated the degree to which American Jews assumed the guilts and, later, the resentments to which other white Americans were susceptible. Though, as he says, Jews were not responsible for the institution of American slavery or for subsequent oppressive regimes directed against blacks, they profited from the system in ways that set them apart from most black people and often made them wonder what they might have done to close the gap between themselves and the less fortunate (Boyers 1999, 174–5).

Moreover, the problem of Negro-Jew hostility does not exist sociologically, not even consciously (because on the conscious level people think that the Negroes love, respect and honor the Jews), but only pre-consciously on the mythological level of legend and nightmare (TG, 165). In America, Jews are engaged in a life of logos—cultivation of the ego, whereas the Negro lives in a world of "sub-literary, unrationalised impulse and free fantasy" (TG, 166). In an attempt to solve this problem mythologically, Fiedler discusses various mythologies at work. According to the legend of the three sons of Noah, the Negro divides the world into two ethnic segments: white and colored, which is in accordance with the WASP racist mythology. On the contrary, the Jewish ethnic-mythic division is threefold, and the Jews were taught they have two hostile and inferior brothers, Ham and Japheth. The Negro's simpler mythology regards the Jew either as a colored man deviously passing as white, or a white man with the fate of the excluded colored man. Therefore, the Jew struggles with the sense of being a third thing, "neither-either," and thinks himself free to "pass" in either direction. At times nominated as "white," he is the victim of a black-white race riot; on the other hand he faces alienation and exclusion like Negroes from white clubs, restaurants, etc. He is doubly baffled when he discovers that both groups, black and white, hate him. Fiedler sees this type of anti–Semitism harbored by Negroes as a kind of "culture climbing," an "illegitimate" attempt to emulate WASP racist attitudes, in short, to join hands with WASPs—against Jews. But it proves to be a futile racist ideal; the WASPs are abandoning them. And Fiedler believes that "no Negro ever died for a Jewish cause ... but some of our boys have died for Negro rights" (TG, 171). And so, "Fiedler describes as unendurable what must assuredly seem unendurable to an intellectual" (Boyers 1999, 176).

In *To the Gentiles*, he pitches his discourse on an affirmative note. The only hope of a resolution of this Negro-Jew problem is offered by young boys and girls. When young Jewish girls go arm in arm with Negro boys, Fiedler believes, "Our daughters will save us, love will save us" (TG, 173). "Sexual taboo" once broken solves all problems, and according to Fiedler, a new mythology is at work. This new myth contains within it a very old myth of a Jewish daughter Hadassah dancing naked for the Jews' salvation before the Gentile kind. Here Fiedler is implying that the new generation will break all taboos and prejudices by removing all barriers of color, race and caste. Hence, Fiedler offers this new solution to the Negro-Jew problem, moving from the racial level to the mythological level. In the introduction Fiedler writes, "These essays move into the tenderest and most difficult area in which American Jewish literature and American Jewish culture are presently involved" (TG, 4), that of relationship between the Jews and the blacks in the United States. These speculations had begun in the essays discussed earlier, "Negro and Jew— Encounter in America," and "Negro and Jew." Fiedler opines, "Taken together these two essays constitute ... a last word on these matters. I see on re-reading them, however, that they represent by no means a conclusive one. But to have anything more or less than inconclusive on this subject would have been not only misleading, but finally not even quite Jewish" (TG, 4). Discussing "Caliban or Hamlet: A Study in Literary Anthropology" with Maini in 1987, Fiedler suggests that the Negro is the real authentic voice of America. In one of his earlier essays, Maini notes Fiedler's suggestion that in America, the voice of the black person represents at once a social meaning and a psychological meaning (1976, 10). According to him, suppressed society speaks of what is repressed in the minds of the oppressors. "The blacks in America speak also for the white. The dark colour has an underclass status" (Maini 1976, 10). And the final irony is stated by Fiedler in *Waiting for the End*: that the young European is trying to become an imaginary American, the American is becoming an imaginary Jew, and the Jew is in the process of becoming an imaginary Negro. Offering this new solution to the Negro-Jew conflict in these essays, Fiedler has proved himself to be a liberal-minded Jew. He has probed the problem from all angles, though the basis has been mythology. Talking to Lakshmi Kannan in 1975, Fiedler in a way clarifies his position. He says that an ethnic writer, like a Jew, tries to present his own group in the best possible light. But there comes a stage when he is no longer addressing his own group, but is merely writing out of his own deep, personal experience. And then he realizes that depicted deeply and sensitively, any situation can become symbolically relevant to everybody. That is to say, it can be converted into myth.

Last Words

Though there never can be a last word, would anyone contend that circumstances have changed for the better in the many years since Fiedler wrote his essay "Negro and Jew?" That they have been changed no one will deny. Some blacks are a good deal better off than they were forty years ago. Many others, by far a greater number, live in circumstances far worse than most white Americans thought possible in the 1950s and '60s. No doubt, too, some American Jews continue to be engaged with black people in efforts to rebuild the black community.

The Jews never really being the spokespersons of anyone, particularly the blacks, Boyers also points out that "quite as Fiedler's essay would seem to have predicted, American Jews do not much speak to black people. Their interests seem less and less to coincide, and they do not much think it worth their while to struggle with one together, to hear one another out and to try to get past their troubling resentments, guilts and inhibitions." The larger purpose staked out by Fiedler's essay "Negro and Jew," however "complicated and tendentious, speculative and occasionally wrong-headed, compassionate and provoking, has much to tell us not only about his characteristic ways of getting inside an issue, but about enduring features of American culture" (Boyers 1999, 176–77).

His interest in the political cause of the Ibo struggle to break away from Nigeria in the late 1960s is a reflection of the unique bonding that Fiedler had with Americans of African descent since his childhood. In literature, he found that most of the best of it was produced by members of the Ibo tribe—foremost among them, of course, being Chinua Achebe, whom Fiedler repeatedly nominated for the Nobel Prize. (Although his masterpiece *Things Fall Apart* is regarded by critics as the best novel written in Anglophone African, Achebe has never gotten the call from Stockholm.) Fiedler had come to regard the Ibos as the "Jews of Africa" (Winchell 2002, 251–53).

His claim to have acquired his platform style from black street preachers was confirmed by Houston Baker and Henry Louis Gates, who jokingly accused him of being the academic equivalent of Elvis Presley—a white man who stole the black man's act.

During his long tenure at Buffalo, he formed particularly warm friendships with two gifted black writers—Samuel P. Delaney and Ishmael Reed. Winchell recalls in his interview with Fiedler in Feb. 1999 that Delaney is one of small number of experimental writers who have combined science fiction and postmodernism. Reed is a Buffalo native, whose work reflects the full range of black experience, not just racial protest. Drawing on folklore, fantasy, parody, myth, and popular culture as well as the conventions of serious literature, he is more often compared to avant-grade writers such as William Gass, Thomas Pynchon and Donald Barthelme than to Richard Wright and James Baldwin. At various times, Leslie was instrumental in persuading both Delaney and Reed to take teaching positions at Buffalo.

Even in 2003, Fiedler believed that the black situation in America had changed (Bauman 2003, 10). His belief is that blacks today finally realize themselves as Americans. When asked about Baldwin, he replied that Baldwin was a good friend and that he liked his "early fiction and essays. One of the things he wrote frankly about, which I wanted to write about—I never got around to it—are the blacks that I think of as 'black Jews,' whose first work was published by Partisan Review, Commentary" (10). Though it is difficult to assess the depth of Fiedler's awareness with respect to the realities of blacks in America, it can be easily inferred that Fiedler has exercised great caution to be objective and has been well guarded in his opinions on the blacks.

The Jews, the Blacks, the Gentiles and Europe

Thus, on American soil the Jew faces the Negro and both face the Gentile. This trio has another important relationship with their parent figure "Europe." Total assimilation for the Jews becomes impossible in America, because his roots are in Europe. He is not able to break totally his umbilical cord, hence he feels a stranger on the American soil. Referring to the Negro and the Jew, Fiedler says, "We are ... outsiders with a difference" (NT, 236). The difference is that for the Negro, America is the gateway to Europe. The Jew, conversely, is the gateway to Europe for America. Jewish history, two thousand years old, is "purely European." A Jew always implies a European, not really an American. Fiedler says that as alien as the Jew might be, he is an alien with a rich culture. The few outbursts of violence against the Jews in America can be understood as "hangovers" from the European experiences from which all have fled, which consist of remnants of debased religion and ancient terror that none have forgotten. Fiedler establishes Europe as the tie between all of them, a tie that can not be broken.

Fiedler writes that just as the Jews have haunted the minds of Europe for two thousand years, so have the Negroes haunted the minds of America for two hundred years. Just as the Negroes live in America with ties of mutual animosity, so are the Jews tied to Europe with ties of mutual hatred. Fiedler emphatically says that if the West tries to oust the Jews, it will do so on the altar of spiritual self-castration that is denying its own Jewishness. For "the Jew is the Father of Europe ... the Negro only an adopted child. If Christendom denies us, it diminishes itself; but if we reject the west, we reject not our legend, only a historical interpretation of it" (NT, 237).

In *Waiting for the End* Fiedler talks of Europe as a retreating horizon of the West, "a place difficult to remain," the place of a "dream" from which we wake in pleasure or terror. Alternatively, it is viewed as an object of "romantic flirtation" where the return is to "marriage or loneliness." Most typically, Europe is represented as a "woman we cannot hold: a saint to be worshipped from afar, or a whore to be longed for and left" (WFTE, 25). In the essay "Jewish-Americans Go Home," Fiedler writes, "No American, not even a Jew in pursuit of Utopian Americanism, can escape European culture completely" (WFTE, 105). Hence, it is the ties with Europe, to a certain extent, that do not let the Jews achieve total assimilation in America. But this is only partly true, because recently in America there is a strong assertion of their American identity, which implies an anti–Europe bias, and a large segment of Jews are propagating it.

What hampers the urge toward assimilation in the Jews and makes them strangers in America is their religion. In "Negro and Jew—Encounter in America," Fiedler writes, "Historically the Jew has been rejected on two grounds, for his religion and for his race" (NT, 241). In recent years, in America there is a "decay of piety" and an increase in "interfaith good will," and both these have rendered the religious aspect irrelevant. Yet it is only partly true, because, for Jews, religion is their strength and weakness as well. Examining the situation mythologically, Fiedler notes the reactions evoked in the Negroes. He says that the main ground for animosity in blacks for the Jews is religion. Being Christian fundamentalist evangelical Protestant, the Negro inherits a simple anti–Jewish mythology; "our" Christ was killed by the myth of Simon the Pyrenean—the kindly Negro by the wayside, who helped Jesus bear his cross as Jews hooted for his blood. As Muslims, they identify with the Arab-African anti–Jewish political mythology that considers the Jew in America more wicked than all the "other" others who came to America. Fiedler emotionally works up his defense and says that both Christianity and Islam are "offshoots of a more punitive Judaism, subject to ... sibling rivalry" (TG, 167). The Jew is accidentally caught between the Christian Negro, for whom he is not (spiritually) white enough, and the Muslim Negro, for whom he is not (mythologically) black enough—not far enough from the white man's God. Fiedler says that no Christian without calling Jehovah a devil can think of Jews as totally "satanic; recalcitrant or rejected." Fiedler puts it aptly: "No good Protestant American can hate the Jew without a sneaking suspicion that he is hating God"

(NT, 240). E. H. L. Masilamoni writes that the Jew is different from all other immigrants in America because he is a "person with a particular religion" (1979, 48). It is true that most of the Jews who came to America came in flight from Europe, but they could never totally discard their religion. The religion practiced by the Jews in America is called reformed Judaism by Fiedler. This enables the Jews to adopt themselves most easily to American customs and habits. On the other hand, religion also becomes an anchor for the Jews that binds them to Europe, preventing them from total integration in America.

"The Jew in the American Novel" (1959)

After two full-length discussions on the Negro and the Jew, Fiedler published a long essay, "The Jew in the American Novel," which forms the core of his anthology *To the Gentiles*. This essay is an exhaustive (Fiedler claims it is not) study of the drama of Jewish cultural life in America. It highlights the scope and shape of the Jewish-American tradition in fiction in a way useful to the Gentile and the Jewish reader and writer alike, not merely as history but as a source of pleasure and self knowledge. This essay is divided into three parts: Zion as Eros, Zion as Armageddon and Zion as Main Street. According to Wallenstein, this essay focuses on one of the "apparent preoccupations or themes" that "unify and serve as guides" (1972, 590) to the large body of Fiedler's writings.

In this significant essay, Fiedler writes that early Jewish writings have a "symptomatic historical importance," for they act as "surrogates" for the whole Jewish-American community in its "quest for an identity." Their writings are an "act of assimilation: a demonstration that there is an American Jew (whose Jewishness and Americanism enrich each other) and that he feels at home" (TG, 66). The existing images of Jews were created by writers who were Gentiles or anti–Semites, "interested in resisting their assimilations impulse and keeping the Jews, Jews." It is Robert Cohn, Hemingway's image of the Jew that survives the twenties, "an outsider still, even among outsiders, and in a self-imposed exile" (TG, 66). But, by and large, long before the Jews came to America, the Jewish character was frozen into the anti–Jewish stereotype such as the archetypal characters of Shylock and Jessica. It became a difficult task for Jewish writers to create their protagonists not only out of the life in which they grew up, but against the literature and language that they learned and read. The Jewish writers in America had to assimilate a traditional vocabulary of images and symbols, changing and adopting whenever required, to create a compelling counter-image of the Jew, which had to be authentically American.

Fiedler points out that Jews were not only businessmen and workers, officials and lawyers, psychoanalysts and theatre-owners, but also actors, singers, musicians, composers of popular songs, writers—all domains of popular culture. What is of significance is that on this platform the Jew speaks, says Fiedler, neither as a Jew becoming an American nor as an American who was a Jew; he communicates in the nonlanguage of anticulture, becoming his own stereotype. The triumph of the Jews in the world of mass culture was the creation of the Jewish-American novel created by the Jewish-American writer. The four pioneers in this field, according to Fiedler, are Sidney Luska, Abraham Cahan, Ludwig Lewisohn and Ben Hecht. All of them were writing books that were Jewish in theme and point of view, and dealt with the Jewish problem of identity and assimilation.

It is only since the thirties that patterns of Jewish speech, experiences of Jewish childhood and adolescence, the smells and tastes of the Jewish kitchen, and the sounds of the Jewish synagogue have become staple features of the American novel and popular culture.

In the late forties and then in the fifties we discover that Fiedler was concerned with how the Jews confront America and the Negro. Fiedler's essays reflect the racial and mythological concerns that have been discussed at length already. In *Waiting for the End*, in a very important essay "Zion as Main Street," Fiedler traces and highlights the success of the Jews on all fronts. In the realm of prose in America, several leading writers are and have been Jews. In *Waiting for the End*, Fiedler surveys the American literary scene from Hemingway to Baldwin. The essays that I am evaluating for this chapter from this collection of critical commentaries—"Zion as Main Street," "Jewish-Americans, Go Home!," "Indian or Injun?" and "The Jig Is Up!"—deal with various problems of Jewish identity, problem of integration and also their intellectual rise in American letters. Ronald Berman says, "We began with a culture in which the Jew was an outsider.... We have now a culture in which the alienated Jewish Intellectual Novel is as much a genre as are the ode and the epic" (Berman 1965, 172). Fiedler also says that the autobiographies of the urban Jews are almost a part of the "mystical life" of America and that they are the ones projecting "most viable images of an American." But Fiedler bemoans the fact that at the moment of great prosperity, the awareness of the Jew—as a Jew— is reaching a vanishing point. In "Jewish-Americans, Go Home!" he says that the popular acceptance of the Jews' alienation has become an affectation, almost a fashionable cliché. Ronald Berman with subdued mockery writes, "Jewishness is now many things ... a sign of suffering, virtue, and estrangement; a sign of superior sensibility; a commodity. It is not as good as being a Negro, but it sells books" (1965, 172). Fiedler points out in "Zion as Main Street" that the long dominance of the Western and the detective story is challenged

3. Integration of the "Other"

by a largely Jewish product, science fiction, which has become the literature of busy males—politicians and executives. As Fiedler also says, "The universe of science fiction is Jewish; the wise old traitor, the absurd but sympathetic Yiddish momma, plus a dozen other Jewish stereotypes" (WFTE, 76). For those who do not read books or comics, Fiedler says that Jewish culture lies in wait, in the gift shop, the saloon, and the supermarket—a cultural fact that no American can deny. The favorite wine in Missoula, Montana (which does not have even a dozen Jewish families), is Mogen David; and for years "Nebbishes" have stared out of the windows of local gift shops, from greeting cards, ash trays, beer mugs and pen stands. Fiedler points out all these facts only to emphasize the wide popularity of the Jewish culture in America. Hence, Fiedler stages, "The 'sick' joke and the 'hate' card, however, represent the entry into our popular culture not only of certain formerly exclusively properties of the avant-garde (the mockery of bourgeois pieties, a touch of psychoanalysis) but also of Jewish humor at its most desperate.... As a matter of fact, the Jew enters American culture 'on the stage, laughing'" (WFTE, 75). The reason for the Judaization of American culture is the resurgence of "intergroup understanding" and " a wave of tolerance" among the Americans. Secondly, the Jew no longer occupy the number one slot of the "insulted and injured."

That there has been some sort of evolution in Fiedler's writings on this theme—the Jewish problem of identity and assimilation—is, by and large, true. Of course a number of his statements are provocative and yet stimulating. They highlight Fiedler's deftness at dealing with the ethnic, racial and typological underlay of American life.

Fiedler believed that it is the task of the Jews to define themselves and their Jewishness. This thought was put forth in a short essay in 1966, "This Year We Are Slaves—Next Year We Shall Be Free." In this essay Fiedler says, "Who the Jews are, to speculate about what the Jews will become, (or alternatively) what will become of the Jews, to remember what the Jews were—surely these have always been the obsessive task of those who by that very token we have continued to call Jews" (141).

Fiedler, the Jew, defines his fellow Jews in the essay "Master of Dreams: The Jew in the Gentile World." Fiedler hails the Jew as a seller of dreams all over the world. He takes his cue from the description of Joseph's dream in the Book of Genesis in which Joseph dreams of an archetypal account of the success of a Jew, hailed first by the Gentiles and as a consequence by his "hostile brethren," that is, the Jews. Fiedler comments that it is the beginning of a myth whose ending we all know, the opening of a large dream that a whole community has dreamed waking and aloud for nearly three thousand years. But it is "unique among communal dreams," for it is the "dream of the dreamer, a myth of myth itself" (TG, 175). Robert Alter in "Jewish Dreams and Nightmares," highly critical of this essay, sums it up as a "single grand mythic plot" that underscores "all Jewish literature" and "all Jewish cultural activity" as well (60). In this plot, according to Alter, Fiedler sees the Jew's "Characteristic cultural role as a vendor of dreams and an interpreter of dream to the world, that is, as poet and therapist" (60). Apart from Joseph's dream, Fiedler derived his cue for this essay from a chance phrase that for a few pennies one can buy any dream "from the Jews" (Alter, 60). This phrase made Fiedler realize that "dream pedlary is Jewish business" (TG, 176). Obviously the relationship of this essay with the "stranger" theme is of importance. Here Fiedler is trying to say that the alienated Jew is "dreaming aloud the dreams of the whole American people" (TG, 192). He concludes by saying that the Jewish dreamer in exile ends up "deciphering the alien dream of that world as well" (TG, 192). By this deciphering of dreams, the Jew ends up even predicting the future, according to Fiedler. Writers such as Nathaniel West and Norman Mailer, Franz Kafka and Sigmund Freud, who is referred to as "master of dreams" and "solver of dreams" by Fiedler, shaped Jewish-American writing in the early twentieth century.

Alter further examines Fiedler's views and points out, "The Jewish folk is imagined as possessing a kind of monopoly on vividness, compassion, humor, pathos, and the like; Jewish critics and novelists are thought to be unique in their preoccupation with questions of morality; and now we are asked to believe that the Jews have all along exercised a privileged control over the cultural market on dreams" (63). Alter calls Fiedler's interpretations "quaint" (this is the first time that a critic has attributed this adjective to Fiedler's criticism) and a "tacit conspiracy" to foist on the public these commonly admired characteristics as Jewish traits. Alter puts it bluntly when he says that Fiedler's criticism has a "paradoxical doubleness of effect" and his favorite critical activity is a "relentless pursuit of archetypes, an ill-considered literary fashion of the fifties" and that there is "an odd hint of datedness in what he writes, despite the swinging up-to-the-minute prose he affects" (61). Alter further claims that what Fiedler has all along been describing is "not a distinctively Jewish imaginative mode but the central tradition of the novel, from *Don Quixote* to *Lolita*" (63). What is most interesting about the essay by Alter is not that it is an attack on Fiedler and his fellow Jews, but that the main charge leveled against Fiedler is that he is a conservative, pompous Jew.

"Master of Dreams: The Jew in the Gentile World" (1967) is quite subjective. Malin has called the Jewish writer's art "parochial." Applied to Fiedler and this essay, it could be partly true. Though the Jews came late to America, Jewish writers have interpreted American experience as no one else did. My attempt is to highlight another facet of this "stranger's" personality. Are they still strangers, outsiders, alienated? Fiedler has tried to answer this perplexing question on a number of occasions, but his answers have never been consistent. At one time he says that the Jews are almost assimilated, and on another he comes up with such statements as this, in which he points out that "total assimilation is difficult in America for Negroes and Jews." Talking to Kannan in 1975, Fiedler felt that there were still some anti–Semitic feelings in the black proletariat and the working class. In 1976, in a conversation with Masilamoni, Fiedler said with respect to the Jews:

> Alienation would be too strong a word.... I think I feel in a way as most Jews do, that though my destiny is an American destiny, it is a special American destiny.... So, as it's often been said, there's no problem in feeling alienated in America, since almost all Americans feel alienated. I mean all of us are relative newcomers here. Some have been around for three hundred years, others for two hundred or one hundred [1979, 44–45].

This way, Fiedler tries to give a universal meaning to the problem of alienation. In the essay "Jewish Americans, Go Home," he writes, "In their very alienation the Jews were always mythically twentieth-century Americans" (Malin 1965, 175). Malin suggests that the Jewish writer began with tensions and never found relief, and his "peculiar tensions alienate him from the larger community (175). Exile is also a crucial moment for the Jews. In it the Jew "recognizes his alienation from the Promised Land," and remains an "outsider." In "Indian or Injun?" from *Waiting for the End,* Fiedler defines the Jew:

> Mythically speaking, the Jew is neither redskin nor paleface, neither black nor white.... The Jew represents to the American imagination an interloper, an alien who was never on the raft, either as Jim or Huck, nor in that primeval forest, either as Natty Bumppo or Chingachgook, and in whom other Americans therefore find an image not of their belonging in their own land, but of their alienation from their parents and their past [115].

Winchell's consideration of the section "To the Gentiles" in *Collected Essays,* volume 2, is that Fiedler has dealt with chiefly Jewish writers who "abandon the traditional tongues of their people, holy or secular, to address the Gentile world in the language of the Gentiles" (CE 2, xi). So, appropriately, this section of the *Collected Essays* is called "To the Gentiles" (233). The very fact that Fiedler wanted to preserve this testimony to the Gentiles suggests that Leib Resenstratuch's grandson could not easily forget from whence he came (233–34).

In his commentary on "Master of Dreams..." Winchell makes a couple of observations: At the outset Winchell focuses on the introduction to "To the Gentiles," in which Fiedler says of "Master of Dreams: The Jew in Gentile world" that here "I have come as near as I suspect I ever shall to a final mythical definition of the situation which defines me as well as many of the writers whom I most love" (3). Beginning with the biblical story of Joseph, this essay argues, the primary archetypal role the Jew has imagined for himself in a predominantly non–Jewish culture has been that of the dream master. The point is made explicitly in the sixth satire of that goyish poet Juvenal, where in the midst of an inventory of all the tempting goods on sale in Rome he tells us that "'for a few pennies' one can buy any dream his heart desires; from the Jews" (176). Because Joseph experienced both persecution and success as a result of his dreams (and his ability to interpret the dreams of others), his story is broad enough to explain the peculiar position that Jews have traditionally occupied in the Western, Gentile world.

In the second observation, Winchell discusses the "strategic qualification" that Fiedler makes by making the Jew "a dream master." The third is more revelatory. According to him, this qualification appears to be "more often a Jewish self-perception than a Gentile stereotype." He explains, "When the gentile dreams the Jew in his midst ... he dreams him as the vengeful and villainous Father: Shylock or Fagin, the Bearded Terror threatening some poor full-grown *goy* with a knife, or inducting some guileless Gentile kid into a life of crime." This is because "Shylock and Fagin are shadows cast upon the Christian world by the First Jewish Father, Abraham, who is to them circumciser and sacrifice rolled into one—castrator, in short" (177). The Jewish imagination, however, always sees Abraham releasing his son before the moment of intended sacrifice. In turn, that son, Isaac, becomes the father of Jacob, who is the father of Joseph. Although Joseph himself had offspring, he lives in the mythic memory not as another father, but as the favorite son who makes good and thus provides salvation for both the Gentiles and his own family. That this schematic description can also be applied to Jesus—who for Christians is the salvific favored son of God—suggests why the biblical Joseph is so important to the Jewish imagination and why he is a luxury that the Gentile mind—insofar as it is shaped by Christian myth—cannot afford. Then Winchell makes his fourth point: that although Fiedler claims that this archetypal formulation holds up for the entire history of Jewish-Gentile relations, he is chiefly concerned with the literary Jew in the modern world (Winchell 2002, 235). This way Winchell foregrounds Fiedler's sound literary turf.

The Stranger in Shakespeare (1972)

To substantiate this, in *The Stranger in Shakespeare* (1972), Fiedler treats Shakespeare's psyche by way of his most uneasy characters, his "strangers," the outsiders and aliens in his plays. This book is an outcome of a promise Fiedler had made to his audience in 1948, to treat all four essential myths in detail, mentioned in his lecture "Shakespeare and the Paradox of Illusion." The purpose is elaborated thus: "to bind my past to my present and to refresh my soul by immersing myself for a little while in a stream of living words and images" (TSS, 9). This book is a culmination of his views on the Jew as stranger, in the essay chosen for this study, "The Jew as Stranger."

Here, he deals with the "stranger" in Shakespeare's plays. This preoccupation with "aliens" has a symbolic significance in his writings. He defines the stranger as an "archetypal figure" who appears sometimes as a villain and sometimes as a clown. I have taken up one essay from this book that is relevant to this study. "The Jew as Stranger" deals with *The Merchant of Venice* and "Shylock" as a stranger. In it Fiedler writes, "The play has captured our imagination, but Shylock has captured the play, turning, in the course of that conquest, from grotesque to pathetic, from utter alien to one of us." He calls the Jew "an archetype of great antiquity and power, a nightmare of the whole Christian community, given a local habitation and a name by Shakespeare, so apt it is hard to believe that he has not always been called Shylock" (97). According to Fiedler the Jew embodies certain "stereotypes and myths, impulses and attitudes, images and metaphors," and what is needed is "to descend to the level of what is most archaic in our living selves and there confront the living Shylock" (TSS, 99). Fiedler sketches the deep-rooted anti–Semitism prevalent in the society that Shakespeare portrays in his plays. He goes a step further and says that the Jew was also felt as a menace to something deeper in the American psyche, even more than the priority of land over money; a threat to manhood itself. But Fiedler requires more explanation for this assumption.

Jay L. Halio, in his article "The Akedah (the Binding of Isaac) in Shakespeare's *Merchant of Venice*," states that this book shows, "above all, that Fiedler is no stranger to Shakespeare" (1999, 81). But he bemoans the neglect that this book has received from the "professional Shakespeareans, many of whom approach Shakespeare's work these days with various agendas, often taking a polemical, not to say anti literary, approach" (81). According to Halio, Fiedler's claims in this book, particularly on *The Merchant of Venice*, are staked out from the position of an "an observant Jew" (81). What he means by it he does not explain, but having gone through Winchell's study of Fiedler's life, one can safely say that Fiedler was and will remain a Jew at heart even though he did not attend regular prayer sessions or Jewish meetings.

In his discussion of *The Merchant of Venice* we find that Shylock, one of Shakespeare's archetypal "strangers," emerges as the leading figure in the play, notwithstanding the fact that its title actually refers to Antonio. In Fiedler's chronology, Shylock follows Joan la Pucelle in *Henry VI, Part I*, and anticipates Othello and, finally, Caliban in *The Tempest* as the principal embodiments of the stranger in Shakespeare.

Halio homes in on one aspect of *The Merchant of Venice* that Fiedler has only touched on but that deserves more attention. It is a subject that most commentators have neglected, although it lies at the heart of the play's most dramatic episode, the so-called Trial Scene in act 4. Like the Moor, the Jew as stranger has been well documented, and Fiedler shows the ways in which Shylock's alien qualities are important in Shakespeare's play. He also shows how, in the view of many in Shakespeare's time, Jews represented a menace to all (Halio 1999, 81). This myth did not die with the Renaissance. As Fiedler reminds us, it persisted in the twentieth century too in the Beilis case in Czarist Russia, in the Nazi exterminations and the calumnies of stretcher, and so on (SS, 124). Halio draws our attention to the reference to the cannibalistic implications of several of Shylock's speeches with regard to Antonio and the revenge the Jew seeks against his Christian oppressor (Halio 1999, 82).

If I have departed in some measure from the present to bring to you these vital debates that Fiedler created more than four decades ago, it is with the intention of putting things in perspective. The question of whether or not the Jews feel assimilated in America today is not of much consequence. After the advent of Albee and his theatre of self-alienation (*Who's Afraid of Virginia Woolf*), not much remains to be said. But Fiedler's writings and articulations need to be understood within the larger debates related to assimilation of the Jews in America, then. His early writings on this subject posed questions of adjustment and acceptance and other conflicts with Negroes and Gentiles. His later writings depict the rise of the Jewish intellectual on the American scene, the Jew heralding the advent of popular culture, and his assimilation. However, as Wallenstein points out, Fiedler in his later writings shifted his focus because the audience that he wanted was the young, and the young "no longer find in the Jewish experience viable images of their own character and fate" (1972, 592–93). An example of this was well brought out by Daniel Walden when in 1985, he asked him to comment on the current state of American-Jewish literature. Fiedler stated: "I was there at the beginning and now I'm seeing the end of it. American Jewish literature is finished" (Walden 1999, 160).

It is true that Fiedler had been making such predictions about the end of the novel in his earlier works such as *Waiting for the End*. In the essay "The Death and Rebirth of the Novel," a serious comment on American-Jewish literature was aired for the first time. Walden challenged him to defend his position at the next MLA convention, to which Fiedler readily agreed. Walden writes,

> The Grand Ballroom was packed, close to thousand people were there to see Fiedler and to hear him engage in a discussion on the subject of the end of the American Jewish novel with Bonnie Lyons, Les Field, Keith Opdahl, and Daniel Walden. However, about ten days before, Fiedler called me and declared that he

wouldn't be able to make it; he said he was ill. I called Cynthia Ozick, in a panic, explained the situation and asked her if she'd appear in Fiedler's place.... Cynthia Ozick was there, and took part in a lively discussion, was proof—argued again and again by all of us so passionately devoted to the appreciation of the genre—that the American Jewish novel was alive and well, but changing, even as each of the many genres in the canon and coming into the canon were [1999, 160–61].

The point proven by such a description perhaps is that Fiedler's statements are often churlish. His absence is testimony to the fact that his articulations cannot be taken seriously on all occasions. But it makes an additional point, too: that had Fiedler been present to defend his case, academia would have heard a new set of his refreshing arguments.

Sanford Pinsker recalls a "dream turned nightmare experience" (Kellman and Malin 1999, 186) which, in his opinion, was the kind of experience that "Fiedler had made his specialty" (186) to stress that Fiedler felt a sense of ownership and authorship for the domain of Jewish studies. When Pinsker tried to enter that arena, he dreamed of being told by Fiedler to "screw off." That territory's mine" (Pinsker 1999, 186).[3] Pinsker explains how much Fiedler mattered to him and just how he, the young would-be academic, "hung on his every word" (186). Pinsker goes on to say,

> He provided measures of aid-and-comfort not easily found in other corners of the academy. Not surprisingly, it was his reflections on Jewish-American literature that most intrigued me, not only because the much-celebrated Jewish-American renaissance was in high gear during the mid-sixties, but also because I was then pecking away on a dissertation about Sholem Aleichem, I. B. Singer, Bernard Malamud, and Saul Bellow. To be sure, there were other critical voices in my head—Alfred Kazin, Irvin Howe, Robert Alter, Ted Solotaroff—but Fiedler's mattered most [183].

It was then Pinsker remembers dreaming of getting this phone call from Fiedler in the middle of the night. Fiedler wanted to know if Pinsker was writing a dissertation on the Schlemiel. Getting the answer in the affirmative, he delivered the brusque line quoted above. Such was Fiedler's allegiance and sense of ownership for the subject. He helped to make Jewish-American literature a worthy subject of study, and inversely, "transformed Jewishness into the literary critic's culture asset" (Rubenstein 2003, 160).

The Two Jews: Fiedler and Trilling

No discussion of Fiedler as a Jew in particular is complete without a comparison with Trilling, the author of *The Liberal Imagination*. Walden gives an astute reading of the two men of letters:

> Fiedler has always been the pugnacious ex-pugilist-cum-intellectual Jew who served his time in Missoula, Montana, before making it in the big time in Buffalo. Trilling was never known as an American Jewish critic; at most he dipped his little toe gingerly in the water [Daniel Walden in Kellman and Malin 1999, 163].

Further, Fiedler's engagement with the Jewish intellectual was intense though "tempered by interminable disquisitions" (163). After pointing out in *Waiting for the End* (1964) that not until the emergence of the Jewish novelists of the fifties and sixties were the literary stereotypes of the Jews created by the twenties and preceding generations dispelled, he explained, "The very notion of a Jewish American literature represents a dream of assimilation, and the process it envisages is bound to move toward a triumph (in terms of personal success) which is also a defeat (in terms of a meaningful Jewish survival)" (WFTE, 70, quoted by Walden, in Kellman and Malin 1999, 163).

His point was that Jewish-American writers, writing the comedy of Jewish dissolution in the midst of prosperity (instead of writing about the persistence in the midst of persecution) were telling the truth "about a world which neither they nor their forerunners considered themselves guiltless of desiring" (Dembo 1973, 146).[4]

Trilling felt he had to accommodate himself to the prevailing mores; after all, it was only a few years before, in 1906, that Ludwig Lewisohn, on the brink of a Ph.D. in English, was told not to go forward, that Jews would never be hired in a major American university. Fiedler, on the other hand, a few decades later, continued to write "from a Jewish point of view, as a Jew," though he was honest enough to admit he had "abandoned all the traditional religion, almost completely lost the traditional culture and no longer [spoke] the languages traditionally associated with Jewishness" (WFTE, 70). Doesn't he say, "I am consequently ... a Jew only in retrospect, in memory; a memory that persists not in my heart or in my head but in my blood" (FR, xv).

Fiedler refused assimilation, whereas Trilling was the "Jewish New Yorker who refuses to leave that city, an exploiter of the themes of anguish and alienation, a naturalist searching for tragedy. But in him the ordinarily annoying pose is mitigated by a soft-spoken style which is modesty itself and combined with the stance of a nineteenth-century English gentleman-dissenter to produce a version of the *PR* writer as a belated Matthew Arnold" (FR, 254, quoted by Walden in Kellman and Malin 1999, 164).

Two more different personality types could hardly be imagined—Trilling, famous (or perhaps infamous) for his Anglophilism and high-minded cultural pronouncements; Fiedler, rambunctious, free-wheeling, every inch the rebel. Nonetheless, Trilling's self-doubt remained a considerable part of his private life (see Diana Trilling's *The Beginning of the Journey*), partly because Trilling was a very different person away from the lectern or writing desk. Fiedler, by contrast, always wore his self-assurance easily. What you saw was what you got—and this merely increased as the years added girth to his middle and gray to his hair and beard. Indeed, the young critic who often seemed to specialize in unpacking outrageous sexual myths came more to look like a satyr from some classic text (Pinsker 1999, 183–84).

The point of accentuating the difference between Fiedler and Trilling is that Trilling is one among many of his fellow Jewish travelers on the intellectual road with whom Fiedler did not walk a step. With some he lost pace (Saul Bellow) while with others he missed the step (Norman Mailer).

Fiedler on the Roof: Essays on Literature and Jewish Identity (1991)

Any discussion of the twin themes of the "other" and "Jewishness" has to take into account his interest in Leopold Bloom, as seen in the two Joyce essays—"Bloom or Joyce, or *Jokey for Jacob*" (1976), and "Joyce and the Jewish Consciousness" (1986). This interest also constitutes the centerpiece of one of his last few significant works, *Fiedler on the Roof* (1991). Originally given as talks in which one can hear the biblical rhythm, the prophetic, almost rabbinic strain in Fiedler's voice, they can also make a very fine concluding statement on Fiedler, the Jew. Schwartz finds that the enjoyment of being Leslie Fiedler is on every page of this book, "an indexless and characteristically idiosyncratic collection of previously published talks and essays that contain his insights, musing, and rants on Jewish subjects" (in Kellman and Malin 1999, 99). He further elaborates that Fiedler, who embraced the role of outsider, is using Joyce the exiled and Bloom the marginal Jew—who valiantly and unsuccessfully tries to cross-dress as a Gentile—to define himself. Thus, Fiedler identifies with Bloom: "I have assumed and am assuming at this moment the voice of Bloom because it is the voice of the eternal amateur, the self-appointed prophet, the Jew, the comic father; and that is a voice which I like to believe, for my own private reasons and some public ones too, is my own authentic voice" (FR, 31–32).

Fiedler's contributions to literary and Jewish studies are many through this book. Extending his critical arm to nudge the "canonical modernists," Fiedler is interested in Joyce because of them, Joyce alone has a place for Jews (xi). Schwartz also tells us that Fiedler compellingly argues that Bloom is Joyce's other self, the alternative to "the voice of Stephen Dedalus, Ph.D." (FR, 31, quoted by Schwartz in Kellman and Malin 1999, 103). According to him, the myth of Ulysses lives in the head of Christian Europe, but the myth of the

Jew, which is Bloom's better half, resides in the guts of Europe: a pain in the dark innards of the Gentile world, or better perhaps, an ache in the genitals, an ache in the loins of the Gentiles (FR, 39). Fiedler realizes that he writes as a Jew and thinks as a Jew, like Bloom—a Jew in spite of itself, not only because of his heritage but because his fellows think of him as a Jew, just as Joyce could not be anything else but an Irishman even in exile (Schwartz 1999, 102).

Schwartz feels that Fiedler is passionately drawn to *Ulysses*: "*Ulysses* was for my youth and has remained for my later years not a novel at all, but a conduct book, a guide to salvation through the mode of art, a kind of secular scripture" (FR, 33, Schwartz in Kellman and Malin 1999, 103). As Fiedler sees it, "Joyce had created in Bloom the archetypal modern Jew: not ghettoized Israelite or Hebrew, but emancipated, secularized yid: his knowledge of his own ancestral tradition approaching degree zero without diminishing his Jewish identity" (FR, 48). Fiedler finds in Bloom a character who was not "the property of an exclusive WASP critical establishment" (FR, xi).

For Fiedler, Bloom "turns out to be what can be adequately described only by another Yiddish word, a mensch; which is to say, a full male human being, as imagined by a tradition hostile to most of the qualities that the gentile world has thought of as being specifically macho" (FR, 50). Schwartz tells us that for Fiedler, "criticism is autobiography," and "books are what they mean to him." So his idiosyncratic perspective sees what "many critics, including Huge Kenner, fail to see, or are at any rate driven to deny, this 'womanly' mawkishness in Joyce, preferring to dwell on his anti-sentimental irony; but he tends to betray it whenever he enters Bloom's Jewish heart and head. Joyce himself seems to have grown ashamed of this weakness in himself after Ulysses, eschewing it completely in the goyish pages of *Finnegans Wake*, where for that reason among others, I prefer not to follow him" (FR, 51). It is as if Fiedler sees himself as the Jewish anti-self of the high Gentile priest of modernist studies, Hugh Kenner (Schwartz in Kellman and Malin 1999, 104).

Fiedler's outsider status is apparent as he deciphers the anti–Semitism in *Ulysses,* "the chief, almost the sole mode of relating to Jews available to the gentiles: and, indeed, it is only in response to it that Bloom can feel himself a Jew at all, since ritually and even ethnically he scarcely qualifies" (FR, 55).

Schwartz's contribution through this essay lies in the fact that he brings to the readers of Fiedler the realization that Fiedler, too, feels himself both a Jew in response to a Gentile world that defines him as Jew and a representative of his people to outsiders. At times, Fiedler writes as a Jew speaking to other Jews; at other times he writes as a stranger, an odd figure, like Bloom, among WASPs—academics and others. But Fiedler also acknowledges that he has benefited by being a chosen person: "I have, that is to say, profited from a philo–Semitism as undiscriminating as the anti–Semitism in reaction to which it originated. And to make matters worse, I have shamelessly played the role in which I have been cast, becoming a literary Fiedler on the roof of academe" (FR, 177; Schwartz 1999, 104).

In this process, Fiedler enacts the "ambiguity of Jews in English studies," as Schwartz puts it, who, on one hand, study a majority culture, accommodate to it, and are shaped by it, but on the other, arrogate that culture for their own understanding and professional ends. He admits, "We conquer it and make it our instrument, and we are in turn conquered by it and are made its voice, and spokespeople. At its best, the tension works in Fiedler—and us. Perhaps Fiedler and other Jewish academics are in part attracted to *Ulysses* because it enacts how Joyce, the Irishman, was in a similar position of both accommodating to and arrogating English and Western literature" (104).

This brings us to the "most brilliant" essay in *Fiedler on the Roof*, "Why Is the Grail Knight Jewish?" in which as per Schwartz's reading, Fiedler interprets the Grail as a metonym of the role he sees himself playing in academic life. Schwartz finds his analysis of the Grail legend characteristically mythopoeic. Fiedler sees himself as the keeper of the Grail, and for Fiedler, the Grail is the truth about books, Jews, and himself:

> I feel committed to an attempt to redream that Passover dream as if it were my own; or to put it somewhat less metaphorically, to try to relocate the myth that exists before, after, outside all of the Christian texts that pretend to embody it, by demonstrating the sense in which it is a Jewish myth. Or perhaps I mean rather a myth about Jews: a reflection of the plight of my own people at a particular historical moment—recorded first by one who may have been a Jew converted to Christianity, and then revised by a score of gentiles, some more, some less aware of what in mythological terms they were doing [FR, 86].

Schwartz suggests that Bloom, too, recuperates the Passover story in the terms Fiedler describes. He asks, "Does Fiedler not truly and commendably understand that the truth one tries to tell about books is the truth one tells of oneself?" Although Fiedler has been regarded as a kind of a mythopoetic interdisciplinary rebel, fusing sociology, anthropology, and myth criticism, interestingly, Schwartz discovers "an old-fashioned humanist who believes books are written by humans for humans and about humans" in such pronouncements of Fiedler. Ignoring any sort of theoretical revolution, what he said in the 1960 preface to *Love and Death in the American Novel* then makes sense today: "The best criticism can hope to do is to set the work in as many illuminating contexts as possible: the context of the genre to which it belongs, of the whole body of work of its author, of the life of that author and of his times" (LD, quoted in Schwartz 1999, 109).

Fiedler on the Roof can be read as Fiedler "giving back" a gift to his grandfather who "remembered." "Not that I believe, but so you should remember."

This is what Leon Rosenstrauch, Fiedler's grandfather, would say as he took his grandson to some storefront synagogue on many a Jewish high holy day (Winchell 2002, 6). The Jewish self that has emerged in his later years, revealing a man not unlike a Bloom counterpart and alter ego, is Leslie Fiedler, Ph.D., who writes, "I feel obliged to wrestle with the question of why the threat of annihilation and the promise of redemption have continued to be the pattern of our history" (FR, 162). So in compliance with Schwartz's statement that Fiedler "blithely ignores prior scholarship on Joyce" (109) to make his own point, in this process he "is and remains an original voice" (109).

Forays into the Non-literary—*Freaks: Myths and Images of the Secret Self* (1978) and *Tyranny of the Normal* (1993)

This leads us to Fiedler's changing priorities: in *Freaks: Myths and Images of the Secret Self* (1978) he moves away from Jewishness though he is not yet done with his concern with outsiders. *Freaks: Myths and Images of the Secret Self* is an extension of Fiedler's concern with the "other" taken up in his earlier works. Here, he confronts not society's but nature's outsiders. The book is a natural history of dwarfs, giants, hermaphrodites, Siamese twins, mutants, the monstrously fat, the grotesquely thin, dog-faced boys and zoophagous geeks. Bruce Bauman calls this "'crossover success,' a survey of the figure of the misshapen person as it has appeared linguistically, psychologically and sexually in human culture from the earliest cave paintings through film and comic books" (2003, 1). Fiedler writes:

> The true Freak, however, stirs both supernatural terror and natural sympathy, since, unlike the fabulous monsters, he is one of us, the human child of human parents, however altered by forces we don't quite understand into something mythic and mysterious as no other cripple ever is.... Only the true Freak challenges the conventional boundaries between male and female, sexed and sexless, animal and human, large and small, self and other, and consequently between reality and illusion, experience and fantasy, fact and myth [*Freaks*, 95].

Fiedler's attempt through *Freaks: Myths and Images of the Secret Self* is to expose to the normal beings the fears and distortions of their own souls. He insists that such revelations are psychological necessities. Relatedly, he points out that men have needed to believe in monsters, and when they could not discover them in nature, they created them for themselves in words and pictures. Hence painters painted them, kings and queens played with them and writers wrote stories about them. Yet, says Fiedler, still today the need for freakishness is unending. It lives in the mutants of literature—Dracula,

Frankenstein's monster, Gunter Grass's dwarf in *The Tin Drum*, Johan Gardner's monstrous Grendel—and in today's science fiction. Fiedler also notes that in the counter-culture of the time, the youth proudly called themselves "freaks" and spent a good time "freaking out." Rock shows are absurdities on stage: a kind of "freaky" entertainment. *Freaks: Myths and Images of the Secret Self* amasses such provocative revelations. Fiedler's *Freaks*, hence, is a "freaky" example of popular culture and for some is quite a "freaky" book.

In one of his last few interviews, in January 2003 with Bruce Bauman, he comments on his book *Freaks* to show how he has changed the stereotypes related to abnormality and freakishness:

> Saying "freaks" used to be impossible; this is one of the books that changed that. I love it now that large minorities of people who are "handicapped" prefer to call themselves "crippled." This is all part of the game, queer theory. It's the same game I play with the word "nigger." I've been playing it for a long time [10].

Tyranny of the Normal (his twenty-fifth book), written in the last decade of his writing career, is a collection of nine essays that began their life as talks delivered to a wide variety of non-literary audiences: a world conference of theologians; the inaugural ceremonies for the Year of the Disabled, held at the United Nations headquarters in New York City; and a meeting of physicians. Fiedler has always been a restless academic, someone who much prefers a lively give-and-take with non-specialists than boring conversations about the literary niceties with his English department colleagues. He has, for nearly fifty years, found ever-newer ways to generate both controversy and attention. Given his lifelong interest in myth-making and what has come to be known as "cultural studies," it is hardly surprising that Fiedler would be drawn to ruminating about theology and biomedical ethics... (Pinsker 1999, 189).

It is no disclosure that throughout his long career, Fiedler tells us, he has been obsessed with the image of the stranger, the outsider, but chiefly as it is embodied in fictional portrayals of the ethnic "other":

> I have concentrated, that is to say, on the myths of the Negro, the Jew, and the Indian in novel and poems written by—and primarily for—WASP Americans. More recently, however, it occurred to me that for all of us to able to think of ourselves as "normal," there is a more ultimate other. That is, of course, the Freak, the Monster, the congenital malformation: a fellow-human born too large or too small, with too many or too few limbs, hair in the wrong places or ambiguous sexual organs [quoted in Pinsker 1999, 189].

Thus Pinsker tells us that Fiedler's prescription—to the theologians, doctors, and social workers he was addressing with some frequency—is "the vicarious release of literature." Interestingly, "when the topic turns to freaks, the ante only goes up." But Fiedler insists that it is "especially important for us to realize that *there are no normals*, at a moment when we are striving desperately to eliminate freaks, to normalize the world" (Fiedler 1996, 153).

Yet it cannot be denied that *Freaks* created a space for Fiedler outside the restrictive canon that was crying out to be opened. *Freaks* demonstrated to many that as a critic he practiced what he preached. It broke the boundaries that he wished were never created, and crossed borders that he disavowed. *Freaks* actually created a fluidity of space in which literature, anthropology, sociology, culture studies and psychology could coexist and comingle. It is acknowledged that it brought him money and a visibility on the popular platform, but what today is also an undisputed fact is that it established him as a scholar out of the ordinary. None but Pinsker would disagree with this, as will be demonstrated in the following pages.

Fiedler, the Freak

> In roughly the same playful spirit that Benjamin Franklin wrote himself down as "Benjamin Franklin, Printer" or that William Faulkner insisted he was "William Faulkner, Farmer,"... the single word Fiedler, at the ripe age of eighty, might affix to his name is *freak*. This, of course, was not always the case.
> —Sanford Pinsker, "Leslie Fiedler, Freak"

The last line is very significant. Sanford Pinsker traces the evolution of Fiedler's critical journey, one in which there were more downturns than upturns. Although Pinsker was much impressed, like many others, with the brilliance of Fiedler's early criticism, in the post-'70s era—when Fiedler moved from the "fresh and provocative" guru who had abundance of "intelligence," the one commodity that T. S. Eliot felt was essential to any sound literary criticism, and from the position of "centrality" in "Jewish studies" (Pinsker 1999, 185) to "Freak" status—the "disciple" Pinsker's awe of a guru shifted forever into nothing (182).

The reasons that Pinsker gives do not date from "the period when Fiedler, an outspoken advocate for the legalization of marijuana, found himself in hot water with the local gendarmes" (182); for *Being Busted* added yet another moniker to his list—namely, martyr—and generated sympathy for him (186). They date from the phase that started with his call in *Cross the Border—Close the Gap* (1972) and in a general embrace of whatever traveled under the wide umbrella of what he called "the New Mutants" (186). At that time even Fiedler did not know—at least not consciously—that he was headed toward the moment when he would discover in the "freak" the ultimate "other" he had been looking for since his salad days, when he specialized in blacks and Jews, homosexuals and Indians (187). Pinsker is very critical of Fiedler's so called pandering to the young because Fiedler reminds him "of the burnt-out English professor (beautifully played by Donald Sutherland) in *Animal House* who tells his students that he doesn't much care for Milton either. Such confessions cannot fail to garner laughs and probably great teaching evaluations; and in the context of an escapist comedy, one out to detail the triumph of the young over their authoritarian elders... (191). Secondly, Pinsker is equally unhappy about Fiedler's forays into the non-literary. He says,

> A "normal" world—this was never Fiedler's dream, even in the days when he defined himself as a "liberal, intellectual, writer, American, and Jew." But his affinity with "freaks"—in what often has the scary look of psychological doubling—is another matter, sensationalist on one hand, small-r romantic on the other. I cannot help feeling that there are worthier subjects for intellectuals to tackle [191].

In spite of his subjective yet astute tracing of the downslide of the evolution of Fiedler's critical thought, when he was unamused, "when he sprinkles dirt on the grave of capital-L Literature," and when "the old magic just wasn't there," Pinsker ends with "some kind words about Fiedler" (191). For a scholar of Fiedler these are equally significant. The following shows not a grudging but an open respect for the original thinker and pioneer Fiedler was. Pinsker acknowledges that as Fiedler himself approaches eighty he is the proud owner of a collection packed with intriguing insights at one point, errant foolishness at another, and, always, marvelously engaged writing. Pinsker concludes, "It is not just that he wrote with brio and brilliance, or even that he often fails to get full credit for pioneering aspects of feminist criticism, culture studies, or queer theory, but, rather, that his passion for what the imagination might tell us about life stayed the course. His career needs no special pleading much less apology. The books are enough, and they always were" (191).

Interestingly, Fiedler's identity as a Jew and his location as an apostle of Jews as well as a spokesperson for the famed New York Jewish establishment went unnoticed by many. William Galperin of Rutgers University, New Brunswick, while reviewing Susanne Klingenstein's anthology *Enlarging America: The Cultural Work of Jewish Literary Scholars, 1930–1990* (Syracuse University Press, 1998), brings some startling facts to our notice. Before I bring to the fore the issues raised by Galperin, I will mention that the most striking part of the review is a point that I have already made. In an anthology that shows the achievements of Jewish scholars from 1930 to 1990, a period in which Fiedler produced his best works (1948: "Come Back"; 1982: *What Was Literature?*; 1996: *Tyranny of the Normal*), Fiedler is just not there. It reminds me of Toni Morrison, who said the same after studying the entire gamut of American literary history. She realized that "she just wasn't there!"

and so chose to write for her people. The difference, however, is that it was not she, per se, who was not there in the pages, but her people and race. In this case however, even amongst his own people, Fiedler is not there. Will others hear?

After this brief but necessary excursus, Galparin, who approached Susanne Klingenstein's book with enormous curiosity but also with a fair amount of Jewish baggage, writes, "I am struck not only by the partiality of Klingenstein's survey—in particular its failure to engage in any real way the contributions of Harold Bloom and Leslie Fiedler who, in my view, are the most important 'Jewish literary scholars' of the last century" (116). He later tells us that the study examines the careers of a dozen or so scholars who were Jewish and variously associated with Harvard and Columbia, such as Harry Levin, M. H. Abrams, and Daniel Aaron, Leo Marx, Alan Guttmann, and Jules Chametzky; then the enigmatic and influential Lionel Trilling, and his followers such as Steven Marcus and Carolyn Heilbrun from Columbia; people of letters such as Norman Podhoretz and Cynthia Ozick; and finally, three other scholars, Robert Alter, Ruth Wisse, and Sacvan Berkovitch. Absent in this study, unfortunately, is any sustained consideration of either Leslie Fiedler or Harold Bloom. Pointing out this deficiency, Galparin writes, "These two highly influential critics were not merely mindful of their Jewishness in a myriad of ways and applications, but also capable of appreciating with an extraordinary degree of self-consciousness the meta-critical narratives (identitarian and otherwise) on which their criticism necessarily opens" (119). Thus it will not be unfair to say that even Fiedler's harshest critics, such as Pinsker, acknowledge his contribution to Jewish studies, and Galparin is well within his right to be critical of Klingenstein's book.

In one of his last few interviews Fiedler was asked if the Jewish imagination was still dominant or what had taken its place. Fiedler responded, "It's gone. It went pretty quickly. I say the name of Saul Bellow to my students and get a blank response. They don't even know of him to say bad things about him. The postmodernists were almost all goyim.... Well, they're gone now, too. The ones that interested me when they came along were Hawkes, Barth" (Bauman 2003, 4).

As a Jewish Auslander, Fiedler has inspired many. Daniel Schwartz, professor of English at Cornell University, strongly contends that just as Bloom is his spiritual father, so Fiedler—as much as Lionel Trilling, Irving Howe, Alfred Kazin, and M. H. Abrams—is a spiritual father for generations of Jewish scholars toiling in the fields of English and American literature in American colleges and universities. Schwartz owes his own interest in his Jewish heritage to Fiedler, particularly ways in which his Jewishness defines him as a scholar. Like Fiedler, he too was drawn to Joyce's Leopold Bloom because "he enacts love of family, immersion and respect for the prosaic of life, the ability to take pleasure in small things, imaginative and emotional resilience, and, yes, a sense of being an outsider" (Schwartz 1999, 107).

Just as Fiedler in his essays (and his fiction) has assiduously summed up the status of the Jews in the United States, Slavitt in 1999, in his joke-title article, "Fiedler on the Roof," links up Newark, freakishness, Marxism and Jewishness with Fiedler. Right at the outset, he remembers a lecture Fiedler gave about the Jews of Newark. He recounts Fiedler's explanation of how the Jews settled in Newark. Baltimore was a major port of entry for immigrant ships. Jews would get on the train, as they had been instructed to do, and would buy a ticket for New York. But at a certain point, a conductor would go through the train announcing that the next station stop was, "Newark, Newark," which sounds, recounts Slavitt, if one know only Yiddish and Polish and Russian, like "New York, New York." So they got out and settled—and lived there for a generation or so before they realized that there was this unused part of the ticket and that they'd made a mistake (156). Fiedler's association with Jews and Newark is so great that Slavitt can almost imagine him hovering in Newark in the following lines:

> So there he is, in that city that's not New York, maybe looking out at night at the glow from the real metropolis, maybe up there on a hot summer's night on what they used to call "Tar beach" trying to catch what Roth describes so vividly in *Goodbye, Columbus*—a cool breeze as welcome as the promise of an afterlife. Hot, stewing, yearning, a Fiedler on the roof [156].

But in this process, Slavitt strikes the key note of this chapter too. He says,

> Is this enough to explain him? His sense of being an *Auslander* [emphasis mine], his distance from what he takes to be the cultural epicentre (epi-centre, *epes*?) is from that. Think of Manhattan in the middle, and these two Jews looking toward it with ambition and an almost hopeless yearning: Alfred Kazin in Brooklyn, and in Newark, Fiedler [156].

Slavitt's position is that as a Jew, one is the "other" in America. The other word for "other" is "freak." The other word for the freak is "different." And Fiedler was different. His book *Freaks* is testimony to the fact, as Slavitt says: "Fiedler's book on freaks makes it clear that you don't have to be different. You only have to feel different. And if you don't, you're not" (157). And being in Newark adds to that differentness. He writes:

> New York is normal. Newark is eccentric, "something else," or, in his word, freakish. As Jews are, in a sense, freakish. (Otherwise, we aren't "choosen," are we?) Fiedler, then, is the world's largest Dwarf, the world's shortest Giant. Why? Because he feels himself to be. His attitudes have been constructed upon that basis, and his odd and sometimes unwelcome truths come from that singularity of vision [157].

Slavitt remembers one of his teachers, Paul Weiss, the first Jew to hold a tenured position in the humanities at Yale, who had been an interested and amused observer of the discussions his colleagues in the English department were having—in the late forties—about whether "a Hebrew could teach English literature" (158). This is echoed by Schwartz, who recounts his discomfort within the world of mostly WASPish Ivy League English departments, particularly in his early Cornell years, beginning in 1968. His view is that during those days, just as women were excluded and marginalized by the academy, Jews were also not welcome at the elite universities and particularly in the humanities. There were no tenured Jews on the rolls of Ivy League English faculties before World War II, and few with Irish or Italian names, he remembers.

This essay by Slavitt needs to be understood in more ways than one. Behind the tongue-in-cheek description of Fiedler as a freak lies the essence of Slavitt's argument that the uncommon (freakish) Fiedler had the unique power to connect with the common. The fact that he read Marx at thirteen and became, not surprisingly, a leftist, is in itself "a kind of intellectual freakishness. This aberrance allowed him to see most of what he has seen, to understand that pop culture is interesting (it's a whole industry now, which is a way of demonstrating that it has become a cliché, but Fiedler was one of those who invented it)" (159). In this bid he also becomes the master inventor of the pop cult in American literature and culture.

Deference for the "Other": The Literary Subalterns

All through his literary career, Fiedler displayed a deference for the neglected and the lost. One can name many a literary subaltern: those authors and books that were lying dormant and buried till Fiedler's critique and interest helped their revival. As a Jewish-American critic and scholar who was preoccupied for a good part of his career with themes of "outsidedness" and "othering," Leslie Fiedler is responsible for drawing attention to the then strangers in the canon or literary outsiders such as Henry Roth's masterpiece *Call It Sleep*, John Hawkes' *The Lime Twig*, Mitchell's *Gone with the Wind*, Stowe's *Uncle Tom's Cabin*, Eric Lotts' *Love and Theft*, and Michael Rogin's *Blackface, White Noise* (Pardini 2008, xiv). He is also responsible for reviving the reputations of such forgotten writers as Nathanael West and Henry Roth.

In the essay "Ethnicity and Marketplace" Thomas J. Ferraro acknowledges the contributions of Fiedler along with Isaac Rosenfeld and Harold Ribalow in promoting and facilitating "renewed academic interest." It is a process of recovery of the classic ethnic novel that depicted the immigrant experience for the mainstream audience in three genres: autobiography, the social science treatise, and fiction in the realist sense. Each offered varying forms of cultural impact (e.g., Stephen Crane's *Maggie: A Girl on the Streets* [1893] and *Mrs. Prexiada* [1886] by Sidney Luska, who was taken to be a German Jew but later turned out to be an Anglo-American, Henry Harland) alongside the canonical high modernists, leading them to become central business after the mid-seventies with the opening up of the canon and the growing effort to recover works depicting the social margins (1991, 383).

Ferraro also attributes to Leslie Fiedler the resuscitation of Henry Roth's 1934 book *Call It Sleep*, an unusual combination of high modernist structure and ethnic themes, a combination that continues to embarrass our terms of critical inquiry. The essay by Leslie Fiedler and Alfred Kazin published in *Partisan Review* called it "the most neglected book of the past 25 years." Winchell calls it Fiedler's "unfinished business" (275) to praise this book. Fiedler begins his essay, which originally appeared in *Commentary* in 1960, by confessing that Roth's novel *Call It Sleep* was not entirely unnoticed when it appeared in 1935. One reviewer, whom he does not identify, called the book "a great novel" and hoped that it would win the Pulitzer Prize, "'which,' that reviewer added mournfully, 'it never will'" (CE 2, 271). In 1959, Fiedler had declared *Call It Sleep* to be "the best single book by a Jew about Jewishness written by an American, certainly through the thirties and perhaps ever" (CE 2, 96). Despite the plausibility of this assessment, even some critics who were hoping for a flowering of Jewish-American literature were cool to Roth's novel. Apparently he had made the mistake of depicting the vulgarity and poverty of New York ghetto life with an unseemly realism. Not only had he offended the sensibilities of ethnic boosters, Roth had compounded the grossness of what he portrayed by rendering it through the sensibility of a child. Making precisely this point in 1960, upon the belated re-publication of *Call It Sleep,* Fiedler writes, "Its vulgarity ... is presented as *felt* vulgarity, grossness assailing a sensibility with no defenses against it" (Winchell 2002, 275).

Ferraro refers to Fiedler's contribution in putting the question of Jewish identity in global perspective, particularly in the context of the postwar novel of the holocaust (1991, 403). In "Avante Garde" Robert Boyers analyzes Fiedler's introduction to John Hawkes' *The Lime Twig* (1961) in which he makes much of Hawkes' distinction as the least read novelist of substantial merit in the United States.

Last Words, Finally

That Fiedler has raised a storm over the years with his provocative opinions is a truism few will disagree with. Yet, in talking about America, its culture, popular culture, myths and archetypes, the Jews, the Negroes, university and education, his only stand is that "to know the weakness and failures of all ... and speak them out is the only way of repaying the debt one feels" (Walden 1978, 209). And he continues to repay his debt—to America.

The connecting thread throughout his critical career has been Fiedler's enduring interest in otherness and outsiders, and the geographical and cultural margins, as embodied by the American West, in the stranger, the black, the Jew, the Indian (in *The Return of the Vanishing American*), and the "freak" (in *Freaks: Myths and Images of the Secret Self*). As John McGowan asserts, Fiedler's work has constantly concerned itself with "people on the margin of culture who embody its deepest fears and deepest urges" (1988, 93).[5] His status as a literary outsider in the American West is strangely conjoined with Hemingway. Winchell says, "One affinity that Leslie felt with Hemingway was that both men were outsiders who had come to live in and identify themselves with the American West" (2002, 238). It is a coincidence that Fiedler was one of the last scholars who went to see Hemingway during his dying moments.

In short, Fiedler's obsession with the marginalized can never be footnoted. In his text and subtext, the confusion among identities—racial, ethnic, and sexual—often grew so pronounced that in the end what Fiedler celebrates is his version of the national myth in which, as Pinsker writes, under the skin all blacks and Jews are Indians (Kellman and Malin 1999, 187). Pinsker's attempt at tracing a decline in Fiedler's position as an "intelligent" critic to a "freaky" one has to be taken as a kind of critical judgment. In fact, it is quite freaky. For many, his forays into pop culture and the non-literary did him in and did not give him the critical cachet that he rightfully deserved. He carelessly threw it away, some would say, making him stand as the "other" in academia.

CHAPTER 4

Toward Popular Culture

Establishment of a Pop Guru

> *Freaks* (1978) had given Fiedler a taste of mass cult popularity, and he hankered for more.... Nonetheless, Fiedler kept his reserved seat on the popular culture bandwagon, hoping against hope that the youth revolution would make a comeback and that he could be its pied piper even as he entered his eighth decade.
> —Sanford Pinsker, "Leslie Fiedler, Freak"

> The fact is that even economic security, high expertise and high culture seem threatened by what may be called marketization. Lately there has been a rejection of literacy itself in certain communities. Most people do not read with pleasure and ease. But they do read images on the screen with pleasure, and that is why cinema and TV are popular.
> —Darshan Singh Maini, "Psychoanalysis and Modern American Criticism"

> Popular Literature is not "words on the page" as some critics would have us believe. Like all literature, it is finally, essentially, images in the head. Once its images pass *through* words ... into our heads, such primordial images, or archetypes, or myths ... can pass out again easily into any other medium.
> —Leslie Fiedler, "Giving the Devil His Due"

If postmodernism is a post–World War II product, a frequent term from 1960s, its present use a common feature, the last decade witnessing a post-postmodern phenomenon, then Fiedler is its progenitor (D'haen 1992). Using the term postmodernism (a term from the world of fine arts that he himself was the first to apply to song and story) wasn't lucky phrase-making. It was a declaration of principles (Tanenhaus 2003). This chapter, in its two sections, examines Fiedler's response and contribution to the advent of postmodernism, which can also be called the "Epoch of Hegemony of Commodities."[1] The examination will primarily be done through his writings foraying into pop culture. He emerges as an advocate of opening up the canon of American literature by re-evaluating literature in his writings and by talking incessantly of the merits and de-merits of the academy and university education. He adopts a futuristic approach, in his conceptualization of the "dream of the new," and heralds the "shift from whisky culture to dope culture" (Fiedler, quoted in Browne 1973, 1). In this process, as the second part of this chapter will enumerate, one witnesses the establishment of the pop guru.

Forays into the Pop

When Bob Ashley wrote *Reading Popular Narrative: A Source Book* (1997) and Christopher Pawling penned *Popular Fiction and Social Change* (1984), they were, at best, building a case for popular culture addressing Eurocentric Western scholarship.[2] They did not really consider the burgeoning readership constituencies of popular cultures in the elitist space of the university classroom all across the world, which in turn troubled socio-psychological discourses about minority and majority culture in academic quarters still bludgeoned by the aftershocks of colonialism and Anglicization. We have traversed a long way since then (Srivastava 2009, 65). Though considered a contested terrain by some, today, popular culture studies not only are considered a legitimate site where conflicting groups struggle for hegemonic surveillance and conflicting interests, but also have been recognized and claimed by world academia, and new and innovative research is underway all over the globe. It is widely known that serious research and interest in the phenomena of popular culture studies was initiated for the first time in America in the 1940s by the Bowling Green University critics—Ray B. Browne, Marshall Fishwick, Russel B. Nye, John G. Cawelti, to name a few. Concurrently, while Arnold's school worried that popular culture represented a threat to cultural and social authority, the Frankfurt School, a group of German intellectuals engaged in speculative philosophy, who expressed their concern about the displacement and menace caused by the explosion of mass culture from newspapers and cinema to popular fiction and jazz, argued that it actually produces the opposite effect: it maintains social authority. In 1944, Max Horkhiemer and Theodor Adorno coined the term "Culture Industry" to designate the processes of mass culture (Storey 2001, 85, quoted in Srivastava 2006, 5).

It can be said that the Frankfurt School critics seem to doubt the critical and discriminatory abilities of the people, whose interests they think they are defending, and their assumption remains that *we*, the educated consumers of high culture, know what is morally and socially good for *you*, the benighted consumers of popular culture. This is the kind of radical elitism that Raymond Williams finds endemic to a whole tradition of British social thought (see

Williams' *Culture and Society*). One alternative to this pessimistic elitism is the kind of mythic populism exemplified by the works of Leslie Fiedler, Richard Slotkin and John G. Cawelti. Fiedler believes "literature is never just 'words on the page'" (Fiedler 1978b, 201, quoted in Srivastava 1992, 159) but is "primordial images of archetypes or myths ... that can pass out again easily into any other medium" (Fiedler 1978b, 201). Dallas Liddle also comments on the relational importance of the novel to other genres.[3] Fiedler suggests that one way of elaborating on this insight might be to treat literature as a certain kind of myth, the property not of a hegemonic class or an educated and officially ordained clerisy, but of the people themselves. Structuralists assert that all myths throughout the world have a family resemblance.

In the wake of new critical practices of contemporary times, several other academicians including Fiedler resisted subservient alignment to academia as the center, provoking the facilitation of the "other" in literary and cultural discourse. An attempt to plunder popular culture for sociological and anthropological study was also made. Turner in his seminal study *Structure and Anti-Structure* opines that popular culture is the world turned upside down in a stratified society. Pierre Bourdieu argues that the celebration of "the remarkable of the unremarkable"—the everyday—forms the core of popular culture (Srivastava 2006, 5–6). The political analysis of the Italian Marxist Antonio Gramsci, particularly his development of the concept of hegemony, refers to the way in which dominant groups in society, through a process of "intellectual and moral leadership," seek to win the consent of the subordinate groups in society. Several cultural theorists have taken Gramsci's political concept and used it to explain the nature and politics of popular culture. Those using this approach, sometimes referred to as neo–Gramscian hegemony theory, see popular culture as a site of struggle between the resistance of subordinate groups in society and the forces of incorporation operating in the interests of dominant groups in society. Popular culture in this usage is not the imposed culture of the mass culture theorists, nor is it emerging from below, the spontaneously oppositional culture of "the people." Rather, it is a terrain of exchange and negotiation between the two; a terrain marked by resistance and incorporation. The texts and practices of popular culture move within what Gramsci calls "compromise equilibrium." The process is historical (labeled popular culture one moment, and another kind of culture the next), but it is also dialectical (moving between resistance and incorporation). For instance, a visit to a hill resort or a seaside holiday began as an aristocratic event, but within 100 years had become an example of popular culture. In general terms, those looking at popular culture from a neo–Gramscian perspective tend to see it as a terrain of ideological struggle between dominant and subordinate classes, dominant and subordinate cultures (Srivastava 2003). The early twentieth century, according to Stuart Hall (1998), also saw some deep cultural questions that remain relevant to this day regarding the relation between corporate-produced culture and the image of popular culture as belonging to the masses. Hall analyzes two common understandings of the concept of popular culture. The first meaning is the one of wide circulation and commerciality bent dangerously towards manipulative consumerism and degradation of authentic working-class cultural content and tradition. The second is an essentialist's view that sees popular culture as all the cultural activities of "the people" but places great value on the binaries of "people" and the "elite." According to Hall, popular culture as a site is very dynamic and in constant conflict and struggle, much in line with the Gramscian notion in which relations of control and subordination are constantly shifting and certain cultural forms gain and lose support from institutions. According to Hall there is a constant movement and interchange between them as a result of shifting power relations, the assimilation of popular content into "high culture" and vice versa.

Recent thinking around the debates on postmodernism and popular culture insists on the claim that postmodern culture ushers in a complete breakdown of categories. As we shall see, for some, this is a reason to celebrate and end to an elitism constructed on arbitrary distinctions of culture; for others it is a reason to despair at the final victory of commerce over culture. Even the high priests of postmodernism, such as Fredrick Jameson, Baudrillard, Lyotard, Susan Sontag, and Hal Foster, call for a "new sensibility" in apprehending culture in their discourse (Srivastava 2006, 10).

It is against such a preface that this chapter will trace Fiedler's journey into popular culture.

Toward Popular Culture

The preceding discussions of his criticism and major preoccupations with the "other"—the natives, Jews, blacks and freaks—and the theme of male bonding in the earlier chapters show that though Fiedler dealt with elite literature as such, he had no intentions of restricting himself to the elite citadel. A slow, sure and definite shift toward popular culture is conclusively observed in his writings. In 1981, in a conversation with Geoffrey Green, a tolerant and open Fiedlerian mind is at play. In this conversation, Fiedler claims that each writer builds an image, a fictional myth of himself, and tries to live up to that myth or image, gradually ceasing to be his original self. In the context of this remark, one can safely say that in the fifties and the early sixties, Fiedler had built up an image of a robust, outspoken, and unaccommodating critic, who mellowed down a little and matured with age. This is evident in his espousal of the middle path between lowbrow and highbrow literature—middlebrow literature.

Going through the total oeuvre of his writings we discover that he has been mainly preoccupied with culture. Critics also say that he is at his best as a culture analyst. The culture of any country is not confined only to the highbrow. It is the way people live, their languages, customs, rituals, beliefs, thought-patterns, science, technology, religion, artifacts, films, etc. Culture is an all-embracing word that includes literature as well. And highbrow literature is only a part of it, confined to the ten percent of the population that includes people of the learned professions. If Fiedler had to justify himself as a critic of culture, he had to make forays into lowbrow or pop culture. Gradually he found equal support for his critical theories in pop culture.

Responding to Postmodernism: The Epoch of Hegemony of Commodities

That Fiedler has been a man of the moment is an assertion that will not be denied by many. His changing prerogatives are but an example of that. P. Meras' "Author" (1966) is a meditative attempt at presenting a glimpse of the dichotomies that often exist in Fiedler's criticism. His reflections on criticism practiced in the fifties and sixties are an example: "This is a very bad time for criticism ... old critics have run out of gas and lost touch with what is going on.... The young writers and poets and novelists today don't seem to be especially interested in criticism" (32). He carries on, "To be criticized easily, literature should be reflective and introspective and highly self-conscious. Impulse and irrationality don't lend themselves to critical writing" (32). In the next breath, he establishes his affinity with "the pop novel that ... gets its mythology not out of Christian and Greek mythology, but out of yesterday's pop culture—comic books, advertising, rock 'n' roll music. There's the assumption that this is the common culture between the reader and the writer" (32). Fiedler calls the above "the mythology of urban culture" and finds it relevant because so few people, nowadays, grow up anywhere but in the city. According to him, not only Ovid and Virgil seem far away to today's youngsters, but Huck Finn and Rip Van Winkle belong to small town life, too. It's comic book heroes such as Phantom, Asterix, Tarzan, Superman, Archie and Mandrake the Magician that are the mythological figures of the metropolis.

Similarly, referring to a series of extracts published by the *New York Times Book Review* under the heading "Leslie Fiedler Re-Introduces Himself," Wallenstein is disconcerted to read Fiedler's views on criticism: "the kind of criticism which the age demands is '...(the) death of art criticism' ... the newest criticism must be ... comic, irreverent, vulgar" (1972, 589). Wallenstein is quite critical of such a viewpoint because, he says, after more than twenty years of searching for total form, and making use of "meaningful generalities," Fiedler has used the term *postmodernism*, which "hangs like a dead weight at the end of his fine line of criticism." According to Wallenstein, postmodernism calls for a departure from the older methods of modern criticism, particularly high art, which the elitist critics preferred. However, Fiedler proposed to deal with all art, including pop art, and "in the process avoid the creation of artistic hierarchies" (589). He further points out, "The tradition that he (Fiedler) is now claiming to abandon is the one that has provided him with a critical method, rich and elastic, that defies all the traditional categories or the current 'age of criticism'" (589). Much has been said about the evolution of Fiedler from an elitist critic to a popular culture critic. Fiedler's major concern, literature—both political and social—reflects his life-long love affair with American culture; from his populist, man-in-the-street approach, to the much more academic-cum-liberal vantage point of the professor-become-pop-guru.

"Versioning" the Pop Revolution

Before Fiedler, intellectuals mostly wrote about "mass culture" with a combination of anxiety, discomfort and condescension. To a thinker trained in formal criticism and high culture, the post–World War II period was bewildering: Mass literacy and affluence led to the explosion of youth fashion, comic books and magazines and, by the mid-'50s, rock 'n' roll. Fiedler, on the other hand, was intoxicated by pop even as he approached it as an old-school scholar. "Though he was a champion of pop culture, he was kind of caught between two worlds," and "he describes himself as a voyeur, not a participant. He was all about equivocation, being in two places and never being in one," says Ritz (quoted in Timberg). But whether he was writing about Faulkner or comic books, Fiedler was addressing pop culture, since to him the novel, from its beginning in eighteenth century England, was the first important popular form. But his allegiance to literature was too strong to be shrugged off. Timberg (2008, 2) quotes Marcus: "There was no way Elvis Presley was going to mean as much to him as 'Absalom, Absalom'" (2008, 2). It will not be unbecoming to say that his mythological approach was used by almost anyone who uses books or movies or TV as a lens into the collective unconscious. Crossing all disciplinary boundaries, his approaches and ideology proved especially influential among writers on popular music; Marcus hears Fiedler's combination of "fun and fearlessness" in legendary rock critic Lester Bangs (quoted in Timberg May 4, 2008, 2). Several music projects such as the Experience Music Project's Pop Conference, an annual gathering of critics and scholars held in Seattle, in 2007 was full of "children of Fiedler," Ritz said (a thought that has been echoed by Susan Gubar in "A Fiedler Brood" (Gubar 1999). "It was interesting to see how his influence permeated a conference of music intellectuals and ethnomusicologists and cultural anthropologists. All these studies—'the Image of the Black Woman from Bessie Smith to Amy Winehouse' or whatever—they're all Fiedlerian riffs" (Timberg 2008, 2). Such statements are powered by strong, heartfelt convictions.

The clarion call of most pop culturalists[4] then was that all cultures are in one continuum, with differing emphases but not with breaks in between. The best symbol is the eyeball. On the one end is folk culture, on the other, elite culture; in the middle, constituting the largest portion, is the iris, in which rests the pupil—popular culture—ever expanding, ever growing, and always seeing more widely, intently and deeply. And the eyeball is horizontal, not vertical. Hence it is inappropriate to think of one culture as "high" and another as "low" (Browne 1973, 6). Another very important aspect of popular culture is that it "provides a kind of audio-video profile of a nation. It pictures the smiles and its echoes the sighs of contentment. It also points to the locations of fissures in the crust of society through which seethes and explodes the lava of public discontent" (9).[5]

Advocates of popular culture insist that popular culture is essential for the health of academics. It is a practical and pragmatic humanities that understands our comprehensive, cogent and cohesive world in all its dimensions.[6] Contrasting popular culture with private (elite) culture, Fishwick (1974) writes that private culture is for the select few; popular culture is for all.[7] Popular art says relax; private art says stretch. Popular art tends to be neither complicated nor profound; private art attempts to be both. Fishwick says that the "vulgar" music of the Beatles became "classic" a decade later. The facts that Shakespeare wrote for the pit and that he knew "little Latin and less Greek" do not seem to have blunted his influence over the masses, over the years. Endless bickering about mob taste, mass audiences, and elitism, critics note, has ranked as the most wasteful activity on the contemporary American scene (Fishwick 1974, 2). Fiedler did not remain unaffected by such views and published two powerful essays on popular culture.

"Towards a Definition of Popular Literature" (1975) and "Giving the Devil His Due" (1978)

Right at the outset of "Towards a Definition of Popular Literature," Fiedler elaborates that by "popular" he does not mean necessarily or primarily what is most widely read, much less what is read by "everybody," and that by "literature" he does not mean what is customarily "studied" in classes in literature (28). By "popular literature" Fiedler implies literature that has been "ghettoized" or excluded from university education but has endured on its own. He adds that popular literature is not a category, a type, a sub-genre, the invention of the authors of the books, who—we have been taught to believe—belong to popular literature. In fact, it exists primarily "in the perception of elitist critics—or better, perhaps, in their mis-perception, their—usually tendentious, sometimes even deliberate misapprehension" (30). And then he makes a very important point: What are considered "serious novels" or "art novels"; works, say, by Henry James or Marcel Proust, Thomas Manor, or James Joyce, are indistinguishable, before the critical act, from "best-sellers" or "popular novels" by Jacqueline Susann or John S. MacDonald, Conan Doyle or Bram Stoker. Despite peripheral attempts to sort them out into different categories such as "classic" or "popular" by invidious binding or labeling, they are all one.

In "Giving the Devil His Due" (1978), Fiedler prefers to define popular culture as modern majority culture. He confesses, "Literature is what I know about, literature is what I am interested in, literature is what I am committed to" (197). But Fiedler restricts himself to popular song and story, mostly story, which, in his opinion, is popular literature. Fiedler uses the term "popular" as opposed to "folk" literature because the latter, as per his perception, describes the literature of the preliterate society. The term *pop literature* is used to mean majority literature in an industrial and post-industrial society.

Both these essays, "Toward a Definition of Popular Literature" and "Giving the Devil His Due," constitute important landmarks in Fiedler's evolution as a pop guru. Some definitional concepts from these two essays have been discussed above. These essays are dealt with, in considerable detail, in the following pages as and when they logically occur in the chronology of the chosen essays, with a view to tracing his trajectory into this burgeoning popular field.

His Other Writings

One of his earliest essays, "William Faulkner, Highbrow's Lowbrow" (1950), incorporated in his anthology *No! In Thunder*, reflects his concern with popular culture. In this essay Fiedler talks of two Faulkners, the real Faulkner and the ersatz "other" Faulkner. According to Fiedler, the other Faulkner writes through a "fog of highbrow rhetoric" (NT, 113). The content, the slavery issue, the Southern atmosphere, the theme of miscegenation, etc., cause Faulkner to be considered "the last serious writer in the United States" (NT, 116) and a "novelist of the first rank," who addresses "directly the American male" (NT, 117). But the obstacle between Faulkner and his complete popular acceptance is his "monstrously involved point of view" (NT, 119) and his prose style, full of poetic passages. However, what is congenial to popular taste is the subject matter. This essay on Faulkner's dialectical position marks the beginning of Fiedler's concern with boundaries of highbrow and lowbrow literature. It also highlights his high regard for popular taste and appeal.

In the same decade, in 1955 to be precise, Fiedler published an essay, "The Middle Against Both Ends," which is included in his anthology *Cross the Border—Close the Gap* (1972). In this article in defense of comic books, in a sentimental protest, Fiedler argues against claims such as Gershon Legman's that comic books encourage crime, destroy literature, express sexual frustration, breed violence, unleash sadism, spread anti-democratic ideas and corrupt youth (CBCG, 15). Fiedler vehemently defends comic books and pop literature in this essay. According to him, popular literature "demands a more than ordinary slickness, the sort of high finish only possible to a machine-produced commodity" (CBCG, 18). Contemporary pop culture is distinguished by its refusal to be shabby and second-rate, says Fiedler. Talking of comic book heroes, he points out that they are archetypal and though these books are categorized as children's literature, they are read by people of all ages. But some critics question this thesis. They claim that since most of the authors of comic books are Jews, Fiedler gives undue attention to this genre. Anyhow, Fiedler's concern with this aspect of popular literature was fully accepted by the majority of critics.

Fiedler's essay on Faulkner and on comic books also marked the beginning of his concern with various categories of literature. In "Partisan Review—Phoenix or Dodo" (Spring 1956, included in *To the Gentiles*, 1971), Fiedler talks of the highbrow, middlebrow and lowbrow in literature. Fiedler has often been called by a number of fellow critics a *Partisan Review*–type writer. This implies that though in the fifties Fiedler was leaning toward popular culture, he was still considered, by some at least, to belong to the highbrow group of literature, which is evident from these lines: "the split among the various kinds of arts in America and their appropriate audiences into low, middle and high has surrendered the creation, consumption and judgement of serious literature into the hands of the very few" (TG, 43). And these "very few" critics of elite literature are the ones who are the targets of attack by critics favoring popular culture. Hence, Fiedler is quite against that superficial and partial judgment of literature that unfortunately divides literature into high or middle or low. In continuation with his war against elite literature, in his other essay, "The War Against—the Academy," included in *Waiting for the End* (1964), Fiedler talks of the youths' revolt against school and university. The university in America symbolizes tradition, the study of classics, orthodoxy and conservation. Hence, Fiedler talks of the war against this academy and says that today's mid-culture triumphs over "high art"; in fact, it parodies high art. With the revolt against the academy there is an alteration of consciousness in the young. This new consciousness is a "possibility to go beyond," it is a kind of dream of the new.

What we notice from his earliest essays is his constant emphasis on newness. This newness is something beyond the cult of sexual freedom and alcoholism.

Hence, this thrust toward newness is another very important tenet of popular culture. The germ of this attitude, later called by Fiedler the "Dream of the New," is actually an urge in the American psyche, seen by many theologians as the desire to go forward. In literature, it is also defined as the frontier approach. In his preface to *An End to Innocence* (1955), Fiedler admits his allegiance to newness. He says, "I am a literary man, immune to certain journalistic platitudes and accustomed to regard men and words with [a] sensibility trained by the newer critical methods" (EI, xv). Later in his works we shall see that Fiedler defines these "newer critical methods" as postmodernism, or New New Criticism, to which he owes allegiance.

Fiedler's perception perceives the emphasis of the new consciousness of the young in America on "full gentility," which should be "the final goal of Man" (WFTE, 176). This is seen by the critic as an "attack on heterosexuality" (WFTE, 177) and an acceptance of the concept of "pure love" (WFTE, 178), a kind of celebration of male homosexuality. All this, says Fiedler, belongs to the cult of popular culture. The exponents of this art are mostly novelists, and quite a few of them are Jews.

Waiting for the End *(1964)*

In this work Fiedler portrays the success of the Jews on all fronts, particularly in the field of popular culture. He traces the rise of the Jewish intellectual on the American literary scene, and talks at length of the Judaization of American culture. He points out that Jewish writers are pioneers in the field of popular culture. In fact Jewish culture has entered the American day-to-day existence, practically in every sphere. He says that the "sick" joke and the "hate" card represent the entry of Jewish humor into the domain of popular culture. But predominantly, it is the novel by a number of Jewish writers that heralds the arrival of popular culture. In the essay "Some Jewish Pop Art Heroes" (1966), Fiedler establishes that Jewish writers play a decisive role in the creation of popular literature with themes that are imbued with myths of the runway male, fear of adulthood, women and sex and companionship of a male. According to Fiedler, "it is the vivid and perdurable vulgarity of the Jews ... which lies at the heart of pop culture" (TG, 136).

Fiedler explicitly emphasizes the relative insignificance of the medium as a very important trait of popular culture for the very first time. In "The End of the Novel" (WFTE), Fiedler says that the novel "represents the beginning of popular culture.... It not merely instructs and delights and moves, but also embodies the myths of a society, serves as the scriptures of an underground religion; and these latter functions, unlike the former ones, depend not at all on any particular form but can be indifferently discharged by stained-glass windows, comic strips, ballads, and movies" (192). This specific characteristic of popular culture has been elaborated by Fiedler repeatedly in many of his later writings also, as will be discussed in the following pages.

Still concerned with literature and its categories, the same year, Fiedler published another essay, "The Death of Avant-Garde Literature" and defined avant-garde literature as "the nostalgic imitation of techniques revolutionary and exciting in the heydays of James Joyce" (CBCG, 55). Proclaiming the death of avant-grade literature, he further points out that avant-garde writing is totally different from popular lowbrow and middlebrow writings. In "The Death and Rebirths of the Novel" (1980–81), which moves on the same thematic pattern as the earlier two essays, he traces the rebirth of the traditional art, the novel, through popular forms such as the theatre and films. Ken Kesey's *One Flew Over the Cuckoo's Nest* meets Fiedler's approval on all counts because it can be read as literature or seen in the theatre or as a film. From the foregoing, it can be inferred that Fiedler is still continuing with the framework that he had used for his writings earlier, when he first talked of "indifference to medium" as an essential characteristic of popular culture. However, what is of great importance in this essay is an evolution in his critical stance as seen in "Cross the Border—Close the Gap" (1969). In this essay, which is a part of his book *Cross the Border—Close the Gap*, Fiedler prophesied that in the future the mass audience would grow closer to the elite, but as noticed here, instead of coming closer to the elite, the mass audience is getting subdivided as forms of pop fiction are becoming varied: "children's books," "science," "mystery," "Westerns," etc. With death of the classic art novel in the country, the elites are moving toward the mass audience, claims Fiedler.

And the masses, like Fiedler, have not abandoned their quest for newness. I touched upon the aspect of the "Dream of the New" earlier. An extension of this idea of the "Dream of the New" was given as a lecture on "the idea of the future," called "The New Mutants" (1965) by Fiedler. The extent and nature of this futuristic revolution in literature as defined in "The New Mutants" becomes evident, says Fiedler, "if we make a brief excursion from the lofty reaches of High Art to the humbler levels of pop culture" (TG, 189). This futuristic revolution, according to Fiedler, is taken up by the young, called "the new mutants." "Mutant" is a word from science fiction, which implies "radically transformed youth." These new mutants are "non-participants in the past, dropouts from history" (TG, 191). They attempt to "disavow the very idea of the past"; in other words, they reject tradition and orthodoxy. The point is not to shout, not to insist, but to hang cool. This "being cool" or nonchalance is the essence of the lifestyle that these futurists adopt.

Yet to say that these mutants are atheists would be untrue. According to Fiedler, these new mutants are quite religious, because they believe in "detachment." In other words, they are mystics—religious but not Christian. They regard Christianity as a white ideology imposed on the rest of the colored world. This ideology, Fiedler notes, sometimes leads to a kind of "psychic assimilation," an urge to become a Negro, to adopt their lifestyle, which is most prevalent among the young. In *Waiting for the End*, Fiedler notes that most of the white American parents of the time observed the mannerisms and living style of the Negroes in their children. This assimilationistic impulse, says Fiedler, is to join oneself with "otherness," identified with blacks and women. Fiedler explains this point further: "To become new men, these children of the future seem to feel, they must not only become more Black than white, but more female than male" (TG, 198). The manifestation of this impulse is found in the desire to shun masculinity, which is another postmodernistic trend. This leads to shunning women, sexually. Hence, new attitudes toward sex and marriage are noted in this post-sexual revolution. The new mutants are eager to be delivered of traditional ideologies of love and sex, and are keen on the casting off of adulthood. Marriage has become a parody and what is happening is a "more personal transformation; a radical metamorphosis of the western male ... that of being beautiful and being loved" (TG, 202). Talking of this impulse in Fiedler, Wallenstein says that Fiedler seems not only on the side of the children of the future, as he conceives of them, contemptuous of language, tradition, humanism, rationality, but their "willing spokesman" too. In fact, Wallenstein quotes Fiedler, who says, "If I live long enough, perhaps I shall finally grow young enough to disavow all vestiges of the humanistic tradition that persist in my thinking—turning my back on the past, recent and remote, quite as if, like some fifteen year old, I, too, inhabit a world I never made" (1972, 593).

Contrapuntally, in "The Two Memories: Reflection on Writers and Writings in the Thirties" (1968) published in his book called *Unfinished Business*, Fiedler looks upon the thirties with feelings of nostalgia as against the idea of the future that rejects the past. Here, Fiedler discusses the thirties with a "kind of return to roots and sources so often required for cultural renewal; the re-examination of a past never quite understood—out of an awareness that unless we understand it now we will not understand the present or our surviving selves." He says, "It is the myth of the period, if not the actual fact, which helped make possible a New Jazz age, a revival of Bohemian life, complete with pop Art ... called camp" (UB, 43). The point that is clear from the essay is that popular culture is not a rejection of the past or tradition; in fact, the present is possible because of the past.

The second social movement of this American popular culture, as traced by Fiedler, is the drug cult. This new cult emphasizes the enjoyment and pleasure and a possible birth of new life through the penetration of a foreign object—the drug. Here, Fiedler has been accused of heralding the shift from the "whisky culture to dope culture." The basic premise of this charge could be that Fiedler has propounded this movement, partially through his association with LEMAR, an organization that fought for the legalization of drugs. This drug cult is part of the alteration of consciousness of the young, as pointed out earlier. All these are the various levels of the American popular culture, foreseen by Fiedler in the mid-sixties.

Fiedler's preoccupation with the future and newness got crystalized in his essay called "The Dream of the New" (1970). In this essay Fiedler argues that the United States has accepted and glorified the notion of newness as its essential character, its fate and its vocation. In short, to be new, to make things new, to get a new start, or if nothing else, then, to dream of the new, forms an essential tenet that shapes the American character. This thrust on the dream of newness was noticed as early as his first essay, "Come Back to the Raft Ag'in, Huck Honey!" in which Fiedler wished to formulate "radically new ideologies" regarding homosexuals and Negroes. Fiedler points out this dream element in *Love and Death in the American Novel* as well. In this book, while discussing the myth of the American male, Fiedler says that the American novelist builds a dream-like atmosphere around the relationship of the runaway white American male and the colored male. The point that I wish to emphasize is that Fiedler, since his earliest writings, has been consciously writing about "dreaming" as an essential element of the American character. In a way, the task of the American writer, says Fiedler, has been to render this dream of the new by inventing a new language, a new vocabulary of symbols and myths, to be able to convey that the dream can take the place of reality. And pop books are dreams, commodities, that are mass produced and distributed and have popular appeal as well. And the master of dreams is the Jew in the Gentile world, as portrayed earlier. But this dream of the new, argues Fiedler, also contains a self-destructive element. He says, "By the act of self-destruction the American novelist makes his fiction dream rather than art, what passes rather than endures, an experience almost as satisfactorily transient as television itself. The art of the new is totally nihilistic but it is joyously so; which may explain why our most authentic books, however tragic the lives of their authors, are if not quite blithe, funny at least" (Fiedler, quoted in Madden 1971, 27). Thus, in addition to the mythic, it is the "dream" element that has often engaged Fiedler's attention—the intangible, often unconsciously conveyed, content of a work of art. "The American Dream," for some writers a debased cliché, has meaning for Fiedler, a meaning beyond the limitations of the past or even the present. It represents to him the future. It thus becomes apparent that the idea of newness, as an important part of popular culture, further crystallizes in various dimensions in his writings, over the years. It can also be observed that the theme of newness keeps recurring periodically in his writings, and that he is consciously or unconsciously averse to discarding this specific theme, as it also touches upon aspects associated with his evolution as a critic and writer.

Building Bridges: Cross the Border—Close the Gap *(1972)*

In the introduction to the article "Cross the Border—Close the Gap," he writes, "Like many in my generation, I have been *thrice* born first into radical dissent, then into radical disillusion and the fear of innocence, finally into whatever it is that lies beyond both commitment and disaffection" (CE 2, 405). The book *Cross the Border—Close the Gap* is the product of his third birth. It attempts to describe "the character and probable destiny of the movement for which there is still no better name than Post-Modernism" (CBCG, 3). To deal with this new movement it is necessary, according to Fiedler, to develop really new criticism, free from elitism and culture religion. Hence, Fiedler says that he has become more interested in books that elitist approaches had difficulty in dealing with that join all audiences, children and adults, women and men, the sophisticated and the naïve. In pursuit of such works, Fiedler is willing to cross the border that once separated high art from pop.

An example of high art that crosses over to popular art are the Japanese art pictures called Ukiyoe, according to Fiedler. Ukiyoe, or floating word pictures, possess the merits of high art. An ancient Japanese art form, Ukiyoe are printed from wooden blocks in several colors. They portray well-known prostitutes and popular actors or, as the Japanese would say, "bijin," i.e., a "beautiful person." Fiedler removes the discrepancy surrounding this art form and says, "Popular is too ambiguous a word to trust, for two of its commonest meanings are middlebrow and folk. But Ukiyoe is lowbrow and urban—a mass produced art of the city" (CBCG, 11). Through such examples Fiedler attempts to bring closer to each other the conflicting poles of high art and popular art. As his artistic sensibilities are manifold, so are his intellectual faculties packed with examples and information. Examples such as Ukiyoe, drawn from a different cultural milieu, reflect Fiedler's multi-faceted, multi-dimensional personality, which rises much above his literary stature, to a scholar of world culture.

Winchell's view is that

> the eight selections gathered here constitute a definitive—some would say anticlimactic—declaration of independence from the critical strictures associated with high modernism. Fiedler was not just pursuing a newer approach to criticism (he had done that from the beginning of his career), he was also questioning the very concept of serious literature, as it had prevailed in England and America since

the early years of the twentieth century. If modernism was dead, so too was an essential part of his own literary education. Rather than seeing this as merely an end, Fiedler tends to regard it as a new beginning [Winchell 2002, 243].

Being a critic himself, Fiedler has always been concerned with the state of literary criticism. In this essay, he talks of the scandal facing contemporary literary criticism, which has attempted to compare one kind of book with another kind of book so radically different that it calls the very assumption underlying that comparison into question. Contrary to the task assigned to critics, Fiedler says, "Established critics may think that they have been judging recent literature; but, in fact, recent literature has been judging them" (CBCG, 61). Here, he called for "a New New Criticism, a Post-Modernist Criticism" that would be "contextual rather than textual." Employing "not words-on-the-page but words-in-the-world," the "New New Criticism" would be "comical, irreverent, vulgar" in its efforts to lead us "out of the Eliot Church" with its elitist dismissal of "low" or "popular" art as well as its widening of the gap between professional critic or artist, on the one hand, and amateur audience or reader, on the other. According to the critic, this contemporary or postmodernist criticism should be congenial to this new culture—popular culture. He says that this "New New Criticism" will be appropriate to postmodernist fiction and verse; it will not be formalist or intrinsic, but contextual rather than textual; not concerned with structure, diction or syntax, but concerned primarily with the reader's response, the "ekstasis" of reading. He assigns to the novel the function of "closing the gap between elite and mass culture" (CBCG, 68). Therefore, "the Dream, the vision, ekstatic: these have again become the avowed goals of literature" (CBCG, 83); this is Fiedler's passionate affirmative credo. Notwithstanding this obdurate flaw of hammering his affirmations into us like a nail in the wall, Fiedler's commentaries on contemporary American culture are refreshing and brilliant.

All this is sufficient indication that Fiedler's concern in the seventies has consistently been mainly with the masses. He was also concerned about the kind of literature that appealed to the masses. His plea to elite critics was that their attempt should not be to categorize literature into two qualities: high literature, studied in classrooms of schools and universities, which never reached the public, so to say; and popular literature, which was mass produced and mass distributed—popular best-sellers, read by a varied audience on a large scale. His appeal to the critics was to build and develop a criticism that bridged the gap between elite and popular literature. Not only this; pop art calls into question the very division of art into high and low, says Fiedler. He says that pop art is

> a threat to all hierarchies insofar as it is hostile to order and ordering in its own realm. What the final intrusion of Pop into the citadels of High Art provides,

therefore, for the critic is the exhilarating new possibility of making judgments about the "goodness" and "badness" of art quite separated from distinctions between "high" and "low" with their concealed class bias [CBCG, 78].

The relevance of Fiedler's myth criticism is really put to use in his credo on popular culture. Fiedler puts his mythopoeic critique to multiple uses on varied sites: as a defense mechanism to protect himself from the unpleasant attacks of the early *Partisan Review* and *Kenyon Review* buddies and chums; to wipe out the then-existing gulf that divided elite culture from pop; to build a bridge, to move to and fro, between the realms of the elite and the pop culture. With its tenacity to be present in elite as well as in popular realms, the mythopoeic approach enjoins all. For Fiedler, myth is the only consistent agent that universalizes all literature into a mythic whole. His own readers, hence, will recognize that he usually concentrates on the mythic element, which is indifferent to medium, and insouciant in the face of the various highs and lows of culture. He relates popular art to myth: "Popular art ... lives only by its mythic appeal, its ability to find, once and for all, the pattern of story and image which will transmit to simple people what they need to know without making them aware that they are learning (horrid word!) anything" (*Vertical File* 1975, 261). I think it would not be inept to say that it is very difficult to find out which is the larger concern of Fiedler's writings, myth or popular culture. Both play a game of hide-and-seek and eventually merge into each other. But a little more thought would reveal another starting fact. As Fiedler and his fellow critics rightly say, popular culture and myths both jointly appeal to the primordial instincts of man and cater to a vast segment of society. Hence, Fiedler's concern with myths gets assimilated into his larger concern of today: popular culture.

The mythic element is "indifferent to medium" (CBCG, 14). Myth also forms the crux of pop literature, according to Fiedler. In an effort to cross the border and close the gap between the past and the present, Fiedler in his talk with DeMott beautifully links up ancient myths and science fiction. Fiedler says that science fiction "refuses to draw lines between the 'real' and the 'hallucinatory.' It is all part of the destruction of the old secular notions and the reintroduction of the mythological" (DeMott 1978, 9). Paradoxically, myths also permeate science fiction. Despite its newness or modern look, science fiction draws upon myths for its popular appeal. Giving the example of *Star Wars* and *Close Encounters of the Third Kind*, two movies that made a mark in the contemporary scientific world, he says, "The science in them is pure pretense. In *Star Wars*, the scientific apparatus gives us an excuse to get back to certain tales of mystery and adventure that thrilled us when we were little kids. *Close Encounters* had almost a religious or a supernatural note, which is not explained by the real details of anything in the plot or the scientific machinery. It's in the tone" (9). DeMott further says, "Our minds have been opened up again in the age where the marvellous was accepted" (9), i.e., the past.

As Fiedler tasted success and acclaim as a literary critic and cultural commentator, it appeared that in his attempt to prove himself "a barbarian at the gates of literary respectability" (Winchell in Kellman and Malin 1999, 87), he adopted an extremely strident tone for his literary criticism. In "Cross the Border—Close the Gap" (1970), he identifies "the unconfused scandal of contemporary literary criticism" as the vain attempt "to explain, defend, and evaluate one kind of book" with standards invented for a very different kind of book (270). "The second or third generation new critics in America," he writes, "...end by proving themselves imbeciles and naïfs when confronted by, say, a poem by Allen Ginsberg, a new novel by John Barth" (271).

In *What Was Literature*? (1982), he contends that by the 1960s, it had become apparent that the New Critics had "exhausted their small usefulness." Although "their analyses had made possible some reforms in pedagogy, and had even illuminated a handful of neglected lyric poems, chiefly by John Donne, they had done nothing to explain the great novels of their own tradition or to encourage any new achievement in that genre." Fiedler even believes that the influence of the new critics on poetry "served to inhibit rather than spur new experiments after 1955" (WWL, 71).

As one of the graduate students at the SUNY at Buffalo in the spring of 1968, Rocco Capozzi recalls the unconventional teacher that Fiedler was. The interview, conducted in Buffalo on October 10, 1990, emphasizes the important role of Fiedler in the early phase of American literary postmodernism. Capozzi cites "Cross the Border—Close the Gap" as the essay that best summarizes Fiedler's proposals to eliminate the "great divide" between academic/elitist literature and mass culture. Capozzi questions,

> However, thirty years later academia still snubs mass culture, and the masses are not rushing to libraries and bookstores to read Dante, Milton, Joyce, Kafka, Becket, etc.! Do you still feel that one way to "close the gap" is for professors to know what students are reading and watching and thus to incorporate in class lectures examples from the so-called official literature with examples of characters, techniques, and language from TV, comic books, movies, etc.—let's say examples from "Columbo," "Star Trek," Woody Allen, Fellini, Spielberg, Batman, Roger Rabbit, Indiana Jones, etc.? [Capozzi 1991, 332].

Fiedler's response is remorseful. He feels that the appearance of "Cross the Border—Close the Gap" in *Playboy* was a "step in the right direction" but the first "flush of euphoria" in which it was written was "a product of the times, and has since evaporated" (332).

He is disappointed that

the two literatures have not fused as I had hoped; yet things are a little different in the late twentieth century. Certain writers have appeared who appeal to both audiences, like Kurt Vonnegut, who remains a favorite of the half-educated young at the same moment that he is being taught in university classes—and Thomas Pynchon is eagerly touted at gatherings of science fiction, who despise all other "mainstream" fiction, to which his dense, convoluted, and immensely allusive novels clearly belong. And, finally, there is the spectacular case of the rise to world-wide best-sellerdom of Umberto Eco's Il *nome Della Rosa*. At the same time, certain hard-core science fiction writers, like Samuel Delany, are adapting the techniques of postmodernism, and that immensely popular producer of horror/shock, Stephen King, interlards his super-best seller, *It*, with quotations from William Carlos William's *Paterson* [333].

Now, I come to a very important phase in Fiedler's literary career—from the mid-seventies to the eighties—in which he published some remarkable essays such as "Toward a Definition of Popular Literature" (1975) and "Giving the Devil His Due" (1978), and books such as *The Inadvertent Epic: From Uncle Tom's Cabin to Roots* (1979) and *What Was Literature?: Class Culture and Mass Society* (1982).

Mid-Seventies to Eighties Phase: "Toward a Definition of Popular Literature" (1975)

The title of "Toward a Definition of Popular Literature" clearly indicates the main idea of that essay. But apart from this, Fiedler in this essay touches upon a number of issues closely related to his evolution as a popular culture critic. Here he discusses, in detail, popular literature as commodity literature and its direct correlation with consumers and marketplace success. Moreover, he accuses the "shamelessly elitist" (Fiedler in Bigsby 1975, 29) of creating distinctions of "high" and "low" art, and, hence, sacrificing the literary merit and literary success of certain popular writers. In the same essay Fiedler also proposes "ekstasis" rather than instruction and delight as the center of critical analysis and evaluation.

At the outset, after defining popular literature, Fiedler says, "If the mother of popular literature is mass-production technology, the midwife which gives it birth, and the wet-nurse which suckles it is the 'free enterprise' marketplace" (29). Sometimes literature that cannot be stopped from attaining marketplace success is denied to university classrooms and libraries, because the notion floated by elitist critics, according to Fiedler, is that the art forms preferred by the majority of people cannot be admirable or worthy of receiving serious attention, and that "there is an inverse relationship between literary merit and market-place success" (29). Fiedler reiterates his point that these guardians of "good" taste "ghettoize" certain writers, even before reading their works. In the United States, says the critic, certain professionals have been trained to do this job for the rest of the people. Even the librarian "gettostacks" these books as "Juveniles" or "Teenage Fiction" or relegates some to a "super ghetto" (31) called "Pornography." Such books are never even thought to be considered for any major prize, bemoans a bitter Fiedler. He calls this an "Untouchable category" (30–31). Fiedler blames this pre-censorship on the "unworkable system" evolved by a select few in the American literary world.

Fiedler points out the plight of those "borderline writers," embarrassingly pop but endowed with energy and skill, invention, and mythopoeic power. Fiedler talks of Dickens and Twain, Cooper and Balzac and Richardson. In a very satirical manner, he writes that for such writers "elitist standards" have been bent a little, shame-facedly adjusted or hypocritically ignored (32). This "priestly brotherhood of critics" (36) evolved a new canon of literature that would exclude philistine, vulgar, trivial or popular works enjoyed by the majority. Hence, Fiedler joins the band of those critics who have become advocates of opening up the canon of American literature. These critics try to prove that the university is not the chief guardian of "taste" and "standards." It is the majority taste that defines literature. "Ekstasis" and not "instruction" will be the concern of the artist who will speak "less of theme and purpose, structure and texture, ideology and significance, irony and symbolism, and more of myth, fable, archetype, fantasy, magic, and wonder" (41), says Fiedler.

"Giving the Devil His Due" (1978)

There is an overemphatic tone in the essay "Giving the Devil His Due" (1978). Apart from stating that popular literature is commodity literature dependent upon the marketplace, Fiedler makes some important observations. He says, "Unlike the high art of the Renaissance, popular art is lacking in qualities which I have called elsewhere 'signature elements' ... an eccentric, obtrusive or special style, a personal voice or point of view" (199). As pointed out earlier, Fiedler believed that art must have the signature, the personal stamp, of the artist. This is evident from his writings of the fifties and sixties, particularly his essays "Archetype and Signature" and "In the Beginning Was the Word: Logos or Mythos," which come to mind immediately in this connection. It is quite evident from his statement that he gives less importance to the "personal voice" in popular literature. Popular culture is less personal and more universal. Instead of catering to a select group, it caters to a large cross-section of society.

In "Giving the Devil His Due," he reiterates his point that popular literature "contains communal dreams, shared myths or archetypes. And it is distinguished by the mythopoeic color of its creators, their ability to sense what already existed in the popular mind, rather than by any unique vision or ability in executive skills. For this reason popular works of literature tend to pass immediately into the public domain" (GDD, 199). Thus, Fiedler is implying that characters of popular works such as Pickwick, Don Quixote, Sherlock Holmes and David Copperfield immediately enter the public domain. In fact, Fiedler says that one of the distinctions between popular and high literature can be made on the basis that certain books and authors are remembered, such as Hemingway and Faulkner and their works, but their characters are forgotten; on the other hand, Sherlock Holmes and Tarzan are familiar household names even with those people who haven't heard of Conan Doyle or Edgar Rice Burroughs, the creators of these two popular figures in fiction.

Another important point that Fiedler establishes in this essay is that "popular literature never seems the kind of literature that you are reading for the first time" (GDD, 200) since it dramatizes communal myths and dreams of time immemorial. Hence such literature is also independent of its author, text and medium too. Popular literature never really belonged to one medium; it never was just "words on the page," says Fiedler. He puts it succinctly that all literature is finally, essentially, "images in the head. Once its images pass through words ... into our heads, such primordial images or archetypes or myths ... can pass out again easily into any other medium. They can be portrayed on the stage; they can be painted; they can be sculpted in stone; they can be turned into stained glass windows, they can be carved in soap" (201). Here, Fiedler implies that such works will retain "their authenticity and the resonance of feeling that was originally connected with them" (201). Further, such popular literature is driven, says Fiedler, by the masses to pass into other forms of media. Taking the example of *Gone with the Wind* and *Roots* as novel and movie and play, Fiedler says that though they depict opposite views of slavery and Reconstruction, yet,

> in the realm of popular Art, overt or conscious ideas could not matter less. What matters is the stirring up of the collective unconscious, the evocation of closely shared nightmares of race and sex; the drama of protecting little sister against the rapist, whoever she may be and whatever color; Black/White, White/Black. You can mix them and match them, it makes no difference to popular appeal. Is it white innocence assaulted by black bestiality? Is it black innocence assaulted by white brutality? The audience loves it in any case [203].

Moving beyond mediums, he talks of going beyond classifications. Much later in 1994, Fiedler believed that as a library text, *Love and Death* defies all classification. He continues, "Librarians have classified it either as literary history or criticism, but I have always considered it a work of art rather than scholarship, since it seeks not to prove its most outrageous theses but to charm the skeptical into a willing suspension of disbelief" (1999a).

Hence, according to him, popular literature is neither good nor bad—it is beyond good and evil, as we define the terms, in whatever culture we may live. It not only brings together the poor and the rich, the educated and the uneducated, male and female, children and adults, but it also joins you with your worst enemies and your worst self. Summing up this essay, Fiedler once again touches upon his major concern:

> When I think of the books I have loved best in my life, I realize that what I admire in them is what I love in pop art at its most gross, fragrant, vulgar, brutal and unrefined: the mythopoeic power of the author ... What really moves us to transport—what Longinus called *ekstasis*—taking us out of our heads and out of our bodies, out of our normal consciousness is the ability of all great books, great pop books, great elite books, to turn us again into savages and children; and releasing us thus from bondage not merely to the restrictions of conscience or superegos, but to consciousness and rationality, which is to say, the ego itself [Fiedler in Pardini 2008, 23].

In the earlier essay, "Towards a Definition of Popular Literature," Fiedler had talked of "ekstasis." In this essay, he develops the term and explains that it stands for the therapeutic function of art, called by various names. Aristotle called it catharsis; later prophets call it alteration of consciousness, or desublimation, or regression in the service of ego. Fiedler, finally, says, "The chief value of majority literature is to remind us of what all literature is really about" (GDD, 207) and literature "teaches us to remain faithful to our animal existence, to those dark Gods, dark only because we have shrouded them, to the dark side of our deepest ambivalence toward violence, toward sex, toward our parents, toward our mates, toward our children, toward our secret selves, toward the daylight deities we are proud to beast we honor alone" (207). And popular arts are, says Fiedler, "a way of giving the devil his due. And that due we must give him or die" (207). In this essay, Fiedler states his priorities in literature quite forcefully. Fiedler at no juncture is trying to create distinctions between high and low art; his only concern is with popular art, which is beyond the high or low compartmentalization of literature.

Freaks: Myths and Images of the Secret Self *(1978)*

A major work of this period is *Freaks: Myths and Images of the Secret Self* (1978). I have already dealt with this book as a commentary on nature's outsiders. Here, the relevance of this book increases manifold as it traces the "other" from classical times to the present era of popular culture: films, theater, soap-operas and arts such as painting, music, and sculpture. All deal with the freak as an intermediary between men and animals or sometimes men and gods; a source of good luck; a showpiece; or entertainment. Fiedler projects the freak as a symbol of the human condition, of the alienated man, and finally as a symbol of the future possibilities of man. Fiedler speaks of the freak as a mutant—which may be suitable to the new world. He traces it in movies—Dr. Jekyll and Mr. Hyde, Frankenstein's monster, Dracula—and in images in popular music, from Frank Zappa to the Rolling Stones. This book is highly provocative, illustrative and interesting and one of the artifacts of today's popular literature. DeMott, in "A Talk with Leslie Fiedler" (1978), discloses Fiedler's special concern with youth culture, myths and popular culture. The conversation, in turn, makes an interesting commentary by DeMott and Fiedler both, on the literature and literary trends of the late seventies. In addition to this, a discussion of *Freaks: Myths and Images of the Secret Self* makes some interesting disclosures. According to DeMott, *Freaks* is a book about "myths, marginal human beings [and] deep-structure psychological motifs" (5). Fiedler has a different viewpoint. He says, "Freaks is the first time I've been completely contemptuous of the boundaries between mediums and so on. It takes off from medical texts, comic books, popular music, movies—it's not just about proper literary works. And it does something I always secretly wanted to do. It's an iconic book. It's not just an illustrated book, it's a book that really isn't fully comprehensible without the pictures" (5). This sums up *Freaks: Myths and Images of the Secret Self* quite comprehensively. But *Time* says, "The richly illustrated work is in fact a combination sideshow, meditation on human nature and medical textbook of that sort that librarians once kept locked away" (Sheppard, 95).

The Inadvertent Epic: From Uncle Tom's Cabin to Roots *(1979)*

In *The Inadvertent Epic: From Uncle Tom's Cabin to Roots*, Fiedler does what he has always done—interprets America and her culture and her myths to Americans and outsiders. *The Inadvertent Epic* is another work in the long tradition of writings in which Fiedler examines popular works such as *Gone with the Wind, Uncle Tom's Cabin* and *Roots,* which are subversive to the anti-family myth and have a potent grasp on popular imagination. According to Barry Hayne (1979), *The Inadvertent Epic* is the obverse of the theme of *Love and Death in the American Novel. The Inadvertent Epic* scrutinizes not a male, subversive, anti-family myth (*Love and Death in the American Novel*) but a feminine society, domestic and familial. This book has as potent and effective a grasp on the wider popular imagination as any other. Later, Fiedler would "come clean about his sentimental side, publicly declaring his long-standing affection for three-hanky novels (Sanford 1999, 184) such as *Uncle Tom's Cabin.*" Hayne adds that while defining this other side of the male-bonding theme, Fiedler puts us in possession of almost a new method of approaching literature itself. Enormously potent works, such as *Uncle Tom's Cabin* and *Gone with the Wind*, known at least in some of their elements to almost everybody on the globe, fall short when measured by academic literary standards and by the canons of high art. If this is so, then let us re-examine those standards and canons to see whether they, not the potent objects of their judgment, may be at fault. And hence, opines Hayne, "Out of this inquiry comes the approach to literature as popular culture—though it is well to remember that we ought to arrive at Gone with the Wind from the classic rather than starting from it (1979, viii).

In *The Inadvertent Epic* Fiedler evaluates these works by redefining literature not as it has been traditionally understood, but by conceiving each as a "hitherto unperceived popular Epic" (Browne et al. 1968, 27). He discusses how critics have condemned these books as failures and their persistent refusal to admit the artistic merits of these books. Fiedler elevates those books to the level of high art. Talking of *Uncle Tom's Cabin*, he says at the very outset, "Most elitist critics have found it an artistic failure, ill constructed, shamefully sentimental and annoyingly shrill, its character stereotypes, its plot, and vulgar melodrama. No wonder that the guardians of high taste, embarrassed by its unwillingness to go away and die the death to which it has been repeatedly condemned, have chosen to pretend it is no longer there" (13). This book, according to Fiedler, had almost become the "nigger" of American literature. Fiedler regards *Uncle Tom's Cabin* and *Roots* as unperceived popular epics. Rooted in demonic dreams of race, sex and violence that have long haunted Americans, these books determine the views on the Civil War, Reconstruction, the rise and fall of the Ku Klux Klan, and the enslavement and liberation of African blacks, thus constituting a myth of American history unequalled in scope and resonance by any work of high literature. Fiedler's special emphasis, however, is on the fact that no epic was created so inadvertently, so improbably "arising out of tradition at once disreputable and genteel, which seemed destined forever to produce not literature of high seriousness, 'doctrinal to a nation,' but only ephemeral best-sellers" (17). Written in the nineteenth century chiefly by amateurs, clergymen and women (Harriet Beecher Stowe was not only a female amateur, but the daughter, wife and sister of clergymen), such best-sellers were accused by high-tone critics and more pretentious novelists, competing for mass audience, of contributing to the degradation of American culture. Such writers, claims Fiedler, preferred books that were not only more elegantly structured and textured, more ideologically dense, more overtly subversive—more difficult and challenging—but that also celebrated the flight from home and mother, civilization and settlement, church and school.

Buffalo Bill and the Wild West *(1981)*

Another attempt at such an evaluation was made in 1981, when Fiedler contributed an essay, "The Legend," to a book called *Buffalo Bill and the Wild West*. Buffalo Bill is a legendary figure in America, the frontiersman, showman, businessman, and pioneer media star, William Cody. The legend of the frontier, as personified in Buffalo Bill, still lives on because it touches upon some crucial phases of the evolution of America—the anguish of the evolution from the Civil War to World War I. This book is based on an exhibition about Buffalo Bill and relates the impact of Buffalo Bill on the national character of America. In his essay, Fiedler gives a mythic significance to the character of Buffalo Bill and illustrates how Cody became a mythological hero of America. David H. Katzive, in the introduction to this book, says, "In writing about Cody's many manifestations, Fiedler focuses on Buffalo Bill as a show business phenomenon created by hack writers and nurtured by press agents. He sees Cody's persona as comprising a complex of legends which satisfied certain psychological needs and mythic expectations of his public but rendered the real man indistinguishable from his images" (84). Even today, Fiedler contends in his article, this Buffalo Bill legend defies any satisfactory interpretation by analysis determined to unmask the reality behind this legend and character. Fiedler discusses the drama of Buffalo Bill as fiction too, and identifies the archetypes of the enduring Western myth in the legend and character. Was Cody an authentic Western hero? Fiedler asks, and tries to seek the truth or reality behind the legend of Buffalo Bill and the Wild West. Fiedler interprets the legend's survival in pulp fiction and popular drama too. He discusses how William Cody became a mythological figure in America and describes his association with the Wild West. In addition to this, Fiedler strengthens his position firmly as a popular culture critic by interpreting a cultural legend of the United States in terms of myth and popular appeal.

What Was Literature? Class Culture and Mass Society *(1982)*

Continuing his preoccupation with myths and popular culture, Fiedler published *What Was Literature? Class Culture and Mass Society* (1982). In this book, Fiedler was very sure of the direction in which he was moving. His priorities were crystal clear, and so were his critical stances. He had declared long before his liking for newness, his distrust of tradition and elitism and his leanings toward popular literature. This book is the last major work that I have examined in the long tradition of writings on popular literature. In this book, at the very outset, Fiedler questions university education, which perpetuates an unfortunate distinction of high literature and low literature, of literature proper and sub- or para-literature. In this book his concern with literature and its categories achieves a rare clarity. According to him the works of Dickens, Twain and Shakespeare were written to titillate the mass audience. The same is the case with Mitchell, Stowe and many other popular writers. Then, Fiedler asks, why are different critical standards used to measure their worth? Fiedler contends that it is because of the inflexibility of our critical standards that his essays "Archetype and Signature" and "In the Beginning Was the Word: Logos or Mythos" were applauded as great critical pieces, whereas his essay "Come Back to the Raft Ag'in, Huck Honey!" "which is [a] less solemn but more truly serious work" (WWL, 14), was completely disregarded by these elite critics. He was understood as a "crypto-pop critic destined to subvert rather than sustain the 'standards' which ... separated 'true literature' from mere 'junk'" (WWL, 14). Fiedler ridicules this dichotomy of standards inherent in present critical theory. He is highly critical of the double standards nurtured by these elite critics. In *What Was Literature?: Class Culture and Mass Society*, Fiedler exposes the reality behind the two critical pieces of his early phase.

The Persistent Huck Motif in Popular Culture

According to Winchell, what Fiedler did not fully realize in 1948 was the degree to which the Huck-Honey motif would permeate American popular culture. Looking back on the situation in 1982, he notes the pervasiveness of inter-ethnic male bonding "in a score of movies such as *The Defiant Ones, The Fortune Cookie*, and the belated film version of Ken Kesey's *One Flew over the Cuckoo's Nest*, as well as in numerous TV shows, ranging from *I Spy* to *Tenspeed and Brown Shoe, Chips* and *Hill Street Blues*" (WWL, 16). Moving beyond 1982, one could cite the TV show *Miami Vice* and the seemingly endless series of *Lethal Weapon* films. Even the daily comic strip *Jump Start* features what John Gregory Dunne once called a "black and white in a black-and-white" (Dunne 2002, 4, quoted in Winchell 2002, 55).

Strangers are constantly writing Fiedler to mention different sightings of the Huck-Honey motif. On October 25, 1967, Geoffrey Williams suggested that someone "write an essay on latent homosexuality in British fiction to be called, "Elementary, Watson Dear." Nearly two decades later, on February 4, 1986, Paul A. Roth, of the philosophy department of the University of Missouri at St. Louis, sent Fiedler a paper called "Come Back to the Millennium Falcon Ag'in, Han Honey: Sex and Society in *Star Wars*." (The possibilities for alien male bonding in deep space had already been noted years before when one of the early reviews of the TV series *Star Trek* was titled "Come Back to the Space Ship Ag'in, Spock Honey!") Then Carol Green suggested that the

Eddie Murphy film *Beverly Hills Cop* "may be the first time that Nigger Jim gets to tell his side of the story." Responding to her elaborately developed theory of the movie, Fiedler notes, "It is always an especial delight to see people working out implications of ideas which I started so long ago" (Winchell 2002, 55).

"How Did It All Start" (WWL)

This small critical piece points toward Fiedler's flair for mild satire and unobtrusive humor. As if to establish his literary credentials, Fiedler traces the beginnings of literature with Plato and Aristotle in "How Did It All Start." Coming to contemporary times, Fiedler asserts that popular literature also deals with the most dark and perilous aspects of our psyche, otherwise confessed only in nightmares. Yet, an examination of such works reveals elements that are totally absent in the so-called classics. Here, Fiedler is implying that popular literature is more enjoyable because it is closer to our psyche and that is the truth behind real and serious literature, be it popular or classic or both. Finally Fiedler states his point:

> Such honored works as Sophocles' *Oedipus Rex,* Euripides' *Medea,* Shakespeare's *Henry IV* and *Macbeth* ... have persisted not merely because they instruct us morally or delight us with their formal felicities, but because they allow us, in waking reverie, to murder our fathers and marry our mothers with Oedipus; to kill a king with the Macbeths; or our own children with Medea; to lie, steal, cheat, deceive and run away from a justified and necessary war with Falstaff and to glory in it [WWL, 50].

Giving the examples of popular writers such as Shakespeare, Sophocles, Bram Stoker and Edger Rice Burroughs, Fiedler implies that these writers allow the readers to fulfill in a vicarious fashion a host of their "shocking and shameful" desires, which none of the readers would even consider remotely possible, in their wildest dreams, to be articulated by either their thoughts, words or actions. These "forbidden" fantasies are made "respectable" by these writers and are marketed to their consumers, i.e., the readers, in a form readily acceptable by them, without the association of any feeling of guilt or embarrassment. Fiedler further elaborates this line of thinking: "the burden of any system of morality becomes finally irksome even to its most sincere advocates, since it necessarily denies, represses, suffocates, certain undying primal impulses which, however outmoded by civilization, need somehow to be expressed. And this release of the repressed, all art, which remains popular, whatever its critical status, makes possible—symbolically only, to be sure; but the joy and terror we feel are real" (WWL, 50).

"What Was the Art Novel?" (WWL)

From the foregoing, it is clear that Fiedler has strong convictions regarding the psychological, moral and social appeal of popular culture and literature since his early days. Hence, in "What Was the Art Novel?" Fiedler describes the inability of the art novel to cater to popular taste. An increasing number of novelists and critics have begun to realize that these art novels are no longer viable models for living fiction. In fact, some writers, particularly in America, have begun to doubt the very distinction between "serious books" and "best sellers" upon which the conception of the "art novel" depends; it was an error from the very beginning. Here Fiedler makes a very important point: the reason for this error is that the culture of the United States has always been "popular" beneath a "thin overlay of imported European elitism" (WWL, 64). He further says, "Our national mythos is a pop myth and our revolution consequently a pop revolution, as compared, for instance, with either the French or the Russian, which originated in high level ideological manifestoes and debates. Our War of Independence was rooted in concrete grievances rather than abstract ideas" (WWL, 64). Moreover, Fiedler says that America has a revolutionary pattern of politics and culture, and that it is a challenge to all nations and cultures. When Europeans or other non–American cultures talk of the incursion in their culture of pop forms such as rock, country, and Western music; comic books; soap operas and cop shows on television; they tend to refer to it as a "creeping Americanization" (WWL, 65) of their cultures. Nonetheless, Fiedler hits upon the harsh truth and says that when "Americanization" is used as a synonym for "vulgarization," it perpetuates a stereotype of America as a land of Calibans, half-educated fugitive slaves, the cast-offs of Europe, Asia and Africa. It is a kind of half-truth, says Fiedler. Moreover, it will be repeated again because a considerable number of Americans, primarily the WASP elitist academics, refuse to acknowledge that pop culture, which has spread all over the world today, is essentially American. It is more particularly a part of youth culture to which most Americans belong. As stated earlier by Fiedler, all Americans like to think of themselves as young (WWL, 65). Moreover, it is a known fact that American culture is itself a relatively "young culture." It is part of the peculiarly American dream, which has not stopped being dreamt by Americans, even today.

According to Christine Bold, Fiedler's writing "celebrates mass literature as a spontaneous expression of modern folk culture," much in contrast to how Ralph Ellison perceived it: as "the debasement of African American Culture in its appropriation by mass forms of entertainment" (Bold 1991, 285).

"Literature and Lucre" (WWL)

In the essay "Literature and Lucre" Fiedler writes of writers who were driven by fantasies of being published, being read, being great and being known. This urge leads them to the market place. Fiedler says what he had said earlier in his essay "Giving the Devil His Due," that a literary work remains incomplete till it has passed from the desk to the marketplace, where it is packaged and sold. There is nothing new in this essay; it is a reiteration of the relationship between literature and lucre established earlier. Fiedler makes the task of writing appear very mundane, commercial and lucrative, but he is known for being unobtrusively frank and outspoken and even highly commercial. Yet, serious, "creative writers considered employment in the university as a kind of selling out" (WWL, 27). But today in America, says Fiedler "commerce is officially more honored than art" (WWL, 27).

To speak to the people means to speak in the language of the people rather than in some artificial tongue invented by academicians precisely for the purpose of creating an elitist or hermetic art. Regarding this view, Fiedler has no doubts. He says that the American artist's language is essentially the popular language, spoken by millions of Americans. Fiedler is accused of employing a highly elitist and sophisticated idiom for his writings. In defense of lowbrow art, Fiedler says that the people to whom he is talking are the ones who resist this culture. He says:

> I am not addressing the people who already know and love popular literature or art. I have those people in mind who have resisted this type of culture. I think of myself as a double agent in their camp. I speak the language of literary critics, explaining in literary idiom the nature and appeal of popular art [Maini 1976, 10].

On High, Low and Middlebrow Culture, Pop Art and the Novel

In a symposium on the American novel organized in 1969 by NOVEL, Fiedler establishes the point that the novel as an art form is popular because it releases popular fantasy. This was demonstrated through a nostalgic trip back to Europe:

> I've recently gone back to the 1840s and I've been reading Eugene Sue, William Reynolds and George Lippard. They all had a popular audience, as almost no writers ever had. Reynolds outsold even Dickens about five to one. And they wrote marvelous, essentially shapeless and formless novels, the *Mysteries of Paris*, the *Mysteries of London*, the *Mysteries of the Court*, which were sentimental, sensational and demi-pornographic, and yet somehow managed to say what it was that life was like in the big cities as they were being created for the first time.... I have a hunch that if the novel is going any place interesting now it's got to go

back to someplace like this, to a place which releases popular fantasy [Fiedler 1970d, 203–04].

In his response to Bruce Bauman in one of his last interviews, Fiedler reminisces on his split with *Partisan Review* precisely because of ideological differences over the clash of highbrow versus lowbrow that has gradually usurped the place of class war in its working mythology. Fiedler says, "There are things in American culture that want to wipe the class distinction. Blue jeans. Ready-made clothes. Coca-Cola. We were talking about Henry Miller: Is it high art or is it—if it imitates the popular form, say a detective story or science fiction—what is it? Then there's the middlebrow, which I hate. Then there's what escapes those [categories] completely. I think Mark Twain is like that." Later he says, "One could call Twain middlebrow—but he *isn't*. He is both high and low at the same time. Joyce is another person who is close to popular literature. It's funny how interest in Joyce has brought together so many people who are so different: Umberto Eco, Helene Cixous, Marshall McLuhan" (Bauman 2003, 7–8).

So popular literature does seem to brings together a wide variety of readers as sharers.

Till the year 2003, just before his death, Fiedler continued to stick by the view that the "novel is the first art form that is an honest-to-god commodity. I guess that's what I mean by 'pop.' That's what makes it different from both high art and folk art." He also says, "The novel is always dying. That's the only way it stays alive. It does really die. I've been thinking about that a lot" (Bauman 2003, 3). He explicates this by giving the example of Cooper, about whom he was writing that year:

> He was not a writer. Here was a man who was 30 years old and had never put anything more than his signature on paper and his wife annoyed him by reading Austen or maybe one of her imitators to him. He said, why are you wasting your time with that? Anybody could write a better one. I could. His wife said, I'd like to see you try. He sat down and wrote a novel which is absolutely indistinguishable from Austen, completely from a female point of view, completely English, no sense that he was an American, the language is British English. Her novel was called "Persuasion," his was one word like that. It was a terrible flop because he discovered that if people wanted to get a novel written by an English woman, they'd go to England and get one. And the new fashion he discovered was this strange Scotsman who couldn't make it writing poetry and decided to write novels, so he [Cooper] turned around completely. And one kind of novel died and another began [Bauman 2003, 3].

Then commenting on some of his favorite writers, he says he finds Stephen King a fascinating popular novelist. Amongst the present-day critics he finds the work of Camille Paglia and Allen Ginsberg closest to his own.

His view is that Ginsberg "will last, or at least those poems will last, the ones in which he finds his real voice. Anybody in the next centuries wanting to know what it was like to be a poet in the middle of the 20th century should read 'Kaddish.'" He confesses that he has "very complicated feelings about Paglia" whom he admired as a critic and poet "when she began" and liked her even better when he "heard her talk." Fiedler was also very happy when she visited on his 80th birthday. What pleased him was her "real sense of humor, which enables her sometimes to see what is really funny not only about other people but about herself as well. If I am in any sense disappointed, it is because her most interesting work seems to have been done early and she has got to a point much too soon to start repeating herself" (Bauman 2003, 12).

Fiedler and the Canon

Fiedler is truly a maker of a canon, built on a credo of inclusion and innovation, but he would not really prefer to be called a creator precisely because for years he has resisted the "currently canonical." In "The Canon and the Classroom: A Caveat," he bemoans that establishing and maintaining a canon has become, for better or worse, one of the chief functions of literary studies in English. He goes on to say, "I am allergic to all words ending in 'ism,' particularly those I have been tempted on occasion to use myself.... Over and over again, I have watched a presumable critical breakthrough, an opening up of new insights tend first to turn into a fad, then a cliché; and finally on the level of day-to-day pedagogy become a canon, enforced in the totalitarian regime of the classroom." He hopes to create "a kind of meta-canon without limits and forever changing ... not an act of conformity and submission to established authority, but a way of challenging and subverting the status quo whatever it might be—a way of saying "No! In thunder" (2008, 128–30).

His firm belief is that the epigones of modernism "consigned to the outer darkness many books which had pleased many ... on the grounds that precisely because they had done so they had proved themselves unredeemable trash." They had "trouble coming to terms with borderline writers, including some who had been my own favorites. I am thinking in particular of Walt Whitman, who theoretically at least wrote for the popular audience; Edgar Allan Poe, who wooed and eventually won that audience, though he boasted of spurning it; and especially Harriet Beecher Stowe, who not merely aspired to best-sellerdom but achieved it" (Fiedler 2008, 130).

This brings me to the all-important question: why are the feminists up in arms against him? After all, he seems to be one who readily agreed and attempted to rectify what he thought was "the old blending of snobbism and misogyny which had prompted Mrs. Stowe's exclusion." In the two critical works that established the modernist canon for American literature, Matthiessen's *American Renaissance* and Lawrence's *Studies in Classic American Literature, Uncle Tom's Cabin* was completely ignored. According to Fiedler, "Nathaniel Hawthorne, a special favorite of both Matthiessen and Lawrence, seems to have been thinking chiefly of Mrs. Stowe when he excoriated 'the damned female scribblers,' against whom, he thought, he and other more serious writers (all male, of course) had to contend for readers" (Fiedler 1992, in Pardini 2008, 130).

Later in *What Was Literature?* he "publicly called for opening up the canon to include her—along with Alex Haley, Thomas Dixon, Jr., and Margaret Mitchell, whose *Gone with the Wind* has finally outsold even *Uncle Tom's Cabin,* becoming simultaneously the most widely sold and loved and the most critically despised of American books."(30) Interestingly, as a result *What Was Literature?* is "the least widely sold and loved ... most vilified, of course, by certain last-ditch defenders of High-Modernism as Hugh Kenner, a political as well as aesthetic reactionary, and therefore particularly offended by my shameless populism" (Fiedler 1992, in Pardini 2008, 130).

By breaking down the boundaries between high art and pop, *What Was Literature?* hoped without prejudice to resurrect "underestimated" and hitherto

> despised works by underprivileged groups in our society: women; Black Americans; Native Americans; homosexuals; Hispanics; even Rednecks, the 'niggers' of the presumably enlightened. Such works had been underestimated; it seemed to me, because the earlier makers of our canon had been chiefly college-educated, straight WASP males, who (speaking only to each other) had found it possible to identify their parochial prejudices with universal aesthetic standards. With this diagnosis of our cultural plight, militant feminists, gays, Indians, and Afro-Americans seemed at first sight to agree [132].

However, these groups later turned out to be "untrustworthy allies" and "another kind of enemy" (132). To begin with, some of them, though dedicated to opening up the canon in terms of gender and race, still smuggled in the old elitist distinctions of high and low. A recent highly respected history of African American literature, for instance (its author himself black), not only ignores the street writer Iceberg Slim but passes over in silence Frank Yerby, the most widely read author of his race; and does not even mention the immensely talented Samuel Delany—presumably because his books, marketed as science fiction, are, whatever their intrinsic merits, generically extracanonical (132).

Even more disconcertingly, such "progressive" revisers of the canon end by excluding as well as including works on ideological grounds; so that their new canon is finally even narrower than the reactionary one they began by deploring (132–33).

The Establishment of the Pop Guru

It may be a paradox, but it is still true that Leslie Fiedler is claimed by both the elitist tradition and the pop tradition. On the one hand some high priests of elitist tradition see him as a member of their clan; on the other hand, the svelte swingers of the pop tradition stoically confirm his affiliation to their group. Yet his criticism amply demonstrates a tilt toward the latter. In his critical writings, at one time or the other he has reflected practically every color of the spectrum. However, his major preoccupations, by and large, have not undergone a change. It has been my endeavor throughout this study not only to trace his evolutionary trajectory within the framework of his major preoccupations at the micro level but also to highlight the general direction of his criticism at the macro level, which shows a determined shift of interest from elite to pop.

His consistent attempt has been to seek an audience outside the portals of the university—a target segment toward which a major part of his criticism is directed. His uniformly uncommon freshness of approach to literature takes him more and more away from orthodox and conservative criticism, leading to the creation of a break with the older generation of critics. The new generation of critics, hence, calls him an advocate of opening up the canon of American literature, an exponent of pop art and mass culture.

A prolific writer, Fiedler's literary career spans more than five decades. His early writings show his elite bearings and enunciate his concern with the function of criticism and literature, the role of the artist and the biographical approach to criticism. He also lays bare his credo of criticism, as dealt with earlier. It was with his essay "No! In Thunder" that he began to set the trend. Before this, his essay "My Credo" categorically established his support for strategic, historical-biographical criticism and his concern for the common man. At first profoundly political, then deeply literary, he came to a point where the textual critic and socio-literary critic merged into one. But he has also taken part in defining and criticizing the new criticism that has emerged since modernism. He categorically disassociates himself from formalism or the structuralist mafia, as he calls them. In fact, he openly acknowledges his allegiance to Romanticism and, as stated earlier, historical-biographical criticism and strategic criticism. For Fiedler, critical writing is just another form of writing fiction. Regarding the creative and critical processes, he sees hardly any overlap between them. Critical essays are fictions about other fictions. Yet, Fiedler is not sure whether the literary world, finally, will belong to the creative artist or to the critic. His view is that any kind of criticism that treats literature in terms of theories of meaning, as if it were merely words on a page, is precisely falling into the world of logos. According to him, the school of French literary criticism, of Jacques Derrida, is caught up in this trap. Fiedler's implications are that criticism has now become inflated with pedagogy and having moved into universities, there are professional critics instead of writers. Towards the later part of his critical career he chose to call himself a literary anthropologist. The sixties were a time of transition for him, and then the populist man in him began to dominate. He became the people's man rather than the elitists' man.

His writings present us a thesis about the infantile element in American culture, its fears and regressions, whose summation can be none but this: there is always *another* way of looking at literature and culture. And this analysis has stood the test of time. Winchell (1985, 6) points out that Fiedler's thesis is "continually being vindicated by movie and television shows that pair a white hero and a dark-skinned sidekick. Indeed, one early review of the series *Star Trek* was entitled, "Come Back to the Spaceship Again, Spock Honey!"

What the critics of the critic do not see is that Fiedler is too bold, forthright, and even idiosyncratic to really care about the cauldron of anger and rage boiling against him and his provocative interpretations of literature. He attempts to restore our faith in what he strongly feels about. The defense that he offers against the barrage of criticism regarding his selectivity of writers is somehow made convincing by him. For example, he says that in *What Was Literature?: Class Culture and Mass Society* he has dealt with a lot of writers he had ignored earlier. For him, three things become primary: literature and society; literature's interpreter, the critic; and the reader, the audience. In the light of this statement his evolution can be easily traced. From a student of literature, Fiedler became a critic of literature, devoting exceptional attention to the audience, its preferences and dislikes. He shares a very special, or as he says, an almost erotic, relationship with his readers. Stressing his differentness, in 1982 he told Patricia Ward Biedernman, author of *Organizing Genius*, that his desire was to write as differently as possible from the structuralist, poststructuralist, and deconstructionist critics who write a private jargon, a secret language, in hermetic code that's only available to the initiated. His differentness cast him away from most of the critics.

He once said (in 1971) that he was convinced that criticism could no longer and would no longer be condescending to popular literature. Since then he has travelled a long way. Turning from the elite he crossed the border to pop in order to better understand books, artifacts and culture. Popular literature, he felt, joined all audiences—children and adults, women and men, the sophisticated and the naive, the initiated and the novice.

It is a battle in Fiedler's long war against genteel criticism and scholarship to defend the tower of pop art that looms large all over now. Fiedler twits at the literary establishment for trying to dictate what people are allowed to enjoy by imposing standards from the elite citadel. This is an extremely witty and spirited defense of the premise that popular culture produces and recognizes excellence and the joys thereof. The opening chapter of that book *What Was Literature? Mass Culture and Mass Society*—which R. W. B. Lewis recommends to one and all—is a sort of autobiographical musing called "Who Was Leslie A. Fiedler?" Lewis writes, "Here Leslie returns to "Come Back to the Raft" and reviews—with a kind of wonder at that old self of his—his deepening involvement with those phases of our culture that have since been so obsessively emphasized. He does so, it can be noted, even while once again showing the way in cultural alertness—that is, by stressing and illustrating the historic and present importance of popular culture" (1999, 154). So this popular culturalist was a public man in more ways than just his ability to connect with the audience and his oratorical skills. It is true that his essays are so imbued with his personality and persona that it almost seems as if he has reinvented the American essay with the critic an integral part of that criticism, as part of the art. His allegiance to the public and the common man complemented his commitment to his calling. He tells Bauman in one of his last interviews that good criticism should be judged the way art is. It shouldn't be read the way one reads history or science. What he likes best is that people who are not experts can not only understand but get engaged by his work. He likes the fact that Joe Paterno can read him and that Bill Bradley calls him up and says, "I've been reading an essay of yours." For him, the American novel is extremely personal—even when it's not memoir, it's as if it were memoir. He gives the example of *Huck Finn*. He is piqued when the last page and line of the new edition of *Huckleberry Finn* doesn't say "yours truly" at the end (Bauman 2003, 7).

The evolution in Fiedler's writings is recognizable, though there are deviations and aberrations, crests and troughs. Fiedler has travelled up and down the academic promenade for decades now. He has established that taste is determined by the common man now and not by the earlier so-called ruling class. In the age of democracy, Fiedler's democratic leanings are evident, and this is the final evolution in his thought pattern: From highbrow, this critic of elite culture moves to lowbrow—the popular culture of the masses.

Fiedler is a man of this age. And it would not be unjust to say that he will be seen as a man for all ages. His evolution is not linear. Though an attempt has been made to point out beginnings, all through his growth there are ups and downs, reversions and diversions, crests and troughs. Whatever the critics might say—that he is a shocker and an iconoclast, provocative and scandalizer—and in spite of all his protestations too, Fiedler constitutes a one-man fifth column in the elitist citadel to earn the nickname of the Pop Guru.

CHAPTER 5

Perspectives of the "Other"

Postcolonial and Feminist Readings

For a nation as self-satisfied and self-isolating as the United States, the need to humbly seek and carefully consider outside perspectives and criticism is essential to the future of the country and its citizens. As Americanists, we need to listen and really hear all voices and make greater efforts to engage with colleagues from around the world, not only to share our knowledge of the United States but to learn other ways of perceiving, thinking, and behaving in the world.
—Emory Elliott, "Diversity in the United States and Abroad"

"Alternative" is defined by what it is not: it is not mainstream, it is not state sponsored, it is not conventional and is not static. It refers to something located outside traditional and established systems; something non-conventional, espousing or reflecting values that are different from those of the establishment.
—John Downing, *Radical Media: Rebellious Communications and Social Movements* in Vijayasree, 2011

Kinsmen of the feminist critics ... the father of us all.
—Susan Gubar, *Madwoman in the Attic*[1]

Did Fiedler become "the other" fighting for the "other?" This chapter offers an alternative thesis on Fiedler.[2] Few practitioners would cite Fiedler as a progenitor or precursor in the field of feminist criticism, queer theory, African American studies, American Indian studies, or Jewish studies. At best, he is seen as a "vaguely embarrassing because unpredictable, irreverent, irascible second cousin twice removed" (Gubar 1999, 169). Postcolonialists also do not engage with him, the way they would not with America and American studies. But in the mid-nineties an alternative paradigm emerged when globally the prefix "re" got attached to American studies: re-thinking American studies, re-visioning America, re-structuring American studies, re-inventing America, re-mapping America. Macro-debates on the future of American studies were the hot discussion point there (Azam 2001, in Vijayasree 2011). This suggested two things: Firstly, doubts had arisen about the older order of things in which American studies flourished then, and secondly, signs of a concerted effort aimed at effecting an overhaul in the discipline of American studies were clearly visible. With this backdrop this chapter makes an alternative reading of Fiedler from two standpoints: feminist and postcolonial. The alternative suggested here is much in line with Vijaysree's understanding of Downing's "alternative" quoted in her address on alternative American studies in India (2011).

Fiedler's writings and criticism thus, is being read under the rubric of this alternative-studies paradigm. In fact, it is more in sync with the Saidian model of contrapuntal reading that encourages interdisciplinarity and fluidity, bringing in polyphony of voices. This also finds a lot of resonance with Indian philosophic thought and the concept of intercomplementarity and pluralism. Discursive strategies such as the Saidian model of contrapuntal reading (Chowdhry 2007), which is a "'reading back' to uncover the 'submerged but crucial presence of empire in canonical texts' and to demonstrate 'the complementarity and interdependence instead of isolated, venerated, or formalized experience that excludes and forbids the hybridizing intrusions of human history'"[3] (Said 2000, 367), are a viable approach. "Unlike univocal readings in which the stories told by dominant powers become naturalized and acquire the status of 'common sense,' a contrapuntal reading thus demonstrates 'a simultaneous awareness both of the metropolitan history and those other histories against which (and together with which) the dominating discourse acts'" (Said 1993, 51). The goal of a contrapuntal reading is thus to not privilege any particular narrative but reveal the "wholeness" of the text, the intermeshed, overlapping, and mutually embedded histories of metropolitan and colonized societies and of the elite and subaltern. A contrapuntal reading, like a fugue, can contain many voices in the same composition, with each maintaining their distinct resonance but they are each distinct. Edward Said's understanding of culture derives from his dedication to the contrapuntal method, a philosophical and methodological premise that "cultural forms are hybrid, mixed, impure" and that modern cultural forms have an "infinity of imperial traces" within them (Said 1993, 14).

Then aren't the Fiedlerian practices of subversive reading, decanonization and building up of a counter discourse actually postcolonial critical practices?

Thus, as such, the rubric spelt out by Emory Elliott in his presidential address to ASA in 2006 can work:

The arrogant assumption that we who live in the City on the Hill are the best, the brightest, and the strongest, who know what is best not only for ourselves but for the rest of the world, is a dangerous and deadly error. For a nation as self-satisfied and self-isolating as the United States, the need to humbly seek and carefully consider outside perspectives and criticism is essential to the future of the country and its citizens.... Moreover, many more members of the new generations of U.S. Americanists must become multilingual. Not only is it self-focused and offensive to assume that everyone else must speak English, but to be unable to converse with others in another language is to lose in translation more than one can ever know [Elliott 2007, 18–19].

He further says: "In this time of deep political division, national paranoia, and global uncertainty, scholars of the humanities, arts, and social sciences across the globe must learn from each other, share perspectives, and continue to broaden the range of ideas needed to bring about change" (2). It is here that he puts transnationalism as "genuine inclusiveness and broad international collaboration" at the center of the American Studies Association's future agenda (6).

While accepting the award of the J. B. Hubbell Medal in 1994, Fiedler said that since his first notoriously iconic essay, "Come Back to the Raft Ag'in, Huck Honey!" (1948) he has been "treating ... [American] literature not in isolation but in relation to Western culture as a whole—specifically, to deal with it as the first postcolonial literature of the modern world." Was there an element of truth in his assertion or was it merely a bold, bombastic, and loud statement?

To find out, we must link some paradigms and notions of postcolonialism and American exceptionalism to Fiedler's attempts to rupture and reform the American canon (in *Love and Death in the American Novel*, 1960; *The Inadvertent Epic: From Uncle Tom Cabin's to Roots*, 1979; and *What Was Literature?: Class Culture and Mass Society*, 1982). *Love and Death in the American Novel* is one of the three major critical books of American literature, along with R. W. B. Lewis's *The American Adam* (1955) and F. O. Matthiessen's *The American Renaissance* (1941).[4] Was he only being churlish in writing a discourse of dissent symptomatic of American literature in the 1950s and 1960s, or was it one of the ways to accede to or supersede the paradigms of American exceptionalism?[5] Towards this end, this section makes a postcolonial reading of Fiedler's position today: un–American American (Madsen defines the un–American as those who are territorially located in the U.S. such as the natives, blacks, Asian Americans and sometimes even the Jews, but ideologically outside, thus never assimilated and made to remain hyphenated), insider-outsider, the wild man of American letters with a bifocal vision, or the one-man fifth-column in the elitist citadel to earn the nickname of a pop guru.

Alternative Readings I

The Register of Postcolonialism

Like all other "post"-marked terms, *postcolonialism* has caused no end of debate among its protagonists and antagonists. While the authors of *The Empire Writes Back* champion a loose use of the term *postcolonial* in expanding it to the literatures of Canada, Australia, and the United States, critics such as Linda Hutcheon, Spivak, and Bhabha are skeptical of the possibility of an "uncontaminated or indigenous" postcolonial theory. The continued surge of interest in postcolonial studies since the 1990s further complicated and enriched the field of American studies (Shaobo 1997). Postcolonial critics do not speak with one voice on America; yet, attempts to de-center the dominant understandings of the American experience and reexamine them have been underway for a long time. One such scholar-critic who has been attempting to understand America his way is Leslie A. Fiedler. Now is the turn to understand him from the postcolonial perspective hitherto untouched.

A postcolonial perspective is useful for several reasons: a postcolonial critique allows for a wide-ranging investigation into power relations in various contexts; the experience of colonialism and imperialism is shared by the ex-colonizer and the ex-colonized, which makes it easy to apply the perspective also to First World European countries (Shohat 1992, 103); generically, the term *postcolonial* is used to signify a position against Eurocentricism; American cultural identity has historically been wrought by the contradictions inherent in its being both former colony and an empire and a nation of immigrants (if Jewish literature can be called immigrant literature, then such literature is increasingly interested in the transnational experiences of its protagonists); and two paradoxical theses on postcolonialism and America exist with the following contentions: Peter Hulme argued as far back as 1995 for a place for America in the discussions on postcolonial studies in his article "Including America."

Through an examination of the critique of important postcolonial scholars (Shohat, McClintock, Helen Tiffin, Bill Ashcroft, and others), Hulme (1993) offers three reasons for including America in postcolonial discussions: firstly, the U.S. has a role as the world's leading imperialist power; secondly, that postcolonial studies related to America should begin their investigations from 1492, which Marx sarcastically designated the "rosy dawn" of capitalism (its immediate consequence would be to provide the U.S. with a nineteenth- and twentieth-century imperial and colonial history that would help in the understanding of America within the world, and the inclusion of America will, and should, affect the shape and definition of the field); and thirdly, and more positively, on closer inspection, many misgivings about America's role in postcolonial studies are misplaced.

Most of these points need careful scrutiny. America is slipping badly. Many, including Donald Pease (2009), have asserted that America is not a shining example or exceptional, or even a competent meddler. It is going to take a generation or so to reclaim American exceptionalism (Power 2003, quoted in Hirsch 2007). Yet, in defining the ideal Malaysian postcolonial literature, postcolonial Malaysian critic Mohammad Quayum discusses America and finds Emerson's *The American Scholar* one of the earliest of postcolonial works imbibing the spirit of dialogism and syncretism (2007, 27).

On the other hand, Ania Loomba, in her extensive research on colonialism and postcolonialism, brings J. Jorge Klor de Alva's (1992) contention that Americans cannot be considered postcolonial since their quarrel with colonial powers was radically different from anti-colonial struggles in Africa or Asia and the view of (quoted in Loomba 1998, 9) dissenters such as Anne McClintock who cautions the reader against a premature celebration of the term *postcolonialism* and question the inclusion of nations donning the double role of oppressor and the oppressed (1994, 87).

Deborah Madsen and Ania Loomba strike two cautionary notes. Madsen's theorization of *preset* and *used* boundaries in postcolonial studies in a number of her books argues for a redefinition of the boundaries that define the postcolonial (1999, 2003). Any postcolonial reading of North America will only accommodate the issues of hybridity, subaltern voices, decolonization, multiculturalism, and border cultures in the literatures of the colonized there. Here, one also accedes to her claim that it is worth a try to stretch the definition of *colonized* and look at certain other metaphorically stifled voices within the American critical establishment. It would be interesting to know why, for instance, a native writer is categorized within American literature if writing on one side of the border, but as Canadian and also postcolonial if writing on the other. Madsen's statements about national identity and multiculturalism are relevant. Loomba cautions that a version of colonialism can be duplicated from within — it is not something that happens only from outside a country or a people or with the collusion of forces outside (1998, 2). (Is Fiedler facing a kind of academic colonialism, then, by being rejected by the academy?) Obviously, there are many dangers attendant upon these perspectives.

On the same register, several critics including Ania Loomba have examined the overlaps between the terms *postcolonialism* and *postmodernism* (2008, xii). Fiedler is said to have coined the term *postmodernism*; if so, is he a postcolonialist, or can he be considered one? (Fiedler 1994; Lapozzi 1990; Pardini 2008). How important is it to be out of America or black in Africa or an Asian in the Caribbean or an Australian somewhere to be postcolonial? Such questions need answers. A postcolonial understanding can also be one in which the post-colony has to come to an intellectual understanding of the power of the independent and the paradox of the identification process. This is true of Fiedler, as he uncovers a diverse range of American experiences to understand and identify with blacks, Jews, natives, and finally, the new mutant—the youth. Fiedler also contributes ably to the seminal issue related to postcolonialism: how gender, race, and class function in colonial and postcolonial discourse. Winchell says, "prior to Fiedler, few critics had discussed classic American literature in terms of race, gender and sexuality" (2002, 53). If postcolonialism is also anti–Europe then there is no doubt that often what he wrote, particularly till the late sixties, was a rejoinder to the "European snobs" of the day (Pardini 2008, 305).

Fiedler and the Register of Postcolonialism

This section attempts to imprint the register created in preceding section in its analysis of Fiedler's attempts to rupture the canon. But I would like to step back from the above discussion for just a moment and bring to you two relevant assessments of Fiedler: one affects this discourse, almost directly. Steven Kellman, who edited, along with Irving Malin, one of the three critical books on Fiedler, titled *Leslie Fiedler and American Culture* (1999), writes:

> During a recent sojourn at the American Studies Center in Hyderabad, India, I was shown an extraordinary piece of furniture: ... Leslie Fiedler Chair.... During one of his two visits, the illustrious American critic donated an actual chair.... It testifies to Fiedler's exalted standing worlds away from Newark, Missoula, and Buffalo.

The other is by Scott McLemee: "Long before the advent of cultural studies, queer theory, disability scholarship, or the phenomenon of the celebrity academic, there was Leslie Fiedler" (2002).

Until 2003, the "garrulous and provocative critic of literature who could write equally well on Nathaniel Hawthorne and circus freaks ... a maverick" (Timberg 2008) whose writing "ridicules its own high-mindedness" (Tanenhaus 2003, quoted in Timberg 2008) was still scandalizing academic elitists, rupturing the canon, and delighting students at the State University of New York (SUNY), Buffalo.

His credo works through the prism of resistance of hierarchies and boundaries of the culture religion as it existed then, till the 1960s. The reflections penetrate the divisions of genre and medium, disband them and accommodate all that art that is closely linked with the market and technology. Years before the iconic worship of kitsch came into vogue, he loved writing on "bad" authors, which is how he described James Fenimore

Cooper, whose books embodied what Fiedler saw as the key to American fiction: "The flight of men West, away from women and domesticity, and often (in one way or another) into each others' arms." "American literature is distinguished by a number of dangerous and disturbing books in its canon," he once wrote, "and American scholarship by its ability to conceal this fact" (Timberg, 2008). Having received enough critical heft for his pathbreaking, critical text *Love and Death in the American Novel* (1960), Fiedler makes it impossible for us to read the classics of literature in the same way ever again.

Just like the structuralists who assert that all myths throughout the world have a family resemblance, he points out that "literature is never just 'words on the page' but primordial images of archetypes or myths ... that can pass out again easily into any other medium..... They can be portrayed on stage; they can be painted; they can be sculpted in stone; they can be turned into stained glass windows; they can be carved in soap" (Fiedler 1975b, 201, in Srivastava 2009, 68). Dallas Liddle also comments on relational importance of the novel to other genres. Fiedler suggests that one way of elaborating on this insight might be to treat literature as a certain kind of myth, the property not of a hegemonic class or an educated and officially ordained clerisy but of the people themselves.[6]

Fiedler's prescience lay in his unafraid alliance with pop culture on his own terms. In this effort he rejected and displaced existing edifices and traditional geneologies of what is "culture proper." With a prose style "muscular and bombastic and extravagant" (Ritz in Timberg 2008), he broke away from the New York intellectuals' twin obsessions: leftist politics and high modernist literature. "What I like," said Pardini, "is that he made the case for popular culture as a barometer of the public condition. *Gone with the Wind* was an awful book, and he knew it, but the point was, 'Why do we like this stuff?'" (quoted in Timberg, 2008). Today, scholars are making a reading of Fiedler from two standpoints: one who was a precursor to the present debates around American Studies and also one who predicted things to come. The overarching discourse that shelters all his micro discourses is one of dissent against American Exceptionalism which is linked with his attempt at de-territorializing American studies. In the latter falls his pet project of exclusion and inclusion of cultures, both, high and low.

In fact, in his bid to re-border the American canon, he attempts to build bridges between *avant garde* and *kitsch*. This way he indulged in a "process of recovery of the neglected and the lost" (Bold 1991, 285–86, quoted in Elliott 1991, 285). His resuscitation[7] of Henry Roth's *Call It Sleep* (1934), "the most neglected book of the past 25 years" (Ferraro 1991, 383), along with the reinstatement of the ghettoized canon (such as *The Lime Twig*

[1961] by John Hawkes [Bold 1991], *Uncle Tom's Cabin* by Harriet Beecher Stowe, Margaret Mitchell's *Gone with the Wind* and *Roots* by Alex Haley) proves that Fiedler revels in the frisson of excluding the obvious and thrusting his uncommon theses and registers. His deconstruction of the American canon included marginal voices and led to an inclusivist and selective thesis, which gave enough space to outsiders, strangers, and others but led Irving Howe, among others, to accuse Fiedler of "simply ignoring those writers and books that might call his thesis into question" and to remark that "what Fiedler disregards ... is awesome" (quoted in Reising 1986, 13). It administered a brisk postcolonial tremor to the sedate and comfortable world of the American literary intelligentsia. Fiedler's credo reflects a largesse of heart in which centers and margins either collapse or merge or even disappear. Instead, he rescues the "common and the periphery" in its attempt to subsume the arrogant highbrow culture power of the center. This also furthers his abiding interest and faith in enlarging the canon as it exists within the rubric of academia. In 2002, he started the introduction to Cooper's *The Deer Slayer* by stating that politics had preceded the formation of a national literary culture in the U.S.: "In 1789, the year James Fenimore Cooper was born, the thirteen North American colonies of Great Britain had declared their political independence, but their literature was still colonial, chiefly belated imitations of styles and genres formerly fashionable in the homeland" (Pardini 2008, xvii).

By stating a devastatingly bold thesis about American literature and culture, two paradoxically different things can be uncovered. First, it is well known that the notion of American exceptionalism has witnessed quite disturbing mutations in the past many years. Fiedler busted its initial ideological heritage of the munificent spirit of "progress" and the "city upon a hill" concept in numerous ways. He rewrote the historical narrative of racism, color, and emancipation with a new pen. On a socio-psycho register, built on his theory of the unconscious and archetypes, Fiedler imprinted his own myths of the white, black, and red, which later critics such as Deborah Madsen and Donald Pease threaded together in a similar thesis. Close on the heels of the notion of American exceptionalism is the concept of preemptive declinism mooted by Herbert London, who calls the belief "that the United States is not an exceptional nation and is not entitled by virtue of history to play a role on the world stage different from other nations" postmodern. Second, Fiedler's pragmatic yet bold tone is evident in his telling the world and Americans that American literary and cultural history needs another writer. This brings us to another interesting approach to his self and work: *Inside or Outside the Whale*.

Inside or Outside the Whale

This approach alludes to Rushdie's essay "Outside the Whale" (1984), a response to an essay by Orwell titled "Inside the Whale" (1940) in which Orwell in the process of discussing and praising both the author Henry Miller and his novel *Tropic of Cancer* (1935) makes some key observations on a writer's behavior and position, within the 1930s (anti-fascist and anti–Hitler, with a communist wave everywhere) milieu. According to Orwell a writer should maintain a position of indifference (in short, irresponsibility) in order to eschew political positioning. Orwell writes,

> For the fact is that being inside a whale is a very comfortable, cozy, homelike thought. The historical Jonah,[8] if he can be so called, was glad enough to escape, but in imagination, in day-dream, countless people have envied him. It is, of course, quite obvious why. The whale's belly is simply a womb big enough for an adult. There you are, in the dark, cushioned space that exactly fits you, with yards of blubber between yourself and reality, able to keep up an attitude of the completest indifference, no matter *what* happens. A storm that would sink all the battleships in the world would hardly reach you as an echo. Even the whale's own movements would probably be imperceptible to you. He might be wallowing among the surface waves or shooting down into the blackness of the middle seas (a mile deep, according to Herman Melville), but you would never notice the difference. Short of being dead, it is the final, unsurpassable stage of irresponsibility.... All his [Henry Miller's] best and most characteristic passages are written from the angle of Jonah, a willing Jonah. In his [Henry Miller's] case the whale happens to be transparent. Only he feels no impulse to alter or control the process that he is undergoing. He has performed the essential Jonah act of allowing himself to be swallowed, remaining passive, *accepting* [1960, quoted in Rushdie 1984, 2].

In a response to Orwell's "Inside the Whale" and the suggestion that Orwell's argument is much impaired by his choice, for a quietist model, of Henry Miller, Rushdie writes,

> The truth is that there is no whale. We live in a world without hiding places; the missiles have made sure of that. However much we may wish to return to the womb, we cannot be unborn. So we are left with a fairly straightforward choice. Either we agree to delude ourselves, to lose ourselves in the fantasy of the great fish—for which a second metaphor is that of Pangloss's garden and for which a third would be the position adopted by the ostrich in time of danger; or we can do what all human beings do instinctively when they realize that the womb has been lost for ever: we can make the very devil of a racket. Certainly, when we cry, we cry partly for the safety we have lost; but we also cry to affirm ourselves, to say, here I am, I matter, too—you're going to have to reckon with me. So, in place of Jonah's womb, I am recommending the ancient tradition of making as big a fuss, as noisy a complaint about the world as is humanly possible. Where Orwell wished quietism, let there be rowdyism; in place of the whale, the protesting wail.

> If we can cease envisaging ourselves as metaphorical fetuses, and substitute the image of a newborn child, then that will be at least a small intellectual advance. In time, perhaps, we may even learn to toddle. I must make one thing plain. I am not saying that all literature must now be of this protesting, noisy type. Perish the thought; now that we are babies fresh from the womb, we must find it possible to laugh and wonder as well as rage and weep [Rushdie 1984, 6].

Stated possibly in the context of the British Raj but actually quite applicable here is that "a number of notions about history ... must be quarreled with, as loudly and as embarrassingly as possible" (Rushdie 1984, 5–6).

Fiedler then also subscribes to the Rushdian "Outside the Whale" syndrome. That Fiedler was no wog and lived in America and also spoke of many things American, does not take away the fact that he was also a protester, a dissenter, someone who longed for the loud rage or howl of voice. Like Rushdie, maybe he also would not have subscribed to the idea of a whale after all.

In fact, Rushdie's "outside the whale" syndrome when applied to Fiedler can be extended a little further: In his case, with particular reference to *Being Busted*, if, like Jonah, you get caught inside the big whale, tear away at the thick blubber of the whale and get out to face the oceanic storms. In *Being Busted* he tore away the blubber of state oppression undeterred by the hostile criticism surrounding him and faced it head on.

Impact on Contemporary Scholarship

Recent scholarship and contemporary theoretical formulations suggest an interesting turn as far as the relevance of Fiedler's formulations is concerned. David Greven (2009) uses Fiedler's formulations on American masculinity to understand the double-protagonist film, a genre in which two male protagonists, each played by a star, vie for narrative dominance. Several scholars in the past two decades have used his insights on adolescence, masculinity metaphors, female stereotypes, and native images in the American novel to conduct exemplary research (Childers 1999).

Susan Gubar calls Fiedler a "kinsmen of the feminist critics" (166). According to her, the work of this "extraordinary individual anticipated and played out so many of the most exciting ventures of literary criticism at the turn of the twentieth century because what made possible the books and essays was precisely Fiedler's rejection of staid, traditional patriarchal business as usual" (in Kellman and Malin 1999, 166).

Yet his writings seem to have been airbrushed out of existence from present-day mainstream American course books. The two latest critical books on Fiedler have been written by Winchell and edited by Samuele Pardini. Pardini feels the crisis in contemporary American literary studies is because important critics such as Fiedler are being ignored. Winchell writes that overdue appreciation in the form of awards has also coincided with "Fiedler's virtual disappearance from the canon of modern criticism" (2002, 334). The irony of the situation is that Fiedler's influence on much of contemporary criticism has been so fully absorbed that it tends to be invisible (334).

Postcolonial tendencies in his case are to be understood from the vantage point of his position as a ghettoized writer also writing about certain subaltern writers and ghettoized texts. Fiedler needs to be understood as an "insider-outsider" owing to his identity as a white American professor at Montana and Samuel Clemens Professor at SUNY Buffalo for over 50 years of his life. His quintessentially "un-American" American position is one that is located territorially in the U.S. but ideologically outside. Can Fiedler's writings, then, be those subaltern voices that come from within?

Alternative Readings II

"The Father of Us All"

Combating caste-consciousness, religious fundamentalism, and pseudo-secularism as a woman in India where even initial feminist debates around rights and equality are alive and throbbing and where the feminine consciousness is sensitive to even small disruptions in hierarchical orders, I was curiously vexed by the following: It is true that long before they became commonplace, Fiedler was comfortable with designations such as "patriarchal" and "matriarchal" to describe cultural structures and assumptions, and he routinely identified the "mood" or "sentiment" that underlay a common practice we had not thought to examine (Boyers 1999). His unconventionality was such. No critique or gender discourse about men or male sexuality can be so opaque as to absolutely obliterate the feminine. In Fiedler's case, the issue was nowhere near this. In fact, the subject position of the woman was of primary importance. He pointed out that in the literary history of America, she was the object to be feared or run away from, or even left behind. So declared the classic American texts. She signified the petticoat government; she was the metaphor for domesticity, home and hearth that the man wanted to escape. In this process she become an object to be feared, repelled, an unwanted subject. This must be unpalatable to many feminists. On the other hand, by bringing this to the fore for the first time in much-canonized texts, Fiedler at least deserved a nod. So why have feminist critics not been sympathetic to his writings?

As has been noticed for a long time now, the most important focus, pointed out by most of the readers, critics, and admirers of Fiedler, is his affinity with the "other." For the purposes of this discussion, the "other" under scrutiny is that described in Simone De Beauvoir's *The Second Sex* or Chandra Talpade Mohanty's "the culturally other"; in both cases, the woman.

This section examines, primarily, the feminist response to Fiedlerian critique—oblique or otherwise—of the woman. It also examines writings of Fiedler that reflect a movement into an arbitrary (for some) feminist discourse as suggested in *Love and Death, The Return of the Vanishing American, The Inadvertent Epic: From Uncle Tom's Cabin to Roots* and several of his other writings that feminists have often grudgingly acknowledged.

His views on comradeship and male bonding are relevant in the present era when sexuality debates are no longer huge conundrums. His essay "Come Back to the Raft Ag'in, Fiedler Honey!" (1948) has assumed canonical stature in the domain of gender, masculinities and queer studies. He wrote *Freaks* when not many thought of exploring this dynamic interdisciplinary terrain of gender, sociology, psychology and literary studies.

Yet, feminists have accused Fiedler along with many of his male contemporaries of neglect and outright condescension. Sandra Wilson Smith (2010) bemoans limited observations of his and of other influential American studies scholars of the mid-twentieth century such as R. W. B. Lewis and Henry Nash Smith on the mythic American character, the frontiersman who penetrates the wilderness and provided analyses of figures such as Daniel Boone and his fictional counterpart Natty Bumppo while discussing the power the romanticized Western frontier had over the American imagination. Smith says they ignored the many narratives in which a female character conquers the frontier. The assumption seemed to be that the literary female figure belonged in the parlor with her sewing basket and not in the forest with her weapon. Unfortunately, this incomplete assessment of the frontier adventure genre is still in evidence today. Smith's essay tries to develop the understanding of the American frontier story and points out a mini-narrative of a heroine who triumphs over the "savage" forces of the wilderness even in the iconic John Filson/John Trumbull Boone tale. This female figure became a cultural archetype, and similar versions of her story were repeated in countless captivity and Western adventure anthologies, almanacs, and the like for the next seventy years. The popularity of this frontier narrative featuring a strong, violent female figure suggests that readers accepted the idea of an active, aggressive woman, at least while she was contending with chaotic forces in the wilderness. The popularity of this kind of narrative also undercuts the traditional gender paradigm (the nurturing, passive female versus the active, aggressive male) too often imposed by scholars on antebellum American letters and culture.

That Fiedler turned pages faster than others is validated by several examples such as the one Schechter refers to in an essay that *The New York Times* (February 1995) published, "Rhett and Scarlet: Rough Sex or Rape?" The gist of the piece was that certain "feminist philosophies," having focused their attention on *Gone with the Wind*, had noticed—much to their outrage—that the book was built around rape fantasies. No less than nine years earlier, however—in the spring of 1986—Fiedler and Schechter had appeared together on a popular culture panel as part of a conference on C. G. Jung and the humanities, held at Hofstra University. In the course of his remarks, Fiedler—who spoke at length about *Gone with the Wind*—declared (Schechter quotes from the transcript, published in book form by Princeton University Press): "Clearly, the basic myth and controlling metaphor, the very leitmotif of Margaret Mitchell's book, is rape" (Schechter 1995, in Kellman and Malin 1999, 134).

In the essay "Literature and Lucre" (WWL), Fiedler gives a new dimension to the struggle between high art and low art. Female writers such as Rowson and her lot were called a "horde of damned female scribblers" (WWL, 29) by Hawthorne, who saw them as caterers to popular taste and mass appeal. Writers from Rowson to Jacqueline Susann are famous for producing bestsellers and popular literature. He perceives the struggle between high art and low art as "a battle of the sexes" (WWL, 29).

Contrapuntally, Harrison feels that though Fiedler may have been well ahead of his time in many ways, in at least one critical matter he was certainly a man of his time (2008). He elaborates that as Fiedler's pronoun choice in "Montana" implies, he suffered from the masculinism that pervaded American culture in the 1950s and 1960s. The way Fiedler portrayed it, it seems the Indians and whites of Montana are all men, and Brady feels that "he pushes women, consciously or unconsciously, to the remote edges of the debates and struggles of the era." One can only partly agree with Brady that in works such as *Love and Death*, Fiedler sounds the white, male tradition of American letters: he takes up, at great length, the work of such luminaries as Cooper, Poe, Hawthorne, Melville, Twain, James, Fitzgerald, Hemingway, Faulkner, Vidal, Bellow, Kerouac, and more but ignores the female tradition almost entirely. Winchell in his second book, *Too Good to Be True*, offers an answer to this unjust summation by stating that in *Love and Death* Fiedler inaugurates his feminist thesis and later builds an exclusive domestic and feminine counter-tradition in *The Inadvertent Epic*. Brady is caustic in his remarks, "Stowe rates a few pages, but that is about it; where are sustained considerations of Davis, Jewett, Chopin, Hopkins, Wharton, Stein, Cather, Hurston, and others? Where are the readings of Ruiz de Burton, Zitkala Ša, Larson, and more? Like many of the other intellectual giants of his day, Fiedler was much more interested in the work of white men than in recovering the work, lives, and writing of women or blacks or Native Americans. Like most of us, perhaps, Fiedler had his blind spots, even as he slashed his way through taboo subjects and posed what were, for many, unsettling literary and cultural questions" (Brady 2008). His risqué thesis of American literary masterpieces was not palatable to the feminists, obviously, because they were not in a powerful subject position.

On the other hand, Susan Gubar (of *Madwoman in the Attic* fame) uses the paternal metaphor "the father of us all" for Fiedler in her article "A Fiedler Brood" (1999).

Gubar states in this essay that she will use a subversive and a mellowed authoritarian image to describe how the work of this "extraordinary individual" anticipated and played out so many of the most exciting ventures of literary criticism at the turn of the twentieth century because Fiedler's rejection of the staid, traditional, patriarchal business as usual is what made the books and essays possible (Gubar 1999, 166).

In *The Inadvertent Epic: From Uncle Tom's Cabin to Roots* Fiedler evaluates many American texts by redefining them not as they had been traditionally understood but as "hitherto unperceived popular Epic[s]" (Browne et al. 1968, 27). Here he constructs a counter-tradition in popular literature. This counter-tradition is dominated by women and domestic values. These two rival myths survive together in popular literature: the myth of family as utopia and the family as dystopia, home as heaven and home as hell, women as redeemer and woman as destroyer. Thus, Fiedler points out that the classroom reading list has examples of books embodying the male tradition, the anti-family myth, whereas our literature is full of books embodying the other tradition as well. Hence, through the analysis of such "inadvertent epics" Fiedler attempts to redefine literature in a tradition other than the one set by the elitist critics.

Gubar, writing during the late 1970s, looks upon him "despite some of his gibes at the feminist critics" as a "kinsman of the feminist critics." She says:

> Quickly cognizant of the same postwar forces of dissent (the beats, civil rights activism, militant protests against Vietnam, the sexual revolution) that eventually readied the stage for the women's movement outside the academy as well as feminist criticism inside it, Fiedler embarked on a series of projects that [he] may not have set out to do..., but nevertheless ended up offering an analysis of women's function in American fiction almost two decades before I and my peer group of feminists in American Studies—Judith Fetterley, Annette Kolodny, Myra Jehlen, and Jane Tompkins—produced comparable contributions [166–67].

Fiedler is responsible for uncovering a cultural aspect of America that relegated women to the fringes. He spoke about certain contradictions in American life that stem from its patriarchal setup: "a regressiveness ... of American life, its implacable nostalgia for the infantile" on the one hand, on the other a running away, an escape from domesticity, civilization and petticoat government in the arms of a non-white male.

Reminding us of his much-validated thesis about the fear of women and of sex that inundates the classic canonical texts, Gubar calls Fiedler "one of the earliest theorists of misogyny" who traced the complex, often contradictory manifestations in literature that would sometimes link women to civilization, a corrupt literary marketplace, the stifling conventions of petty urban pieties and properties, but sometimes to the savagery or silence of a natural, virgin landscape in need of penetration. Before it was fashionable to do so, *Love and Death in the American Novel* uncovered not only the ubiquitous but also an aesthetically generative anxiety among the canonical authors of American letters, that the love of women spelled death for men (Browne et al. 1968, 167).

Gubar generously states "Father of us all" and adds that Fiedler "adumbrated the first stage of feminist criticism—the phase Elaine Showalter called 'critique' in which resisting readers criticized the reification of female images in books written by men" (167). Fiedler was an active participant in the second step of feminist criticism that Showalter medically names "gynocriticism"— "the period of recovery where texts that have been neglected or devalued because composed by women received new interpretative appreciation." Gubar specifically refers to Fiedler's pet project of opening up the canon of American literature by reinstating Harriet Beecher Stowe into "a principal position in twentieth century literary history that reflects her centrality in the nineteenth century literary scene" (167).

As he demonstrated his sensitivity to the connections between gender and genre as well as to the sex-antagonism at work in the economy that produces publishing houses, reviews, bestsellers, and reputations, his work contributed to the intellectual climate in which Sandra Gilbert and Gubar completed their three-volume appraisal of the literary interaction between the sexes in the modern period: *No Man's Land*, and in which the first edition of our *Norton Anthology of Literature by Women* appeared. Susan Gubar raises an interesting question:

> At times in his publications Fiedler seemed to promulgate precisely the misogynist strains he uncovered, that at other times he reinvented gendered stereotypes for the women writers he reclaimed; that Fiedler sometimes ignored, baited, or teased the feminists who followed him: don't these phenomena simply accord with the role of older brothers who rarely allow their regard for their siblings to deter their heckling or harassing them?

With what ambivalent feelings was this big brother watching another sibling growing up in the brood, an addition to the family born later enough in time to regard Fiedler more as a kind of uncle? Whether or not they disavow him as homophobic, such queer theorists as Joseph Boone, Wayne Koestenbaum, Gail Reuben, and Eve Kosofsky Sedgwick remain indebted to Fiedler's perspicacity about white male fantasies of a dark male beloved whose embrace will make well all manners of evils that have accrued from white supremacy (Gubar 1999, 168).

According to Gubar, Fiedler's essay "Come Back to the Raft Ag'in, Huck Honey!" "presages the emphasis in gay studies on the feminine functioning in sexual and textual contexts as an object of exchange, serving primarily as glue bonding man to man. Although Fiedler termed that bonding 'homoerotic,' whereas queer theorists now use the phrase 'homosocial,' *he intuited the complex spectrum* [emphasis mine] of amorously passionate feelings of white men attracted toward African American masculinity and not simply prompted by the dynamics of racial guilt over white privilege" (168).

Attributing to Fiedler the placing of the white man–black man couple at the center of the American imagination, Gubar is also indebted to Fiedler for her project in which she attempted to engender racial categories that were paradoxically as unstable as they were recalcitrant, especially in her last book *Racechangers: White Skin, Black Face in American Culture*. In one of the chapters on white artists fascinated by hyper-sexualized stereotypes of a black "penis-not-a-phallus" (168), Susan Gubar quoted passages from Fiedler's writings that demonstrated his understanding of cross-racial and homosexual desire. Referring to the seminal intuition that Fiedler had in *Waiting for the End*, Gubar says that the following is the most "multiply inflected critical stance" (168) anticipated by Fiedler: "Born theoretically white, we are permitted to pass our childhood as imaginary Indians, our adolescence as imaginary Negroes, and only then are expected to settle down to being what we really are: white once more." This demonstrates a deep engagement with ethnic, racial, religious, regional, and national manifestations of what today are called "subject positionalities" or "cultural identifications," refusing to let his knowledge of the sensitivity of these topics inhibit his intellectual absorption of them (Gubar 1999, 168).

There will be many who would endorse the view that "the scholars who owe most to Fiedler's groundbreaking work are feminist critics of American literature" (Winchell 2002, 334). For was not Fiedler the one to put the woman in the forefront in his thesis of the "culturally other" before he actually spoke about the other "others?" This has only been acknowledged by some, primarily Susan Gubar, but also Ann Douglass. Winchell notes many examples of the short shrift that Fiedler is given in feminist criticism even when feminists owe the kernel of their argument to him. A prime example that he brings to us is Carolyn Heilbrun's *The Masculine Wilderness of the American Novel*, which discusses James Dickey's novel *Deliverance*. "Whatever Dickey's intention," Heilbrun writes, "his achievement is one more version—dare we hope it is the last?—of what Leslie Fiedler identified for us more than a decade ago in *Death and Love in the American Novel* [*sic*]: the woman despising [the] American dream" (quoted in Winchell 2002, 335). Winchell is worried about the negative subtext that this essay creates about Fiedler's ideas about this American dream, particularly when there is no explication or elaboration. In his book, however, he makes clear his belief that the failure of the American novel to deal with mature heterosexual love is one of its major limitations. Heilbrun obviously agrees. She writes, for example, "American novels are not in the mainstream; they are outside it; turning away from fully human women whom the great non–American novels have seen as a redeeming force ... Becky Sharpe, Jane Eyre, Madame Bovary, Anna Karenina." Unfortunately, this is presented as an original insight on Heilbrun's part. Obviously, she has forgotten more than the title of Fiedler's book, because later she writes, "No one, certainly no American critic, has noticed that ... the novel is the great androgynous form, the embodiment of the peculiar human need to joining the sexes in a shared destiny, whether through passion or work or conversation." Heilbrun does make an exception for Hawthorne's *The Scarlet Letter*. According to her, in "the America James fled," that book "stands isolated as the only classic American novel that is not a fantasy of two or more men fleeing women, borne by natural forces down some river toward deliverance" (41–42, 44, quoted in Winchell 2002, 335). At this point, the astute reader might wonder: where have I heard all this before? Try the first chapter of *Love and Death in the American Novel*, says Winchell.

> Where is our *Madame Bovary*, our *Anna Karenina*, our *Pride and Prejudice* or *Vanity Fair?* Among our classic novels, at least those before Henry James, who stands so oddly between our own traditions and the European ones we rejected or recast, the best attempt at dealing with love is *The Scarlet Letter*, in which the physical consummation of adultery has occurred and all passion burned away before the novel proper begins. For the rest, there are *Moby Dick* and *Huckleberry Finn, The Last of the Mohicans, The Red Badge of Courage*, the stories of Edgar Allan Poe—books that turn from society to nature or nightmare out of a desperate need to avoid the facts of wooing, marriage, and child-bearing [LD, 25, quoted in Winchell 2002, 336].

The other issue that critics, even feminists, problematized was the battle of the sexes. This has been evident from Fiedler's criticism of Washington Irving's *Rip Van Winkle*. Winchell draws our attention to Judith Fetterley's *The Resisting Reader* (1978), considered a watershed in feminist criticism of American fiction. Although some of her readings seem tendentious and wrongheaded, he says, she has many perceptive things to say about Washington Irving's *Rip Van Winkle*.

Fetterley begins her discussion of Irving's story with epigraphs from

Philip Young and Leslie Fiedler, the two critics who had most to say about *Rip Van Winkle* (Young 167, 204–31, quoted in Winchell 2002, 335). Although both dealt with the story in terms of myth, the difference in their perspectives was more important than the similarity. Young operated as a conventional anthropologist, cataloging various sources of the Rip myth. Fiedler, the futurist, contended that "what is remarkable and significant ... is not the European past, but the American future of the tale" (RVA, 56). This makes more sense than cultural and literary archiving, and Fetterley obviously agrees with Fiedler's emphasis because, like him, she focuses on Irving's original contribution of the tale of the enchanted sleeper to the battle of the sexes. As she points out, "the German tale on which he based 'Rip' has no equivalent for Dame Van Winkle: she is Irving's creation and addition.... What drives Rip away from the village and up into the mountains and what makes him a likely partaker of the sleep-inducing liquor is his wife; all the ills from which Rip seeks escape are symbolically located in the person of the offending Dame Van Winkle" (Fetterley 1978, 3, quoted in Winchell 2002, 336–37). Ten years earlier, in *The Return of the Vanishing American,* Fiedler had made essentially the same observation: "It is Irving who invents the character of Rip's wife and his difficult relationship with her, Irving who first portrays Dame Van Winkle as an intolerably efficient and shrewish wife" (RVA, 36, quoted in Winchell 2002, 336).

Fetterley also recognizes the durability of Irving's prototype in American culture. "Like his more famous successor, Huckleberry Finn," she writes, "Rip wages ... subterranean and passive revolt against the superego and its imperatives." The image of the woman-persecuted male has even survived into the late twentieth century: "It is not hard—there are lots of pointers along the way—to get from Irving's Dame to Ken Kesey's Big Nurse, who is bad because she represents a system whose illegitimacy is underscored by the fact that *she,* a woman, represents it" (1978, 6, quoted in Winchell 2002, 337). Again, we find Fiedler having said much the same things a decade earlier: "Rip ... is the first of those escapees from what women call responsibility, the first American character shiftless enough to be loved by the audience which loves Cooper's Natty Bumppo, Melville's Ishmael, and Mark Twain's Huck Finn, as well as Saul Bellow's Henderson the Rain King and the hero of Ken Kesey's *One Flew Over the Cuckoo's Nest*" (RVA, 60).

Many unobtrusive readers—as well as those who know Fiedler's views only at second hand—often assume that he is *celebrating* the motifs that he identifies in American fiction. Such an inference simply ignores the critic's essential ambivalence. Although he is capable of being moved by our "boys'" books, Fiedler also knows where they fall short of full maturity. (Remember that many of the early reviewers of *Love and Death in the American Novel* thought that he was trashing his own tradition, fouling his own nest.) Ironically, when feminist critics such as Carolyn Heilbrun and Judith Fetterley set Fiedler up as the patriarchal straw man against whom they are doing battle, their arguments invariably echo points that he himself had made with greater subtlety and nuance.

One has only to make a nuanced reading of the female counter-tradition that Fiedler created in *The Inadvertent Epic: From Uncle Tom's Cabin to Roots* and understand how much of *Love and Death in the American Novel* is devoted to reviving the reputations of nineteenth-century women writers who are reviled both today and when they wrote. Although Fiedler can see their shortcomings and the limitations of the canonical male novelists he discusses, he treats both categories of writers with respect. To her credit, Susan Gubar acknowledges that Fiedler's "treatment of *Uncle Tom's Cabin* helped put Harriet Beecher Stowe's name back into the principal position in twentieth-century literary history that reflects her centrality in the nineteenth-century literary scene" (1999, 167, quoted in Winchell 2002, 337). Unfortunately, not all of Stowe's defenders have been so ready to acknowledge Fiedler's efforts on her behalf.

Although a committed minority of critics have always been willing to defend *Uncle Tom's Cabin,* its place of honor in the feminist canon probably dates to 1978, when Jane P. Tompkins published her much-heralded essay "Sentimental Power: *Uncle Tom's Cabin* and the Politics of Literary History" (Winchell 2002, 338). Tompkins begins by decrying the patriarchal view of American fiction she herself had accepted unquestioningly as a graduate student. Now she asks us to view the popular female novelists of nineteenth-century America as not just a "damned mob of scribbling women," as Hawthorne had resentfully called them, but as exemplars of an entirely different approach to literature. Although some observers might argue that it was the hegemony of modernism and New Criticism that doomed Stowe and her sisters to excommunication from the High Church of literature, Tompkins is convinced that it was all *a male plot*. She is even willing to name names, arguing, "The tradition of Perry Miller, F. O. Matthiesen, Harry Levin, Richard Chase, R. W. B. Lewis, Yvor Winters, and Henry Nash Smith has prevented even committed feminists from recognizing and asserting the *value* of a powerful and specifically female novelistic tradition" (Tompkins 1994, 502–3, quoted in Winchell 2002, 338).

Winchell asks: "Is it mere oversight that the one major Americanist whose name is conspicuously absent from Tompkins's list is that of Leslie Fiedler? To have included him would have been to admit that there was one male critic who took the women seriously." Although Tompkins seems to owe very little to what Fiedler said about *Uncle Tom's Cabin* in *Love and Death in the Amer-*

ican Novel, her views on Stowe and the American canon are remarkably similar to those he would publish in monograph form as *The Inadvertent Epic* in 1980. One might even suspect Fiedler of having been voicing his most recent assessment of *Uncle Tom's Cabin* in lectures and television appearances since at least the mid-1970s. What we have is "confluence" rather than influence, but one that Tompkins is loath to admit. In twenty-two pages of text and over thirty footnotes, she does not even mention Fiedler's name (2002, 338). In fact, the Norton critical edition that includes Tompkins's essay doesn't publish any works by Fiedler.

There is a hint of overreaction in Winchell's initial question: "Is it mere oversight that the one major Americanist whose name is conspicuously absent from Tompkins's list is that of Leslie Fiedler?" Maybe deliberately, because he is precisely the only critic of that time who draws attention to this fact too and thus cannot cohere with the likes of Nash Smith in that list. The rest of it is a similar story that one finds in anthologies of Jewish literature or commentary on Twain in that Twain journal that I discussed early on in this book. But the next chapter will establish that there are several admirers of Fiedler who would want to say, come back to the raft ag'in, Fiedler honey!

What is noteworthy is the fact that his entire discourse on opening up the canon while critiquing the politics of canon formation also aligns him with advocates of feminism. Not only does he elevate Harriet Beecher Stowe to a platform where the likes of Mark Twain are discussed, in *What Was Literature?* he does not hesitate to question his own criticism in *Love and Death*. Although he resurrected several women novelists who had found no place in literary history, he also faulted Harriet Beecher Stowe for a lack of tragic ambivalence and radical protest without ever questioning the supreme importance of these qualities (Winchell 2002, 338–9). Winchell points out that having made such an observation, Fiedler does not feel compelled to right the balance with reverse discrimination. To replace the old canon with an opposite one that is just as rigid would simply promote ideology at the expense of art (339).

It is important to bring to the fore the fact that when in April 1995, his friend and long-time colleague at SUNY Buffalo Bruce Jackson and his wife Diane Christian organized a special tribute for their friend, they asked Fiedler for the names of the people he would like to speak on his behalf. The one that Fiedler chose was the controversial cultural critic and independent feminist Camille Paglia (who had first heard Fiedler when he spoke at Yale during her undergraduate years and recalls that no one from the English department attended). At the height of her celebrity status in April 1995, Paglia came to Buffalo to honor one of the seminal influences on her career (Winchell 2002, 333).

It needs to be understood that Fiedler chose Camille Paglia, "the most future-oriented of them all, the *enfant terrible*, in fact, of her generation as I was of mine" (1999a). It was probably not because she had said in a blurb for a paperback reprint of *Love and Death in the American Novel* published in 1992: "Fiedler created an American intellectual style that was truncated by the invasion of faddish French theory in the 70s and 80s. Let's turn back to Fiedler and begin again" (Winchell 2002, 333). Instead, it was probably because Fiedler all through his life, literary and otherwise, had always been on the side of the feminists. As has been the trajectory of his expansive literary career, his voice *for* the feminists remained an important one of his many polyphonic voices. The other reason is that he was too careless or even bold to bother to garner support from any direction. The result is for all of us to see: he seems to have been disowned by all. But will America disown him too? This needs to be answered.

Later in his acceptance speech for the Hubbell Award, he said:

> Her [Paglia's] words [do] not merely reassure me that I am still not politically correct. They also make me aware that whatever I have written about it has always been from an essentially American point of view and in an essentially American voice; and that therefore I am in the deepest sense an "Americanist"— a true colleague (despite their original doubts and my own continuing ones) of all those who have earlier received this award and you who so graciously bestow it on me now.

Using "Come Back..." as an important junction for my discussion, I wish to state that there is enough in the essay for feminists to cheer about. In the essay, Fiedler says:

> The nineteenth-century myth of the Immaculate Young Girl has failed to survive in any *felt* way into our time. Rather in the jokes shared among men in the smoking car, the barracks, or the dormitory, there is a common male revenge against women for having flagrantly betrayed that myth; and under the revenge, the rather smug assumption of the chastity of the revenging group, in so far as it is a purely male society [CB, 27, quoted in Kellman and Malin 1999, 27].

Fiedler quotes Cooper's Natty Bumppo of *The Last of the Mohicans*, the man who boasts always of having "no cross" in *his* blood, and who flees by nature from the defilement of all women, but never with so absolute a revulsion as he displays towards the squaw.

Fiedler propounded an anti-marriage thesis so pro-women that I wonder why they did not run and embrace him. The timing of such a thesis was just right. In the 1960s, feminism was a fledgling movement and was ready to take off at any bidding or calling. The thesis that he propounded in *Love and Death* about the flight from petticoat government was actually a gauntlet, which many did not take. It would have paid rich dividends.

For example, the theme of seduction in *Love and Death* leads him to talk not only about Hawthorne (*The Scarlet Letter*) and Melville (*Pierre*) but also about the obscure George Lippard, Theodore Dreiser, and, ultimately and wittily, Herman Wouk. The sentimental theme has undergone strange modifications. The nice girl remains, even after being treated ambivalently by Fitzgerald, Hemingway, Faulkner, and Nathanael West, who sought to destroy her, and Wright Morris, who pointed a jeering finger at her mother in *Man and Boy* (Hicks 1960a, 16). Three decades later,

> the uniquely American hero/anti-hero ... rescues no maiden, like Perseus; kills no dragon, like Saint George; discovers no treasure, like Beowulf or Siegfried; he does not even manage at long last to get back to his wife, like Odysseus. He is, in fact, an anti–Odysseus who finds his identity by *running away from home* [WWL, 152].

In Fiedler's writings, early on, in *The Return of the Vanishing American*, the American West and the Western implies primarily an encounter with the savage: the other. In fact, whichever space is occupied by this "untamed Indian" becomes a western in the American author's imagination. Fiedler asserts that, unlike Europe, America is a big land with a short history. Consequently, it is possible to think of our fiction, like our poetry, as being Northern, Southern, Eastern, and Western. When Fiedler speaks of the American West, he is thinking of the region between the Mississippi River and the Rocky Mountains.

Because of the radically strange and alien nature of the Indian, he is the one element of the American experience that Europeans have never been able to assimilate. Whether he is a survivor of the Lost Continent of Atlantis, a remnant of the wandering tribes of Israel, or some extraterrestrial being, he is the ultimate other. He may have a soul, but—as D.H. Lawrence concluded—not one precisely like our own, except as our own have the potentiality of becoming like his (RVA, 22).

As stated at a number of places, Fiedler's topological definition and mythological reading of the geography of United States tells us that four myths arose. Fiedler argues that four myths arose that collectively created the image of the Far West. These are the myth of love in the woods, or the story of Pocahontas and Captain John Smith; the myth of the white woman with the tomahawk, which is based on the experience of Hannah Duston, a New England woman who was captured by Indians and fought her way to freedom; the myth of the good companions in the woods, the Paleface/Redskin version of the "Huck Honey" motif, derived from the youthful friendship of fur trader Alexander Henry and the Indian Wawatam: and the myth of the runaway male, first imagined by Washington Irving in *Rip Van Winkle* (Winchell 2002, 203–204).

Beginning with the last of these myths, Fiedler duly acknowledges that the Rip Van Winkle prototype goes back many centuries in German legend but argues that a distinctively American element was added to the story in Irving's retelling. This is the battle of the sexes, a conflict that Fiedler contends is the American equivalent of the class struggle in European culture. Although Irving's story is set in New York, it is mythologically less a "Northern" than a Western. Rip's antagonist is not the climate or the land, but petticoat government. (Irving invented that marvelously evocative term.) By fleeing from the hearth into the wilderness, Rip becomes the comic version of the womanless American hero. In effect, Irving has taken the Teutonic legend of the enchanted sleeper and, by adding a shrewish wife, turned it into "a comic version of the legend of the Persecuted Maiden—a corresponding male fantasy of persecution, appropriate to a country that likes to think of itself, or endures being through of, as the first matriarchy of the modern world" (56).

But the Rip myth lacks potency because of the lack of an adequate male companion, which is fulfilled by Cooper. Winchell brings to the fore an interesting example of the Rip story that Joseph Jefferson reinterpreted for the stage. In the melodramatic version of the tale, Rip returns to not a dead but a chastened wife. Instead of a profound depiction of the misogynist myth, we simply have *Pamela* with the sex roles reversed—the shrew is not defeated, only converted (Winchell 2002, 204).

The feminist perspective is visible in the observations on the Fiedlerian discourse on the myth of the American male; in his articulations on the creation of an inadvertent domestic epic in the book *The Inadvertent Epic: From Uncle Tom's Cabin to Roots* (1979) "on the all-feminine/domestic myth that pervades a major chunk of American literature"; in his analysis of "sentimental love religion" and women in American fiction; and in the archetypal binaries of women into the good-good girl and the good-bad girl archetype typified by Zenobia and Priscilla of Hawthorne's *The Blithedale Romance*, which need to be understood before being totally decried.

Gubar rightly points out that few practitioners would name Fiedler as a progenitor or adopt him as a precursor despite his having intellectually engaged with ethnic, racial, religious, regional, and national manifestations—practically all aspects of life. In fact, his views on Simone Weil or about "terminal Jews" could outrage Jewish studies proponents no less than the assumption that "we" are "really white" might offend blacks and Jews alike (Gubar 1999, 169). Susan Gubar further says,

> Perhaps even the non-patriarchal family metaphors break down as analogues of Fiedler's influential prominence in twentieth–century criticism because he remains what the abiding figure in his work has always been: the single trope that sustains even the most polychromatic of his investigations. Add to it his other extensive writings on science fiction and the alien, on the freak show and the

monster, and on the stranger on stage and screen. The composite figure emerging from this daunting variegated set of subjects appears to be none other than the Other: an eccentric, even a renegade, the Other might be the female or the freak, the black or the Jew, the homosexual or the Native American or, of course, the critic himself [1999, 169–70].

Towards the end, I step back from the discussion and look at my position in a postcolonial historiography and geography and attempt to address some questions my critique may have raised. Spivak has asked repeatedly and famously if the subaltern can speak. Though her own response was in the negative, several interventionist attempts have been made in the over two decades since she asked this question. In one sense, can Indian Americanists speak and be listened to, ever the subaltern in traditional English literary studies as practiced in postcolonial India? Probably yes. And is this also the case with Fiedler? We, the postcolonials, have listened to him and about him, to what they (the Americanists) have told us; now they (Americans) need to hear us. The gaze of the "other" on the "other" defines this research. This is the response of a postcolonial to a Jekyll-and-Hyde "exceptional scholar-critic of all ages" on the verge of being anointed a postcolonial. As someone who inaugurated the present discourse, he would surely be guffawing to himself in his grave.

Conclusion

"Come Back to the Raft Ag'in, Fiedler Honey!"

> The irony of the situation is that Fiedler's influence on much of contemporary criticism has been so fully absorbed that it tends to be invisible.
> —Mark Royden Winchell, *"Too Good to Be True": The Life and Work of Leslie Fiedler*

> Literary criticism is in crisis.... The clearest indication ... is the lack of proper memorialization of scholars who are part of and makers of the history of this valuable profession. One such case is that of Leslie Fiedler.
> —Samuele F. S. Pardini, *The Devil Gets His Due*

> Brave Heavy Runner has left deep tracks.[1]
> —Steven G. Kellman, "The Importance of *Being Busted*"

One very tidy summing-up of Fiedler reads like this:

Leslie Fiedler's contribution to American and international intellectual life has been enormous: he invented the first-person critical voice in American letters; he originated what we now call cultural criticism and queer theory; he was an early champion of multiculturalism; he singlehandedly assaulted the elitist literary canon; he established the field of American studies in Europe; and he pioneered efforts to understand art in terms of popular and mass culture, society, race, religion, psychology, and our own shared human dreams. Fiedler's life work is now emerging ineluctably into its full degree of radiance and immanence, as is appropriate to his colossal contribution.... We are—all of us—in his debt for the writing he has given us and continues to give us and for his inimitable presence. His example sets new standards to which we all aspire: he is a true tzaddik, a righteous man [Green 1999, 180–81].

This summing up by Geoffrey Green in every way is a very proper assessment of Fiedler; but knowing Fiedler, he would be a little uncomfortable with this propriety. After all, didn't he say himself that he longed for the raise and howl of a voice as a response to his writings? So the following is another way to sum up Fiedler today.

A recipient of many fellowships and awards: Rockefeller Fellow at Harvard University, Fulbright to universities of Rome, Bologna and Athens between 1946 and 1963 and Guggenheim fellowship in 1970–71; teaching assignments to prestigious universities such as Princeton, Sussex, Yale and Vincennes all through his career; elected to the American Academy and Institute of Arts and Letters in 1988; awarded the Chancellor Charles P. Norton medal in 1989; honored by his colleagues at the Department of English, State University of New York, Buffalo, in "Fiedlerfest" in 1992, Fiedler's list of achievement is long. In 1994, the American literature section of the Modern Language Association conferred the Lifetime Achievement Award, the Hubbell Medal. Three years after the Buffalo "Fiedlerfest," in 1998, the National Book Critics' Circle gave Fiedler, "best remembered for his protean transformations," its Ivan Sandorf Award for Lifetime Achievement in a public ceremony at the NYU Law School. The following year, in 1999, he received a similar career award from PEN West, a regional branch of the famed International Association of writers for his "fierceness as a critic and ... [h]is belief that culture speaks to an entire populace, a belief borne out by his own engaged prose style" (Winchell 2002, 334). While gratefully accepting all of these awards, Leslie couldn't help noticing that these organizations were "giving a prize for a whole body of work, of which no single essay ever received such a prize or even very high praise" (334).

Yet, ironically, appreciation in the form of awards has also coincided with "Fiedler's virtual disappearance from the canon of modern criticism as it is represented by standard books in the field" (Winchell 2002, 334). Winchell recalls that when he entered the "profession" as an undergraduate English major in the early 1970s, anthologies of criticism typically included either "Come Back to the Raft Ag'in, Huck Honey!" or "Archetype and Signature." This seems no longer to be the case. It is not just that Leslie Fiedler is not fashionable these days, the standard texts seem intent on denying that he was ever of importance. Not only this, academicians confirm both that the critic most frequently cited has been Leslie Fiedler and that the critic whose ideas have been most cribbed without attribution is Fiedler (Winchell 2002, 335).

The all-pervasive but diffused influence of Fiedler is well echoed by Schechter who says Fiedler's "ideas and concerns have become common currency among people who haven't the foggiest notion where they came from" (1999, 133). The most obvious example of this can be found in Hollywood, where every second action movie is a pumped-up version of Leslie's myth of interracial male bonding—Huck and Jim on steroids and armed with semiautomatic weapons (130).

Exasperation is the feeling that many experience, particularly those who recognize the source of these ideas but see them go largely unacknowledged. Ironically, it exactly parallels what Fiedler himself had said of pop artists such as Bram Stoker and Edgar Rice Burroughs: creators of some of the most enduring myths, whose creations are familiar to everyone, even while the authors themselves remain mostly unknown (Schechter in Kellman and Malin, 1999, 133).

Like the protagonist in his story "The Last Jew in America," Fiedler was the rare academic scholar who dared write fiction. But just as his criticism is not being studied, his fiction has also been given a short shrift by the intelligentsia (Winchell 2002; Pardini 2008).

To know that he was precocious and "ahead of the curve" causes pain to some of his admirers such as Schechter, who writes, "I've experienced this directly on a number of occasions, when—having been struck with what I consider a staggeringly original insight and struggled to find the perfect way to phrase it—I happen to pick up some twenty-year-old essay by Leslie and discover that he not only said it first but said it better" (1999, 134).

Referring to a major conference on *Dracula* (March 1997), Schechter comments, "The extent to which Stoker's creation has become such a hot academic subject is sufficient proof of the precociousness of this man who was already mulling over the archetypal meaning of the Vampire king at least twenty years ago—back in the halcyon days of the early 1970s" (1999, 134). All this is to prove that Fiedler can only walk ahead followed by many. His non-inclusion is the birth of a crisis, which will grow if not addressed soon. He has left a void in contemporary literary critical studies in America (Pardini 2008).

Is his work dated today? This is a question that may come to mind while going through several of the essays written decades ago and that have also been used in this book. They will interest us and might appear more as historical documents of something said half a century ago. But the case as it stands with Fiedler, the writer, is that he has always been a man of the moment. Boyers points out,

> Like other first-rate critics, Fiedler is very much a man of his time, which is to say that, even when he is writing about Dante or Shakespeare, he reflects the preoccupations of his own moment. His sense of the mythic is a 1950s construction. He is no more "dated" as a critic than Matthew Arnold or Roland Barthes, but there is no doubt that his essays of the 1950s—or 1970s—could have been written only in those decades. This is most obvious in essays devoted to topical matters, where Fiedler is assiduous to chart recent shifts in the way his contemporaries behave and think about burning issues [1999, 172–73].

Today, some of his critical writings may not be as relevant as they were when they were written, such as his views on new criticism and his mythopoeic views on the cultural contagion of America, not because they are dated, but because being among the first ones to hold the baton in the relay race, he has set the right pace for others to follow. As is always the case, the winner is the one who holds the baton in the end. Unfortunately, he was not the one. Yet as one of the frontrunners, for example in the essay "Come Back...," he will always be remembered for turning the page in terms of race, gender and sexuality debates; in establishing a middle-brow critique.

Having put this matter to rest, while writing this book and thumbing through the pages of many journals and books, I decided to go through some recent criticism on Twain (after all, Fiedler's first notorious essay, "Come Back...," impacted the way *The Adventures of Huckleberry Finn*—from which all American literature came out, so said Hemingway—was read) and books on Jewish studies. Hoping for some earth-shattering disclosures about the impact of Fiedler, I was in for a rude shock. I will adumbrate the startle with this example: Going through P. Messent's "A Re-evaluation of Mark Twain Following the Centenary of His Death" in *The Mark Twain Annual*, volume 9, published in 2011, it is surprising that in such an utterly complete summation of the oeuvre of Mark Twain's writings, in an article of 20 pages that discusses all his major fiction and nonfiction works at length, there is not a word on what Leslie Fiedler said of Twain. My immediate reaction was that this article requires a re-examination and a re-writing. There are many such omissions and flip-flops.

What we see, thus, in this diffused influence, is not a *force majeure* on a battalion but only on a column. If the present American critical account can bowdlerize his thesis and position from America's cultural contagion, a rethink is required. And we are not done yet. Though some critics rightly bemoan his death, literally, others even symbolically and metaphorically, there is already a prophetic resurrection in the offing. This resurrection is not a post-death emergence; it has been there for quite a while.

De-territorializing Literary Studies

Throughout his life, Fiedler's endeavor was to de-territorialize literary studies from the watertight compartments that it was encased in. His attempt was to study literature, which traditionally had been always attached to a particular territory—a culture, a language, a tradition, a school—in a broad manner. His writings suggest interdisciplinary enquiry with the twin aim of offering both linkages and transcultural connections between different literatures no longer trussed by national, linguistic, or disciplinary boundaries. Further on, often, hegemony and hierarchy that ruled comparative literature scholarship came under his minute scrutiny. As rightly said by Richard, "He was particularly interested in why some works endure in popular regard despite having been dismissed by critics" (2004, 295). Not one to be cowed by the redacted geographies of American texts, which excluded more than included, Fiedler defined his own boundaries and margins.

Leslie Fiedler agreed to be interviewed by Geoffrey Green in what is his most expansive formal interview. In that interview, he mused that he was fascinated by "terminal boundaries: beginnings and ends, and the fading of ends into beginnings. Maybe it's the ambiguity of the negative that interests me more than anything: the yes that's under the no, the beginning that's under the end. In a funny way, I think of myself as a secret affirmative writer pretending to be a nihilist. I know that someplace there are absolute categories, I equally know that we never perceive them" (1999, 179–80).

Even after all this, many are curiously vexed by the following: Fiedler has been a prolific critic. His writings have a critical and informational heft that many of his contemporary critics would strive for. Why is Fiedler not yet canonized? Why is he not part of the curriculum? Is there more to it than meets the eye?

In "The Postmodern *Weltanschauung* and Its Relation to Modernism: An Introductory Survey" (1986), Hans Bertens identifies Fiedler's key place in the early debates surrounding postmodern culture and literature: "Fiedler, who was joined by another American critic, Susan Sontag, found in Postmodernism a 'new sensibility' (Sontag's term), a new spontaneity identified with the American counterculture of the 1960s. In 'Cross the Border—Close the Gap: Postmodernism,' published in 1975, but written much earlier, Fiedler explored further his own brand of Postmodernism, which tended heavily toward pop art" (31). Bertens continues:

> For Fiedler—who obviously sympathizes with his Postmodernism—the new sensibility derides the pretensions of especially Modernist art; the postmodern novel will draw upon the Western, upon science fiction, upon pornography, upon other genres considered to be sub-literary, and it will close the gap between elite and mass culture. It will essentially be a pop-novel, "anti-artistic" and "anti-serious." Furthermore, in its anti–Modernist, anti-intellectual orientation, it will create new myths—although not authoritative Modernist myths—it will create "a certain rude magic in its authentic context," it will contribute to a magical tribalization in an age dominated by machines, making "a thousand little Wests in the interstices of a machine civilization" [31].

Bertens' analysis of "Cross the Border—Close the Gap" not only identifies Fiedler's seminal role in the early analysis of postmodernism, but also notes Fiedler's support (not surprisingly, given his own gift for going against the current) for the contrarian new literature. More importantly still, he shows Fiedler to be an early pioneer in American cultural studies: well before the influence of the Birmingham School had crossed the Atlantic, Fiedler championed hybrid, mass, and low cultures, a hallmark of many populist, post-Marxist analyses.

Because Fiedler received so much flak for his homoerotic cultural critique of the cultural contagion of America early on, it is heartening to hear a scholar of the stature of R. W. B. Lewis say that initially he was "taken aback by the author detecting a homoerotic attraction between Dimmesdale and Chillingworth in *The Scarlet Letter*," and that he "regretted Leslie's sceptical view of Henry James," but that he felt that Leslie Fiedler "as a cultural analyst was here twisting American culture into some very strange new shape, like a pretzel" (1999, 153). Only slowly did he realize that this was "the true, the real shape of American culture ... and that Leslie was in effect twisting it back into its proper shape" (153).

Fiedler's critical style was as important as his ideas. Christopher Lehmann-Haupt, writing in the *New York Times*, caught the essence of the Fiedler style: "What is remarkable about Fiedler's career is the way his use of the [pronoun] 'I' serves to expand the reader's vista to a rich intellectual landscape instead of reducing it to the narrow confines of the ego" (Bauman 2003, 2).[2] Brooding on Fiedler as a cantankerous muse, Gubar remembers, "Though we continue our debates quite definitely outside 'the Eliotic Church'—not in small measure because of the vigorously eccentric part Fiedler has played in American criticism—we still need to learn from him how to make our words comic, irreverent, and vulgar enough to come alive in the world, as his so robustly have" (1999, 170).

Even if there ever existed a view that Fiedler would always remain on the fringes of academia from within the mainstream, he continued to be venerated overseas. Foreign students who came to Buffalo especially wanted to work with him, and once a visiting scholar from India crawled under his desk to kiss his feet (Winchell 2002, 325).

In fact, in Hyderabad, India, where Fiedler donated an actual chair to the American Studies Research Centre, now converted into the Advanced Centre for American Studies (ACAS), at Osmania University Centre for International Programmes (OUCIP), one of his students, a professor at the university of Hyderabad, has instituted an "Annual Leslie Fiedler Memorial Lecture" in his memory. True to his eclectic interests and ideology, scholars of various disciplines and multi-disciplinary interests have been invited to deliver that lecture. There might be many more such instances that one is not aware of.

In an astute summing up in his book *Too Good to Be True* (2002), Winchell quotes Joan Didion in one of her more perceptive essays: "Certain places seem to exist because someone has written about them.... A place belongs forever to whoever claims it hardest, remembers it most obsessively, wrenches it from itself, shapes it, renders it, and loves it so radically that he remakes it in his image" (Didion 1979, 146, quoted in Winchell 2002, 341). Attributing the archetypes of American literature to Leslie Fiedler, Winchell in many ways is also overriding the role of Northrop Frye in its making. But then, since Aristotle and his discussion about *Oedipus Rex,* it seems that certain realms of literature also belong to certain critics. T. S. Eliot's ownership of the metaphysical poets cannot be denied, and Yoknapatawpha County belongs not just to William Faulkner but also to Cleanth Brooks. Similarly, at least one generation of readers first saw the early modernist writers through the eyes of Edmund Wilson (Winchell 2002, 342). Adding yet another dimension to this analogy is Fiedler, to whom the humanistic dismantling of hierarchies and categories of literature and culture can be ascribed and, as Winchell might say, given "the signature of a runaway boy from Newark—dreaming dreams too good to be true" (342).

Was he just dreaming; or imposing his dreams on others; or helping others to dream; or even putting his and their dreams into reality? Maybe no or maybe yes, but many would vouch for those dreams.

Fiedler: An Echo

> *Although the canon proves productive for pragmatic purposes, it may also turn out to be stifling and blinding in the long run if we do not establish a healthy distance from it.*
> —A. Classen, "Defining and Teaching the Canon in German Studies"

The literary canon, firmly circumscribed and defined by numerous literary histories that establish the standards of our field, provides "a most useful hermeneutic framework for everything we do in literary studies" (1). Classen (2011) elaborates on a pedagogical credo that is fast becoming the mantra of the younger pedagogues today:

> Both in research and in teaching there are always two stages in the critical treatment of the canon. Pedagogically it seems most advisable at first to present our students with the canon and to help them to digest it thoroughly, so that they can easily draw connections and move from one author/poet to the other, can explain historical, aesthetic, and social developments, and are informed enough to recognize genres, common motifs, the essential *stoff* of a text, and thus can comprehend how to differentiate among the various literary periods [1].

But Classen also states that fresh critical interpretations and punctilious studies have regularly brought about "cultural or literary turns" and helped in recognition and discovery of "heretofore unknown poets and texts." In fact it has also compelled us to reveal "ideological biases, religious manipulations, and political agendas" hidden in literary texts that make up our canon (1).

The obvious case in point of one such pedagogue who brought about "cultural and literary turns" is Leslie Fiedler. Of course such examples also abound in literature across the globe. One example of the recognition of heretofore unknown poets and texts from India is the rediscovery of Chandrabati's *Ramayana* by the famed Bengali scholar Nabaneeta Deb Sen.[3] The discovery unpacks what Classen calls "ideological biases, religious manipulations, and political agendas hidden in literary texts that make up our canon," in this case *Ramayana*, but also the prejudices of those who formed the canon. Since then, I have begun to explore, propelled by the insights provided by Nabaneeta Deb Sen, the rather impressive "other story" of *Ramayana*. A well-known poet and an academic, Sen's discerning eye accidentally located the rare text of *Chandrabati Ramayana*. This text is Sita's story narrated in the guise of a Rama-tale by a Bengali village woman of the sixteenth century. This had been dismissed as a mere fragment or an incomplete story by those to whom Deb Sen (1994) refers as the male, urban custodians of literary history. By selecting to write on this text, Sen offer a significant space to the otherwise silenced voice of the woman, emerging from within the rural Bengali cultural contexts.

Whether these "other" texts will be canonized is not for us to judge here; neither is it the object of this study. It is sufficient to say that some of these have found a place in university curricula, which in many ways implies entering the canon. It is not that great writers decline in our estimation. It is courageous enough to grant heretofore muted or forgotten voices a mike to sing and speak with, and a podium to recite from. Fiedler had that courage. "If we accept the canon for pragmatic purposes, then it must be malleable enough to facilitate new names and texts to compete with" (Classen 2011, 2). This echoes something similar said by the "wild man of American letters," years ago. Then Classen says, "Both from a pedagogical and a scholarly perspective, the canon and the margin need to talk to each other" (3). Could you hear Fiedler's voice? Finally Classen adds, "It is true that research has long left behind the narrow confines of a literary canon; and the task of the future must be to bring new voices into our academic classrooms, adding to—not substituting for—the wealth of the grand old masters.... Every canon becomes ossified and gets out of tune" (3). A voice so very reminiscent of Fiedler, Albrecht Classen makes a Fiedlerian case for opening up the canon.

Brady Harrison, himself from Montana, also joins in to point out that just as "the West left its mark on Fiedler, he certainly left his mark on scholarly work at the University of Montana." Brady finds "the ghost of Fiedler" in many writings of his colleagues. Brady makes a particular mention of Bill Bevis's landmark study of Montana writing, *Ten Tough Trips* (1990). It certainly builds on Fiedler's legacy in its analysis of Montana literature and history. Moreover it has the Fiedleresque mix of the literary, the cultural, and the personal. Brady adds "If traces of Fiedler can be found in Bevis's work on Montana and Western literature, new work by Jill Bergman, Casey Charles, Nancy Cook, Lynn Itagaki, David Moore, and others may well, I suspect, reveal at least a few marks of the great wildman" (Harrison 2008).

It is due to critics like Fiedler that English studies all over the world, in general, and in India in particular, are not the same any more. The last three decades have been both dynamic and unsettling. There has been a dismantling of hierarchies and a breakdown of categories. A kind of opening up of the canon has taken place in English classrooms. Paradigmatic shifts in course content; changes in pedagogical strategies; inclusion of the local (Harish Trivedi's *Pancha Dhatu* concept of English in India)[4]; "the phenomenon of the World Englishes project[5]; the rising interest in local or Indian English[6]; shifts in the center-vs.-margin paradigm; inclusionist approaches (Angela McRobbie and Dick Hebdige)[7]; and the advent of postmodernism have showcased that, on the contemporary register, English pedagogy and classrooms are revolutionary seats of interdisciplinarity and cross-cultural inter-genre discussions. In university classrooms across India in particular, the Holy Bible has been replaced by selections from *Mahabharata*[8] and the *Ramayana*[9]; Shakespeare has been reduced from occupying an entire paper being desperately accommodated (by the shrieking conservativists) in two papers, alongside Marlowe, Milton and others. Space has been created for a vast array of local and Indian texts—selections from poetry, novels, drama, and so on, of Mahatma Gandhi; Rabindra Nath Tagore; and Prem Chand, in translation; Chinnua Achebe is in the company of Soyinka, Derek Walcott, Marquez, Toni Morrison, and many others. One interesting shift is in the locations of classics in an English major course. Some compulsory classics have been nudged, to be replaced by popular fiction such as Agatha Christie, Ian Fleming, Lewis Carroll, Isaac Asimov, Margaret Mitchell, and so on. It is a relatively contemporary phenomenon in university education where critical applications are negotiated in the realm of texts received, absorbed and later interrogated in newer ways, not tried earlier.

Finally, it is due to the broadened insights of critics such as Fiedler that Tony Bennett's argument for intertextuality that can build a premise that every "spectator's interpretation of the text is in effect a new construction of it, based on the formation of reading competencies. They do not act solely upon the reader to produce different readings of the same text, but also act upon the text, shifting its very signifying potential so that it is no longer what it once was (and conceived) because in terms of its cultural location, it is no longer where it once was" (1990, 248). Fiedler is an echo that continues to resound and will continue to be heard.

The Road Not Taken

Being a long-distance, unfailing and a restless traveler, Fiedler went a long way. In this protracted journey, he took the road not taken by many. Much like the traveler of Robert Frost's much anthologized poem "The Road Not Taken," Fiedler could not have travelled both, the Frostian two roads. So he took the "grassy" one that "wanted wear." And, when two roads diverged in a wood, he "took the one less traveled by, /and that has made all the difference." In his acceptance speech for the J. B. Hubbell Award in 1994, Fiedler said he considered himself "an interloper, an uninvited guest." He began by saying that he was an unreconstructed amateur, a dilettante who had stumbled accidentally into American literature. Never a member of the American Literature Section of the MLA, he disclosed that "in graduate school I took no courses and wrote no papers on American literature, concentrating instead on the poetry of the Middle Ages and the English Seventeenth Century under mentors who believed and sought to persuade me that only second-rate minds wasted their time in studying American books.... I did not even then, however, share their elitist beliefs, convinced indeed that the canon should be opened even wider than the pioneers of American Studies were then proposing" (1999a). As a supporter of non-canonical study, in a review of *The Literary History of the United States,* along with Daniel Aaron and R. A. Miller (1949b) he chided its editors for having sought to canonize only those classic American authors already dead and sanctified by the passage of time, while ignoring still living and problematical modernists such as T. S. Eliot and Ezra Pound. In his passionate bid to open up the canon and its subsequent defense, Fiedler raises doubts about the presence of all those "writers, living or dead, who embody in our own tongue our own deepest nightmares and dreams" in American classrooms. He says, "Would it not be better ... to keep them sources of private delight rather than turning them into required reading for students in quest of good grades and teachers seeking promotion and tenure" (1999a).

The gauntlet seems to have ricocheted badly. Somebody seems to have read these lines a bit too minutely. Fiedler, as Winchell points out, is nowhere in the classrooms or course books. But this is too convenient a reason to pack him off to the gallows. As the next few pages will demonstrate, if it has not been demonstrated already, he is very much there, outside and inside the pages of critical texts and in the hearts of his admirers, alive and kicking.

In relation to the broader context staked out in the earlier chapters it can be safely said that his criticism is an achingly human one, mired in quotidian details. No neophyte to the world of popular culture, Fiedler is criticized for playing to the gallery. In light of this, it is gainful to recall that veiled by his twinned themes of whiteness and blackness, Fiedler's cultural imaginary of America has been canned anew with his every book. His later phase and critical positioning led another generation of critics, even his earlier admirers, to speak of him luridly. All such sources granted, I want to focus on a small topic: "Come back to the raft ag'in, Fiedler honey!"

"Come Back to the Raft Ag'in, Fiedler Honey!"

"I am working on a book on Fiedler."
"Who?"
"The Leslie Fiedler of America," shouted I, over the whirling fan in the waiting room, against the background din of many trains huffing, puffing and whistling away on that railway station in Hyderabad, that day.

"Oh! Leslie Fiedler. He is dead and GONE" responded the miss know-it-all scholar critic, and a once-upon-a-time American studies scholar.

"I don't think he is being much talked about now, even in America," crooned the second just-returned-from-America professor.

"His work has hardly any relevance now"—was the echoed verdict of the two.

This and many such statements have often affected my research, hampered its pace and lowered my confidence. And it is against several such encounters that this book has grown. What has provided it nourishment is the sheer impact of Fiedler on a vast generation of young scholars that he tutored and advised in their graduate, post graduate and doctoral days who today hold worthy positions as critics, academics, celebrities, writers, etc. They acknowledge his influence on their lives and writings, even their personalities.

What, then, has blocked Fiedler's entry into the canon? All his life he jousted for the literary "other"; isn't it ironic that he has himself become one? So when I write "Come back to the Raft Ag'in, Fiedler Honey!," is it then to bring back his own peripatetic wandering "literary self?"

Dillard's "Anthropophagi" is a poetic tribute to Fiedler in more ways than one. The poet opens with an exhortation:

> With their heads tucked into their vests
> Our friends, the everyday Scholars,
> Frost, Snow or Williwaw, note the literary "best"
> In perfect harmony with their peers, but must

> *Nonetheless stand in awe of Leslie Fiedler*
> *Who has actually read it all* [1999, 13]

Dillard finds Fiedler's insights original, "not something / We've already read somewhere else" in his commentary on all "the good, the bad, the wheedlers, / The winners, the bold and visionary." Fiedler's iconoclasm and difference have been summed up this way: "He's often out of step, / Inaccurate on occasion, or even downright / Duplicitous (eh, Huck honey?)." Yet the poet admires his sharp memory by calling him "literary Mr. Memory / Who remembers with a skill apparently instinctive / Everything he's ever read (or maybe he just / Takes good notes, who knows?) and knows how / And when to use it to bowl the reader over" (13–14). In the most important point that Dillard makes, he calls "those devotees of a priori / Criticism, those ideologues and theory / Touters with their heads buried in their chests," *anthropophagi*:

> But here's my Point, those anthropophagi
> I mentioned, those devotees of a priori
>   Criticism, those ideologues and theory
> Touters with their heads buried in their chests,
>   Should take note of Fiedler and just look up,
> Should (as Vivian de Sola Pinto, unimpressed
>   By a visiting lecturer at Nottingham,
> Once shouted out, "Read the book, sir, read
>   The book!") read the book! Read the books,
> Not just the books "about" the books, screeds
>   Of continental garble, read Poe,
> Actually read him, read Twain, read Robinson,
>   Read the women and the men, like Fiedler
> Read everything from Shakespeare to Stapledon,
>   And read them well, not just to fit a template
> Or make a point dozens have already made.

Dillard earnestly urges all who follow the beaten track to be as original and creative as Fiedler. According to him they should not hesitate to applaud him. The poet especially notes the expansive literary scholarship of Fiedler from the ancients to present day writers. Towards the end the poet predicts a kind of second coming of Fiedler. Dillard recalls the vision of Fiedler "...high above, / Locked in low clouds and drifting fog, / Leslie Fiedler circled (14–15).

The poem ends by giving a standing ovation to Fiedler: "Then suddenly / At the door the lost traveller appeared, every hair / In place, with the rosiest cheeks I've ever seen / On a man, the brightest eyes, clearly having a ball. / The room arose as one and burst / Into standing applause. So should we all" (15).

Even the singer-songwriter Leonard Cohen, in a poem written for a book dedicated to works about Fiedler, paid tribute to the critic's legacy, describing how so many readers have learned to imagine him: "leaning over the American moonlight / like the shyest gargoyle / who will not become angry or old" (Bauman 2003, 1–2).

Brady Harrison, to honor Fiedler's legacy at Montana, has a dream: "Alongside the glowering photo of Richard Hugo in the English seminar room [at Montana] a drink in one hand, cigarette in the other, looking unhappy about something—I would like to see one of Fiedler, the famous one of him in profile, looking like Walt Whitman's younger brother" (2008).

Harold Schechter, a Ph.D. student of Fiedler's at SUNY Buffalo, now a writer of true-crime books about America's most infamous sociopaths with a trio of titles behind him—*Deviant, Deranged,* and *Depraved*—owes his calling to Fiedler. According to him, "As a mentor [Fiedler] inspired us to pursue our observations wherever they led" (1999, 130). He further says that as a member of the Queens College Department of English, it was "Leslie's example that emboldened me to break out of the increasingly constricted world of academic 'discourse' and attempt to address the larger, 'mass' audience. Second, because Leslie's work—especially his brilliant, scandalously undervalued book, *What Was Literature?*—taught me that, to be true to the essential nature of his or her chosen material, a pop culture critic ought to write—ought to *perform*—in a pop culture mode. And finally, because my career as a 'commercial' author recently led to an experience that struck me as marvellously revealing of Leslie's impact on contemporary American culture" (130). He cites two incidents that are important in judging the all-pervasive influence of Fiedler. The first incident is when a book editor approached Schechter about the possibility of writing a history of Troma Entertainment, Inc. By way of introducing himself to Troma's founder, creative mastermind, and visionary auteur, Lloyd Kaufman, who maintained a polite but distinctly noncommittal mien throughout the interview, Schechter mentioned that he had done his doctorate under Fiedler. Schechter describes Lloyd's reaction, "Leslie Fiedler? You studied with Leslie Fiedler? That's really something." Schechter noticed that in an instant, his expression had shifted from utter indifference to serious respect (131). That the filmmaker responsible for giving the world movies such as *Bloodsucking Freaks, Blondes Have More Guns,* and *Femme Fontaine: Killer Babe for the CIA* was an ardent Fiedler-fan should have come as no surprise, since Leslie is, after all, the original champion of American trash cinema (131). The second incident that Schechter narrates is related to a brilliantly eccentric artist named Joe Coleman.[10] Shortly after meeting Joe, Schechter happened to mention—in the course of a conversation about sideshow freaks—that Fiedler had been his dissertation director at SUNY-Buffalo. Joe's response was identical to Lloyd Kaufman's—i.e., he regarded Schechter with new-found respect. He also insisted on getting Leslie's home address, so that he could send Leslie—whose bestseller *Freaks* was one of Joe's favorite books—a letter of admiration (132–33).

Schechter writes that he has encountered striking proof of Fiedler's enduring, inspiring influence on those artists, writers, and thinkers who—like Kaufman and Coleman—are all (in the sense that Fiedler himself has always been) "outsiders": creators who look to the taboo, the transgressive, the freakish, and forbidden for those vital (even redemptive) energies that are the wellspring of art (133).

Schechter recalls that in *What Was Literature?* Fiedler writes, "It is a major mystery of my career that I have come to be regarded as a 'seminal' ... critic even though every one of my books has been more scorned than praised in academic and literary reviews" (134–35). The solution to that mystery, Schechter believes, can be located in Emerson's "The American Scholar," which portrays an intellectual ideal that Fiedler has come closer to fulfilling than any other contemporary critic: "If a single man plant himself indomitably on his instincts, and there abide, the huge world will come round to him" (135). Indeed it will. Similarly, Geoffrey Green, Fiedler's Ph.D. student and later a professor of English at San Francisco State University, cherishes the most important advice given by Fiedler: "Write in the first person, be yourself. Speak to the reader directly and don't duck the big questions" (1999, 179). Would both Schechter and Green want to call out with me, "Come back to the raft ag'in, Fiedler honey!?" Oh yes, they would!

In another such homage, John Barth recounts Fiedler's impact, which "affected in large and small ways my professional trajectory; and that I remain the ongoing beneficiary of" (1999, 139). Fiedler (who had met Barth back in the 1950s when he was teaching at Princeton and Barth was on the faculty at Penn State) urged Cook to give Barth a tenured full professorship at SUNY Buffalo (Winchell 2002, 190). As Barth noted years later, "more than any other single factor, it was Leslie's presence there that tipped my scales Buffaloward" (1999, 139). When Barth's novel *Chimera* (1972) was nominated for the National Book Award, Fiedler was one of the five jurors making the selection. "But he soon realized that the rest of the panel did not seem favorable to Barth. (Leslie even phoned him ahead of time to inform him that he didn't have a prayer.) Jack was therefore surprised when a divided jury decided to give him half the prize. When pressed for an explanation, Leslie cheerfully confided to his friend: 'You had two for you and two against you ... and I drank the swing-vote under the table'" (141). In fact Barth wrote that Fiedler "is a mentor from whom this incidental, often skeptical, sometimes reluctant mentee never failed to learn" (Bauman 2003, 1). Surely Barth would join me in calling Fiedler back to the raft again.

It is people such as Ritz, who left SUNY before taking his Ph.D.—deciding to be "a pop culture participant and not a pop culture analyzer"—encouraged by Fiedler, who would want Fiedler to be back ag'in, always "training people to do things he couldn't do [and] go places he couldn't go" (Timberg 2008).

Pinsker's example of an entry dated September 1948, drawn from the notebooks of Lionel Trilling, shows the regard Fiedler's contemporaries had for him:

> Read my paper on the novel ["Art and Fortune"] to the English Institute, the response seemed very warm, hearty and prolonged applause.... I did it well, but ended hoarse and exhausted—wanted desperately to be praised by [Mark] Scholar and Fiedler [1999, 183–84].

In another of those rare acknowledgments, Lewis writes:

> If the study of that phenomenon [popular culture] has become so pronounced in the American academy in recent years, it is in good part the consequence of *What Was Literature?* Leslie never abandons hard-headed literary values and standards—the way so many academics are doing today—in some self-serving pursuit of some fashionable line [1999, 154]

Fiedler has always championed works that have never been in the canon of high art (*Gone with the Wind, Dracula*, and the classic works of science fiction) (Winchell 2002, 341). But he has also argued for the recanonization of writers whom the modernists toppled from their pedestals. Anyone can be an iconoclast these days; it takes a true original to restore a fallen icon to his place of former glory. This is what Fiedler has done for Henry Wadsworth Longfellow and a host of other writers who once crossed the border and closed the gap between the elite and popular culture (Fiedler 1950a, quoted in Winchell 2002, 341).

But for all his supposed academic tawdriness, let me, with all of the above, call out, "Come back to the raft ag'in, Fiedler honey!"

Which Is the Real Leslie Fiedler?

A cultural analyst, an admixture of cacophonous polyphony (many would nod their heads) and kaleidoscopic versatility; for this man, answers are aplenty. One answer lies in the impressive body of insights and criticism that mark the works of this bucolic cultural guru (Pinsker 1999, 185) who in his customary perverse and ambivalent way is, as he says, "a jack-of-all-fields and master of none" (1999a). Another answer involves his occasionally wrongheaded but provocative pronouncements: the novel is dead, or the Jewish American novel is history (Walden 1999, 160–65). Is he the one, susceptible—more than a little—to the siren call of the Dionysian and the vatic, the subversive and the counterculture, or could he generally be counted upon to keep his feet firmly planted and to tell the difference between a genuine idea and a specious concoction (Boyers 1999, 171)? This he did with several texts, in turn, annoying profusely. Or is he the one-off critical picaro, who in his literary, cultural, anthropological, and socio-political sojourns, in America and outside, enjoyed being Leslie Fiedler, the Auslander (Schwartz 1999, 99)? Concurrently, Green asked if he was "some medieval knight, jousting with a score of feisty competitors before a packed arena: with one arm he held his antagonists at bay with the other, he questioned, probed, and challenged the critical assumptions of the forum" (1999, 178). Or the populist, one who attacked the platitude that writers were either realist or antirealist and presented his vision of the writer as "magician, a dealer in illusions," who warned that "there are a lot of people who call themselves revolutionaries who are the reactionaries of tomorrow" (178). Finally, is he the wild man of American letters, a pioneer of a new literature, "a middle-of-the-roader" of a road that "hasn't been built yet" (Capozzi 1991, 335).

In spite of all these adjectives and his own protestations too, he is the one-man fifth column in the elitist citadel. An energetic iconoclast, but even more a ferocious scholar and thinker, he opened new ground in the study of literature, gender, sexuality, national myths, and more (Harrison 2008). When asked by Bauman if someone would go on to finish his work, Fiedler had this to say, probably his last few words for his readers:

> I have two answers to that: I hope so ... and I hope not. If there's one thing I can't stand, it's somebody doing something because I pushed them in that direction. What I really dream of is that somebody would blow everything I've done out of the water in a beautiful way which would clear the way for something better to come along. My assignment is what every writer's assignment is: tell the truth of his own time [Bauman 2003, 13].

Fiedler was asked to offer some advice to the critics of the future. Fiedler spontaneously responded,

> It's funny to be a critic, I never met anybody in my life who says, when you say what do you want to be when you grow up, "I want to be a critic." People say I wanna be a fireman, poet, novelist. Critics? How do they happen? I know how it happened to me. I would send a poem or story to a magazine and they would say this doesn't suit our needs precisely but on the other hand you sound interesting. Would you be interested in doing a review? And then I'd do it and decide that it's easy and you figure you might as well keep your name in front of people and you figure some day they'll run a story. And after a while they did publish some stories, but it's strange ... When somebody asks me what I do, I don't think I'd say "critic." I say "writer" [13].

A guru that every disciple would wish to have, Fiedler stood for the principles of the Sanskritic paradigm of *Vasudheva Kutumbkam*, which forms the fulcrum of Hindu Upanishadic philosophy. He was true to its sublime thought that to call one person a relative and another a stranger can only be the deed of small men. For those who live magnanimously, the entire world constitutes but a family (*ayam bandhurayam neti ganana laghuchetasam udaracharitanam tu vasudhaiva kutumbakam*). This tall man rewrote America's exceptional dream exceptionally: one of inclusion and innovation, avoiding insider-outsider dichotomies.

Let this book be treated as both an ode and an elegy to this columnist, the real "Brave Heavy Runner" who has lit out into the territory ahead of the rest.

Chapter Notes

Preface

1. Schechter elaborates that to speak in the first person is a particularly Emersonian notion and that Fiedler can be considered "the most Emersonian of our critics" (1999, 335).
2. Maini calls him a gadfly; many others have called him "the *enfant terrible*" (Maini 1987, 7–10).
3. "Sympathy for the Devil. Looking Backward for a New Tradition" is the title of his introduction. The "Devil" here is obviously Leslie Fiedler. Pardini laments the disappearance of "the beneficial effects of Cultural Theory, Neo-Marxism, Feminism and Post-Colonial Studies, the main critical practices of the last few decades" and "gender-race-nation" the triad that occupied the front stage of the critical scene in the recent past is also gone. "Working-class studies ... gaining a long-overdue attention ... still lack widespread organized institutional backing" [2008, xiii].
4. Pardini in his introduction refers to Terry Eagleton's *After Theory* (London: Allen Lane, 2003). Pardini (pp. xiii–xiv) informs us of "The Center for Working-Class Studies" at Youngstown University as one exception, with the work of Janet Zandy and Robert Coles at the center. He refers to numerous works written or edited by Janet Zandy, such as *Hands: Physical Labor, Class, and Cultural Work* (New Brunswick, NJ: Rutgers University Press, 2004); *What We Hold in Common: An Introduction to Working-Class Studies* (New York: Feminist Press, 2001): *Liberating Memory: Our Work and Our Working-Class Consciousness* (New Brunswick, NJ: Rutgers University Press, 1995); *Calling Home: Working-class Women's Writings: An Anthology* (New Brunswick, NJ: Rutgers University Press, 1990); (with co-editor Nicholas Coles) *American Working-Class Literature: An Anthology* (New York: Oxford University Press, 2007).
5. The number of theses and dissertations quoting Fiedler and using his theories has increased over the last two decades. The following list is a very selective one: Aspaas Kathie Menduni, "Harvey Breverman: Rendezvous with History and Literature in the Aftermath of Holocaust" (Master's thesis, State University of New York, Buffalo, 2007); Willis Lloyd Elliot, "Looking Away: The Evasive Environmental Politics of American Literature, 1823–1966" (Doctoral dissertation, University of Florida, 2006); Shere Jeremy, "Jewish American Canons: Assimilation, Identity, and the Invention of Post War Jewish American Literature" (Doctoral dissertation, Indiana University, 2006); Michael K. Johnson, "Where He Could Be a Man: The Frontier Myth and Constructions of White and Black Manhood in American Literature" (Doctoral dissertation, University of Kansas, 1997).
6. George Orwell said that of Henry Miller in "Inside the Whale: A Selection of Essays: From the Complete Works," XXII, 600 (first published on March 11, 1940; http://theorwellprize.co.uk/george-orwell/by-orwell/essays-and-other-works/inside-the-whale).

Introduction

1. Kellman and Malin write, "While men of his age still wore hats, Fiedler was baldly both stretching and relaxing the diction of lit-

erary discourse. He was challenging the canon when the proper reaction was still reverence. He was practicing cultural studies and gender studies without a license, reading American Indian literature and science fiction when to do so was raffish" (1999, i).

2. Some of these are *Freaks: Myths and Images of the Secret Self, Nude Croquet, Cross the Border—Close the Gap, What Was Literature: Class, Culture and Mass Society,* and *Tyranny of the Normal.*

3. "During a review of A *Fiedler Reader* (1977) and *Freaks* (1978), Alison Lurie, a novelist and specialist in children's literature, faulted Fiedler for" the same (Kellman 1999, 8).

4. *Love and Death in the American Novel, Times Literary Supplement,* March 17, 1961, 161–62.

5. Quoted by Scott McLemee in "Leslie Fiedler," *Chronicle of Higher Education,* July 19 and December 13, 2002.

6. Boyers further writes that as a writer Fiedler "seemed to do everything well, and ... will always be associated with *Love and Death in the American Novel,* which ought to be required reading ... in English departments, where not so long ago the bright Americanists could recite from memory their favorite Fiedlerian passages. But many of us first discovered Fiedler in the magazines, where he taught us how to think freshly about Alger Hiss and Whittaker Chambers, about Italian writers and Jewish writers, about the near past and the distant past" (1999, 171).

7. David Gates, "Fiedler's Utopian Vision," *Newsweek,* January 9, 1984, 11.

8. Greil Marcus, who name-checked Fiedler in *Mystery Train,* his groundbreaking 1975 study of rock music and American myth, further adds, "He was a pugnacious person who was determined to be at once the life of the party and never to be accepted. When you read Fiedler, if you have any germ of wanting to write, you have to wonder, 'Do I have the nerve to do this?' You're making criticism into a kind of public performance—leaving yourself completely exposed" (quoted in Timberg, 2008, http://articles.latimes.com/2008/may/04/entertainment/et-fiedler).

9. William Van O'Conner, in his essay "Accent on the Negative" (1960, 46–47), highlights Fiedler's pretentiousness in order to gain attention. He says, "Fiedler has a good eye for pretense, he can worry an idea like a cat toying with a mouse but he has a terrible need to be a show-off." The same point is made by Granville Hicks (1960a, 4), who calls him the wild man of American literary criticism, insisting that all Fiedler wanted to do was to give his readers a kick in the pants.

10. Zsolt Kelemen of Hungary (2010) while reviewing Pardini's collection finds the devil's (Fiedler's) indelible imprints in all the selections.

11. The review of *Love and Death in the American Novel* in the *Times Literary Supplement* (March 17, 1961, 161–62) throws ample illumination on his populist approach: "He has written a long book. Nor is he content with a scholarly audience; he reaches out to the general public, for what he has to say bears not only upon the American novel but upon 'the American Experience,' so inextricably entangled are literature and life."

12. "A conference paper by Fiedler in 1965 had been among the first discussions of hippie culture by an academic. 'According to *The Oxford English Dictionary*,' writes Winchell, 'it was in this lecture that the term postmodernism was first applied to literature'" (quoted by McLemee 2002, http://www.mclemee.com/id120.html).

13. John Barth recounts in "The Accidental Mentor" the ways Fiedler affected his life, which "affected in large and small ways my professional trajectory; and that I remain the ongoing beneficiary of" (1999, 139).

Chapter 1

1. Pardini in his introduction to *Devil Gets His Due* (2008) calls him an inheritor and maker.

2. Brady Harrison calls the Montana phase the "Wild Montana Phase" (2008).

3. Ransom is often regarded as the godfather of the American version of New Criticism and the *Kenyon Review* as its unofficial house organ. The term "New Criticism" (with its built-in obsolescence) was inadvertently coined by Ransom when he used it as the title of a book he published in 1941 (Winchell in Kellman and Malin 1999, 88).

4. Dembo (1973) in "Dissent and Dissent: A Look at Fiedler and Trilling" sees Fiedler as a dissenter.

5. In this context O'Conner's attempt in "Accent on the Negative" is to offer a very balanced view of his negativism.

6. *Times Literary Supplement* in a review of *Love and Death in the American Novel* (1961, 162).

7. Despite Leslie's and Margaret's claims of innocence, the jury returned a verdict of guilty on April 9, 1970. On April 30, Margaret was fined $500, while Leslie was ordered to serve six months in prison. In the spring and summer of 1972, five years after his arrest, Leslie's conviction was reviewed by the New York Court of Appeals. When the appeals court rendered its verdict in July of 1972, Leslie walked free for a reason more basic than any of the procedural issues raised. Speaking for a 5 to 2 majority of the court, Judge James Gibson declared that "no crime had been charged or proven." The law that Leslie was accused of violating applied only to a building that the owners specifically maintained for criminal purposes. "It was never contemplated," Judge Gibson wrote, "that the criminal taint would attach to a family home should members of the family on one occasion smoke marijuana or hashish there." Finally getting it right, *Time* titled its account of the decision "Being Unbusted" (Winchell 2002, 232).

8. Molly extensively brings to our notice such readings: Richard H. Pells, *The Liberal Mind in the Conservative Age: American Intellectuals in the 1940s and 1950s* (New York: Harper and Row, 1985), especially pages 277–80, a discussion of Fiedler's and Warshow's essays as instances of anticommunist intellectuals' insistence "that all political movements threatened to rob the individual of his distinctive identity" (277). For a contemporary influential and commensurately more equivocal account of the same phenomenon, see Arthur Schlesinger, *The Vital Center: The Politics of Freedom* (Boston: Houghton Mifflin, 1949), especially the concluding chapter, "Freedom: A Fighting Faith" (243–58).

9. New York: Jero, 1953.

10. Pease brings in Cornelius Castoriadis' *The Imaginary Institution of Society* (Cambridge: MIT Press, 1987), 3. Like Fiedler, Castoriadis developed this symbolic construct at a time in the 1950s when he believed authentic political change could only take place on the level of the Cultural Imaginary.

11. Malin goes to the extent of saying that he has also been subtly influenced by Fiedler (37–38).

Chapter 2

1. See Sanford (1999, 183) for a discussion of this quirkiness.

2. In both the essays, "Puritanism as Allegory: Yvor Winters, Richard Chase and Leslie Fiedler" and "The Apolitical Unconscious: Leslie Fiedler" from *The Unusable Past* (New York and London: Methuen, 1986), Russell Reising makes an extensive reading of Fiedler's works.

3. This article is a much-cited one.

Chapter 3

1. Jerome Richard, in "Leslie Fiedler: an Appreciation," claims to establish the "tallness" of Fiedler, the critic and pedagogue, but in relation to Montana and the recognition that he got from the Blackfeet Indian Tribe, he writes that Fiedler, "did not hesitate to bite the hands that were feeding him." The reference is to the notorious essay "Montana, or the End of Jean-Jacques Rousseau" (Richard 2004, 297).

2. The reference is to Leo Marx's *The Machine in the Garden: Technology and the Pastoral Ideal in America* (New York: Oxford University Press, 1964), 34–72.

3. Read this full article by Sanford Pinsker, "Leslie Fiedler, Freak" (1999, 182–191) to enjoy the powerful influence of Fiedler on students at the time and present-day academics and scholars.

4. For a longer discussion see Irving Malin, ed., *Contemporary American-Jewish Literature* (Bloomington: Indiana University Press, 1973).

5. Read John McGowan's "Leslie A. Fiedler" in *Modern American Critics since 1955*, ed. Gregory S. Jay (Dictionary of Literary Biography, vol. 67; Detroit: Gale, 1988), for a greater understanding of his position among American critics of today.

Chapter 4

1. This was a term that I used in one of my paper presentations in an international confer-

ence at Nagpur in 2004, in which I discussed Fiedler's contribution to popular culture.

2. Both these books: Bob Ashley's *Reading Popular Narrative: A Source Book* (London: Leicester University Press, 1997) and Christopher Pawling's *Popular Fiction and Social Change* (London: Macmillan, 1984) are important reference texts used in Indian University undergraduate classrooms while teaching papers in popular fiction. Some of these points were made in my research papers titled "British Popular Fiction in an Indian Classroom: A View from the Other," *Literary Paritantra (Systems)* 1.1 (January 2009) (India: DEI): 65–76, and "The Postmodern Condition and the Politics of the Popular," *Creative Forum* 16.1–2 (January–June, 2003) (New Delhi: Bahri Publications): 119–30.

3. For more details see Dallas Liddle's (2007) "Bakhtinian 'Journalization' and the Mid-Victorian Literary Marketplace" in which he tells us about the famous remarks of M. M. Bakhtin on novelization, in which he theorized a mechanism by which one literary genre influences the content and structure of other genres. Though the influence Bakhtin describes goes only one way—the novel "novelizes" other genres. In addition, novelization is not an isolated phenomenon, but an example or case study within Bakhtin's larger "Galilean" conception of genre interaction (*Literature Compass* 4, 2007).

4. Ray B. Browne, Marshall Fishwick, Russel B. Nye, and John Cawelti.

5. Browne elaborates that popular culture "can be used as a tool to assist in education. It can be utilized in numerous ways to encourage learning, to overcome illiteracy, to retain people in school, and to energize our educational system" (Browne 1973, 8). He also stresses that popular culture is a derivative of the sum total of our experiences, thinking, and attitudes toward life. It is the environment around us, the culture we inherit, the culture we transmit to our descendants. Popular culture is the television we watch, the cinema we give patronage to, the type of food—fast, junk, or conventional—that we eat, the type of attire we wear, the music we appreciate, the things we spend money on; in short, the whole society we live in.

6. For a discussion of the Pop Revolution in the sixties and early seventies, see Browne et al. 1968; Browne 1973; Browne and Fishwick 1978; and Browne and Ambrosetti 1970.

7. Fishwick's "Confessions of an Ex-Elitist" is a candid expression of how a person changes his attitude toward "elite" culture and eventually becomes an exponent of "popular culture." In *Parameters of Popular Culture* (1974), Fishwick refers to popular culture as a new international style that emerged in the late twentieth century. This trend, according to him, is far more pervasive and spontaneous than the earlier ones (classical, gothic, romantic and modern), and it transcends national, class, language and racial barriers. This new trend has been widely acclaimed all over the world. Students proclaim it in the streets of Paris, Prague, New Delhi and New York. Under this broad umbrella are those works and events (both artistic and commercial) that are designed for mass consumption and to cater to the taste of the majority. Fishwick further points out the most important tenet of popular culture: "Entertainment is the key, and money is the spur" (1974, 1).

Chapter 5

1. Susan Gubar, famed for her text *Madwoman in the Attic*, hails Fiedler as one who predicted the feminist revolution of the mid-seventies.

2. Some of the points incorporated in this chapter were part of my paper presentation at an international conference held at ACAS, OUCIP, Hyderabad, December 12–14, 2011.

3. According to Aamir Mufti, "Said's most influential contribution to these debates is of course the concept and metaphor—evocative, dense, and elusive at the same time—of contrapuntiality, first employed in 1984 in the essay 'Reflections on Exile,' but finding its fullest elaboration in *Culture and Imperialism*" (Mufti 1984).

4. Lately the text has been criticized for its selection and overemphasis on a few white male writers and high-cultural artifacts.

5. American exceptionalism is reverence for difference on the one hand, but on the other, becoming shadows of the masters (in ways that America has become a shadow of the imperial masters). No wonder strict and conventional postcolonialists would decry North America and push it out of the much-protected boundary of postcolonialism. Alexis de Tocqueville was the first writer to describe the U.S. as "ex-

ceptional" in 1831 and 1840 in his work *Democracy in America*. He writes, "The position of the Americans is therefore quite exceptional, and it may be believed that no other democratic people will ever be placed in a similar one" (36). Contrapuntally, Donald Pease defined it as a "state fantasy" and a "myth" in his 2009 book *The New American Exceptionalism*, (Minneapolis: University of Minnesota Press, 10).

6. See my paper, "British Popular Fiction in an Indian Classroom: A view from the Other" note 14: "As Roland Barthes and Richard Slotkin have shown, myth and word are inextricably interrelated; popular icons and narratives provide effective justifications for the dominant values of a society. The danger of myth, for Slotkin as for Barthes, is that we take it for natural truth, for example, in the divinely ordained racial and cultural superiority of the European settler, and the regenerative value of their violent subjugation of the "wilderness" and its "savage inhabitants." (Srivastava, 2009, 74) The American popular culture Slotkin studies in *Regeneration through Violence* tends to embody this myth and so to justify black slavery and Native American genocide, for example. He convinces us in later writings, furthermore, that the same myth was at work in the Vietnam War and continues today (see *The Fatal Environment: The Myth of the Frontier in the Age of Industrialization, 1800–1890* (New York: Atheneum, 1985, chapters 1 and 2). He does not, however, argue that all popular culture necessarily works to propagate these myths and their maleficent ilk (Quoted in Srivastava 2009, 65–76).

7. Ferraro (1991) throws light on Fiedler's contribution to ethnic literature.

8. According to a Biblical myth, "a Hebrew minor prophet. He was called by God to preach in Nineveh, but disobeyed and attempted to escape by sea; in a storm he was thrown overboard as a bringer of bad luck and swallowed by a great fish, only to be saved and finally succeed in his mission" (Oxford Dictionary online, http://oxforddictionaries.com/, s.v. "Jonah").

Chapter 6

1. The reference is to Fiedler's being named a chief by the Blackfoot tribe.

2. The reference is to the essay "Hemingway in Ketchum," in which Fiedler regales us with an account of his visit with Hemingway in Idaho, and examines Hemingway's career and persona, never hiding or repressing his own presence.

3. Nabaneeta Deb Sen, well-known writer, critic and academic, is a professor at the Department of Comparative Literature in Jadavpur University. She has many books to her credit in a variety of genres: short stories, essays, travelogues, poetry, fiction, children's literature and verse-plays. Even her most scholarly essays are remarkable for their charming and humorous prose. She is one of the most popular authors in Bengal today. She has received the Padma Shree (2000), the Sahitya Academy Award, the Kair Samman, the Rabindra Puraskar and the Sanskriti Award. She is a fellow of the Royal Asiatic Society of Great Britain and vice president of the Indian National Comparative literature Association. She was the Radhakrishnan Memorial Lecturer of Oxford in 1996–97 ("Nabaneeta Dev Sen," http://manashtech.blogspot.com/2011/08/nabanita-deb-sen.html).

4. Harish Trivedi, "Panchadhatu: Teaching English Literature in the Indian Literary Context," in *Colonial Transactions: English Literature and India* (UK: Manchester University Press, 1993), 199–219. Trivedi suggests that in a canon fashioned of *panchadhatu*, or the five elements (earth, water, fire, wind, and sky), one would study five literatures of different linguistic and/or provincial/national origins assembled together in such measure and proportion as may be found appropriate from time to time. The objective is not to abandon English altogether, but to plant it in native ground and give it a surrounding context. The five elements of reading literature in English would be thus: (1) Literature written in English in England; (2) Literature written originally in English, in countries other than England; (3) Literature not originally written in English, but available in translation; (4) Literature in local Indian languages to be studied in original; and (5) Classical literature to be studied in its original language—Sanskrit, Persian, Latin, Greek, and so on.

5. The World Englishes project and the New Englishes project, with their division of speakers/speech into Acrolect (standard), Basilect (deviant from standard) and Mesolect

(informal—midway between the Acrolect and the Basilect), rupture age-old language traditions often leading to lexical and grammatical change and create a fantastical illusion where ownership of the language for us always remains in the virtual realm. Whether it is Kachru's Three Circle Model of World English, McArthur's Circle of World English, or Modiano's Centripetal Circles of Modern English, all these models are exo-normative in nature (Srivastava 2010, 4).

6. At a macro level, nudging the enterprise of the World Englishes, it will be interesting to look at the substrate influence—mother tongues' and local languages' influence on the morphology and syntax of Indian English(es). While mapping the language scene of India, it is crucial to be alert to the role of politics in building language hierarchies and their implications for linguistic and cultural plurality.

7. We have come a long way from Arnold's view of popular culture as "anarchy" to Dick Hebdige's claim that "Popular Culture is no longer marginal, still less subterranean. Most of the time and for most people it simply is culture" (Storey 2001, 15).

8. Refer to Veda Vyasa's classical epic *Mahabharata* (said to predate the age of Buddha, that is, sixth century BC).

9. In Sanskrit literature, Maharishi Valmiki's classical epic *Ramayana* is known to be the first epic. In Winternitz's opinion, the first format of the *Ramayana* evolved in the fourth century BC and its final format in the second century AD.

10. Joe Coleman, whose work is rapidly gaining the international attention it so richly deserves (Coleman's life and art are the subject of a feature-length documentary, *Rest in Pieces*). Largely because of his "naif" style and disquieting subject matter (which tends to dwell on disfiguring disease, grotesque bodily deformity, and an astonishing range of deviant behavior), Coleman is generally classified under the currently trendy label of "outsider artist." Coleman is also the only major American painter to perform as an actual geek, having once been sued by TV game show host and animal rights activist Bob Barker after biting off and swallowing the head of a live mouse during a public exhibition (abridged from Schechter 1999, 132).

Bibliography

Works by Leslie Fiedler

1948. "Poetry Chronicle." Reviews of four poetry collections. *Partisan Review* 15.3: 381–385.

1949a. "Jahrzeit for Papa Jay" (poem). *Poetry* (October): 17+.

1949b. Review of *The Literary History of the United States* by Daniel Aaron and R. A. Miller. *American Quarterly* 1.2 (Summer): 169–83.

1949c. "What Can We Do About Fagin? The Jew-Villain in Western Tradition." *Commentary* (May): 411–18.

1950a. "The Children's Hour: or, The Return of the Vanishing Longfellow: Some Lament for Little Farfel; To the Unbeautiful in Spring; Poems." *Poetry* (February): 264–65.

1950b. "My Credo." *The Kenyon Review* 12 (Autumn): 561–74.

1950c. "On Leaving Cambridge; Pair of Posies for John Skelton; Memories of Winter; Poems." *Poetry* (June): 125–29.

1950d. "Poem for St. Valentine's Day," "Child's Play," "Boy by the Sea," "Children at the Show," "Bloody Husband" (poems). *Poetry* (November): 69–72.

1950e. "Toward an Amateur Criticism." *Kenyon Review* 2 (Autumn): 561–74.

1951a. "Bad Poetry and the Tradition." *Poetry* (January): 215–16.

1951b. "Your Greenstone Hair," "To Margaret," "Against Waking" (poems). *Poetry* (July): 208–209.

1952. "Our Country and Our Culture" (symposium). *Partisan Review* 19.3: 282–326.

1953a. "Afterthoughts on the Rosenbergs." This controversial article was republished along with two related articles, "McCarthy and the Intellectuals" (which had appeared in *Encounter* in August 1954) and "Hiss, Chambers and the Age of Innocence" (which first appeared in *Commentary* in December 1950) in Fiedler's first critical work, *An End to Innocence*, in 1955.

1953b. "Sea," "Quarry," "Extra Ecclesiam" (poems). *Poetry* (October): 10–12.

1955a. "Adolescence and Maturity in the American Novel." *New Republic* (May 2): 16–18.

1955b. "Dancing of Rebhershal with the Withered Hand" (short story). *The Kenyon Review* (September): 193–207.

1955c. *An End to Innocence: Essays on Culture and Politics.* Boston: Beacon.

1955d. "Lion" (poem). *Poetry* (January): 197.

1956. "Some Footnotes on the Fiction of '56." *Reporter* (December): 13, 44–46.

1957a. "Memoir and Parable." *Poetry* (February): 326–29.

1957b. "Three Train Poems." *Poetry* (August): 294–95.

1958a. *The Art of the Essay.* (Editor.) Rev. ed., New York: Thomas Y. Crowell, 1969.

1958b. "Road to Shaw." *Saturday Review* (May 10): 27–29.

1959. "Four Midrashum for the Passover" (poems). *Commentary* (February): 116–17.

1960a. "Henry Roth's Neglected Masterpiece." *Commentary* (August): 102–07.

1960b. *Love and Death in the American Novel*. New York: Stein and Day.
1960c. *No! In Thunder: Essays on Myth and Literature*. London: Eyre and Spottiswoode.
1960d. "On the Road; or The Adventures of Karl Shapiro." *Poetry* (June): 171–78.
1962a. "Almost Imaginary Interview: Hemingway in Ketchum." *Partisan Review* (Summer): 395–405.
1962b. *Pull Down Vanity and Other Stories*. Philadelphia: Lippincott.
1963. *The Second Stone: A Love Story*. New York: Stein and Day.
1964a. *The Continuing Debate: Essays on Education*. (Edited volume; co-editor, Jacob Vinocur.) New York: St. Martin's.
1964b. "Kind of Solution: The Situation of Poetry Now." *The Kenyon Review* (Winter): 54–79.
1964c. *Waiting for the End*. New York: Stein and Day.
1965a. *Back to China*. New York: Stein and Day.
1965b. *The Continuing Debate: Essays on Education*. (Edited volume; co-editor, Jacob Vinocur.) New York: St. Martin's.
1965c. "Girl in a Black Raincoat" (short story). *Partisan Review* (Winter): 35–41.
1965d. "The New Mutants." *Partisan Review* (Fall): 505–25.
1965e. *Waiting for the End: The Crisis in American Culture and a Report on Twentieth-Century American Literature*. New York: Dell.
1966a. "American Abroad." *Partisan Review* (Winter): 77–91.
1966b. *The Last Jew in America*. New York: Stein and Day.
1966c. *Love and Death in the American Novel*. New York: Stein and Day. 1992. New York: Anchor.
1967a. "Master of Dreams: The Jew in the Gentile World." *Partisan Review* (Summer): 339–56.
1967b. "Second Thoughts on *Love and Death in the American Novel*: My First 'Gothic Novel.'" *Novel: A Forum on Fiction* 1 (Fall): 8–11.
1968a. *0 Brave New World*. (Edited volume; co-editor, Arthur Zeiger.) New York: Dell.
1968b. *The Return of the Vanishing American*. New York: Stein and Day.
1969b. *Being Busted*. New York: Stein and Day.
1970a. "The Divine Stupidity of Kurt Vonnegut." *Esquire* (September): 195–97.
1970b. "Male Novel." *Partisan Review* 371: 74–89.
1970c. *Nude Croquet and Other Stories*. New York: Stein and Day, 1969. London: Secker and Warburg.
1970d. Fiedler et al. "Symposium Highlights: Wrestling (American Style) with Proteus." Report by Roger Henkle. *NOVEL: A Forum on Fiction* 3, no. 3. (Spring): 197–207.
1971a. *The Collected Essays of Leslie Fiedler*. 2 vols. New York: Stein and Day.
1971b. *To the Gentiles*. New York: Stein and Day.
1972a. *The Stranger in Shakespeare*. New York: Stein and Day.
1972b. *Unfinished Business*. New York: Stein and Day.
1972c. "Which Writer Under Thirty Five Has Your Attention and What Has He Done to Get It." *Esquire* (October): 135+.
1974. *The Messengers Will Come No More*. New York: Stein and Day.
1975a. *In Dreams Awake: A Historical-Critical Anthology of Science Fiction*. New York: Dell.
1975b. "Towards a Definition of Popular Literature." In *Superculture: American Popular Culture and Europe*, ed. C. W. E. Bigsby. Bowling Green, OH: Bowling Green University Press, 29–38.
1976. "Fairy Tales Without Apologies." *Saturday Review* 15 (May): 24–27.
1977a. *A Fiedler Reader*. New York: Stein and Day.
1977b. "Malamud's Travesty Western." *Novel* (Spring): 212–19.
1978a. *Freaks: Myths and Images of the Secret Self*. New York: Simon & Schuster.
1978b. "Give the Devil His Due." *Journal of Popular Culture* (Fall): 197–207.
1979. *The Inadvertent Epic: From "Uncle Tom's Cabin" to "Roots."* New York: Simon & Schuster.
1980. "The Death and Rebirths of the Novel." *Salmagundi* 50–51: 143–52.

1981a. *English Literature: Opening Up the Canon.* (Edited volume; co-editor, Houston A. Baker, Jr.) Baltimore: Johns Hopkins University Press.
1981b. "The Legend." In *Buffalo Bill and the Wild West,* ed. Fiedler, et al. 84–95. Brooklyn: Brooklyn Museum.
1981c. "On Infanticide." *Journal of Popular Culture* (Spring): 676–80.
1982. *What Was Literature? Class Culture and Mass Society.* New York: Simon & Schuster.
1983. *Olaf Stapeldon: A Man Divided.* New York: Oxford University Press.
1990a. "Mythicizing the Unspeakable." *Journal of American Folklore* 103, no. 410 (October–December): 390–399.
1990b. "What Used to be Called Dead" (short story). *Kenyon Review* 12.1 (Winter): 104.
1991. *Fiedler on the Roof: Essays on Literature and Jewish Identity.* Boston: David R. Godine.
1993. "Fulbright I: Italy 1952." In *The Fulbright Difference,* ed. Richard T. Arndt and David Lee Rubin. New Brunswick, N.J.: Transaction.
1996. *Tyranny of the Normal: Essays on Bioethics, Theology and Myth.* Boston: David R. Godine.
1999a. "Hubbell Acceptance Speech 1994." In *Leslie Fiedler and American Culture,* ed. Steven G. Kellman and Irving Malin, 21–25. Newark: University of Delaware Press; London: Associated University Presses. The Hubbell Medal, which has been awarded since 1964, is named after the founding editor of *American Literature,* Jay B. Hubbell. Hubbell, a long-time professor at Duke University, was one of the pioneers of American literary scholarship. In this speech Fiedler admits that alongside ancient Greek tragedy, the classic Chinese novel, Old Provencal poetry, the English Victorian novel, Kafka and James Joyce, Jaroslav Hasek and Chrétien de Troyes, and especially Shakespeare and Dante, he has "also dealt with subjects as remote from my presumable field of expertise as theology and psychology, voting studies and the war in Vietnam, Japanese woodblock engravings, pornography and comic books, sideshows and circuses, bioethics and organ transplants. I have talked about them, moreover, not just in the classroom and at gatherings of my fellow-academics, but to trade-unionists, nurses and dermatologists, as well as on talk shows presided over by Dick Cavett and William Buckley, Merv Griffin and Phil Donahue—earning myself a listing in *Who's Who in Entertainment."* Several of these also stand as the "extras" in the academia, perpetually waiting in the wings to be called on stage. This "extra" is actually a reflection of his abiding interest in the "other."
1999b. *A New Fiedler Reader*: Amherst, N.Y.: Prometheus.
2008. "The Canon and the Classroom: A Caveat." *English Inside and Out: The Plaeces of Literary Criticism,* eds. Susan Gubar and Jonathan Kamholtz, Routledge, UK. Reprinted in *The Devil Gets His Due: The Uncollected Essays of Leslie Fiedler,* ed. Samuele F. S. Pardini, 128–135. Berkeley, CA: Counterpoint.

Secondary Sources: Essays, Articles, Books, Interviews and Reviews

Adam, Ian, and Helen Tiffin, eds. 1990. *Past the Last Post: Theorizing Post Colonialism and Post Modernism.* Calgary: University of Calgary Press.
Adamowski, T. H. 2006. "Demoralizing Liberalism: Lionel Trilling, Leslie Fiedler, and Norman Mailer." *University of Toronto Quarterly* 75.3 (Summer): 883–904. This article focuses on the demoralization of the liberalism ideology with reference to the works of social scientists Lionel Trilling, Leslie Fiedler, and Norman Mailer. The author hypothesizes that before and after the Second World War, demoralization of liberalism may have begun in the work of men and women involved with *Partisan Review* and New York literary culture. In particular, the article suggests that the work of these three may have contributed despite themselves

and from within liberalism to the crisis of liberalism.

Adams, Robert M. 1969. "The Return of the Vanishing American." *New York Review of Books*, (April 10): 34.

Aldridge, John. 1966. "Speaking of Books: The Novel and the Critic." *New York Times*, March 6.

Allen, Gay Wilson. 1955. Review of *Leaves of Grass One Hundred Years After: New Essays by William Carlos Williams, Richard Chase, Leslie A. Fiedler, Kenneth Burke, David Daiches, and J. Middleton Murry*. *American Literature* 27.3 (November): 433.

Almansi, G. 1969. "Interview with Leslie Fiedler." *Twentieth Century Studies* (November): 56–67.

Alridge, John. 1966. "The Critic's Novel: *The Second Stone*." In *Time to Murder and Create: The Contemporary Novel in Crisis*. New York: David Mckay.

Alter, Robert. 1963. "The Creative Writer as a Jew." *Congress Bi-Weekly* (September 16): 42–59.

———. 1965. "Sentimentalizing the Jews." *Commentary* (September): 71–75.

———. 1968. "Jewish Dreams and Nightmares." *Commentary* (January): 48–51.

———. 1974. Review of *The Messengers Will Come No More*, by Leslie Fiedler. *New York Times* (September 29): 5–6.

American Literature. 1969 Review of *The Return of the Vanishing American* (January): 586.

Ames, Christopher. 1992. "Restoring the Black Man's Lethal Weapon." *Journal of Popular Film and Television* 20.3 (Fall): 52. Discusses race and sexuality in contemporary cop films. The American literary myth described by Leslie Fiedler prevalent in recent popular films; the powerful masculine bond that animates the interethnic buddy film; and the continuation of certain characteristically American imperial and misogynist themes in *Die Hard*, *Lethal Weapon*, and *Shoot to Kill*.

Ashcroft, Bill, Gareth Griffiths, and Helen Tiffin. 1989. *The Empire Writes Back: Theory and Practice in Post-Colonial Literatures*. London: Rutledge.

Aspaas, Kathie Menduni. 2007. "Harvey Breverman: Rendezvous with History and Literature in the Aftermath of Holocaust." Master's Thesis. State University of New York, Buffalo.

Azam, Kousar J., ed. 2001. *Rediscovering America: American Studies in the New Century*. New Delhi: South Asian Publishers. The introduction very succinctly presents the twenty-first century perspective of American studies outside America.

Barrett, William. 1955. "Life, Letters, and Politics." Review of *An End to Innocence* by Leslie Fiedler. *New York Times Book Review* (April 24): 20.

Barth, John. 1967. "The Literature of Exhaustion." *Atlantic Monthly* (August): 29–34.

———. 1999. "The Accidental Mentor." In *Leslie Fiedler and American Culture*, ed. Steven G. Kellman and Irving Malin, 139–41. Newark: University of Delaware Press.

Bauman, Bruce. 2003. "The Critic in Winter." http://www.salon.com/books/int/2003/01/02/fiedler/print.html. Accessed on December 2, 2010, 1–13. In this interview, Fiedler talks about his encounters with Hemingway and Faulkner, his falling out with Bellow, the modern novel, which contemporary novelists will last, and his being called a "writer" rather than a "critic."

Bellman, Samuel L. 1963. "The American Artist as European Frontiersman: Leslie Fiedler's *The Second Stone*." *Critique: Studies in Modern Fiction* 6: 131–43.

Bennett, Tony. 1990. *Popular Fiction: Technology, Ideology, Production, Reading*. London and New York: Routledge.

Berman, Ronald. 1965. "Zion as Main Street." *The Kenyon Review* 27 (Winter): 171–75.

Biederman, Patricia Ward. 1982. "Leslie Fiedler: The Critic as Outlaw." *Buffalo Courier-Express* (March 7): 9–11, 13–15.

Bigsby, C. W. E. 1975. *Superculture: American Popular Culture and Europe*. Bowling Green, OH: Bowling Green University Popular Press.

———. 1976. *Approaches to Popular Culture*.

Bowling Green, OH: Bowling Green University Popular Press.

Birnbaum, Milton. 2005. "Two of a Kind?" *Modern Age* 47.2 (Spring): 167–70. Birnbaum reviews two books: *Too Good to Be True: The Life and Work of Leslie Fiedler*, by Mark Royden Winchell, and *Aldous Huxley: A Biography*, by Nicholas Murray.

Bloom, Alexander. 1986. *Prodigal Sons: The New York Intellectuals and Their World*. New York and Oxford, UK: Oxford University Press.

———. 1989. "Fiedler, Leslie." In *The Blackwell Companion of Jewish Culture*, ed. Glenda Abramson, 223–224. Oxford, UK: Basil Blackwell.

Bode, Carl. 1960. *The Anatomy of American Popular Culture 1940–1961*. Berkeley: University of California Press. Reprinted under the title *Antebellum Culture*, 1970.

Boewe, Charles. 2004. "American Studies in India: A Personal Memoir." *American Studies International* 42.1: 49–91.

Bold, Christine. 1991. "Popular Forms I." In *The Columbia History of the American Novel*, ed. Elliot Emory, 285–308. New York: Columbia University Press.

Booth, W. C. 1979. *Critical Understanding: The Powers and Limits of Pluralism*. Chicago: University of Chicago Press.

Boyers, Robert. 1991. "Avante Garde." In *The Columbia History of the American Novel*, ed. Emory Elliot, 726–51. New York: Columbia University Press.

———. 1999. "Thinking About Leslie Fiedler." In *Leslie Fiedler and American Culture*, ed. Steven G. Kellman and Irving Malin, 171–78. Newark: University of Delaware Press; London: Associated University Presses.

Bradbury, Malcolm. 1963. "Review of *No! In Thunder*, by Leslie Fiedler." *The Listener* (July 18): 101–2.

Branch, Taylor. 1989. "The Uncivil War." *Esquire* (May): 89–116.

Brooks, Cleanth. 1979. "The New Criticism." *Sewanee Review* 87 (Fall): 598.

Browne, Ray B. 1973. *Popular Culture and the Expanding Consciousness*. New York: Wiley.

———. 2009. Review of *The Devil Gets His Due: The Uncollected Essays of Leslie Fiedler*, ed. Samuele Pardini. *The Journal of American Culture* 32.2 (June): 184. http://onlinelibrary.wiley.com/. Accessed December 2, 2011. In a crisp, short, no-holds-barred review that is more like a note, Browne calls Fiedler "the Serpent in the Garden who not only tempted but also urged" (184). Nailing Fiedler for his impulsive, wrongheaded criticism, he welcomes Pardini's not-so-full collection about an author, "worthy to be heard," as a kind of beginning until a more comprehensive one is out.

Browne, Ray B., and Marshall Fishwick, eds. 1978. *Icons of America*. Bowling Green, OH: Bowling Green State University Popular Press.

Browne, Ray B., and Ronald J. Ambrosetti. 1970. *Popular Culture and Curricula*. Bowling Green, OH: Bowling Green State University Popular Press.

Browne, Ray B., et al., eds. 1968. *Frontiers of American Culture*. Purdue: University Studies.

Bryden, Ronald. 1969. *The Unfinished Hero and Other Essays*. London: Faber and Faber.

Capozzi, Rocco. 1991. "An Interview with Leslie A. Fiedler: Let's Revisit Postmodernism." *University of Toronto Quarterly* 60.3 (Spring): 332–36. As one of the graduate students at the SUNY at Buffalo in the spring of 1968, Rocco Capozzi recalls the unconventional teacher that Fiedler was, advising students to go home and watch "soap operas" and other popular TV shows, in order to study the new modern "myths" offered by the "mass media." The interview, conducted in Buffalo on October 10, 1990, emphasizes the important role of Fiedler in the early phase of American Literary Postmodernism. It also sums up his pedagogical strategies as a teacher in proposing new approaches for looking at literature and at culture in general, and his role as an educator and writer. Most important, it uncovers the man and the impulses behind Postmodernism, a term coined by Fiedler in *Cross the Border—Close the Gap*, his subsequent disappointment with it, as it turned into a merely academic subject. He was the first who saw the importance of the rising role of mass media in the American *avant-garde* phenomenon called Postmodernism. The interview further reveals Fiedler's approaches to the examination of literature and culture and on the incorporation of mass culture in classic literature; his views on an experiment on pop culture; and his comments on the role of Postmodernism in the evolution of modern society.

Chase, Richard. 1960. "Leslie Fiedler and American Culture." *Chicago Review* (Autumn/Winter), 8–18. Microfilm, vol. 14, ASRC Hyderabad.

Childers, Molly. 1999. "Female Adolescence in the American Novel: James, Nabakov and Oates." Master's thesis. Boston University. Childers uses Fiedler's argument that adolescence serves to express themes of independence, rebellion and initiation in the American novel. Her study is on female adolescence in Henry James's *The Bostonians* (1886). Nabokov's *Lolita* (1955), and Joyce Carol Oates's *You Must Remember This* (1987).

Chow, Rey. 2008. "American Studies in Japan; Japan in American Studies: Challenges of the Heterolingual Address." *Nanzan Review of American Studies* 30: 47–61.

Chowdhry, Geeta. 2007. "Edward Said and Contrapuntal Reading: Implications for Critical Interventions in International Relations." *Millennium* 36: 101–16.

Classen, A. 2011. "Defining and Teaching the Canon in German Studies." *The German Quarterly* 84: 1–3.

College Language Association Journal. 1975. "The Last Jew in America." (March): 412–21.

Commentary. 1955. "Search for the Thirties." (Summer): 285–86.

———. 1956. "Pope and Prophet." (February): 190–95.

———. 1970. Review of *Being Busted*. (March): 86.

Congress Bi-Weekly. 1964. "Leslie A. Fiedler: Lazarus or Prophet." (December 21): 10–12.

Corber, Robert J. 1992. "Resisting History: Rear Window and the Limits of the Postwar Settlement." *Boundary 2* 19.1 (Spring): 121. Examines literary works in the U.S. after the Civil War. Analysis of critical works of Leslie Fiedler; liberal pluralism and the denial of political agency; psychopathology of surveillance.

Cox, James M. 1999. "Celebrating Leslie Fiedler." In *Leslie Fiedler and American Culture*, ed. Steven G. Kellman and Irving Malin, 142–153. Newark: University of Delaware Press; London: Associated University Presses.

Daiches, David. 1961. "Breakthrough?" In *Breakthrough: A Treasury of Contemporary American Jewish Literature*, eds. Irving Malin and Irwin Stark, 30–38. New York: McGraw-Hill.

Davis, Robert. 1967. "Leslie Fiedler's Fictions." *Commentary* (January): 13–77.

Davis, Robert, et al. 1986. *Contemporary Literary Criticism: Modernism through Post Structuralism*. New York and London: Longman.

Dembo, L.S. 1973. "Dissent and Dissent: A Look at Fiedler and Trilling." In *Contemporary American-Jewish Literature*, ed. Irving Malin, 134–155. Bloomington: Indiana University Press.

DeMott, Benjamin. 1961. "Jewish Writers in America." *Commentary* (February): 127–34.

———. 1967. "The Negative American." *Commentary* (April): 442–47.

———. 1978. "A Talk with Leslie Fiedler." *New York Times Book Review* (March): 5, 9+.

DeMott, Benjamin, and George Stade. 1978. "A Book by and Talk with Leslie Fiedler." Interview and Review of *Freaks*, by Leslie Fiedler. *New York Times* (March): 5, 9+.

Desautels, L.C. 1998. "Upon the Burning of His House." *Plaza* 4 (Autumn): 22.

Desmond, Jane C., and Virginia R. Dominguez. 2001. "America and the Changing Object of Study." In *Rediscovering America: American Studies in the New Century*, ed. Kousar J. Azam, 14–22. New Delhi: South Asian Publishers.

D'haen, Theo. 1992. "Post-Colonial Literature and Postmodern Literary Histori-

ography." *Neohelicon* 27: 19–29.
_____. 1997a. "'History,' (Counter-)Postmodernism, and Postcolonialism." *European Journal of English Studies* 1.2: 205–16.
_____. 1997b. "What is Post/Colonial Literature, and Why Are They Saying Such Terrible Things about It?" *Link and Letters* 4: 11–18.
Dickstein, Morris. 1991. "Rebel with a Thousand Causes." Review of *Fiedler on the Roof*, by Leslie Fiedler. *New York Times* (August 4). http://www.nytimes.com/1991/08/04/magazine/rebel-with-a-thousand-causes.html?pagewanted=all&src=pm.
Didion, Joan. 1979. *The White Album*. New York: Simon & Schuster.
Dillard, R. H. W. 1999. "Anthropophagi." In *Leslie Fiedler and American Culture*, eds. Steven G. Kellman and Irving Malin, 13–15. Newark: University of Delaware Press; London: Associated University Presses.
Donadio, Stephen. 1964. "End Game." *Partisan Review*, (Fall): 668–72.
Downing, John. 2001. *Radical Media: Rebellious Communication and Social Movements*. Thousand Oaks, CA: Sage.
Dunne, John Gregory. 2002. *True Confessions*. New York: Da Capo.
Edwards, Brian T., and Dilip Parameshwar Gaonkar. 2010. *Globalizing American Studies*. Chicago: University of Chicago Press.
Edwards, T. R. 1968. "The Indian Wants the Bronx." *Partisan Review* (Fall): 606–10.
Ehrlich, Heyward, ed. 1984. *Light Rays, James Joyce and Modernism*. New York: New Horizon.
Elliot, T. S. 1992. "Tradition and Individual Talent." In *Critical Theory since Plato*, ed. Hazard Adams, 761–64. Fort Worth, TX: Harcourt Brace Jovanovich.
Emory, Elliott. 2007. "Diversity in the United States and Abroad: What Does It Mean When American Studies Is Transnational?—Presidential Address to the American Studies Association, November 12, 2004." *American Quarterly* 59.1 (March): 1–22.
Encounter. 1968. "Greek Mythologies." (April): 41–55.
Encyclopedia Judaica. 1971. Vol. 6, s.v. "Fiedler, Leslie Aaron." Jerusalem: Keter. 1,271–72.
Entzminger, Betina. 2007. "Come Back to the Raft Ag'in, Ed Gentry." *Southern Literary Journal* 40.1 (Fall): 98–112. This article has been used for two purposes. First, as it examines the message of Fiedler's essay "Come Back to the Raft Ag'in, Huck Honey," published in 1948. It also establishes its critical impact on later works of American literature. The article makes a comparison of Fiedler's work on *The Adventures of Huckleberry Finn* (1885) and *Deliverance* (1970). The author's opinions about the writings of Leslie Fiedler, Mark Twain and James Dickey as well as the philosophical statement of Judith Butler are also presented.
Feinstein, Herbert. 1961. "Contemporary American Fiction: Harvey Swados and Leslie Fiedler." *Wisconsin Studies in Contemporary Literature* (Winter): 79–98.
Ferraro, Thomas J. 1991. "Ethnicity and Marketplace." In *The Columbia History of the American Novel*, ed. Emory Elliot, 380–406. New York: Columbia University Press.
Fetterley, Judith. 1978. *The Resisting Reader: A Feminist Approach to American Fiction*. Bloomington: Indiana University Press.
Fishwick, Marshall. 1974. *Parameters of Popular Culture*. Bowling Green, OH: Bowling Green University Popular Press.
Friedensohn, Doris. 1996. "Towards a Post-Imperial Transnational American Studies: Notes of a Frequent Flier." *Revista Critica de Ciencias Sociais* 45: 167–83.
Frye, Northrop. 1957. *The Anatomy of Criticism*. Princeton: Princeton University Press.
Galperin, William H. 2001. Review of "Enlarging America: The Cultural Work of Jewish Literary Scholars, 1930–1990." *Criticism* 43.1 (Winter): 116–19.
Gates, David. 1984. "Fiedler's Utopian Vision." *Newsweek* (January 9): 11.
Glicksberg, Charles I. 1968. "A Jewish American Literature?" *South West Review* (Spring): 195–205.
Goldsmith, Arnold L. 1979a. *American Literary Criticism: 1905–1965*. Boston: Twayne.

_____. 1979b. "The Myth Critics." In *American Literary Criticism: 1905–1965*, vol. 3, 146–68. Boston: Twayne.

Green, Geoffrey. 1981. "Reestablishing Innocence: A Conversation with Leslie Fiedler." *Genre*, September, 133–49. Reprinted in *Interdisciplinary Humanities* 20.1 (Spring 2003): 93–105. This article establishes Fiedler's inclusive, embracing approach and focuses on his attempts to break down hierarchies. In many ways this article suggests his pioneering efforts in cultural criticism.

_____. 1999. "The Once and Future Fiedler." In *Leslie Fiedler and American Culture*, eds. Steven G. Kellman and Irving Malin, 178–181. Newark: University of Delaware Press; London: Associated University Presses.

Greven, David. 2009. "Contemporary Hollywood Masculinity and the Double-Protagonist Film." In *Cinema Journal* 48.4 (Summer): 22–43. David Greven is assistant professor of English at Connecticut College. He is the author of *Men Beyond Desire: Manhood, Sex, and Violation in American Literature* (New York: Palgrave Macmillan, 2005) and the forthcoming *Manhood in Hollywood from Bush to Bush* (Austin: University of Texas Press). He is currently working on a book on Hawthorne, Freud, and narcissism. This article is a much cited one.

Gubar, Susan. 1999. "A Fiedler Brood." In *Leslie Fiedler and American Culture*, eds. Steven G. Kellman and Irving Malin, 166–170. Newark: University of Delaware Press; London: Associated University Presses.

Guttmaun, Allen. 1963. "Jewish Radicals, Jewish Writers." *American Scholar* (August): 563–75.

Haley, Alex. 1976. *Roots: The Saga of an American Family*. New York: Dell.

Hall, James. 1960. "Recharging American Gothic: Leslie Fiedler." *Northwest Review* (Summer): 82–6.

Hall, Stuart. 1998. "Notes on Deconstructing 'The Popular.'" In *Cultural Theory and Popular Culture*, ed. John Storey Pearson, 442–453. New York: Prentice Hall.

Halperin, John, ed. 1974. *The Theory of the Novel*. New York: Oxford University Press.

Handy, William I., and Max Westbrook, eds. 1974. *Twentieth Century Criticism*. New Delhi: Light of Life.

Harding, Brian. 1990. "Ernest Hemingway: Men With, or Without, Women." In *American Declarations of Love*, ed. Ann Massa. New York: St. Martin's.

Harrison, Brady. 2008. "Love, Death, and the Deep, Abiding Happiness of Edgar Allan Poe, or, Leslie Fiedler at Montana State University (and SUNY-Buffalo)." *The Montana Professor* 19.1 (Fall 2008). http://mtprof.msun.edu.http://mtprof.msun.edu/Fall2008/harrison.html.

Hassan, Ihab. 1962. *Radical Innocence: Studies in the Contemporary American Novel*. New Jersey: Princeton University Press.

Hayman, Allen. 1961. Review of *Love and Death in the American Novel*, by Leslie Fiedler. *The New England Quarterly* 34.2: 261–63.

Hayne, Barry. 1979. Introduction. In *The Inadvertent Epic: From Uncle Tom's Cabin to Roots*, by Leslie Fiedler, i–xi. New York: Simon & Schuster.

Heibrun, Carolyn. 1972. "The Masculine Wilderness of the American Novel." *Saturday Review* (January 29): 41–44.

Henkle, Roger. 1970. "Symposium Highlights: Wrestling (American Style) with Proteus." *NOVEL: A Forum on Fiction* 3.3 (Spring): 197–207.

Hicks, Granville. 1960a. "A Fresh View of American Fiction." *Saturday Review* 43.12 (March 19): 16.

_____. 1960b. "They Needn't Say No." *Saturday Review* (July 2): 14.

Hirsh, Michael. 2007. "No Time to Go Wobbly, Barack." *Washington Monthly* (April). http://www.washingtonmonthly.com/features/2007/0704.hirsh.html.

Hite, Molly. 1993. "A Parody of Martyrdom: The Rosenbergs, Cold War Theology, and Robert Coover's *The Public Burning*." *Novel: A Forum on Fiction* 27.1 (Fall): 85–101. This article focuses on Leslie Fiedler's retrospective justification of the United States government's execution of Julius and Ethel Rosenberg for conspiracy to commit espionage and Robert Coover's novel *The Public Burning*, which both literalizes and exaggerates the ideological shift that Fiedler's comment represents.

Horkheimer, Max, and Theodor W. Adorno. 1972. "The Culture Industry: Enlightenment as Mass Deception." In *Dialectic of Enlightenment*, 120–67. Trans. John Cumming. New York: Herder.

Howe, Irving. 1959. "Mass Society and Post-Modern Fiction." *Partisan Review* (Summer): 420–436. http://www.questia.com/googleScholar.qst?docId=5006598670.

———. 1960. "Literature on the Couch." *The New Republic* 143.24 (December 5): 17–19.

Huey, John. 1990. "America's Hottest Export: Pop Culture." *Fortune* (December 31): 22–30.

Hulme, Peter. 1993. "Imperial Counterpoint." *Wasafiri* 18: 57–61.

———. 1995. "Including America." *ARIEL: A Review of International English Literature* 26.1 (January): 117–23.

Hutton, Bill. 1972. "Leslie A. Fiedler." *Esquire* (October 4): 135+.

Inge, Thomas M. 1968. *Handbook of American Popular Culture*. Vol. 1. London: Greenwood.

Jackson, B. 1967. "Blackballing the Fiedlers." *New Republic* (September 9). 13–14.

JanMohamed, Abdul R., and David Lloyd, eds. 1990. *The Nature and Context of Minority Discourse*. New York: Oxford University Press.

Janowsky, Oscar I. 1964. *The American Jew: A Reappraisal*. Philadelphia: Jewish Publication Society of America.

Jewish Digest. 1964. "Science Fiction—A Jewish Product." (May): 67.

Johnson, Michael K. 1997. *"Where He Could Be a Man": The Frontier Myth and Constructions of White and Black Manhood in American Literature*. Doctoral dissertation, University of Kansas.

Jones, Emryso. 1973. Review of *The Stranger in Shakespeare* by Leslie Fiedler. *Encounter* (July): 68.

Kalmar, Ivan. 1987. "Jews on the Train." *Journal of Popular Culture* 21: 139–54.

Kannan, Lakshmi. 1976. "The Contemporary Jewish American Writer: A Conversation with Leslie Fiedler." *Indian Journal of American Studies* 1–2: 76–81.

Kaplan, Amy. 1993. "'Left Alone with America': The Absence of Empire in the Study of American Culture." In *Cultures of United States Imperialism*, ed. Amy Kaplan and Donald E. Pease, 3–21. Durham, NC: Duke University Press.

Kar, Prafulla. 2001. "The Future of American Studies in India." In *Rediscovering America: American Studies in the New Century*, ed. Kousar J. Azam, 25–33. New Delhi: South Asian Publishers.

Kazin, Alfred. 1966. "The Jew as Modern Writer." *Commentary* (April): 37–41.

Kelemen, Zsolt. 2010. "The Devil in the Details: Review of *The Devil Gets His Due: The Uncollected Essays of Leslie Fiedler*." *Americana, E-Journal of American Studies in Hungary* 6.2 (Fall). http://americanaejournal.hu/vol6no2/kelemen-rev. Accessed December 2, 2011.

Kellman, Steven G. 1999. "The Importance of *Being Busted*." In *Leslie Fiedler and American Culture*, eds. Steven G. Kellman and Irving Malin, 74–80. Newark: University of Delaware Press; London: Associated University Presses.

———. 2003. "Too Good to Be True. (Book)." *Review of Contemporary Fiction* 23.1 (Spring): 167. Kellman reviews the non-fiction *"Too Good to Be True": The Life and Work of Leslie Fiedler*, by Mark Royden Winchell.

Kellman, Steven G., and Irving Malin, eds. 1999. *Leslie Fiedler and American Culture*. Newark: University of Delaware Press, London: Associated University Presses.

Kenner, Hugh. 1964. "A Word for the Wild Man." *National Review* 16.30 (July 28): 654–56.

———. 1982. "Who Was Leslie Fiedler?" *Harper's* (November): 69–73.

Kermode, Frank. 1972. Review of *The Stranger in Shakespeare*, by Leslie Fiedler. *New York Times* (December 10): BR3.

Kirby, David. 1978. Review of *A Fiedler Reader*, by Leslie Fiedler. *Vancouver Quarterly Review* (September): 381.

Klingenstein, Susanne. 1998. *Enlarging*

America: The Cultural Work of Jewish Literary Scholars, 1930–1990. Syracuse, NY: Syracuse University Press.

Klor de Alva, J. Jorge. 1992. "Colonialism and Postcolonialism as (Latin) American Mirages." *Colonial Latin American Review* 1.1–2: 3–23.

Kostelanetz. Richard. 1974. "Leslie Fiedler (1965)." *Studies in Twentieth Century* (September): 21–38.

Kristol, Irving. 1960. "A Traitor to His Class?" *Kenyon Review* 2 (Summer): 505–9.

Landess, Thomas H. 2008. "Mark Royden Winchell." *Modern Age* 50.4 (Fall): 306–10. This article reviews the life and career of Professor Mark Winchell, who passed away in 2008. Winchell taught English at Clemson University. Winchell wrote several biographies including *"Too Good to Be True": The Life and Work of Leslie Fiedler.*

Larson, Charles R. 1970. "Leslie Fiedler: The Critic and the Myth, the Critic as Myth." *Literary Review* 4 (Winter): 133–43.

———. 1971. "The Good Bad Boy and Guru of American Letters." *Saturday Review* (December 25): 27–28, 35.

Lask, Thomas. 1971. "John Steinbeck to John Lennon." Review of *The Collected Essays of Leslie Fiedler*, by Leslie Fiedler. *New York Times* (August 24): 35.

Levine, Paul. 1967. "Meanwhile Back on the Raft." *Commentary* (April): 439–42.

Lewis, R. W. B. 1955. *The American Adam: Innocence, Tragedy, and Tradition in the Nineteenth Century.* Chicago: University of Chicago Press.

———. 1960. "Gothic Criticism and American Fiction." Review of *Love and Death in the American Novel*, by Leslie Fiedler. *The Yale Review* (Summer): 610.

———. 1999. "Leslie Fiedler: A Tribute." In *Leslie Fiedler and American Culture*, eds. Steven G. Kellman and Irving Malin, 153–156. Newark: University of Delaware Press; London: Associated University Presses.

Library Journal. 1960. Review of *No! In Thunder.* (October 15): 3,660.

———. 1969. Review of *Being Busted.* (December 1): 4,420.

Lloyd, Elliot Willis. 2006. "Looking Away: The Evasive Environmental Politics of American Literature, 1823–1966." Doctoral dissertation, University of Florida.

Looby, Christopher. 1995 "'Innocent Homosexuality': The Fiedler Thesis in Retrospect." In *The Adventures of Huckleberry Finn*, Case Studies in Critical Controversy. Edited by Gerald Graff and James Phelan. Baston: St Martin's.

Loomba, Ania. 1998. *Colonialism/Postcolonialism.* New Critical Idiom. Series editor: John Drakakis. London and New York: Routledge. This is the first significant seminal study on postcolonialism coming from an Indian University scholar.

Lynn, Kenneth S. 1983. "Back to the Raft." *Commentary* (January): 66, 68.

Madden, David. 1970. *American Dreams, American Nightmares.* Carbondale: Southern Illinois University Press.

Madsen, Deborah L. 1998. *American Exceptionalism.* Jackson: University of Mississippi Press.

———, ed. 1999. *Post-Colonial Literatures: Expanding the Canon.* London: Pluto.

———. 2003. *Beyond the Borders: American Literature and Post-Colonial Theory.* London: Pluto.

Mailer, Norman. 1968. *The Armies of the Night: History as a Novel, the Novel as History.* New York: New American Library.

———. 1984. "Huckleberry Finn, Alive at 100." *New York Times* (December 9): 19.

Maini, Darshan Singh. 1976. "Psychoanalysis and Modern American Criticism." In *Studies in American Literature: Essays in Honor of William Mulder*, eds. Jagdish Chander and S. Pradhan Narinder. Delhi: Oxford University Press.

———. 1987. "The American Gadfly." *Span* (September): 7–10.

Malin, Irving. 1965. *Jews and Americans.* Carbondale: Southern Illinois University Press.

———. 1999. "The Prophetic Textbook." In *Leslie Fiedler and American Culture*, eds. Steven G. Kellman and Irving Malin, 37–46. Newark: University of Delaware Press; London: Associated University Presses. The essay closely reads a textbook, *The Art of the Essay*, that Fiedler published in 1958. This textbook, which appeared a few years before *Love and Death in the American Novel*, clarifies Fiedler's abiding interests and obsessions. It is, thus, an intriguing document, one that, like his dissertation on Donne, offers a "secret" passage into his written world. Malin calls this book an "occult" autobiography; it is for students and Fiedler himself.

Malin, Irving, and Irwin Stark. 1961. Introduction. In *Breakthrough: A Treasury of Contemporary American Jewish Literature*, 1–24. New York: McGraw-Hill.

Maloff, S. 1970. "Fiedler on the Woolf." *Common Weal* (May 9): 189–91.

Marudanayagam, P. 1980. "Leslie Fiedler as a Literary Critic." Dissertation, Madurai Kamaraj University.

Masilamoni, E. H. L. 1979. "Fiction of Jewish Americans: An Interview with Leslie Fiedler." *South West Review* (Winter): 44–59.

Matthiessen, Francis Otto. 1941 *American Renaissance: Art and Expression in the Age of Emerson and Whitman*. New York: Oxford University Press.

Mattos, Ed. 1975. "Conversation with Leslie Fiedler." U.S. Information Agency. VTR. 28 minutes, Color Microfilm, ASRC Hyderabad.

Maurer, Robert. 1968. "A Second Soul Haunts Us All." Rev of *The Return of the Vanishing American*, by Leslie Fiedler. *Saturday Review* 51.13 (March 30): 26–27.

McClintock, Anne. 1994. "The Angel of Progress: Pitfalls of the Term 'Post Colonialism.'" *Social Text* 31/32 (1992): 84–98. Reprinted in *ColonialDiscourse/PostcolonialTheory*, ed. Francis Barker, Peter Hulme, and Margaret Iversen, 253–66. Manchester: Manchester University Press.

McGowan, John. 1988. "Leslie A. Fiedler." In *Dictionary of Literary Biography*, vol. 67, *Modern American Critics since 1955*, ed. Gregory S. Jay. Detroit: Gale.

McLemee, Scott. 2002. "Leslie Fiedler." *Chronicle of Higher Education* (July 19 and December 13). http://www.mclemee.com/id120.html.

Meras, P. 1966. "Author." *Saturday Review* (July 30): 32.

Messent, P. 2011. "A Re-evaluation of Mark Twain Following the Centenary of his Death." *Mark Twain Annual* 9: 44–64. http://onlinelibrary.wiley.com/doi/10.1111/j.1756-2597.2011.00059.x/full. Accessed December 15, 2011. It is surprising that in such a complete summation of the oeuvre of Mark Twain's writings that discusses all his major fiction and nonfiction works at length, there is not a word on what Leslie Fiedler said of Twain.

Meyer, Adam. 2004. "Putting the 'Jewish' Back in 'Jewish-American Fiction': A Look at Jewish American Fiction from 1977 to 2002 and an Allegorical Reading of Nathan Englander's 'The Gilgul of Park Avenue.'" *Shofar: An Interdisciplinary Journal of Jewish Studies* 22.3 (Spring): 104–20. 25 years have now passed since Irving Howe made his famous statement that "Jewish-American fiction has probably moved past its high point," and no doubt some would argue that time has proven him right, that no younger writer has yet equaled the career of Saul Bellow. Nevertheless, it also seems safe to say that any reports of the complete demise of Jewish American fiction—such as Leslie Fiedler's lesser-known comment that "the Jewish American novel is over and done with, a part of history rather than a living literature," were greatly exaggerated.

Michelson, Peter. 1968. "The Only Good Injun." *New Republic* (May 11): 29–32.

Midstream. 1966. "Negro-Jewish Relations in America." (December): 22–28.

Mitchell, Margaret. 1936. *Gone with the Wind*. Reprint, New York: Avon.

Mohanty, Sachidananda. 2001. "Revisioning America: American Studies and the New American Exceptionalism." In *Rediscovering America: American Studies in the New Century*, ed. Kousar J. Azam, 61–66. New Delhi: South Asian Publishers.

Mufti, Aamir. 2005. "Global Comparativism." In *Edward Said. Continuing the Conversation*, ed. Homi Bhabha and W. J. T. Mitchell, 109–26. Chicago: University of Chicago Press.

Mulder, William. 1969. "Point Counterpoint: An Exchange on American Studies in India." *Indian Journal of American Studies* 1.1 (July): 74–89.

Murphy, Richard. 2000. "Leslie Fiedler and American Culture" (Book Review). *Review of Contemporary Fiction* 20.2 (Summer): 187.

Nachbar, Jack, and John L. Wright, eds. 1975. *The Popular Culture Reader.* Bowling Green, OH: Bowling Green University Popular Press.

Nation. 1950. "Third Thomas Hardy." 2 (Summer): 210–11e.

_____. 1955. Review of *An End to Innocence.* (June 25): 188.

_____. 1959. "Belated Smear." (August 15): 62+.

New England Review. 1982. "On Becoming a Pop Critic: A Memoir and a Meditation." (Autumn/Winter): 195–207.

New Republic. 1955. "Romance in the Operatic Manner." (September 26): 28–30.

_____. 1956. "Old Pro at Work." (January 9): 16–17.

_____. 1957. "Encounter with Death." (December 9): 25+.

New York Herald Tribune. 1961. Review of *No! In Thunder* (January 1): 31.

New York Times. 1967. "Fiedler Assails Action." (August 23): 19.

_____. 2003. "Leslie Fiedler Dies at 85." (January 31): C25.

New York Times Book Review. 1958. "Readers and Writers Face to Face." (November 9): 4, 40–41.

_____. 1961. "The Writer Must Say No." Review of *No! In Thunder,* by Leslie Fiedler. (January 8): 6.

_____. 1971. "Leslie Fiedler Reintroduces Himself." (May 23): 7.

_____. 1974. "Lord of the Absolute Elsewhere." (June 9): 8.

New Yorker. 1955. Review of *An End to Innocence.* (May 21): 137.

_____. 1964. Review of *Waiting for the End.* (June 6): 180.

_____. 1968. Review of *The Return of the Vanishing American.* (June 1): 126.

_____. 1970. Review of *Being Busted.* (February 14): 131.

_____. 1972. Review of *The Stranger in Shakespeare.* (August 5): 83.

Newsweek. 1967. "Fiedler's Affair." (June 12): 29.

Norman, A. H. 1970. "Maintaining a Premise." *Newsweek.* (January 26): 77A+.

O'Conner, Erin. 2003. "Preface for a Post-Postcolonial Criticism." *Victorian Studies.* (Winter): 217–46.

O'Conner, W. V. 1960. "Accent on the Negative." *Saturday Review* 43 (November 19): 46–7.

Orwell, George. 1940. "Inside the Whale." http://theorwellprize.co.uk/george-orwell/by-orwell/essays-and-other-works/inside-the-whale/.

Paranjpe, Makarand. 2001. "Rethinking America: A Trans-Civilizational Approach." In *Rediscovering America: American Studies in the New Century,* ed. Kousar J. Azam, 34–60. New Delhi: South Asian Publishers.

Pardini, Samuele F. S., ed. 2008. *The Devil Gets His Due: The Uncollected Essays of Leslie Fiedler.* Berkeley: Counterpoint. This book is the latest attempt to provide several uncollected writings to Fiedler fans.

Partisan Review. 1960. "Novel and America." (Winter): 41–61.

Pearson, Gabriel. 1973. "Fiedler's American Shakespeare." *The Spectator* 230.7554 (April 7): 426–27.

Pease, Donald E. 1990. "Leslie Fiedler, the Rosenberg Trial, and the Formulation of an American Canon." *Boundary 2* 17.2 (Summer): 155–98. This article is concerned with the relationship between Leslie Fiedler's account in *Love and Death in the American Novel,* published in 1960, of what constitutes a representative work of American literature, and his critical interventions, written over a decade earlier, in the collective debates over the significance for American cultural life of the national public trials involving the Rosenbergs, Hiss, Chambers, and McCarthyism. This essay's central contention is that Leslie Fiedler, in his work of canon-formation, constructed a "cultural imaginary" that enabled him and his readers to imagine themselves reconstituted within an alternative cultural realm, and that this alternative to the Cold War mentality inevitably turned Fiedler into a subject of that mentality.

Pease, Donald E., and Robyn Wiegman. 2002. "Futures." In *The Futures of American Studies*, ed. Donald E. Pease and Robyn Wiegman, 1–42. Durham, NC: Duke University Press. An authoritative and informative discussion of the history and future potentials of American studies.

Peddie, Ian. 2001. "Poles Apart? Ethnicity, Race, Class, and Nelson Algren." *Modern Fiction Studies* 47.1 (Spring): 118–44. http://muse.jhu.edu/journals/mfs/summary/v047/47.1peddie.html. Accessed December 2, 2010. In this essay, as the title suggests, Ian Peddie problematizes the dynamics between class, ethnic and racial experience across the broad landscape of 1930s and '40s literature in the U.S. Internalized by critics as a kind of agitprop proletarianism, the paper also uses Leslie Fiedler's suggestion that it "provided only a handy set of formulas" around which "writers could organize their protests," a template to which certain writers, along with their chosen forms and subjects, were expected to conform (119).

Pinsker, Sanford. 1980. "Book Review: 'The Inadvertent Epic: From *Uncle Tom's Cabin* to *Roots*.'" *The Georgia Review* 34.3 (Fall): 690–92.

———. 1993. "Is the Jewish-American Experience Over?" *Virginia Quarterly Review* 69.4 (Autumn): 749. This review is noteworthy as it reviews the book *Fiedler on the Roof: Essays on Literature and Jewish Identity*, by Leslie Fiedler, alongside *A History of the J Potter*.

———. 1999. "Leslie Fiedler, Freak." In *Leslie Fiedler and American Culture*, eds. Steven G. Kellman and Irving Malin, 182–191. Newark: University of Delaware Press; London: Associated University Presses.

Pizer, Donald. 1983. Book Review of *What Was Literature? Class Culture and Mass Society*, by Leslie Fiedler. *American Literature* 55.3 (October): 446.

Power, Samantha. 2003. *A Problem from Hell: America and the Age of Genocide*. New York: HarperCollins.

Prasad, Yuvaraj D., ed. 1990. *American Studies in India*. Proceedings of the 1988 and 1989 conferences of the Indian Association for American Studies. Patna, India: Janaki Prakashan.

Prescott, P. S. 1971. "Americans as Innocents." *Newsweek* (August 2): 76–79.

Psychology Today. 1977. "The Fascination of Freaks." (August): 56.

Quayum, Mohammad A. 2007. "Self-Refashioning a Plural Society: Dialogism and Syncretism in Malaysian Post-Colonial Literature." *New Zealand Journal of Asian Studies* 9.2 (December): 27–46.

Rebalow, Harold V. 1963. "The Jewish Side of American Life." *Ramparts* 2 (Autumn): 24–31.

Reising, Russell. 1986a. "The Apolitical Unconscious—Leslie Fiedler." In *The Unusable Past*, by Russell Reising, 129–140. New York and London: Methuen.

———. 1986b. "Puritanism as Allegory: Yvor Winters, Richard Chase and Leslie Fiedler." In *The Unusable Past*, by Russell Reising. New York and London: Methuen.

Rexroth, Kenneth. 1968. "Ids and Animuses." *The New York Times Book Review*, (March 11): 4, 47. A severe criticism of Fiedler and his like, the extremely ethnocentric people (the self-styled New York Establishment, triangulated by the *Partisan Review*, *The New York Review of Books*, and *Commentary*) who use their favorite term of abuse, "WASP," the way Stalinists used to use "Trotskyite," for the most incongruous assortment of writers and tendencies. Kenneth calls most of these people outlanders who have been permitted into the inner citadels of WASP culture as the WASPS themselves have wearied and wandered away.

Richard, Jerome. 2004. "Leslie Fiedler: An Appreciation." *The Massachusetts Review* 45.2 (Summer): 294–97. http://www.jstor.org/stable/25092050. Accessed March 10, 2011.

Rollin, Roger. 1989. "'Words, Words, Words...': On Redefining 'Literature.'" *Journal of Popular Culture* (Winter): 1–9.

Rubinstein, Rachel. 2003. "Fiedler, Leslie A." In *Jewish Writers of the Twentieth Century*, ed. Sorrel Kerbel, 158–160. New York: Fitzroy Dearborn.

Rushdie, Salman. 1984. "Outside the Whale." *Granta* 11 (Spring):1–6. http://www.granta.com/Archive/11/Outside-the-Whale/.

Russ, T. J. 1984. "Leslie Fiedler and the School of Ekstatics." *Literature Film Quarterly* 12.4: 238.

Said, Edward. 1978. *Orientalism*. London: Routledge.

———. 1984. "Reflections on Exile." *Granta* 13 (Autumn): 159–72.

———. 1993. *Culture and Imperialism*. New York: Knopf.

———. 2000. "Jane Austen and Empire" in *The Edward Said Reader*, eds. Moustafa Bayami and Andrew Rubin. New York: Vintage Books.

Sale, Roger. 1971. Review of *The Collected Essays of Leslie Fiedler*. *New York Times Book Review* (October 10): 10.

Salmagundi. 1973. "Rebirth of God, the Death of Man." (Winter): 3–26.

———. 1982. "Leslie A. Fiedler." 57 (Summer): 57–69.

Saturday Review. 1960. *Love and Death in the American Novel*. (March 19): 16.

Schechter, Harold. 1999. "Myth, Archetype, and *Chopper Chicks in Zombietown*: What We've Learned from Leslie." In *Leslie Fiedler and American Culture*, eds. Steven G. Kellman and Irving Malin, 130–35. Newark: University of Delaware Press; London: Associated University Presses.

Schulman, Elias. 1966. "Notes on Anglo-Jewish Writers." *Chicago Jewish Forum*, Summer, 276–80.

Schulz, Max F. 1969. "Leslie A. Fiedler and the Hieroglyphs of Life." In *Radical Sophistication: Studies in Contemporary Jewish American Novelists*, by Max F. Schulz, 154–72. Athens: Ohio University Press.

Schwarz, Daniel R. 1999. "Leslie Fiedler as Leopold Bloom." In *Leslie Fiedler and American Culture*, ed. Steven G. Kellman and Irving Malin, 99–111. Newark: University of Delaware Press; London: Associated University Presses.

———. 2003. "Eating Kosher Ivy: Jews as Literary Intellectuals." *Shofar: An Interdisciplinary Journal of Jewish Studies* 21 (Spring). This essay considers the place of the Jewish literary intellectual, the diaspora of Jewish public intellectuals from New York urban culture to universities in the U.S., and the consequent transformation of public intellectuals into literary intellectuals. The role of Jews as public intellectuals is considered at a time when Jews were still having difficulties finding a place in prestigious universities, especially those in the Ivy League. The field of Jewish studies was a way for scholars to rediscover themselves both as Jews and public intellectuals. It is important to read this article because of the absence of a discussion of Fiedler.

Seaton, James. 1989. "Innocence Regained: The Career of Leslie Fiedler." In *Politics and the Muse: Studies in the Politics of Recent American Literature*, eds. Adam J. Sorkin. Bowling Green, OH: Bowling Green State University Popular Press.

Seminar on the American Novel. 1987. Four Audio Cassettes, 60 min. each. Sponsored by USIS Delhi, Jaipur.

Sen, Nabaneeta Deb. 1994. "A Woman's Retelling of the Rama-Tale: Narrative Strategies Employed in the *Chandrabati Ramayana*." In *Narrative: A Seminar*, ed. Amiya Dev, 170–79. New Delhi: Sahitya Akademi.

Sesachari, Neila. 1976. "Leslie A. Fiedler: Critic as Mythographer." In *Studies in American Literature: Essays in Honor of William Mulder*, eds. Jagdish Chander and Narinder S. Pradhan, 17–27. Delhi: Oxford University Press.

Sharma, D. R. 1983. "Leslie A. Fiedler: The Vitality of Negativism." In *Research Bulletin* PU2, 13–22. Chandigarh: Panjab University.

Shere, Jeremy. 2006. "Jewish American Canons: Assimilation, Identity, and the Invention of Postwar Jewish American Literature." Doctoral dissertation, Indiana University.

Shippard, R. Z. 1978. "Leslie Fiedler's Monster Party." *Time* (February 20): 95.

Shohat, Ella. 1992. "Notes on the 'Post-Colonial.'" *Social Text* 31/32: 99–113.

Slavitt, David R. 1999. "Fiedler on the Roof." In *Leslie Fiedler and American Culture*, eds. Steven G. Kellman and Irving Malin, 156–59. Newark: University of Delaware Press; London: Associated University Presses.

Smith, Henry Nash, ed. 1963. *Mark Twain: A Collection of Critical Essays*. Englewood Cliffs, New Jersey: Prentice Hall.

Smith, Sandra Wilson. 2010. "Frontier Androgyny: An Archetypal Female Hero in *The Adventures of Daniel Boone*." *Journal of American Studies* 44: 269–86.

Snyder, Michael. 2007. "Crises of Masculinity: Homosocial Desire and Homosexual Panic in the Critical." *Critique* 48.3 (Spring): 250–77. Applying the theories of Guy Hocquenghem, Eve Kosofsky Sedgwick, and Louis Althusser, this essay closely examines Robert Coover's novel *The Public Burning* and Norman Mailer's novels of the sixties, *An American Dream* and *Why Are We in Vietnam?*, as Cold War critical national narratives. The essay discusses the crises of masculinity provoked in the American fifties and sixties by anticommunist discourse, which rhetorically linked communism and homosexuality as symptomatic of a perverse behavior. In this way they critique the way homosociality functions to consolidate patriarchal power, and the resulting institutional homophobia, homosexual panic, and violence. The essay also discusses Mailer's and critic Leslie Fiedler's homophobia in drawing a conclusion that Coover, with his use of subversive Bakhtinian carnival laughter, presents a critique of Cold War rhetoric that is more aggravated than Mailer's.

South West Review. 1963. "The Frontiers of Leslie Fiedler." 48 (Winter): 86–89.

Srivastava, Prem K. 1992. "Leslie Fiedler: Evolution of a Pop Guru." Unpublished thesis. Indian Institute of Technology, New Delhi, India.

———. 1993. "The American Male Psyche: A Psychological Analysis." *Indian Journal of Psychology* 68.3–4: 91–93.

———. 1994a. "The American Dream: A Psychological View." *Indian Psychological Review* 41: 9–10.

———. 1994b. "A Psychological Analysis of Alienation in Modern Jewish-American Literature." *Psycho-Lingua* 24.1: 23–28.

———. 1998. "Popular Literature: A Fiedlerian Perspective." *Jadhavpur Journal of Comparative Literature* 36 (1998–99).

———. 2002. "Giving the Devil His Due—Revisited." *Dialog* (May): 73–80.

———. 2003. "The Postmodern Condition and the Politics of the Popular." *Creative Forum* 16.1–2 (January–June): 119–30.

———. 2006. "The Culture Conundrum: Can It Be Popular?" *Yearly Academic Journal*: 1–16.

———. 2009. "British Popular Fiction in an Indian Classroom: A View from the Other." *Literary Paritantra (Systems)* 1.1 (January): 65–76.

———. 2010. "A Legacy We have (almost) Made Our Own!: English Language ... in India" *Fortell* no. 18 (May 2010): 3–5.

Storey, John. 2001. *Cultural Theory and Popular Culture*. London: Prentice Hall.

Symes, Colin. 2006. "The Paradox of the Canon: Edward W. Said and Musical Transgression." *Discourse: Studies in the Cultural Politics of Education* 27.3: 309–24.

Tanenhaus, Sam. 2003. "Fear and Loathing." *Slate* (February 4). Tanenhaus shows how Leslie Fiedler turned American criticism on its head. Written in the form of an obituary, shortly after Fiedler's death, it looks at the critical career of Fiedler in a cool, detached and wild style that typified the subject of his study.

Teller, Judd L. 1968. "From Yiddish to Neo-Brahmin." In *Strangers and Natives—The Evolution of the American Jew from 1921 to the Present*, 251–272. New York: Delacorte.

———. 1970. *Strangers and Natives*. New York: Delacorte.

Thahil, Jeet. 1987. "The Wild Man of American Literary Criticism." *Express Magazine* (February 22): 6.

Thorp, William. 1960. Review of *Love and Death in the American Novel*, by Leslie Fiedler. *New York Herald Tribune Book Review* (April 10).

Timberg, Scott. 2008. "High-minded Lowdown." *Los Angeles Times* (May 4): 2.

Time. 1960. *Love and Death in the American Novel*. April 18, 115.

———. 1964. Review of *Waiting for the End.* (May 15): 122.

———. 1968. "West Goes Psychedelic." (March 15).

———. 1972a. "Being Unbusted." (July 17): 50.

———. 1972b. "Being Unbusted." (July 27): 17.

Times Literary Supplement. 1961a. "The Bridges Still Stand." No. 3081 (March 17): 161–62.

———. 1961b. "*Love and Death in the American Novel.*" (March 17): 161–62.

———. 1973. Review of *The Stranger in Shakespeare* (March 30): 346.

Tompkins, Jane P. 1994. "Sentimental Power: *Uncle Tom's Cabin* and the Politics of Literary History." In *Uncle Tom's Cabin.* Norton Critical Edition, ed. Elizabeth Ammons. New York: Norton.

Twain, Mark. 1884, reprint 1995. *Adventures of Huckleberry Finn.* New York: St. Martin's.

Vertical File. 1975. American Studies Research Center (ASRC). "Leslie A Fiedler—A Profile." April 15.

Vijay, Kumar T. 2011. "New Directions in American Studies in India." 56th Annual Conference of British Association of American Studies (BAAS), University of Central Lancashire, Preston, UK, April 14–17. Working paper.

Vijayasree, C. 2011. "Towards an Alternative American Studies: A 'Field' Report from India." Unpublished presentation at the International Conference on "Globalizing American Studies." Northwestern University, May 19–20.

Wakeman, John, ed. 1975. *World Authors, 1950–1970.* New York: H. H. Wilson.

Wald, A. 1987. *The New York Intellectuals.* Chapel Hill: University of North Carolina Press.

Walden, Daniel 1978. "Leslie Fiedler." *Journal of Popular Culture* (Fall): 208–9.

———. 1999. "Leslie Fiedler: Enfant Terrible, American Jewish Critic and the Other Side of Lionel Trilling." In *Leslie Fiedler and American Culture*, eds. Steven G. Kellman and Irving Malin, 160–165. Newark: University of Delaware Press; London: Associated University Presses.

Waldmeir, Joseph J. 1963. "The Breakthrough: The American Jewish Novelist and the Fictional Image of the Jew." In *Recent American Fiction: Some Critical Views*, by Joseph J. Waldmeir, 84–109. Boston: Houghton Mifflin.

Wallenstein, Barry. 1972. "Leslie Fiedler between Raft and Shore." *Journal of Modern Literature* (November): 589–94.

Wasserstrom, William. 1966. "In Gertrude's Closet." In *Hidden Patterns: Studies in Psychoanalytic Literary Criticism*, eds. Leonard and Eleanor Manheim, 277–78. New York: Macmillan.

Watt, Ian. 1967. *The Rise of the Novel.* Berkeley: University of California Press.

Webster, Grant. 1967. "Leslie Fiedler: Adolescent and Jew as Critic." *Denver Quarterly* 1 (Winter): 44–53.

Werthman, Michael S., and Norman F. Cantor, eds. 1968. *The History of Popular Culture.* New York: Macmillan.

Whalen, Patricia. 1968. "An Interview with Leslie Fiedler." *North West Review* (September): 67–73.

Whittemore, R. 1970. "Tough Martyr." *New Republic* (April 18): 27–28.

Widmer, K. 1965. *The Literary Rebel.* Carbondale: Southern Illinois University Press.

Williams, Patrick, and Laura Chrisman, eds. 1993. *Colonial Discourse and Post-Colonial Theory.* New York: Columbia University Press.

Wilson, Janet, Cristina Sandru, and Sarah Lawson Welsh, eds. 2010. *Re-Routing the Postcolonial: New Directions for the New Millennium.* London: Routledge.

Wimsatt, William K., and Cleanth Brooks. 1978. *Literary Criticism.* Chicago: University of Chicago Press.

Winchell, Mark Royden. 1985. *Leslie Fiedler.* Boston: Twayne. This full-length study is significant as it is the first to bring to the readers of American culture a critic such as Fiedler.

———. 1999. "Fiedler and the New Criticism." In *Leslie Fiedler and American Culture*, ed. Steven G. Kellman and Irving Malin, 87–99. Newark: University of Delaware Press; London: Associated University Presses.

_____. 2002. *"Too Good to Be True": The Life and Work of Leslie Fiedler.* Columbia: University of Missouri Press. The second book by the author that allows the readers the privilege of knowing Fiedler, the man, the husband, father, brother and son, behind his voluminous creative and critical writings.

_____. 2005. "Leslie Fiedler, Ahead of the Herd." *Southern Review* 41.2 (Spring): 403–16. This essay presents the eminent author Leslie Fiedler, who remained a *Partisan Review* intellectual in his early career of the 1940s and '50s. During this phase he made the transition from Trotskyism to liberal anti–Communism.

Witholt, Thomas. 2009. "A Second Look at Leslie Fiedler." *Minnesota Review* (Winter/Spring): 71–72. http://www.theminnesotareview.org/journal/ns7172/witholt.shtml. Accessed November 30, 2011. In this Witholt mourns that Fiedler has been largely forgotten by scholars and the public alike. It brings out the interesting fact that Fiedler was somewhere aware that his paradoxical position as an academic scholar and pop guru would not be taken seriously by his readers. An astute reader of the public mind, he realized that his popularity would soon diminish as it did. Sums up the expansive landscape of writings of this maverick scholar.

Woolf, Leonard. 1954. "Politics for the Unpolitical." *New Republic.* (February 8): 17–18.

Xie, Shaobo. 1997. "Rethinking the Problem of Postcolonialism." *New Literary History* 28.1 (Winter). http://www.jstor.org/pss/20057397.

Yinger, J. Milton. 1982. *Countercultures: The Promise and Peril of a World Turned Upside Down.* New York: Free Press.

Young, Philip. 1967. "Fallen from Time: Rip Van Winkle." *Three Bags Full: Essays in American Fiction.* New York: Harcourt, Brace.

Index

Achebe, Chinnua 203
Adorno, Theodor 138
Advanced Centre for American Studies (ACAS) 200
The Adventures of Huckleberry Finn 10, 34, 69, 72, 74, 90, 91, 198, 225, 228
African American studies 171
Alighieri, Dante 9, 22, 45, 47, 48, 76, 95, 153, 197, 221
Alter, Robert 222
Alva, J. Jorge klor de 175
The American Adam 69, 80, 173, 228
American dream 82, 84, 93, 149, 163, 187, 228, 233
American exceptionalism 53, 173, 175, 178, 217, 228, 229
American Indian studies 171, 172, 234
American literature 6, 10, 13, 19, 20, 23–26, 30, 35, 36, 42, 53, 56, 63, 69, 71, 73, 79–81, 86–88, 90, 93, 95, 100, 106, 123, 124, 132, 134, 135, 145, 155, 159, 167, 168, 173, 175–178, 185, 186, 193, 196, 198, 201, 204, 213, 220–222, 225–228, 230–233
The American Renaissance 69, 173
The American Scholar 175, 208; *see also* Emerson, Ralph Waldo
American studies 2, 4–7, 171–174, 176, 182, 184, 195
American Studies Association 173, 225
American West 9, 57, 100, 136, 192
"Annual Leslie Fiedler Memorial Lecture" 200
"Anthropophagi" 205, 206, 225
Anti-communism 235
Anti-semitism 105, 110, 121, 126
Archetype 3, 14, 17, 18, 20, 23, 39, 40, 41, 42, 47, 64, 66, 73, 80, 81, 83, 84, 87, 101, 107, 109, 118, 121, 136, 137, 139, 155, 156, 160, 161, 177, 178, 182, 193, 196, 201, 232
Archetype and signature 14, 39, 40, 42, 47, 64, 66, 155, 161, 196
Arnold, Matthew 38, 63, 124, 138, 197, 218, 225
The Art of the Essay 57, 61, 71, 95, 219, 228
Ashcroft, Bill 174, 222
Ashley, Bob 138, 216
Asian Americans 173
Asimov, Isaac 203
Austen, Jane 232
Avant Garde 4, 147, 177
Azam, Kausar 172, 222, 225, 227, 229, 230

Back to China 99, 220
Baldwin, James 107, 113
Barth, John 222
Barthes, Roland 197, 217
Bauman, Bruce 99, 113, 128, 129, 132, 165, 166, 170, 207, 208, 210, 222
Beatles 143
Beauvoir, Simone de 182
Beckett, Samuel 34
Being Busted 20–21, 43–47, 54–55, 57, 62, 71, 103, 130, 180, 195
Bellman, Samuel Irving 23, 24, 222
Bellow, Saul 74, 81, 123, 125, 132, 188, 229
Bennett, Tony 222
Bertens, Hans 199
Beverly Hills Cop 162
Bhabha, Homi 229
Biederman, Patricia Ward 222
Blackfoot tribe 217
Blake, William 10, 22
Bloom, Leopold 106, 125, 132
Boyers, Robert 29, 110, 135, 214, 223
Brando, Marlon 10, 22
Brave Heavy Runner 99, 195, 211

Index

Brooks, Cleanth 223
Browne, Ray B. 223
Bryden, Ronald 223
Buffalo, New York 10, 22, 27, 44, 57, 58, 59, 70, 99, 104, 112, 113, 124, 153, 160, 176, 181, 190, 196; *see also* State University of New York, Buffalo
Buffalo Bill 160, 221
Bumppo, Natty 119
Burroughs Edgar Rice 60, 156, 197
Butler, Rhett 183

Caliban 55, 102, 111, 121
Call It Sleep 15, 134, 135, 178
Capone, Al 10, 22
Capozzi, Rocco, 54, 79, 153, 223
Captain Ahab 64, 75, 203, 218
Carroll, Lewis 203
Cavalcanti, Guido 10, 22
Chandrabhati Ramayana 202, 203, 218, 232
Charles P. Norton medal 196
Chase, Richard 224
Childers, Molly 92, 180, 224
Chimera 208
Chingachgook 53, 74, 82, 83, 85, 101, 119
Christian Gauss lectures 99
Christie, Agatha 203
Civil War 34, 108, 159, 160, 223, 224
Cixous, Helene 165
Classen, Albrecht 202
Clemens, Samuel L. 181, 200; *see also* Twain, Mark
Close Encounters of the Third Kind 152
Cohen, Leonard 100, 206
Coleman, Joe 207, 218
The Collected Essays 119, 220, 228, 232
"Come Back to the Raft Ag'in, Fiedler Honey!" 205, 208, 209
"Come Back to the Raft Ag'in, Huck Honey!" 69, 71, 73, 84, 149, 186, 196, 225
Conan Doyle, Arthur 144, 156
The Continuing Debate 220
Contrapuntal reading 172, 224
Cooper, James Fenimore 177, 178; *The Deer Slayer* 178; *The Last of the Mohicans* 76, 187, 191
Cox, James M. 224
Credo (Fiedler's) 16, 23, 25, 29, 30, 31, 32, 35, 37, 38, 39, 40, 43, 45, 47, 49, 51, 53, 55–61, 63–67, 151, 166, 168, 176
Cross the Border—Close the Gap 64, 130, 145, 147, 150, 153, 199, 214, 217, 223

Darwin, Charles 22
The Deer Slayer 178
Deliverance 90–91, 186–87, 225; *see also* Dickey, James
Dembo, L. S. 224
Derrida, Jacques 4, 169
Dickey, James 90, 91, 186, 187, 225
Didion, Joan 225
Dixon, Thomas, Jr. 167
Donne, John 153, 229
Downing, John 225
Dracula 128, 158, 197, 209
Dustan, Hannah 85

Eco, Umberto 154, 165
Eliot, T. S. 43, 105, 130, 151, 200, 201, 204
Elliott, Emory 171, 172, 178, 225
Ellison, Ralph 100, 163
Emerson, Ralph Waldo 175, 208; *see also The American Scholar*
The Empire Writes Back 174, 222
An End to Innocence 5, 10, 30, 38, 46, 48, 79, 88, 104, 146
English Literature: Opening Up the Canon 221
"Epoch of Hegemony of Commodities" 22, 137, 141
Euripides 162

Fagin 120, 219
"The Father of Us All" 181–194
Faulkner, William 34, 107, 130, 144, 201
Feminism 11, 190, 191, 213
Fetterley, Judith 225
"A Fiedler Brood" 142, 184, 226
Fiedler on the Roof 5, 79, 95, 104, 106, 125, 127, 133
A Fiedler Reader 4, 214, 220, 221, 227
Fiedlerfest 196
Fishwick, Marshall 225
Fitzgerald, F. Scott 62, 100, 183, 192
Fleming, Ian 203
Force majeure 27, 198
Forster, Hal 140
Freaks: Myths and Images of the Secret Self 95, 128, 129, 136, 157, 158, 214, 217, 220
Freud, Sigmund 87, 118
Frost, Robert 204, 205
Frye, Northrope 201
Fulbright lecturer 5
Fulbright program 5

Gadfly 2, 6, 7, 213, 228
Galparin, William 132
Gandhi, Mahatma 203

Ginsberg, Allen 85, 153, 165
"Giving the Devil His Due" 137, 143, 144, 154, 155, 157, 164, 178, 217
Gone with the Wind 10, 134, 156, 158, 159, 167, 178, 183, 209, 229
Good Bad Boy 35, 68, 77, 78, 228
Gothic 36, 37, 38, 62, 64, 216, 220, 226, 228
Grail Knight 106, 127
Great Britain 178, 217
Green, Geoffrey 226
Griffith, D. W. 107
Gubar, Susan 226
Guggenheim Fellowship 196
Guru 24, 26, 27, 45, 68, 87, 130, 137, 138, 142, 144, 168, 170, 173, 209, 210, 228, 233, 235

Haley, Alex 178, 226
Halio, J. L. 121, 122
Hall, Stuart 140, 226
Hamlet 94, 102, 111
Harlem Renaissance 108
Harrison, Brady 29, 48, 57, 58, 70, 71, 72, 79, 86, 88, 92, 96, 98, 183, 202, 203, 207
Harvard University 196
Hawkes, John 15, 134, 135, 178
Hawthorne, Nathaniel 22, 33, 167, 176
Hebdige, Dick 203
Heilbrun, Carolyn 132, 186, 189
Hemingway, Ernest 226
Hicks, Granville 226
High Modernism 52, 150, 167
Highbrow 10, 25, 36, 51, 57, 80, 98, 140, 141, 144, 145, 165, 170, 178
Hindu Upanishadic philosophy 211
Hollywood 71, 92, 196, 226
Holocaust 135, 213, 222
Horkhiemer, Max 138
"How Did It All Start" 162
Hubbell Medal 59, 88, 93, 173, 191, 196, 204, 221
Huck Finn 14, 68, 69, 74–78, 82, 84, 91, 97, 141, 170, 188
Hutcheon, Linda 5, 174

Ibo tribe 112
In Cold Blood 37
In Dreams Awake 220
The Inadvertent Epic: From Uncle Tom's Cabin to Roots 154, 158, 182, 184, 193, 226, 231
India 2, 5–7, 14, 17, 18, 25, 55, 56, 73, 75, 80, 82, 85, 94–101, 104, 108, 116, 119, 129, 131, 136, 153, 167, 172, 176, 181, 183, 186, 192, 193, 194, 200, 202, 203, 213, 214, 215, 216–18, 223
Indian 2, 6, 14, 17, 18, 25, 37, 55, 56, 73, 75, 80, 82, 85, 94–102, 104, 108, 116, 119, 129, 131, 136, 153, 157, 172, 183, 186, 192–197, 213–218, 228, 230–233
Indian English 203, 218
Indian Institute of Technology 2
Injun 83, 109, 116, 119, 229
Inside or Outside the Whale 178
Inter-disciplinarity 4
Intertextuality 4
Irving, Washington 69, 85, 101, 187, 192, 193
Ishmael 45, 53, 69, 74, 75, 81, 82, 84, 112, 188
Israel 96, 100, 126, 192
Italy 44, 93, 221
Ivan Sandorf Award for Lifetime Achievement 196

Jackson, Bruce 103, 190, 196
James, Henry 78, 92, 144, 187, 200, 224
Japan 55, 95, 108, 150, 221, 224
Jekyll and Hyde 158, 194
Jerusalem 225
Jewish-American Literature 106, 123, 124, 135, 213, 225, 232
Jews 11, 17, 18, 23, 26, 48, 49, 54, 94, 95, 97, 104–134, 136, 140, 145, 146, 173, 176, 194
Joyce, James 225; *see also Ulysses*

Kafka, Franz 118
Kazin, Alfred 80, 84, 123, 132, 133, 135, 227
Kellman, Steven 3, 10, 11, 12, 22, 27, 43–45, 56, 57, 84, 94, 123–126, 136, 153, 176, 180, 183, 191, 195, 197, 200, 214, 215, 221–228, 231–234
Kenner, Hugh 126, 176
Kenyon Review 30, 31, 152, 215, 219, 221, 228
Kitsch 4, 176, 177
Klingenstein, Susanne 227
Kristol, Irving 52
Ku Klux Klan 159

Larson, Charles R. 13–16, 42, 47, 68, 183, 228
The Last Jew in America 100, 106, 197, 220, 224
The Last of the Mohicans 76, 187, 191
Lawrence, D. H. 34, 43, 63, 79, 83, 100, 167, 192
Leonard, William Ellery 56
Lewis, R. W. B. 69, 74, 80, 170, 173, 182, 189, 200

Liddle, Dallas 139, 177, 216
The Lime Twig 134, 135, 178
"Literature and Lucre" 164, 183
Looby, Christopher 228
Loomba, Ania 175, 228
Lotts, Eric 134
Love and Death in the American Novel 1, 3, 5, 11, 16, 17, 25, 30, 33, 35, 36–39, 42, 53, 54, 61, 64, 71, 73, 74, 76, 78, 79, 80–84, 103, 104, 127, 149, 158, 173, 177, 185, 187, 188–189, 191
Lowbrow 25, 57, 140, 144, 145, 147, 150, 164, 165, 170
Luska, Sidney 116, 135

Madwoman in the Attic 171, 184, 216
Madame Bovary 187
Madsen, Deborah 173, 175, 178, 228
Mahabharata 203, 218
Mailer, Norman 228
Maini, Darshan Singh 6, 20, 22–24, 111, 137, 164, 213, 228
Malamud, Bernard 228
Male bonding 25, 68, 71, 73, 74, 77, 79, 81, 83, 85, 87, 89, 91, 93, 140, 158, 161, 182, 197
Malin, Irving 228, 229
Marcus, Greil 214
Marlowe, Christopher 203
Marquez 203
Marx, Karl 134, 174
Marxism 54, 98, 133, 139
Marxist approach/analysis 38, 220
Matthiessen, Francis Otto 80, 167, 173, 226
McCarthy, Joseph 16, 48, 51–53
McClintock, Anne 174, 175, 229
McLemee, Scott 229
McLuhan, Marshall 1, 165
McRobbie, Angela 203
Medea 162
Melville, Herman 33, 74, 86, 179; *Moby-Dick* 23, 26, 31, 33, 74; *Pierre* 139, 192
The Merchant of Venice 106, 121
The Messengers Will Come No More 220, 222
Middlebrow 29, 36, 67, 104, 140, 145, 147, 150, 164, 165
Miller, Henry 165, 179, 213
Miller, Perry 189
Milton, John 2, 31, 131, 153, 203, 222, 235
Mississippi River 100, 192
Missoula, Montana 10, 104, 117, 124
Moby-Dick 23, 26, 31, 33, 74, 75, 76, 82, 84, 187

Modern Language Association 59, 71, 122, 204
Modernism 30, 52, 60, 113, 137, 140, 141, 142, 146, 150, 151, 153, 154, 166, 167, 168, 175, 189, 199, 203, 214, 221, 223, 224, 225
Mohanty, Chandra Talpade 182, 229
Montana 5, 10, 27, 29, 45, 54, 56, 92, 96, 97, 98–100, 104, 106, 117, 124, 181, 183, 202, 203, 205, 207, 214, 215, 226
Montana State University 70, 81, 86, 226
Morrison, Toni 203
Myth criticism 3, 14, 17, 23, 40, 41, 42, 81, 127, 152

Nabokov, Vladimir 78, 92
National Book Critics' Circle Award 196
Negro 11, 18, 23, 49, 54, 72, 73, 82, 85, 90, 97, 100, 102, 104, 106–116, 119, 122, 129, 136, 148, 149
Neo-Marxism 213
New Criticism 38, 40, 60, 104, 146, 198, 215, 223, 234
New Jersey 54, 226, 233
New Mutants 4, 130, 147, 148, 220
New New Criticism 151
New York Times 13, 141, 183, 200, 222, 224, 225, 229, 228, 230, 231, 233
New York Times Book Review 13, 141, 222, 224, 230, 231, 232
Newark 54
Nigger Jim 74, 83, 109, 162
No! In Thunder 10, 17, 18, 30, 33–36, 38, 42, 47, 64, 104, 107, 144, 166, 168, 220, 223, 228
No Man's Land 185
Norton Anthology of Literature by Women 185
Nude Croquet and Other Stories 220

Oedipus Rex 162, 201
Olaf Stapledon: A Man Divided 15
One Flew Over the Cuckoo's Nest 38, 101, 147, 151, 188
Orwell, George; 179, 213, 230
Osmania University Centre for International Programmes (OUCIP) 200

Paglia, Camille 1, 25, 56, 165, 166, 190, 191
Pardini, Samuele F. S. 3, 4
Partisan Review 11, 30, 49, 53, 70, 71, 72, 86, 92, 102, 104, 113, 135, 145, 152, 165, 219, 220, 221, 225, 227, 230, 231, 235
Pawling, Christopher 138, 216
Pease, Donald 53, 55, 113, 131, 144, 175, 178, 217, 227, 230, 231

PEN West 196
Personal voice 4, 30, 38, 42, 43, 155
Pierre 139, 192
Pinsker, Sanford 123, 130, 137, 158, 215, 231
Playboy 153
Pocahontas 85, 101, 192
Poe, Edgar Allan 29, 81, 166, 187, 226
Popular Culture 2, 4, 9, 12, 16, 18, 21–26, 30, 36, 48, 60–61, 63, 73, 87, 113, 116, 122, 129, 136–139, 140, 142–52, 154, 158–61, 163, 170, 183, 205, 223, 209, 216
Post-colonialism 171, 174, 175, 176, 217, 224, 221, 222, 228, 229, 235
Post-modernism 113, 137, 140, 141, 142, 146, 153, 154, 175, 199, 203, 214, 223, 224
Post-structuralism 224
Pound, Ezra 204
Presley, Elvis 112, 142
Puduer 18, 20
Pull Down Vanity and Other Stories 220
Puritanism 215, 231
Pynchon, Thomas 113, 154

Quayum, Mohammad 175, 231
Queequeg 53, 69, 75, 81–87
Queer theory 11, 129, 131, 171, 176, 195

Racechangers: White Skin, Black Faces in American Culture 186
Rahv, Philip 86, 102
Ramayana 202, 203, 218, 232
Ransom, John Crowe 30, 31
The Return of the Vanishing American 3, 42, 71, 79, 81, 84, 85, 93, 100, 101, 102, 136, 182, 188, 192, 220, 222, 229, 230
Richard, Jerome 3, 58, 67, 70, 99, 215, 231
Richards, I. A. 66, 155
Rip Van Winkle 54, 69, 81, 83, 101, 141, 187
Rockefeller Fellow 196
Rogin, Michael 134
"Roman Holiday" 17, 105
Romanticism 31, 43, 77, 168
Roots 13, 16, 101, 108, 113, 148, 154, 156, 158, 159, 173, 178, 183, 187, 193, 220, 226, 231; see also Haley, Alex
Rosenberg, Julius and Ethel 16, 30, 47, 48, 50–54, 219, 226, 230
Roth, Henry 134, 135, 178, 219
Rousseau, Jean-Jacques 63, 71, 96, 215
Rushdie, Salman 177, 180, 232
Russell, Reising 19–20, 35, 79, 178, 215, 236

Said, Edward 4, 172, 224, 229, 232
Salmagundi 220, 232

Sawyer, Tom 35, 77, 78
The Scarlet Letter 74, 100, 187, 192, 200
Schechter, Harold 2, 183, 196, 197, 207, 208, 213, 218, 232
Schwartz, Daniel 104, 125–128, 132, 134, 210
Science fiction 220
Seaton, James 9, 46
The Second Stone 106, 220, 222
Sedgwick, Eva Kosofsky 186, 233
Sen, Nabaneeta Deb 202, 217, 232
Shakespeare, William 2, 3, 60, 92, 94, 95, 102, 106, 120, 121, 143, 161, 162, 197, 203, 206, 220, 221, 227, 230
Shohat, Ella 174, 232
Shylock 109, 115, 120, 121, 122
Slavitt, David R. 133, 134, 233
Smith, Henry Nash 70, 182, 189, 233
Sontag, Susan 140, 199
Sophocles 162
The Sopranos 86–87
Soyinka, Wole 203
Spivak, Gayatri 174, 194
Stalinism 52
Stapeldon, Olaf 221
Star Trek 153, 161, 169
Star Wars 152, 161
State University of New York, Buffalo 10, 22, 27, 44, 57, 58, 59, 70, 99, 104, 112, 113, 124, 153, 160, 176, 181, 190, 196
Stoker, Bram 144, 162, 197
Storey, John 138, 218, 226, 233
Stowe, Harriet Beecher 34, 107, 159, 166, 178, 185, 189, 190
The Stranger in Shakespeare 92, 94, 95, 106, 120, 121, 220, 227, 230, 234

Tagore, Rabindra Nath 203
Talmud 9
Tanenhaus, Sam 12, 45, 51–53, 65, 137, 176, 196, 233
Thoreau, Henry David 69, 83
Tiffin, Helen 174, 221–22
To the Gentiles 17, 35, 95, 104, 111, 115, 119, 126, 145, 220
Tolstoy, Leo 27
Tompkins Jane 234
Too Good to Be True 3, 11, 21, 94, 183, 195, 200, 201, 223, 227, 228, 235
Trilling, Lionel 49, 123, 124, 125, 132, 234
Trivedi, Harish 203, 217
Trotsky, Leon 231, 235
Twain, Mark 2, 34, 55, 58, 69, 72–75, 78, 79, 90, 107, 155, 161, 165, 183, 188, 190, 198, 206, 225, 229, 233, 234

Tyranny of the Normal: Essays on Bioethics, Theology and Myth 95, 128–29, 131, 214, 221

Ulysses 106, 125–127; *see also* Joyce, James
Uncle Tom 10, 34, 77, 107, 109, 134, 154, 158, 159, 167, 173, 178, 182, 184, 189, 190, 193, 220, 226, 231, 234
Uncle Tom's Cabin 10, 34, 77, 107, 109, 134, 154, 158, 159, 167, 173, 178, 182, 184, 189, 190, 193, 220, 226, 231, 234
Unfinished Business 102, 103, 135, 148, 220
University of Bologna 5, 196
University of Montana 5, 58, 70, 92, 203
University of Wisconsin, Madison 56, 61

Vasudheva Kutumbkum 210
Vidal, Gore 21, 84

Waiting for the End 17, 23, 24, 35, 42, 71, 79, 81, 83, 84, 95, 104, 105, 109, 111, 114, 116, 119, 122, 124, 145, 146, 148, 177, 186, 220, 230, 234
Walcott, Derek 203
Walden 69, 83

Walden, Daniel 12, 17, 23, 79, 122–124, 136, 209, 234
Wallenstein, Barry 234
WASP 24, 25, 26, 37, 68, 85, 107, 110, 111, 126, 129, 134, 163, 137, 177, 231
Weil, Simone 193
Western frontier 182
What Was Literature? Class Culture and Mass Society 160, 221, 231
Whitman, Walt 166, 207
Williams, Raymond 138
Wilson, Edmund 201
Winchell, Mark Royden 3, 11, 94, 195, 223, 227, 228
Winters, Yvor 189
World Englishes Project 203, 218
World War I 44, 51, 99, 103, 134, 137, 142, 160
World War II 44, 51, 99, 103, 134, 137, 142, 160

Yale University 134, 190, 196
Yiddish 20, 64, 101, 117, 126, 133

"Zion as Main Street" 115, 116, 222

www.ingramcontent.com/pod-product-compliance
Lightning Source LLC
Chambersburg PA
CBHW051217300426
44116CB00006B/607